FETISHISM AS CULTURAL DISCOURSE

FETISHISM AS CULTURAL DISCOURSE

EDITED BY

Emily Apter and

William Pietz

CORNELL UNIVERSITY PRESS

ITHACA AND LONDON

First published 1993 by Cornell University Press

International Standard Book Number 0-8014-2522-0 (cloth)
International Standard Book Number 0-8014-9757-4 (paper)
Library of Congress Catalog Card Number 92-31984
Printed in the United States of America
Librarians: Library of Congress cataloging information appears on the last page of the book.

⊗ The paper in this book meets the minimum requirements of the American National Standard for Information Sciences—Permanence of Paper for Printed Library Materials, ANSI Z39.48-1984.

Contents

v

Illustrations

Preface

Our title, *Fetishism as Cultural Discourse*, and the arrangement of the essays into three groups might require a word of explanation. *Fetishism* has been a key word in the cultural discourse through which "developed" societies have identified themselves by characterizing their Others. The reasons why modern cultures have at times explained and justified themselves as mature, sane, civilized, and rational in terms of an absence of "fetishism" have been explored of late by scholars and artists working in a variety of disciplines and media. These diverse investigations seem to us to bring into thematic focus three sites of controversy: the historical construction of gender identity; the social life of capital; and lived ideologies in visual culture.

The first part, "Engendering Fetishism," historicizes current debates about the gender politics of "perversion" by situating them in the fin-de-siècle institutionalization of "sexuality," which set the terms for contemporary discussions. As the essays in this part indicate, France was a particularly important site for fomenting enduring sexological typologies and epistemologies. In scientific circles, the prestige of Jean-Martin Charcot's clinic in the 1880s put France at the center of ensuing Freudian and post-Freudian determinations of gendered psychoanalysis. On the literary front, French pathological realism, with its emplotment of tainted heredities, decadent manias, psychic phobias, and "anomalous" sexual preferences, is arguably the most developed expression of a fetishistic fiction popular throughout Europe and America at the turn of the century.

The point of "Magic Capital" may be less obvious. The authors of the essays in this part try to move beyond the critical discourse about commodity fetishism, which has perhaps been one of the most attractive and least useful legacies of Western Marxism, by taking seriously Marx's characterization of the "supernatural" power that the social order of capital exercises over human subjectivity. The strategies employed are diverse and at times in conflict with one another. They range from reconstructing Marx's argument about the social reproductive system of capital as a process of fetishization to deconstructing the rhetoric of ghosts and the uncanny in the opening chapter of *Capital*, and from delineating the rational forms of cognitive subjectivity and objectified value required in market societies to interrogating the breakdown in social theory's dialectic of subject and object when the modern state is recognized as itself a sexual fetish and magical power-object, alternately conceivable as a thing and a god.

These explorations of the complex, historically specific relations connecting human desires, material objects, and social power are extended to the field of visual culture in the last part, "Scopic Fixations." Essays here are also anchored in the concerns of the first part insofar as fetishism is profoundly linked to what psychoanalysis terms *scopophilia* (the love of looking). According to the Freudian model, fetishism works to obstruct, displace, or refocus the scopophilic gaze rather than facilitate its attachment to the longed-for object. In this book, the gender of the object is interrogated well beyond the bounds of Freudian theory to include theorizations of the homoerotic and lesbian fetish, as well as the visual erotics of racial and class fetishisms. Such investigations extend and transform the significance of the Freudian commonplace that visual interdiction may serve to intensify the scopic pleasure of looking and being looked at. The insight that such a dynamic, so crucial to art practice and spectatorship, also informs the play of visual fascination and visceral response in the everyday experience of social identities has itself become an object of aesthetic interrogation in the work of many of the contemporary artists considered in the final part of this volume.

The following essays have been published previously: Jack Amariglio and Antonio Callari, "Marxian Value Theory and the Problem of the Subject: The Role of Commodity Fetishism," *Rethinking Marxism* 3 (Fall 1989): 31–60; Elizabeth Grosz, "Lesbian Fetishism?" *Differences* 3 (Summer 1991): 39–54; Abigail Solomon-Godeau, "The Legs of the Countess," *October* 39 (Winter 1986): 65–108; Kobena Mercer, "Reading Racial Fetishism: The Photographs of Robert Mapplethorpe," from *Lost Boundaries: Essays in Black Cultural Studies*, forthcoming from Routledge, reprinted by permission of Routledge, Chapman and Hall, Inc.;

Naomi Schor, "Fetishism and Its Ironies," *Nineteenth-Century French Studies* 17 (Fall–Winter 1988–89): 89–97; Jane Weinstock and Barbara Bloom, "Amor nel Cor," in *Ghost Writer*, ed. Barbara Bloom (Berlin: Berliner Künstlerprogramm des DAAD, 1988), 66–80. We express our gratitude for permission to reprint these essays and the following photographs: Robert Mapplethorpe, *Man in Polyester Suit* (1980), the Estate of Robert Mapplethorpe; Rotimi Fani-Kayode, *Technique of Ecstasy* (1987), the Estate of Rotimi Fani-Kayode; Barbara Bloom, *Lost and Found* (1985), Galerie Isabella Kacprzak; Mary Kelly, detail photographs from *Pecunia* (1989); Aubrey Beardsley, "The Woman in the Moon" (1894) and "J'ai Baisé ta Bouche Iokanaan" (1893), illustrations for Oscar Wilde's *Salomé*, Harvard College Library; Mayer & Pierson, photographs of the countess de Castiglione (c. 1856–1860), Musée d'Unterlinden Colmar; A. A. E. Disdéri, *Les jambes de l'Opéra* (1856), International Museum of Photography at George Eastman House. We would like to express personal gratitude to Anthony Vidler, whose help, humor, and moral support were vital to the project. Our thanks also to our editor at Cornell University Press, Bernhard Kendler, to managing editor Kay Scheuer, to Patricia Peltekos, and the editorial and production staff. Finally, we thank Michael Taussig and the New York University Department of Performance Studies for hosting a discussion on fetishism in the fall of 1989 that brought together many of the contributors to this volume.

Unless otherwise noted, all translations are by the authors of the essay in which they appear.

Emily Apter and William Pietz

Oakland and Santa Cruz,
California

FETISHISM AS CULTURAL DISCOURSE

Introduction

Emily Apter

Like many collective volumes of essays, this one has grown out of a critical conjuncture of interdisciplinary work on a common theme. History, feminism, anthropology, literary criticism, political philosophy, art practice and theory—each field has been drawn on for approaches to the problem of fetishism.

Though it carries the historical baggage of fin-de-siècle bourgeois fantasms—case histories culled from the racier pages of Krafft-Ebing's *Psychopathia sexualis*, on the one hand, or caricatural projections of "primitive" idol worship, on the other—fetishism has since the early 1980s enjoyed a curious resurgence of popularity as a trope of criticism and aesthetics, particularly in film and art criticism (I am thinking here of work by Roland Barthes, Christian Metz, Stephen Heath, Laura Mulvey, and in this collection, by Abigail Solomon-Godeau, Mary Kelly, Kobena Mercer, Jane Weinstock, and Barbara Bloom).[1]

The importance of fetishism as a conceptual feature of contemporary art practice first came to my attention in Mary Kelly's *Post-Partum Document* (1976), an installation in which female fetishism (a term introduced by Naomi Schor) was construed as a kind of maternal bric-a-bracomania.[2] An album of nursery dejecta—fecal stains, baby hair,

---

1. In feminist film studies the critique of fetishism and male spectatorship has been extensive. Laura Mulvey, Mary Ann Doane, Janet Bergstrom, Gertrude Koch, Miriam Hanson, E. Ann Kaplan, Annette Kuhn, Constance Penley, and Vivian Sobchack are among the many whose work has been essential to the theorization of fetishism, vision, and gender.

2. Naomi Schor inaugurated the term "female fetishism" in theory and feminist

charts of early development—was tenderly proffered with museal exactitude and psychoanalytically glossed. This transgressive sendup of postpartum sentimentality paralleled comparable reappropriations in art, film, and literature of campy sexual and commodity fetishism. Throughout the 1980s, David Salle and Eric Fischl painted suburban male subjects caught out spying at home, their eyes furtively trained on female genitalia, erotically scotomized by sheets, bathing suits, or panties. At the same time women artists, including Kelly, Bloom, Rosemarie Trockel, and Cindy Sherman, implicitly countering these gynophobic scenes of domestic voyeurism, reframed the commodity fetishism of the female body in its function as hackneyed trademark of advertising culture.

In literature, Bruce Chatwin's last novel, *Utz*, explored the psychopathology of the collectomaniac, obsessively bent on amassing a microsociety of uncannily animated Meissen figurines. As if returning to an earlier nineteenth-century genre (as in the Biedermeier novels of Adalbert Stifter or Oscar Panizza's chilling 1890 novella, "Das Wachsfigurenkabinet" [The cabinet of wax figures], Chatwin recuperated the fetishism of *das Dinge* for late capitalist America—a period and culture that witnessed both an extraordinary frenzy of conspicuous consumption and a return to fictions of saccharine "coziness" in a bibelot-encumbered hearth and home.

Fetishism, in this regard, offers parallels between late nineteenth and late twentieth turn-of-the-century commodity cultures. Behind Chatwin's porcelain statuettes lurk the writings of Walter Benjamin on the cosseted interiors of his Berlin childhood or the "phantasmagoria" presented by merchandise displayed in urban passages and arcades. Like Georg Simmel and Werner Sombart before him, Benjamin anticipates the contemporary hypersensitivity to the sexuality of things. Objects are revealed as provocations to desire and possession. The objectified female anatomy is sexually domesticated through sartorial masquerades, just as the household fetishes of cars, TVs, and swimming pools are shown to be sites of displaced lack, dream surrogates for better values. Fetishism in avant-garde culture, one might say, is impregnated with the self-consciousness of absent value.

At the risk of making trite generalizations, I would venture that fetishism appeals to disparate fields and sensibilities first and foremost because the etymological origins and philosophical history of the word itself point to the artifice (*facticius*) present in virtually all forms of

---

debate in "Female Fetishism: The Case of George Sand," *Poetics Today* 6, no. 1–2 (1985): 301-10, reprinted in *The Female Body in Western Culture: Contemporary Perspectives*, ed. Susan Suleiman (Cambridge: Harvard University Press, 1986), 363–72.

cultural representation. Desublimating the aura of falsity and bad faith in consumer consciousness; unmasking the banal sexisms of everyday life; undercutting aesthetic idealism with the seductive spectacle of kitsch, camp, or punk; exposing the postmodern infatuation with transgression, "gender trouble," and erotic fixation; smoking out the Eurocentric voyeurism of "other-collecting"— fetishism as a discourse weds its own negative history as a synonym for sorcery and witchcraft (feitiçaria) to an outlaw strategy of dereification. Whether it is in the silent quotation marks that form around postured, literary speech, or in the ironic distance that collects between the eye and its erotic object, or in the spectral semblance of value that descends over the commodity (here explored by Thomas Keenan, Jack Amariglio, and Antonio Callari), or in the halo of hyperreality attached to hypostatized nation-markers such as "Europe," "India," or as Jeffrey Mehlman notes, the historically resonant Alsation province of "Phalsbourg"[3]—a consistent displacing of reference occurs, paradoxically, as a result of so much *fixing*. Fetishism, in spite of itself, unfixes representations even as it enables them to become monolithic "signs" of culture. As my coeditor, William Pietz, has written:

> The fetish is always a meaningful fixation of a singular event; it is above all a "historical" object, the enduring material form and force of an unrepeatable event. This object is "territorialized" in material space (an earthly matrix), whether in the form of a geographical locality, a marked site on the surface of the human body, or a medium of inscription or configuration defined by some portable or wearable thing. . . . This reified, territorialized historical object is also "personalized" in the sense that beyond its status as a collective social object it evokes an intensely personal response from individuals. This intense relation to the individual's experience of his or her own living self through an impassioned response to the fetish object is always incommensurable with (whether in a way that reinforces or undercuts) the social value codes within which the fetish holds the status of a material signifier. It is in these "disavowals" and "perspectives of flight" whose possibility is opened in the clash of this incommensurable difference that the fetish might be identified as the site of both the formation and the revelation of ideology and value-consciousness.[4]

3. Dipesh Chakrabarty made this point in a talk titled "Postcoloniality and the Artifice of History" delivered at a conference called "Nation, History, and the Postcolonial Condition: Views from Subaltern Studies" at Princeton University, May 10, 1990.

4. William Pietz, "The Problem of the Fetish," pt. 1, *Res* 9 (Spring 1985): 12–13. See also parts 2 and 3a, *Res* 13 (Spring 1987): 23–45, and *Res* 16 (Autumn 1988): 105–23.

In identifying where and how fixation unfixes in the clash between fierce individual attachments and the adherence to collectively valued social objects (or, in another guise, what Michael Taussig calls state fetishism), Pietz also inadvertently points to the proverbially testy relationship between psychoanalysis and Marxism, rent apart often enough by disagreements over what to do about the loyalties, passions, and object cathexes characteristic of the (historically recalcitrant) "bourgeois private."[5] To some extent this clash has, I think, creatively informed the editorial collaboration that has shaped this book.

Though, as Pietz says, fetishism fixes in time and place—commemorating a founding moment in the etiology of consciousness, harking back as a "memorial" (Freud's expression) to an unrepeatable first form—it is hardly immune to repetition compulsion. If anything, fetishism records the trajectory of an idée fixe or *noumen* in search of its materialist twin (god to idol, alienated labor to luxury item, phallus to shoe fetish and so on). Though the twin provides only an inferior reflection of the imaginary first form, its degraded simulation may be recuperated for politics: it speaks in the name of colonized, lesser gods. Moreover, fetishism's recursivity—its habit of playing representational sosie to itself—also allows it to become a vehicle for resisting confining essentialisms.

Feminist essentialism is resisted through fetishism's implicit challenge to a stable phallic referent. Characterized by Michel Foucault as the "model perversion" of nineteenth-century clinical discourse, fetishism played, and continues to play, a significant role within the history and epistemology of sexual codes (as demonstrated by the essays by Robert Nye and Jann Matlock). Though Freud referred to maternal castration as a "fact" in his 1927 essay "Fetishism," this "fact" proves hypothetical, mythically allegorical (Charles Bernheimer makes this point in his essay). The imaginary phallus, venerated elsewhere, ultimately comes to occupy no fixed place at all. And the idea stipulated by classical psychoanalysis that virtually any object—fur, velvet, chair legs, shoelaces, apron strings, hatbands, feather boas, etc.—can become a candidate for fetishization once it is placed on the great metonymic chain of phallic substitutions ultimately undermines the presupposition of a phallic ur-form, or *objet-type*. If the phallus itself no longer necessarily resembles a phallus (Elizabeth Grosz suggests in her essay that even another woman can become a fetish, thus giving rise to a revisionary concept of "lesbian fetishism"), then perhaps an epoch obsessed

5. An expression used in postcolonial discourse to refer to a typically "metropolitan" assumption about what communitarian Third World societies supposedly lack.

with castration anxiety has reached its twilight days. At any rate, the implication here is that fetishism, conceived as a mock performance of phallic woman vested with preposterous props and veils, springs gender codes loose from the moorings of biological essentialism.

Fetishism as that "other phallus" standing in for a supposed "real" phallus no longer there, also engages a subversive logic (future anterior) of retroactive agency. Sarah Kofman has noted: "The mother's penis, the 'thing itself,' is always already a fetish invented by the child, a *belief* implying at once denial and affirmation of castration. There was never a 'thing itself,' but only ersatz, a sham, a prosthesis, an originary supple-mentarity as the panicked reaction of infantile narcissism."[6] Antiessen-tialist feminism has historically made good use of this sham sexuality both in its configuration of femininity (always already posited some-where else) and in its (formerly) futuristic vision of reproductive tech-nology. Although in this volume, no essay is specifically devoted to the implications of fetishism for a feminist critique of such "body works," the writings of Donna Haraway on cyborgian prosthetics (invoked by Naomi Schor), of Alice Jardine on "technobodies," of Mary Ann Doane on "technophilia," or the slash-and-probe architectonics of Elizabeth Diller and Ricardo Scofidio would seem to imply a vital connection between fetishism and a new, sci-fi, screen- and sero-tested, bodies-without-organs mode of cultural reproduction.[7]

Fetishism also resists racial essentialism even as it reverts in the his-toric European Imaginary to a fantasy about black objects ("les objets qu'adorent les nègres" in the words of Emile Littré, the nineteenth-century French lexicographer). As William Pietz has shown, the word *fetisso* came into parlance as a Portuguese trading term associated with "small wares" and "magic charms" used for barter between blacks and whites. White merchants, compromising both their religion and their "rational" economic principles, took oaths on fetishes in order to seal commercial agreements. Willy-nilly their capital became magical, a mask for black objects in a white society, hexed and "mist-envelopped"

6. Sarah Kofman, "Ça cloche," in *Les fins de l'homme: Lectures de Derrida* (Paris: Galilée, 1984), 136–37, as cited and translated by Barbara Spackman in *Decadent Genealogies: The Rhetoric of Sickness from Baudelaire to D'Annunzio* (Ithaca: Cornell University Press, 1989), 193. See Spackman's discussion "A Memorial to Medusa."

7. Donna Haraway, "A Manifesto for Cyborgs: Science, Technology and Socialist Feminism in the 1980s," *Socialist Review* 80 (March–April 1985): 65–108; Alice Jardine, "Bodies and Technologies," in *Discussions in Contemporary Culture*, ed. Hal Foster (Seattle: Bay Press, 1989), 151–58; Mary Ann Doane, "Technophilia: Technolo-gy, Representation, and the Feminine," in *Body/Politics: Women and the Discourses of Science*, ed. Mary Jacobus, Evelyn Fox Keller, and Sally Shuttleworth (London: Rout-ledge, 1990), 163–76.

as Marx would describe the commodity fetish several centuries later in *Das Kapital*. As African fetishism was introduced into Europe, the anchored antipodes of black objects and white objects, or black and white religions, or black and white races, could no longer hold fast: a historic cultural syncretism (though obviously biased in favor of Europe) had begun.

Smuggled into the First World through the back door of mercantilism, the so-called African fetish, though it bolstered the European economy and its attendant panoply of Enlightenment values, refused to stay in place as (in Pietz's words) "a safely displaced synecdoche of the Enlightenment's Other." Just as throwing African statues and masks in with the china and *tchotchkes* of bourgeois curiosity cabinets had the effect of rubbing some of their exoticist aura off onto Western objets d'art, so the European literary imagination increasingly found itself attracted to a defamiliarizing Africanist idyll, whereby Europe made itself strange to itself. Africa was seen as prelinguistic, prerational, unskeptical, its "signs" naive in their simplicity and mediated by sensualism. Writing in 1894 in *Le jardin d'Epicure*, Anatole France pictured all true poets as "fetishists of words and sounds," superstitiously adhering to a belief in the magical properties of incantations:

> Very pious or artistic people put a refined sensualism into religion or art. Yet, one is not sensual without being a little bit fetishistic. The poet possesses the fetishism of words and sounds. He endows certain combinations of syllables with marvelous virtues and tends, like all true believers, to have faith in the efficacy of consecrated formulas.
>
> There is more liturgy in versification than one might suppose. And, for a poet blanched in poetics, to make a verse is to perform a sacred rite.[8]

Poetry at the turn of the century was accordingly taken with verbal "charms" (a favorite figure of Stéphane Mallarmé, Paul Valéry, and Saint-John Perse). In its quest for aura-soaked, originary signs it fell for the unlikely analogy between pagan idolatry and its own spellbound venera-

---

8. "Les personnes très pieuses ou très artistes mettent dans la religion ou dans l'art un sensualisme raffiné. Or, on n'est pas sensuel sans être un peu fétichiste. Le poète a le fétichisme des mots et des sons. Il prête des vertus merveilleuses à certaines combinaisons de syllabes et tend, comme les dévots, à croire à l'efficacité des formules consacrées.

"Il y a dans la versification plus de liturgie qu'on ne croit. Et, pour un poète blanchi dans la poétique, faire des vers, c'est accomplir les rites sacrés." Anatole France, *Le jardin d'Epicure* (Paris: Calmann-Lévy, 1894), 71–72.

tion of the aesthetic Ideal. In this way, fetishism, standard linchpin of a colonizer's tourist sublime, became less safe the more it "returned" to European shores. Taking its place in symbolist poetics it increasingly emerged as a trope of "wish fulfillment," an expression of oneiric nostalgia for archaic substrata of the self.[9]

James Clifford and Hal Foster have critically assessed the attempts of an endangered Eurocentrism to reappropriate (and thereby tame) black alterity through modernist strategies of primitivism, "ethnographic surrealism," and ethnopsychiatry. Despite their chic look, such strategies in the wake of postcolonial and subaltern studies have increasingly come under attack for their complicity with an age-old European cultural imperialism. According to V. Y. Mudimbe, the Western transformation of *feitiços* into "symbols of African art . . . viewed as primitive, simple, childish and nonsensical," coincided historically with the colonial repression of native slave revolts.[10] Aestheticization, coming at the price of infantilization on the evolutionary chain of global cultural achievement, also facilitated what Abdul R. JanMohamed has identified as a Western "fetishization of the Other":

> The power of the "imaginary" field binding the narcissistic colonialist text is nowhere better illustrated than in its fetishization of the Other. This process operates by substituting natural or generic categories for those that are socially or ideologically determined. All the evil characteristics and habits with which the colonialist endows the native are thereby not presented as the products of social and cultural difference but as characteristics inherent in the race—in the "blood"—of the native. In its extreme form, this kind of fetishization transmutes all the specificity and difference into a magical essence.[11]

Though this political critique, once applied to a modernist fetishism, can seem disconcertingly reductive, it nonetheless signals hitherto in-

9. Examining Freud's allusion to this "primitive state" in *The Interpretation of Dreams*, Christopher Miller notes: "That 'primitive state' of wish-fulfillment is how Europe conceives of African thought: as a free reign of fulfilled desire, a place to 'linger delighted' with the gods, where dualities of representation have been abolished in a single 'fetish-religion,' where ornamentation and physique coincide, where the alien native cries welcome in your own language, where the people are nothing but a 'soft wax,' and where 'any figure that you wish' can be realized." *Blank Darkness: Africanist Discourse in French* (Chicago: University of Chicago Press, 1985), 63.

10. V. Y. Mudimbe, *The Invention of Africa: Gnosis, Philosophy, and the Order of Knowledge* (Bloomington: Indiana University Press, 1988), 10.

11. Abdul R. JanMohamed, "The Economy of Manichean Allegory: The Function of Racial Difference in Colonialist Literature," in *"Race," Writing, and Difference*, ed. Henry Louis Gates, Jr. (Chicago: University of Chicago Press, 1986), 86.

visible racist undertones in the essentializing and "chosifying" of negri-
tude canonized by Parisian art nègre or the 1920s cult of jazz.

Though capable of undercutting racist psychogeography by "provin-
cializing" or "negrifying" metropolitan culture, the fetish will never
shed its stigma as a synonym for racist "chosification" ("colonisation =
chosification," wrote Aimé Césaire in his Discours sur le colonialisme).[12] Kobena Mercer confronts this issue in an essay for this volume
dealing with the problematic positioning of black spectators with respect to the colonial fantasy of mastery in Robert Mapplethorpe's photographs of black men. Is it not the case, he implicitly asks, that black
subjects, in the context of gay subculture, may also participate in the
kinds of pleasure offered by such fantasies of power? Is black identity in
the process compromised and rendered inauthentic, or is it split as is
any other subjectivity?

Whereas Mercer has used the recursivity of fetishism to expose the
colonial ethnocentrism of classical psychoanalysis, Homi K. Bhabha has
invoked a comparable recursivity to demonstrate the subliminal con-
tamination of the colonial mind by the very belief in a "magical essence"
that it so abhorred in the native subject. An example of colonial
"mimicry"—that strange dance in which mutually obsessed "subjects of
difference" frequently engage—this doubly refracted fetishism of "magic" and racial essence undermines the myth of Western cultural superiority.[13]

Although, as I have tried to point out in this introduction, the treatment of fetishism presented here is far from exhaustive, we have endeav-
ored to show why fetishism is "good to think" (to borrow Lévi-Strauss's
phrase) in the context of contemporary cultural studies. Part of what has
motivated this project of "fetishism as cultural discourse" is the desire
(albeit utopian) to invent a politically implicated language of cultural
interpretation that somehow desublimates the inherent voyeurism of the
critic's fixative stare. What have come to the fore are issues as varied as
cultural appropriationism; the political dangers and aesthetic temptations of an ironic, expropriative feminist, gay, and lesbian fetishism; the
eroticization of state power; the elusiveness of commodity value as it
relates to the supremely nomadic or situational character of the con-

12. Aimé Césaire, Discours sur le colonialisme (Paris: Editions Présence Africaine,
1989), 19.
13. Homi K. Bhabha, "Of Mimicry and Man: The Ambivalence of Colonial Discourse," in October: The First Decade, 1976–1986, ed. Annette Michelson, Rosalind
Krauss, Douglas Crimp, and Joan Copjec (Cambridge: MIT Press, 1987), 317–25. For
Bhabha's elaboration of "ambivalence," see his "Introduction: Narrating the Nation,"
in Nation and Narration, ed. Bhabha (London: Routledge, 1990), 3.

sumer in everyday life; the spatial repression of scopic drives (the love of looking); commodity fetishism and the art market in relation to the historic traffic between Europe and the Third World. But even where these themes have served to unify the disparate pieces assembled, the juxtaposition of these essays to one another has also brought out parallels and thematic intersections that have yet to be fully articulated in the human sciences, producing a quality of the conceptual unforeseen that, for the editors, has made this project particularly worthwhile.

ENGENDERING
FETISHISM

The Medical Origins
of Sexual Fetishism

Robert A. Nye

Like many of the other modern "perversions," fetishism was first documented and named by doctors and psychiatric specialists in the 1880s and 1890s, a period we know by hindsight to have been the classificational golden age of contemporary sexology.[1] As other contributions to this volume demonstrate, the *concept* of fetishism had been around a long time in anthropology, philosophy, and economics, but it was not until the fin de siècle that fetishism became an object of the medical "gaze," and therefore "real," despite the numerous literary or philosophical descriptions of the phenomenon that preceded this development.[2]

Perhaps the most interesting epistemological question that arises with respect to any psychiatric neologism is one provoked by modern linguistic philosophy: was the phenomenon "discovered" by medical specialists who had been unaccountably blind to its social existence until some propitious accident brought it to light, or was it "invented" by its namers, literally called into being by the cognitive organizing force of medical language? In the history of sexuality this epistemological debate

1. Most obviously, "inversion" was described in 1882 by Jean-Martin Charcot and Valentin Magnan ("Inversion du sens génital," *Archives de neurologie* 3 [1882]: 53–60); "sadism" and "masochism" in 1886 by Richard von Krafft-Ebing (*Psychopathia sexualis*, 12th ed., trans. Harry Wedeck [New York: Putnam, 1965]); medical "fetishism" in 1887 by Alfred Binet ("Le fétichisme dans l'amour: Etude de psychologie morbide," *Revue philosophique* 24 [1887]: 143–67).
2. The best schematic account of this process is that in Michel Foucault, *The History of Sexuality*, vol. 1: *An Introduction*, trans. Richard Howard (New York: Vintage, 1980), 36–50.

has been dubbed the "essentialist"/"instrumentalist" controversy; the side one chooses to support has important implications for social policies and practices because, to take one obvious example, it matters for a number of reasons whether or not a homosexual is born with his or her sexual nature in place or whether that nature is constructed in individuals from the social and cultural materials at hand. John Boswell advises us to treat this matter as an open question, but it does not prejudice the answer to this question—so far as we may ever know it—to see how far a social-constructionist attitude may take us.[3] When one looks at the historical evidence, there are clear indications of a "prehistory" of (sexual) fetishism in both medical theory and practice prior to the emergence of the word itself; but there are also excellent reasons for concluding that the fin de siècle provided a unique cultural and social setting for making fetishism a culturally evocative concept for contemporary observers. I hope here to show how a strand of continuity was preserved in the midst of some apparently revolutionary changes in cultural meanings.

The whole question of invention/discovery is complicated by the remarkable fact, noted by historians of medicine in this period, that literary figures and psychiatrists borrowed freely from one another; thus it was the rare sexological treatise that did not cite contemporary novels, and the unusual novel that did not display a grasp of psychiatric technique.[4] This characteristic reciprocity makes more difficult the effort to track causal influences, but it dramatically increases the historian's ability to document the influence and popularity of concepts of sexual aberration.

My primary contention in this essay is the following: that the concept of fetishistic perversion first arose in French psychiatry and was only later integrated into psychiatric nosologies elsewhere, including that of Sigmund Freud, where this historical investigation will terminate. But why France? I hope to explain how a pressing cultural anxiety about the health and the size of their population provoked the French to consider *how* and *why* fetishistic deflections of the sexual instinct occurred. I hope to show how long-term concerns with reproductive fertility, male impotence, and sexual exhaustion influenced the status fetishistic perversions possessed in pre–World War I psychiatry.

When historians consider the past two hundred years of French history, they generally emphasize the positive. They consider France's expansive and progressive political heritage, its vast material impact on the

3. John Boswell, "Revolutions, Universals, and Sexual Categories," *Salmagundi* 58–59 (Fall 1983): 89–113.
4. Henri Ellenberger, *The Discovery of the Unconscious: The History and Evolution of Dynamic Psychiatry* (New York: Basic Books, 1970), 278–84.

non-European world, and, perhaps particularly, the enormous achievements of its cultural life. But the French were burdened with two related concerns that were more or less unique among industrial nations in the nineteenth century. These concerns attracted increasing attention through the course of the century, provoking an unusual amount of public concern and anxiety during the thirty years or so before 1914. First, the geopolitical status of the nation underwent a steady deterioration during this era, from undisputed primacy under Napoleon I to the position of a second-rate power following the ignominious defeat at the hands of Prussia in 1870. After 1870, the rise of a united Germany and Italy, a reforming and modernizing Russia, and an ever-expanding Great Britain seemed to presage, at best, a maintenance of this diminished status, or worse, a continued slide. France had a slower rate of economic growth than the new German empire and fewer natural resources than it needed to compete in the new industrial order. But the most troubling aspect of French inferiority was the prospect that by 1910 Germany would be able to put two soldiers in the field for every Frenchman, a factor that not only lessened the likelihood of recovering Alsace-Lorraine but exposed France to future dismemberment at the hands of its more aggressive and fertile neighbors.

Though inseparably linked to geopolitical considerations throughout the century, "depopulation" became the focus of fresh concerns in the 1880s and 1890s when it was learned that in certain years there were more deaths than births and that the rate of marital fertility was constantly plunging.[5] Medical and scientific commentators, noting that the rates of alcoholism, insanity, crime, and venereal diseases were also on the rise, concluded that these were in some way related to the problem of depopulation, either as effects of a common cause or as causes themselves of reproductive infertility. The medical concept of degeneration, as I have pointed out elsewhere, was the perfect scientific model for explaining how a kind of retrogression was operating to degrade both the bodies and the minds of its victims, spreading its hereditary stain generation after generation until an infected line died out through sterility.[6] Emile Zola's Rougon-Macquart cycle was remarkably loyal to the medical model of degeneration that inspired it.

5. On the statistics of this issue, see Joseph Spengler, *France Faces Depopulation* (Durham, N.C.: Duke University Press, 1938).

6. I have discussed this theme at some length in *Crime, Madness, and Politics in Modern France: The Medical Concept of National Decline* (Princeton: Princeton University Press, 1984). For a recent account of the role of degeneration theory in France, see Daniel Pick, *Faces of Degeneration: A European Disorder, c. 1848–c. 1918* (Cambridge: Cambridge University Press, 1989), 37–108.

A principal speculation of the medical experts in this era was that the masculine "will" or "instinct" to reproduce had been somehow affected by the spread of degeneracy. As the "active" agent in reproduction, men were assumed, both in biological science and in popular culture, to be the efficient cause of lowered natality.[7] The contemporary campaigns against wet-nursing and infanticide are clear testimony that women were held responsible in some measure for the depopulation problem, but most of the responsibility fell on males. While women might be "sterile" (though this possibility was badly understood until after 1914), their "impotence" (frigidity) was only a partial barrier to pregnancy. Male sterility was better understood and documented, but male *impotence* was generally assumed to be the major cause of childless marriages, and had been so regarded since the old regime.[8]

The nineteenth-century understanding of male impotence was linked to a venerable principle in French (and European) physiology, which held that sexual function, like all other bodily activities, was dependent on the maintenance of an equilibrium of vital forces, a sort of biological "golden mean" among the various functions of the organism (nutritive, reproductive, etc.). According to this concept, the overall "animal economy" could be depleted by an excessive expenditure within any of these autonomous systems. Indeed, the experimental criterion for deciding on the biological norms of the normal and the pathological was the *rate* of energy expenditure. Moderate (average) rates of expenditure were deemed normal, and excessive or insufficient rates were judged to fall in the range of the pathological.[9]

With respect to the sexual function—and this precept held equally for women—excessive sexual activity exhausted the organism, destroying the dynamism characteristic of sexual function and leading to impo-

7. It was assumed, for instance, that the sex of the offspring and its general health and viability were largely determined by the age, vitality, and "masculine" qualities of the father. Women were, at best, a dependent variable in this equation. For some of these views, see Angus McLaren, *Reproductive Rituals: The Perception of Fertility in England from the Sixteenth Century to the Nineteenth Century* (London: Methuen, 1984). For late nineteenth-century medical opinion, see Dr. A. Cleisz, *Recherches des lois qui président à la création des sexes* (Paris: Rongier, 1889).

8. See Georges David, "La stérilité masculine: Le déni du mâle," *Le genre humain* 10 (1984): 23–38. In the old regime impotence was recognized as a cause for divorce, but Napoleonic law did not recognize either the natural or acquired type as legitimate grounds for separation or divorce. See Pierre Darmon, *Trial by Impotence: Virility and Marriage in Pre-revolutionary France*, trans. Paul Keegan (London: Chatto and Windus, 1985).

9. See on this point Georges Canguilhem, *Le normal et le pathologique*, 3d ed. (Paris: Presses Universitaires de France, 1975), 19–25. I have discussed the relation of these rates to impotence in "Honor, Impotence, and Male Sexuality in Nineteenth-Century French Medicine," *French Historical Studies* 16 (Spring 1988): 52–60.

tence or, in more severe cases, to sterility. As the "genital" instincts, as they were called, drained from the organic structures that housed them (the genitals), it was believed that the organs themselves were altered, together with all the secondary sexual characters of the individual. This process produced anatomical abnormalities that doctors believed to be the stigmata of degeneration. Though excessive copulation could bring about this result, medical specialists from the late eighteenth century on believed that the most likely explanation was masturbation.[10] Both activities, by making pleasure rather than reproduction the end of sexual activity, disrupted the "normal" and *intrinsic* aim of the genital instincts and led directly to exhaustion and premature death.

Most medical specialists in the early nineteenth century, in keeping with the principle of the old humoral medicine that men embodied the qualities of heat and dryness and women those of coolness and moistness, believed that men "spent" far more in the sex act than did women. Men were therefore especially prone to exhaustion and functional impotence.[11] This basic distinction between the sexes was maintained throughout the nineteenth century, assuming the form of evolutionary discourse after 1870 or so. The evolutionary explanation for the differences between men and women was that a woman was more biologically primitive than a man, a case of arrested embryological development. Women were therefore more "instinctive" (read "natural") than men; women's animal economies functioned more smoothly than those of men because less of their vital energy was directed away from the organism and toward the cerebrally based function of higher reason. Engaged as they were in the world of affairs, so the argument went, men had a far greater opportunity to exhaust themselves in overwork, where their superior capacity to reason was an ironic liability in the struggle for survival. Males' "genital instincts" ("sexual instincts" after 1880 or so) were therefore less reliable, less certain in aim and duration than those of women, despite the apparently greater short-run violence of their sexual behavior.[12]

As one might expect in view of these deeply rooted assumptions, the medical literature on male impotence in the nineteenth century was

10. The best medical and cultural history of this development is Jean Stengers and Anne Van Neck, *Histoire d'une grande peur: La masturbation* (Brussels: Éditions de l'Université de Bruxelles, 1984).

11. See, for example, Julien Joseph Virey, *De la femme* (Paris, 1823), 141.

12. For a late nineteenth-century example of this argument, see Julien Chevalier, *L'inversion sexuelle: Une maladie de la personnalité* (Lyon: Storck, 1893), 414–15. For a general account of the way evolutionary theory treats sex difference, see Victor J. Seidler, "Reason, Desire, and Male Sexuality," in *The Cultural Construction of Sexuality*, ed. Pat Caplan (London: Tavistock, 1987), 82–112.

extensive. Much of this material was highly popular in form, and publishers advertised regularly in newspapers and magazines. But there was also a serious psychiatric literature on the problem. One finds in these frequently republished tomes the whole spectrum of dangers to male potency: organic, chemical, behavioral. Though many cases of impotence were congenital or the result of serious accident, the majority were believed to be the consequence of mental disorder.

The starting point for the psychiatric analysis of impotence was Etienne Esquirol's notion of "erotomania," which he elaborated in his classic *Des maladies mentales* of 1838.[13] For Esquirol and his pupils erotomania was a serious disease, invariably delusional, which focused the attention of its male victims on a single object of erotic desire, a kind of obsessional idée fixe. Physicians treating impotence were not often confronted with delusional patients, but the concept of a deflected or improperly focused genital drive was a useful one that they adapted to their own ends. Dr. Félix Roubaud cited a case from his colleague Dr. Alibert of a young artist who complained of impotence with women. The young man discovered an extreme sexual excitement at drawing the forms of nude men, and this practice coincided with the appearance of his first symptoms of functional impotence. This was not, Alibert observed, a case of "vulgar" sodomy, because the bodies of living men did not move him, but was a situation in which the patient "had so inverted the application of his talents that he no longer knew how to return them to their proper object."[14] Alibert treated this case by requiring his patient to draw pictures of women's bodies, and, by degrees, "nature" triumphed over his "artificial penchants."

Roubaud, whose text was the most famous of its kind, concluded that this case was an instance of "complete perversion" successfully cured by "moral treatment" (treatment of the mind, not the body). But he averred that "incomplete perversions" were more common still. Here the organic function and external stimulus were "normal," but the imaginative faculty was momentarily focused elsewhere than on the "external stimulus"; this deflection of attention was sufficient to produce momentary impotence.[15] Roubaud and his colleagues, it is important to note, believed that impotence occurred only when the genital instincts were

13. Etienne Esquirol, *Des maladies mentales* (Paris: Baillière, 1838), 2:182–98.

14. From Dr. Alibert, *Nouveaux éléments de thérapeutique et de matière médicale* (2d ed., 2:556) as quoted in Dr. Félix Roubaud, *Traité de l'impuissance et de la stérilité chez l'homme et chez la femme* (Paris: Baillière, 1855), 223–26.

15. Roubaud, *Traité de l'impuissance*, 226–29. For a discussion of other nineteenth-century texts on impotence, see Nye, "Honor, Impotence, and Male Sexuality," 58–61.

diverted from their marital, genital, reproductive functions. They believed that marriage was a kind of prophylaxis against the dangers of impotence and sexual exhaustion that confronted adolescents, bachelors, old men, and sexual perverts. It is my argument here that this traditional emphasis on conventional marital sexuality was strongly reinforced by the deeply felt anxiety about the falling birth rate at the end of the century, so that men who deviated from this sexual norm were also perceived to be engaged in behavior that threatened the national welfare. It was in this atmosphere of crisis that the modern concept of the fetishistic perversion was formulated in French psychiatry.

Michel Foucault has presented us a version of how the classification and study of the "perversions" took place. Political experts and their allies in the medical establishment hoped to repress, if not eliminate, the perversions spreading in their midst, but instead of limiting them, these authorities produced an "age of multiplication: a dispersion of sexualities, a strengthening of their disparate forms, a multiple implantation of 'perversions.' Our epoch has initiated sexual heterogeneities."[16] The system of psychiatric classification that emerged in this era was deeply indebted to organicist medicine. Its central operating principle was that mental disorder was rooted in a parallel organic disorder that was inherited or could be acquired in predisposed individuals.[17] The psychiatrists of this era simply assumed that the appearance of any symptoms of "perversion" suggested the presence of a progressive degeneration that, if not arrested, would produce increasingly serious and bizarre behavior within this lifetime and over the span of generations.

It is not well understood that Foucault identified fetishism as the "master perversion" of this period. In the "psychiatrization of perversions," he wrote, sex was

> referred to an instinct which, through its peculiar development and according to the objects to which it could become attached, made it possible for perverse behavior patterns to arise and make their genesis intelligible. Thus "sex" was defined by the interlacing of function and instinct, finality and signification; moreover, this was the form in which it was manifested, more clearly than anywhere else, in the model perversion, in that "fetishism" which, from at least as early as 1877, served

16. Foucault, *History of Sexuality*, 1:37.
17. I have discussed this era in *Crime, Madness, and Politics*, 132–44. See also Georges Lanteri-Laura, *Lecture des perversions: Histoire de leur appropriation médicale* (Paris: Masson, 1978).

as the guiding thread for analyzing all the other deviations. In it one could clearly perceive the way in which the instinct became fastened to an object in accordance with an individual's historical adherence and biological inadequacy.[18]

Foucault does not document this statement, or justify the date 1877 as a point of some epistemological rupture, but the medical literature is fully supportive of the general point and the date is adequately approximate. The sexual perversions were regarded at this time as kinds of *folies raisonnantes*, to distinguish them from debilitating delusional states that incapacitated individuals for everyday life. Doctors believed that these illnesses, though usually organic in origin, were diseases of the reasoning faculty, which expressed themselves as obsession with certain ideas or as compulsive behavior but left cognition and ratiocination otherwise unharmed. In 1876 the forensic psychiatrist Henri Legrand du Saulle presented a paper to the Société médico-psychologique in which he discussed several cases of *folies raisonnantes*, among them a well-educated young man of twenty, with "contemplative tendencies," who felt repulsion for women in general and found himself "invincibly" attracted to images, tableaux, and statues featuring nude men and male genitalia. He was arrested one day in a public urinal in the place de la Bourse in reciprocal genital display with an elderly man.[19] Legrand du Saulle was at a loss as to how to diagnose this individual, other than to say he had a "genital perversion," but the similarity to Roubaud's earlier case is striking.

The most important initiative in defining fetishistic perversions occurred a few years later in a now-classic paper of 1882 by Jean-Martin Charcot and Valentin Magnan, the two most influential psychiatrists of the era. The paper was presented in separate parts in the *Archives de neurologie*. The first section was titled "Inversion du sens génitale," and the second section added the phrase "and other sexual perversions."[20] Charcot and Magnan state clearly that since "the form taken by these obsessions in no way modifies the basis of the illness, we are going to present some observations of sexual perversions different from the inversion of the genital sense." Though they might appear to be different illnesses, "they are simply some of the semiological variations that

18. Foucault, *History of Sexuality*, 1:154.
19. Henri Legrand du Saulle, *Séance* of the Société médico-psychologique, 27 March 1876, in *Annales médico-psychologiques* 15 (May 1876): 446.
20. *Archives de neurologie* 3 (January–February 1882): 53–60; 4 (November 1882): 296–322, reprinted as *Inversion du sens génital et autres perversions sexuelles*, ed. Gérard Bonnet (Paris: Frénésie, 1987).

degeneracy presents to us."[21] These "different" perversions are what we have since come to know as classical sexual fetishes, obsessions for night bonnets, aprons, shoes, and shoe nails. Charcot and Magnan did not, however, give them this name.

It is clear enough that for Charcot and Magnan "inversion," which term they coin here, is simply a genital perversion in which the genital appetite has fixed itself on a person of the same sex; it is a point not heretofore appreciated in the history of homosexuality.[22] The authors reveal their debt to the medical tradition by explaining these perversions as consequences of masturbation or other sexual excesses, which have "weakened" the "natural" instincts and opened the door to obsessive ideas.[23] All the victims of these perversions are impotent except in the presence of the object of their desire, and even then their orgasms are weak and usually accomplished without genital contact. The link between these types of perversion and impotence was made by medical commentators elsewhere who drew principally on the French tradition.[24]

A striking thing about Charcot and Magnan's treatment of these (fetishistic) perversions is their articulation of a cultural critique that held these perversions to be "the degrading consequences of a weakening of morals in a profoundly vitiated society."[25] This argument, which would be amplified in later medical discussions of these phenomena, testifies to the unease medical specialists felt about identifying forms of sexual behavior that recalled the sexual peculiarities and excesses of decadent Rome, and which seemed analogically related, in their manifestations of impotence, to the cultural and political exhaustion of that ancient society.[26]

It was not until 1887 that Charcot's student Alfred Binet finally gave a name to this strange phenomenon. Binet published "Fetishism in Love" not in an obscure medical journal but in the prestigious *Revue philosophique*, thereby ensuring a broad audience for his synthesis. He set

21. Ibid., 305.

22. In a signal failure to appreciate this point, see the preface by Gérard Bonnet to the reprinted version of Charcot and Magnan's paper, pp. v–xxv. I have discussed this paper elsewhere as an aspect of the history of homosexuality in France, "Sex Difference and Male Homosexuality in French Medical Discourse," *Bulletin of the History of Medicine* 63 (1989): 32–51.

23. Charcot and Magnan, *Inversion du sens génital*, 54–57.

24. For instance, William A. Hammond, M.D., *Sexual Impotence in the Male and Female* (New York: Birmingham, 1883), especially 32–35, 40–52, 59–66. Hammond discusses a number of shoe fetishists, though without calling them by that name.

25. Charcot and Magnan, *Inversion du sens génital*, 54.

26. On this connection, see Dr. Dupouy, *Médecine et moeurs de l'ancienne Rome d'après les poètes latins* (Paris: Baillière, 1885).

the whole problem of fetishism against the background of cultural crisis and exhaustion. The very appearance of these multiple attachments, he wrote, is the consequence of the unique need, "so frequent in our epoch, to augment the causes of excitation and pleasure. Both history and physiology teach us that these are the marks of enfeeblement and decadence. The individual does not look for strong excitations with such avidity but when his power of reaction is already in a weakened state."[27]

Binet admitted that all love was to some extent fetishistic, but he maintained that a kind of "psychic impotence" was invariably associated with the obsessive attention fetishists paid to a particular feature of the loved one or an article of clothing or, worse still, an unrelated object. Binet agreed with Charcot and Magnan that a "perverse predisposition" was the "characteristic fact" of fetishism, no matter what form it took, but he insisted that heredity itself could not explain the particular attachment each fetishist displayed, for the origins of an individual fetish harkened back to some accident in the victim's psychic past.[28] As Charcot and Magnan had done, Binet treated inversion as a fetish, arguing that the only difference between an invert and a boot fetishist was a variation in life experience.[29]

Binet left little doubt that his essay was also a critique of contemporary culture. He cited recent novels where some variety of fetishistic love figured prominently.[30] He scorned the modern fascination for makeup, where the lover fixes his attention on the artificial rather than the real, on the actress rather than the woman who hides behind the mask. True love, he argued, is a kind of symphony, an emotional "polytheism," which celebrates all the glories of the beloved, not an impoverished "monotheism," which focuses impotently on a single unworthy object. "Normal love," he wrote, "leads always to the deification of the whole individual, a natural enough consideration given its aim of reproduction."[31]

Other medical commentators amplified these themes. Nearly all the books written on perversions in this era treated homosexuality as a fetish.[32] They also regularly distinguished between the fetishistic and the sadomasochistic perversions as a difference between a *monstrum*

27. Binet, "Le fétichisme," 166.
28. Ibid., 164.
29. Ibid., 165.
30. For instance, Adolphe Belot, *La bouche de Madame X*, cited in Binet, "Le fétichisme," 170.
31. Ibid., 164–65, my emphasis.
32. Paul-Emile Garnier, *Les fétichistes, pervertis, et invertis sexuels: Observations médico-légales* (Paris: Baillière, 1896), 22; Georges Saint-Paul, *Perversion et perversités sexuelles: Une enquête médicale sur l'inversion* (Paris, 1896), 20–31.

par excessum (sadism, masochism) and a *monstrum par defectum* (fetishism).[33] Fetishists and inverts were not truly potent, because their orgasms were dependent on "abnormal" sexual stratagems and were marked by "hyperesthesia" or "irritable weakness."[34] The criticism doctors leveled at their culture reads like Old Testament prophecy with a twist. Men admired clothes and refinements, avidly sought riches, intellectual emancipation, sensual pleasures, and excessive amounts of food and drink; but they did so not out of sheer unregulated vitality or powerful penchants for evil—the standard Judeo-Christian point of view—but from a kind of weakness in which "cerebral" stimuli had overridden depleted natural instincts.[35] As the sexologist Charles Féré summed up this outlook, "The sexual preoccupations [of individuals] are often in inverse ratio to their sexual powers. Nations that perish through sterility are remarkable for licentiousness."[36]

In spite of the stern tone of some of these medical jeremiads, many of the texts on fetishism reveal an ambivalence toward male sexual aberration that seems somehow more in the worldly spirit of the *belle époque*.[37] Many of them freely admit the fetishistic elements in normal love, and some even suggest the utility of creating fetishes in individuals as a form of sexual therapy.[38] Since the line between the normal and the pathological was only one of degree, as we have seen, a passage such as the following on buttock fetishism does not stand as a refutation of the grimmer views on such matters:

> Have you ever contemplated at the National Museum of Naples the Venus Callipyge, that divine piece of marble which throws off sparks of life, grace, and love? Is it not the most beautiful, the most lifelike, the most voluptuous, the most desirable of antique Venuses? In the pres-

33. Emile Laurent, *Fétichistes et érotomanes* (Paris: Vigot, 1905), 7.

34. Henri Legludic, *Notes et observations de médecine légale: Attentats aux moeurs* (Paris: Masson, 1896), 224–25; Dr. Louis Reuss, "Des aberrations du sens génésique chez l'homme," *Annales d'hygiène publique et de médecine légale*, 3d ser., 16 (1886): 311; Garnier, *Les fétichistes*, 144–45; Chevalier, *L'inversion sexuelle*, 414–15.

35. Garnier, *Les fétichistes*, 18–19; Alexandre Lacassagne, preface to Chevalier, *L'inversion sexuelle*, v; Emile Laurent, *L'amour morbide: Etude de psychologie pathologique*, 3d ed. (Paris: 1895), 319; Joanny Roux, *Psychologie de l'instinct sexuel* (Paris: Baillière, 1899), 82.

36. Charles Féré, *The Evolution and Dissolution of the Sexual Instinct*, 2d rev. ed. (Paris: Carrington, 1904), 31. For a similar statement, see Reuss, "Des aberrations," 315–16.

37. For a remarkable account of the Parisian *vie de bohème* which stresses the ambivalence of bohemian and bourgeois attitudes toward each other, see Jerrold Siegel, *Bohemian Paris* (New York: Viking, 1986).

38. Roux, *Psychologie de l'instinct sexuel*, 87–90.

ence of that incomparable spectacle the fetishism of buttocks is self-explanatory, for it is highly unlikely that all the admirers of the Venus Callipyge are sick.[39]

A male point of view is obvious here. It was somehow inconceivable for this generation of doctors to imagine that women might somehow be able to transcend their roles as "natural" sexual objects and have a subjective orientation toward love (as opposed to mere "subjectivity").[40] It is also clear here that the medical theory of sexual fetishism was in a certain sense also an aesthetic psychology. The "search for beauty" cannot, Binet admitted, be satisfied in the same way as the "material" instincts (genital, hunger, thirst); it springs from the same kind of cerebral and imaginative condition that drives the fetishist and causes him to exaggerate and overvalue the object of his love.[41] That this thirst for beauty sprang from weakness and decline rather than a healthy vigor is an irony that was not lost on the psychiatrists or the partisans of the decadent movement in literature, with the difference, perhaps, that the latter aficionados of decay relished rather than feared its ultimate consequences.

The perspectives on sexual identity and sexual perversion presented in the literature of the 1880s and 1890s are remarkably similar to the technical medical writing on the same subjects, raising the question of who was learning from whom. The theme of strong women/weak men appears regularly in fin-de-siècle literature as does a helpless and confused resignation on the part of men at the new emancipation of women.[42] The so-called decadent writers—J. K. Huysmans, Remy de Gourmont, Joséphin Péladan, Jean Lorrain, Pierre Louys, Rachilde—explored the whole range of sexual perversions in their novels and plays, stressing the themes of social and moral decay, ambiguous sexuality, and male impotence.

Perhaps the most famous of these texts, Huysmans's A rebours (1884), contains several examples of the fetishistic obsessions of its hero Des

---

39. Laurent, Fétichistes, 44. See also Binet, "Le fétichisme," passim.

40. As Julien Chevalier wrote, women are more instinctive, "and so resemble one another in love, while men, more conscious, more cerebral, love in a particular and personal fashion." L'inversion sexuelle, 414–15.

41. Binet, "Le fétichisme," 161.

42. Isabelle de Courtivron, "Weak Men and Fatal Women: The Sand Image," in Homosexualities and French Literature: Cultural Contexts, Critical Texts, ed. George Stambolian and Elaine Marks (Ithaca: Cornell University Press, 1979), 210–27. See also Annelise Mauge, L'identité masculine en crise au tournant du siècle (Paris: Rivages, 1987). These themes are also considered in Sander L. Gilman, Difference and Pathology: Stereotypes of Sexuality, Race, and Madness (Ithaca: Cornell University Press, 1985).

Esseintes, which, without actually taking the name, fall into the categories of olfactory, auditory, and visual fetishes. The three episodes of recollection in chapter 9 chronicle the progressive sexual exhaustion of Des Esseintes in a style that is practically interchangeable with that of the psychiatrist's case study.

The first of these episodes involves the American acrobat Miss Urania, she of the "supple body, sinewy legs, muscles of steel, and arms of iron."[43] The fragile Des Esseintes imagines a kind of "change of sex" in which she would take the man's role in their relationship because he was himself "becoming increasingly feminized."[44] He is bitterly disappointed, however, because her sexual comportment is in fact conventionally coy and passive, aggravating the "premature impotence" he already suffers.[45] His second mistress, evoked by powerful olfactory memories, was a café-concert ventriloquist, a dark and boyish woman who captivated Des Esseintes by her ventriloquistic ability to project exotic literary dialogue into statues of the Chimera and the Sphinx, giving "life and voice to the two monsters."[46] Inevitably, however, "his [sexual] weakness became more pronounced; the effervescence of his brain could no longer melt his frozen body: the nerves no longer obeyed his will; the mad passions of old men overtook him. Feeling himself grow more and more sexually indecisive, he had recourse to the most effective stimulant of old voluptuaries, fear":

> While he held her clasped in his arms, a husky voice burst out from behind the door: "Let me in, I know you have a lover with you, just wait, you trollop." Suddenly, like the libertines excited by the terror of being taken en flagrant délit outdoors . . . he would temporarily recover his powers and throw himself upon the ventriloquist, who continued to hurl her shouts from beyond the door.[47]

Rejected finally by this woman, who preferred a man with "less complicated requirements and a sturdier back," Des Esseintes embarked on a

43. Joris-Karl Huysmans, A rebours (Paris: Fasquelle, n.d.), 140.
44. Ibid., 141.
45. Ibid., 143.
46. Ibid., 144.
47. Ibid., 146. In what may be an instance of medicine's borrowing from literature, Alfred Binet wrote in his 1887 article about how impotent men "seek rare sensations" to provide "the new source of energy and pleasure" that will sustain erections, including "luxury . . . [and] the risk of being caught in flagrante delicto. . . . all these refinements invented by the subtle imaginations of the jaded attest to an unconscious search for sensory excitations that are able, by stimulating the subject, to augment the physical pleasure of love." "Le fétichisme," 160.

homosexual affair with a young Parisian *gavroche*, entering the last stage, so to speak, of his sexual decline: "Never had he experienced a more alluring and imperious liaison; never had he tasted such perils or felt himself so painfully fulfilled."[48]

The "hero" of Remy de Gourmont's *Sixtine* (1890), Des Entragues, seems to be patterned on the same model of psychic impotence as Huysmans's Des Esseintes, for he drives away the delectable Sixtine with exotic foreplay she correctly takes to be evasion. "I don't know how to live," Des Entragues complains. "My existence is perpetual cerebration, the complete negation of ordinary life and its ordinary loves."[49] In the later *Le songe d'une femme* (1899), Gourmont punishes his misogynous hero by subjecting him in a dream to a female monster that one might call the nightmare of the (male) fetishist. In his dream Paul enters a conservatory filled with heaving, fleshlike flowers that transform themselves into the limbs and parts of women. By stages, a pair of disembodied arms randomly assembles a melange of these parts into a grotesque whole:

> Don't you recognize me, my love? We're all those separate parts you so love, that you've just been worshipping. Put together somewhat hastily, I confess, we're the beauty you enjoyed last night; every part of her, every one of the chapels where you knelt with such fervor. Does the order of our design matter so much? Would you like legs instead of arms, arms in place of legs? There you are—look. . . . Do you want my head down to my belly, my belly in place of my head? There you are— look. See, I express myself very well, even though I've no teeth. Am I lovely? . . . You love me don't you? Give me your lips, my love.[50]

There is one last interesting, albeit speculative, reason why sexual fetishism may have appeared first in France, and developed such deep roots there. Many of the decadent writers were social and political conservatives and nationalist and "revanchist" in foreign policy.[51] The medical community, in its public hygiene function as "first servant of the state," was equally disposed to a conservative, nationalist outlook.[52] Could it be that the concept of fetishism sprang to mind because both

48. Huysmans, *A rebours*, 147.

49. As quoted in Jennifer Birkett, *The Sins of the Fathers: Decadence in France, 1870–1914* (London: Quartet, 1986), 104.

50. As quoted ibid., 124.

51. See Birkett, *Sins of the Fathers*, on Lorrain (199), Rachilde (178–80), and Péladan (134–35).

52. On medical conservatism around the turn of the century, see Nye, *Crime, Madness, and Politics in Modern France*.

doctors and writers viewed French expansion in the colonies as a (fetishistic) compensation or displacement for the proper aim of regaining Alsace-Lorraine? Might fetishistic love, in other words, be to real love what colonialism is to *revanche*?

Though fetishism seems to have originated in France, it was soon incorporated into the great sexological classics of the turn of the century: Richard von Krafft-Ebing's *Psychopathia sexualis* (1st edition 1886); Havelock Ellis's *Studies in the Psychology of Sex* (1897–1910), and Sigmund Freud's *Three Essays on the Theory of Sexuality* (1905). In these different national settings, fetishism and the other "perversions" of the "normal" genital instinct were not regarded by medical specialists with the same degree of hostility or concern that they received in France. With the partial exception of Great Britain, where there was a flurry of concern about the "quality" of the population after the Boer War (1900), no other European power had anything like the unique set of geopolitical and demographic concerns of the French. As I have argued elsewhere, there was, as a result, relatively less concern in these countries that nonprocreative sexual activity might have far-reaching biological consequences in the general population. Thus, it was possible for Krafft-Ebing, Ellis, and even Freud to pose as sexual reformers demanding more tolerance for homosexuals and acknowledgment by the courts that homosexuality was an innate condition requiring sympathy or treatment, not prosecution.[53]

Lawrence Birken has argued that in the last quarter of the century, European sexologists reacted ambivalently to the array of perversions— fetishism among them—that they were busily classifying and analyzing. On the one hand, the weight of tradition encouraged them to consider "heterogenital coitus" the "normal" way to satisfy sexual desire; on the other hand, the sexual science they were creating "was to dissolve these distinctions even as it desperately sought to uphold them, by understanding desire in its radically idiosyncratic form as 'fetishes' or 'perversions.'"[54] It is interesting for us to consider for a moment the way Freud's work on sexual fetishism displays this ambivalent outlook; though his early work bears the imprint of French thinking on the subject and the influence of traditional medical thinking about the dangers of nonprocreative sexuality, he was gradually able to break with these ideas and make bold new departures in his theorizing about fetishism.

53. Robert A. Nye, "The History of Sexuality in Context: National Sexological Traditions," *Science in Context* 4 (Autumn 1991): 387–406.

54. Lawrence Birken, *Consuming Desire: Sexual Science and the Emergence of the Culture of Abundance, 1871–1914* (Ithaca: Cornell University Press, 1988), 50.

In the early "Sexuality in the Aetiology of the Neuroses" (1898), Freud
sought to discredit the notion that neurosis arose from degenerative or
constitutional disorders or from functional exhaustion such as overwork. Most cases of neurasthenia or anxiety neurosis, he wrote, were the
consequence of digressions from the "normal *vita sexualis*," such as
masturbation (with its attendant impotence) or coitus interruptus. He
recommends in particular inducing patients to abandon the habit of
masturbation, observing that "medical treatment, in this instance, can
have no other aim than to lead the neurasthenic who has now recovered
his strength, back to normal sexual intercourse. For sexual need, when
once it has been aroused and has been satisfied for any length of time,
can no longer be silenced: it can only be displaced along another
path."[55] Freud was convinced that masturbation in both sexes needed
particular attention because such excess produced impotence, and since
neurasthenia "is a disorder which we are told is growing more and more
prevalent, we see that it is positively a matter of public interest *that men
should enter upon sexual relations with full potency*."[56] Freud here
seems remarkably close to a "populationist" position that equates sexual
health with reproductive potency.

Writing seven years later on the same question, Freud mentioned the
specific activities that provoked adult neurosis but placed general blame
on any action that led to "an insufficient discharge of the libido that had
been produced."[57] It seems clear enough that Freud still shared the
central belief of French psychiatrists that, however produced, male impotence was the key causal agent in the creation of sexual deviations or
their subsequent neuroses. Nonetheless, this basic assumption, which
he followed up in all his patients in this era, enabled him to identify
libido as a sexual force that was neutral with respect to aim and object
until fixed by a combination of the individual's life history and constitutional makeup, the position he articulates in the great *Three Essays on
the Theory of Sexuality* (1905).

In the first of the three essays, Freud discusses the sexual aberrations.
These he divides into two categories: deviations with respect to sexual
object and to sexual aim. In the first category he considers inversion at
some length and children and animals briefly. In the second category he
treats fetishism, observing that "no other variation of the sexual instinct
that borders on the pathological can lay so much claim to our interest as

55. Sigmund Freud, "Sexuality in the Aetiology of the Neuroses" (1898), in *Standard Edition*, 3:275–76.
56. Ibid., 278, Freud's emphasis.
57. Freud, "My Views on the Part Played by Sexuality in the Aetiology of the
Neuroses" (1905), in *Standard Edition*, 7:272.

does this one."[58] But he immediately questions his own distinction between object and aim by suggesting that fetishism might as easily have been mentioned in the previous section on deviations in respect of sexual object. Indeed, on close examination there is little to distinguish between them. In both some "genital" weakness or diminution of the "normal sexual aim" (heterosexual intercourse) is a prerequisite;[59] there is in both a kind of overvaluation of the love object that refuses to restrict itself to "union of the actual genitals."[60] Sexual satisfaction, therefore, can be obtained in this deflected love only by masturbation or "simple outpourings of emotion."[61]

Freud's treatment of the similarity of inversion and fetishism in the *Three Essays* thus, in many respects, remarkably resembles the French view. But Freud uses the similarity between them to reach a diametrically opposite conclusion from that of French psychiatry, one that places him, in contradistinction, in the camp of sexual "enlightenment" and toleration.[62] "It has been brought to our notice," he writes,

> that we have been in the habit of regarding the connection between the sexual instinct and the sexual object as more intimate than it in fact is. Experience of the cases that are considered abnormal has shown us that in them the sexual instinct and the sexual object are merely soldered together—a fact which we have been in danger of overlooking in consequence of the uniformity of the normal picture, where the object appears to form part and parcel of the instinct. We are thus warned to loosen the bond that exists in our thoughts between instinct and object.[63]

By 1905, though not breaking entirely with the prevailing psychiatric tradition, Freud's criterion for distinguishing between the normal and

58. Freud, *Three Essays on the Theory of Sexuality*, in *Standard Edition*, 7:153.

59. In the section of Freud's *Three Essays* on inversion, see the remarks on pages 140–41 and the remark on impotence and bestiality on 148; in the section on fetishism, see the remark on 141 about "executive weakness" of the sexual apparatus as a "precondition."

60. Ibid., 150–51. Freud refers here to the subject as "intellectually infatuated."

61. On this application to inverts, ibid., 142–43; on fetishistic fixations, ibid., 145–46.

62. See for this point Arnold Davidson's important argument, which nonetheless exaggerates the decisiveness of the rupture Freud achieved with mainstream psychiatry. "How to Do the History of Psychoanalysis: A Reading of Freud's *Three Essays on the Theory of Sexuality*," *Critical Inquiry* 13 (Winter 1987): 252–77.

63. Freud, *Three Essays*, 147–48. I have discussed this broader question of tolerance for sexual "perversion" in national context in "The History of Sexuality in Context."

the pathological in sexual life was less closely tied to an absolute and biologically determined standard of genital heterosexuality than was the French. If anything, his evolution away from biological determinism accelerated in later years, so that in his last writings on fetishism Freud treats fetishes as "screen memories," "precipitates," or substitutes for the dreaded loss of the penis in men.[64] He has, in short, converted the "perverse" manifestations of impotence, narrowly premised on the normalcy of "heterogenitality," into a powerful analytic matrix of symptoms, mental disturbances, and neuroses associated with the castration complex.

It seems to me impossible to avoid the conclusion that the concept of the sexual fetish was born in a cultural crisis in Western Europe, which was experienced more intensely by the French for reasons unique to their cultural and historical experience and which was reflected in the preoccupations of their medical elite. In this medical conception, any departures from conventional reproductive behavior cast great doubt on the normality of the subject and on the nature of the bond he experienced with the object of his desire. We have reason to suppose that fetishistic behavior has always played some role in human love, but the precipitous emergence of a medically inspired concept of fetishistic perversion in fin-de-siècle France allows us to situate the concept more precisely in its historical setting and to understand better why the concept provoked such a powerful and widespread resonance in other regions of French cultural life.

64. See the footnotes in *Three Essays*, added in editions after 1905, esp. 154 n. 2 (1920), where he criticizes Binet's assumptions about the largely accidental nature of fetishistic fixations. See also "Fetishism" (1927), in *Standard Edition*, 21:152–57.

Masquerading Women, Pathologized Men: Cross-Dressing, Fetishism, and the Theory of Perversion, 1882–1935

Jann Matlock

Women can't be fetishists, declared psychiatrist Gatian de Gaeton de Clérambault in 1908.[1] We might well greet Clérambault's assessment with relief. After a century of analyses of female madness, at last doctors had found a form of abnormality from which women were exempt. We might also wonder at Clérambault's reading of his predecessors. By 1908, Lacan's teacher might have found some *twenty* female fetishists in the psychiatric literature of his era.[2] What on earth

I thank Emily Apter, William Pietz, Sara Blair, Linda Nochlin, Robert Nye, Vanessa Schwartz, Ann-Louise Shapiro, Abigail Solomon-Godeau, Rebecca Spang, and Linda Williams, for their generous comments and suggestions on different drafts of this essay. I am especially grateful to Emily Apter for encouraging me to write on Clérambault. I am also greatly indebted to Dr. Jacques Postel and the staff of the Bibliothèque Henri Ey for their assistance in researching early French psychiatry, and to the staff of the Archives de la Préfecture de police in Paris.

1. Gatian de Gaeton de Clérambault, "Passion érotique des étoffes chez la femme" (1908), in *Oeuvre psychiatrique* (Paris: Presses Universitaires de France, 1942), 698, hereafter abbreviated PE. Unless otherwise indicated, all translations of French texts are my own.

2. Indeed, four of Binet's twenty-two cases of fetishism concerned women. Four women appeared among ten cases of (fetishistic) perversion analyzed by Magnan and Charcot. All three of Moreau de Tours' 1883 cases described women's sexual madness. Of eighteen observations that would serve as the foundation for the analysis of fetishistic perversions in Magnan's study of *perversions sexuelles*, nine were female. Moll insists on the prevalence of female perversions. Though Laurent's 1905 work looked primarily at male fetishists and female erotomaniacs, his *Amour morbide* (1891) gave much attention to women. Of all the major studies published in the thirty years prior to Clérambault's analysis of female cloth obsessionals, only Garnier, *Les fétichistes* (1896), altogether omitted women's propensities to sexual pathology. See Alfred Binet, "Le fétichisme dans l'amour," *Revue philosophique* 24 (1887), 143–67,

could Clérambault have had in mind when he absolved women of fetishistic aberrations?

Although Clérambault embraced a view of fetishism opposed to that of many of his contemporaries, he nevertheless articulated a recurring obsession in turn-of-the-century European psychiatry. His insistence on gender difference in sexual madness reveals his ties to a century of observations of madness *in* difference. Throughout the nineteenth century, *aliénistes* (as the early members of the French psychiatric movement called themselves) looked at male and female patients through an optic of essential gender difference. The most frequently asked question of the midcentury—Can men be hysterical?—carried with it a charge affecting all conceptions of gender both inside and outside the asylum. Its corollary—Are women more prone than men to madness?—marked decades of psychiatric study with an answer that doomed women to surveillance, inactivity, and limited spheres.

In the course of the 1880s, however, psychiatrists throughout Europe shifted their attention from madness to perversion. With this shift came a discursive shift from the *study of women* to the *study of men.* Charcot's conclusion that men could suffer from hysteria, combined with a general psychiatric fascination with heredity as a source of mental illness, shook up the strict gender divisions that had governed the concerns of *aliénisme.* In the place of debates about men's predilection for hysteria, psychiatrists now asked, "Are women prone to perversion?" "Can women be fetishists?"

New categories of perversion brought "new kinds of people" into being, Arnold Davidson has argued.[3] We need therefore to study how the doctors of the turn of the century described their new subjects, how they imagined the practices they attributed to those subjects, and ultimately, how they generated a prescribed version of "normal" sexuality. My goal

---

252–74 (hereafter abbreviated FA); Jean-Martin Charcot and Valentin Magnan, "Inversion du sens génital," *Archives du neurologie* 3 (1882): 53–60; 4 (1882), 296–322 (hereafter abbreviated ISG); Valentin Magnan, *Des anomalies, des aberrations, et des perversions sexuelles* (Paris: Delahaye, 1885; hereafter abbreviated *AAPS*); Jacques-Joseph Moreau de Tours, *Des aberrations du sens génésique* (Paris, 1883; hereafter abbreviated *ASG*); Albert Moll, *Les perversions de l'instinct génital* (Paris: Carré, 1893), a translation of *Die Konträre Sexualempfindung* (Berlin: Fischer, 1891); Richard von Krafft-Ebing, *Psychopathia sexualis,* 12th ed., trans. Harry Wedeck (New York: Putnam, 1965; hereafter abbreviated PS); Emile Laurent, *Fétichistes et érotomanes* (Paris: Vigot, 1905; hereafter abbreviated FE); Laurent, *L'amour morbide: Etude de psychologie pathologique* (Paris: Société d'éducation scientifique, 1891); Laurent, *Les bisexués: Gynécomastes et hermaphrodites* (Paris: Carré, 1894); Paul-Emile Garnier, *Les fétichistes, pervertis, et invertis sexuels: Observations médico-légales* (Paris: Baillière, 1896; hereafter abbreviated LF).

3. Arnold Davidson, "Sex and the Emergence of Sexuality," *Critical Inquiry* 14 (Autumn 1987): 47.

here is an understanding of how those "new people" came to be gendered as male.

To demonstrate how the shift from madness to perversion produced its own version of sexual difference, I concentrate on two kinds of behavior identified as perversion and categorized as types of fetishism: clothing obsessions and costume obsessions. Differentiated only loosely in the decades between 1880 and 1935, these two kinds of "abnormality" focused concerns over homosexuality, masturbation, criminality, and degeneracy. By definition, clothing fetishists desire cloth or clothing which they hoard, steal, masturbate with, or make the precondition of sexual contact. Costume obsessionals desire sexual contact with partners wearing certain costumes or want to dress themselves in certain costumes, frequently those of the opposite sex.

I will argue in this essay that clothing obsessionals played a central role in the gendering of perversion in turn-of-the-century France, and a pivotal role in our understanding of sexual difference. Just as mid-nineteenth-century debates about hysteria provided the foundation for understandings of women's sexuality, these later debates about clothing fetishism generated new appreciations of the gendering of bodies and imaginations.

Perverts Uncloaked as Female

Women hide their perversions better than men, argued Jean-Martin Charcot and Valentin Magnan in the 1882 essay that first articulated a concept of sexual perversion. Clinical observations demonstrated, the French *aliénistes* claimed, that "unnatural or contrary sexual impulses" are identical in both sexes—though women may veil their "instinctive troubles" with greater facility (ISG, 303). Two cases imported from the German allowed Charcot and Magnan to elucidate the similarities of female and male perversion. Both patients were young women who showed preference from an early age for other women: "They wanted to dress as boys, they would have wanted to be men. The gazes of certain girls impressed them acutely; they courted them, blushing when near them, struck by a keen passion" (ISG, 304). Cross-dressing, sexual desire for other girls, masturbation, and suicidal wishes convinced Charcot and Magnan of the psychopathic dimensions of these women's degeneracy (ISG, 304–5).[4]

4. Charcot and Magnan here produce four detailed observations of men, amplified by analysis of six other cases, four concerning women. Of those four women, three

These German cases of female cross-dressers had a particularly charged way of eliciting French debate over the differences between fetishism and cross-dressing. Not only did these women reappear in other psychiatric studies, but their specific form of "perversion" emerged in the next decades as the dominant shape given to women's sexual aberrations.[5] One wonders if transvestism became the perversion psychiatrists were willing to leave to women, even as they turned their attention to more varied forms of male cloth and costume fetishism. In fact, over the next fifty years of psychiatric studies of perversion, one detects an epistemological split between fetishism, increasingly classed as exclusively male, and transvestism, which included male and female variants.[6] As we shall see, these gender divisions between male fetishism and female perversions masked complicated social anxieties at the turn of this century.

Because of the fluidity of psychiatric categories, however, we need to look beyond the specific terms doctors gave to their diagnoses to demonstrate how they managed to extract women's fetishistic practices from their concerns and how they nonetheless generated categories of patho-

---

turn up among Magnan's 1885 cases in the category containing fetishists. One serves as a reference point for Binet. I do not wish to argue that the cases of women analyzed by Charcot and Magnan are those of fetishists *as such*. But I do want to emphasize the fluidity between what is studied here as sexual "perversion" and the type of perversion that will come to gain the label of "fetishism."

5. The original cases derive from C. Westphal, "Die conträre Sexualempfindung," *Archiv für Psychiatrie und Nervenkrankheiten* 2 (1869): 73–108; and H. Gock, "Beitrag zur Kenntnis der conträren Sexualempfindung," *Archiv für Psychiatrie und Nervenkrankheiten* 5 (1875): 564–75. For their reappearances, see Magnan, AAPS, 17–18. Moll sees transvestites as fetishists who wear the clothing to which they are attracted. See his 1924 edition of Krafft-Ebing, PS, 572–632. See also Havelock Ellis, "Eonism" (1906), in *Studies in the Psychology of Sex* 2, pt. 2 (New York: Random House, 1936): 14–15.

6. After the 1880s, observers treated the line between cross-dressing and clothing obsession as ambiguous, though most saw both as sexual perversions, symptoms of severe psychopathic or neuropathic ailments, and at least partially related to hereditary problems. Ellis took pains to differentiate transvestism ("Eonism") from fetishism. Krafft-Ebing, like Moll, gave more attention to producing cases to fit his categories than to differences between the categories he labels "fetishism," "viraginity," "gynandry," "homosexuality or urning," and "effemination." Agnès Masson reproduced sixty-six observations of cross-dressing ranging between 1800 and the 1930s, in *Le travestissement: Essai de psycho-pathologie sexuelle* (Paris: Hippocrate, 1935; hereafter abbreviated *LT*). Although she argued that cross-dressing was not a form of mental illness (88–90), she nevertheless underlined its intimate relationship to fetishism (69). Magnus Hirschfeld's six-hundred-page *Die Transvestiten* (Berlin: Alfred Pulvermacher, 1910) led to further analysis of separate categories of transvestism and fetishistic practices in his later compendium *Geschlects anomalien und perversionen*, translated as *Anomalies et perversions sexuelles*, trans. Ann-Catherine Stier (Paris: Corréa, 1957; hereafter abbreviated *APS*).

logical practice in which women were understood to participate. Early theorists of perversion gave considerable space to female aberrations, cataloging cases of female transvestism as corollaries to studies of male fetishism. The clothes obsessions of male fetishists emerge as intimately related to the masquerades psychiatrists attributed to women. By exploring the gender divisions read into perversion, I hope to reopen questions posed by more recent critical appropriations of female fetishism and feminine masquerade.[7]

The psychiatric profession could not have created its perverts without including women. The female cross-dresser came to embody women's sexual perversion in Charcot and Magnan's 1882 study. By Magnan's 1885 lecture, women's perverse desires had begun to take a range of forms alongside the perverse desires of men. And as we shall see, the female fetishist retained center stage in Binet's 1887 "Fétichisme dans l'amour." With Binet's synthesis, however, it was a woman's *garb* and not her own sexual practices that began to characterize the obsessions of sexual perverts. By the end of the century, the ways women dressed would define male as well as female perversions. Case studies demonstrated that women were not only dressing *themselves* up perversely but they were also lending perverse manners to men.

Four kinds of male and female *aliénés* demonstrate sexual aberrations, Magnan explained in 1885: "idiots" suffering from the uncontrollable desire to masturbate; individuals unable to control their sexual urges for members of the opposite sex; "erotomaniacs" infatuated with some individual, imaginary or real, who occupies their every thought—though they remain chaste; and patients under a psychic influence that acts upon them "in the same way as in normal people" except that "for these individuals, the idea, the sentiment, or the penchant is *perverted*"

7. I am thinking of the important work of Sarah Kofman, Naomi Schor, Kaja Silverman, and Mary Ann Doane, without which the very questions I am asking might not have been possible. See Kofman, *The Enigma of Woman: Woman in Freud's Writings*, trans. Catherine Porter (Ithaca: Cornell University Press, 1985); Schor, "Female Fetishism: The Case of George Sand," *Poetics Today* 6, no. 1–2 (1985): 301–10, and "Fetishism and Its Ironies," in this volume; Silverman, "Fragments of a Fashionable Discourse," in *Studies in Entertainment*, ed. Tania Modleski (Bloomington: Indiana University Press, 1986), 138–52; Doane, "Film and the Masquerade: Theorising the Female Spectator," *Screen* 23 (September–October 1982): 74–88, "Masquerade Reconsidered: Further Thoughts on the Female Spectator," *Discourse* 11 (Fall–Winter 1988–89): 42–54, and "Veiling over Desire: Close-ups of the Woman," in *Feminism and Psychoanalysis*, ed. Richard Feldstein and Judith Roof (Ithaca: Cornell University Press, 1989), 105–41. See most recently, Emily Apter, "Unmasking the Masquerade: Fetishism and Femininity from the Goncourt Brothers to Joan Riviere," in *Feminizing the Fetish: Psychoanalysis and Narrative Obsession in Turn-of-the-Century France* (Ithaca: Cornell University Press, 1991), 65–98.

(AAPS, 4). Unlike the masturbating idiots, convulsing nymphomaniacs, and ecstatically vapid erotomaniacs of the first three categories, this last group of individuals proved particularly worrisome to Magnan and his contemporaries, for they reasoned with agility, desired with social restraint, and experienced sexual urges in a causal relationship to their chosen stimuli. But they did so with a twist. Unlike the impoverished degenerates of the asylum, these clients were frequently bourgeois or aristocratic, typically quite literate, and almost always in reproductive trouble.[8]

The perverts in this category might at first seem to have little in common besides the pain with which they and their families view unacceptable desires. Yet when it comes to reproductive sex, every one of these individuals has other concerns. A twenty-nine-year-old woman suffers from acute anxiety about her sexual desire for her five small nephews. A thirty-two-year-old mother of two suffers from a sexual obsession for a thirteen-year-old schoolboy whom she has caressed, propositioned, and pursued until the scandal persuaded her family to place her in an asylum. A young mother of three, despite a history of "morality and good conduct," announces to her husband that she has fallen in love with a youth of twenty-four with whom she wishes to spend six months satisfying her "needs of the soul" before returning to her conjugal duties. A hysterical woman harmoniously married for twelve years falls wildly in love with a "cart driver" even though she is aware that her husband is "superior to her lover." An engineer craves the sight of bottoms, especially those of little boys, and is so dismayed that he undergoes shock treatments to his bone marrow in hopes that he will be able to fulfill his marital obligations. A university professor suffers from the obsessional desire to see other men naked. He finds uninteresting even the most beautiful women, though he hopes each time for sexual excitement. His desires are accompanied by his pleasures in "la toilette féminine," by cross-dressing, and fashion chatter with women.

The two German cases of female cross-dressers serve again as reference points for an understanding of perversion, allowing Magnan to

---

8. Although asylum doctors of the midcentury seemed unconcerned whether their patients produced progeny, psychiatrists of the period following 1880 constantly assess the past and future sexual activity of their cases. If the goal is not always to help these individuals return to the sphere of the "normal," then it is at least to keep them from "perverting" others. Charcot and Magnan tell of a university professor who is possessed by a violent desire to see nude men. His cross-dressing is read as a significant aspect of his problem, his present obsession with the female toilette as just another symptom of his "inversion." The doctors write in 1882 that their suggestions may be working a cure on the man's disinterest in women. By 1885 Magnan anticipates no such cure.

broach the issue of *obsessive ideas*, which he sees as the root problem in three cases of fetishism.[9] These three classic obsessionals take as their sexual objects white pinafores, shoenails from women's shoes, and a nightcap on an aged woman's wrinkled head. Like the two young women who want to be men, the male shoenail fixator and nightcap fetishist have become so stuck on their objects that they cannot be coerced into reproductive sexuality. Homosexuality—whether male or female—becomes, in this reading, just another perverse obsession with a non-productive object.[10]

In Magnan's analysis of sexual perversion, the relationship between clothing obsessions and transvestism is so integral that the gender of the individuals studied is not an issue. Magnan is far more concerned with these individuals' legal and moral responsibility for their madness, and with their future care. Although he does not propose ways of curing their ills, he nevertheless insists that despite their reasonable appearance, they should be placed under the eye of doctors and within the framework of the asylum system (AAPS, 27). Magnan's work rescued the theory of degeneration and the psychiatric profession that had been staking its reputation on it, just at a moment when *aliénisme* was becoming increasingly unpopular. Ruth Harris has argued that the extension of degeneration theory to the sexual sphere empowered the psychiatrists who embraced such theories by lending a biological authority to their ideas.[11] The new emphasis on perversion also expanded the doctors' realm well beyond the asylums where they practiced. The work of numerous Parisian *aliénistes* of the 1880s (Charcot, Magnan, Moreau de Tours, Lasègue, Legrand du Saulle) reflects their attempts to transfer their

9. These three cases turn up repeatedly as classic instances of fetishism. Strikingly, Magnan defines them in the same context as the obsessions of the German female cross-dressers. Magnan further uses them to connect cross-dressing and cross-desiring by referring to German formulations from the 1860s and 1870s that obsessive ideas of men for men and women for women derive from "a woman's brain in a man's body" and "a man's brain in a woman's body" (AAPS, 18). The cross-dressers, the individuals obsessed with women's apparel, and the "sexual inverts" (homosexuals) suffer from troubles with containers and cloaks. In Karl Ulrichs' original formulation of 1868, the body has become just such a container, incorrectly cloaking an individual's desires.

10. By the late nineteenth century, psychiatric studies gave separate consideration to male homosexual practices (cf. Garnier on homosexual fetishism, Krafft-Ebing, Moll, Ellis, Hirschfeld, etc.). Women's homosexuality continued to be studied under rubrics that mixed clothing and costume obsessions. We could say that psychiatric studies of female cross-dressing and clothes obsessions became the euphemistic space in which lesbians had their day. George Chauncey, Jr., confirms this observation in "From Sexual Inversion to Homosexuality: Medicine and the Changing Conceptualization of Female Deviance," *Salmagundi* 58–59 (1982–83): 119.

11. Ruth Harris, *Murders and Madness: Medicine, Law, and Society in the Fin de Siècle* (Oxford: Clarendon, 1989), 51–79.

sphere of influence out of the public hospitals and police dépôt, and into the privacy of bourgeois homes, where the financial means of the clientele made psychiatric practice much more lucrative.[12]

In these changing circumstances, men's sexual practices came into the scope of the medical profession more frequently than those of women because, as Marjorie Garber has suggested, men were supposed to be sexual, to have sex lives, and to account for their own sexual dysfunction. Women were not expected to know much about their own or anyone else's sexuality.[13] We should not, therefore, be surprised, that the sexual perversions of women rarely came to light. Women may, as Charcot and Magnan contended, have hidden their perversions better than men, but what this new clientele wanted to know about women may have equally influenced what doctors sought to expose. One thing was certain: women's raiments were already, quite publicly, on view.

Fashionable Woman, Perverse Men

In his 1887 essay "Le fétichisme dans l'amour," Alfred Binet attempted to delineate pathological perversion in order to elucidate the workings of "normal" love. As he grappled with the problem of drawing boundaries between the normal and the perverse, Binet staked out a space of fetishism that, like Magnan's work, admitted women. At the same time, however, Binet studied lovers of the eye, hands, hair, odors, voice, and finally, "costume lovers." Here the psychologist opened the cases of a man who follows women wearing Italian dress, a handkerchief thief, a worshiper of nightcaps, a coveter of women's shoenails, an adorer of white pinafores, a hysteric who steals spoons, the male crossdresser whose case had appeared in Magnan, as well as men and women attracted to those of the same sex.[14]

12. In Les hystériques (Paris: Ballière, 1883; hereafter abbreviated LH), Legrand du Saulle turns from the monomania diagnosis and "médecine légale" he favored in the 1860s and 1870s to varieties of hysteria hitherto unexplored—particularly kleptomania. Likewise Charles Lasègue now turned from cataloging types of hysteria to exhibitionism and kleptomania. Etudes médicales 2 (Paris: Asselin, 1884).

13. Cf. Marjorie Garber, "Spare Parts: The Surgical Construction of Gender," Differences 1, no. 3 (1989): 147. On male sexual dysfunction, see Robert Nye, "Honor, Impotence, and Male Sexuality in Nineteenth-Century French Medicine," French Historical Studies 16 (Spring 1988): 48–71.

14. Like Magnan's category of sexual perverts, this category contains Binet's largest number of observations. Cloth, clothing, and costume fetishes probably appear with such frequency because they are both the most socially acceptable of the potential obsessions (clothes, unlike dead bodies and women's hair, are household items—

Although Binet discusses several cases involving women—a woman obsessed with a male singer's voice, a woman driven to sexual excitement by the ballet of Walpurgis, a woman obsessed with the desire to cut out her child's tongue, and literary characters from Barbey d'Aurevilly and Dumas—only the kleptomaniac hysteric falls within his discussion of costume fetishism and only because of the mechanism of her symptoms, not her actual object choice.[15] Though he cites Westphal in his analysis of the male cross-dresser, he omits the obvious cases of cross-dressing women relayed from the German by both Charcot and Magnan. Whereas both his predecessors assert that female perversion is equivalent to male, Binet remains stunningly silent. The psychologist's interest in women seems to fix itself far more readily upon the garb women can endow with fetishistic powers for men.

Men are driven to fetishistic madness by women, Binet argues: "One might say that every adornment and ornament that woman has invented, everything she has imagined as pretty, curious, bizarre, and extravagant to please a man, and vice versa, has been able to become the occasion of a new fetishism. Who can enumerate all the madness caused by a beautiful red head of hair, or by the violent brilliancy of a painted face?"[16] Binet's cases are obsessed with ornamented women. And those women, Binet suggests, have worked hard at driving men crazy.

Fashion and makeup that exaggerate certain pleasing forms of the body and create "psychic illusions" that generate excitement. And this excitement is, we learn, of a *normal* kind. Binet insists on the importance of artifice that increases sexual attraction and excitement: "These artifices can in fact lack good taste, but they do not always lack utility, for they have an undeniable influence upon the senses of men" (FA, 266). Yet Binet is unable to locate the all-important line between normal and pathological kinds of fetishism. He continually wavers between two no-

---

easy-to-obtain, portable, and hoardable) and also the most easily stolen (you can't bring home a foot; women's tresses are cut with difficulty; odors and voices can't be packaged). Because fetishists pilfered their objects with a certain abandon, these individuals frequently fell into the hands of the police, enabling police-infirmary doctors like Garnier to study them. Bourgeois families who might have otherwise looked the other way were also undoubtedly driven to get medical help for sons arrested with several hundred stolen handkerchiefs in their possession.

15. Binet's essay assumes a certain nonchalance about gender difference though it already shifts the scales in favor of male perversion simply in its choice of cases.

16. Although Binet allows with that afterthoughtlike "vice versa" for women to fetishize men and for men to have invented "beautiful, curious, bizarre, and *insensé* things" to please women, every single fetish object experienced by his subjects is either related to female apparel or else shared by men and women (voices, hands, odors) and marked by gender difference.

tions of "amorous fetishism"—one purely pathological and one that might range in degrees from the normal to the insane.[17] Women's fashion particularly sends him into tailspins. Although he believes female beauty is the primary source of sexual excitement for all men, normal or perverse, he insists that crazy love exacts an "unharmonious" fetishism from its objects. Though women's artifice usefully encourages a normal fetishism that enhances desire, when it becomes excessive, female ornamentation unhinges otherwise reasonable men (FA, 266). Though he aspires to avoid such decadence, Binet leaves one question unanswered: how are doctors, lovers, or fetishists to know when women's displays have become too much? "The love of the pervert is a theater piece where a simple extra comes forward into the limelight and takes the place of the lead," he suggests, whereas normal love is a "symphony" of "polytheistic fetishes" (FA, 274). Perverse fetishism is somehow distinguished by that space of the theater, the locale of ornamentation, artifice, and masquerade.

Female Masqueraders

"Clothes make the body," declared Magnus Hirschfeld in a twist on a familiar saying (APS, 362). Because people are used to thinking about their anatomy and their clothing as a whole, clothes assume a central role in sexual life (APS, 363–64). Hirschfeld discovered that of one thousand (presumably "normal") men questioned by his institute, 65 percent preferred women either fully clothed (25 percent) or partially clothed (40 percent). He concluded with indignation that "the hypocrisy of our civilization" has "exerted a deplorable influence upon the sexual lives of men, for between this choice [of clothed women] and pathogenic fetishism of clothes lies only a minimal difference" (APS, 364). The Berlin sexologist's work asserts a critical factor for men's fetishism as well as women's masquerades: the close connection between female dress and sexuality.

When women try to be men, the psychiatric profession of the late nineteenth century debates whether they are lesbians. When men try to be women, psychiatrists puzzle over the sources of their attraction to

17. At times Binet suggests the only difference between normal love and abnormal fetishism is the degree of exaggeration (FA, 143, 150, 156). At other moments, he suggests that normal love includes normal fetishism (157–58, 261, 272, 274) because of the desire for beauty (260), the instinct to reproduce (160), the need for sexual excitement (266).

clothes. Of female transvestites doctors ask: Is she attracted to women? Is she hysterical? Does she have a history of degeneracy in her family? Has she ever shown any interest in a female social role? Of male transvestites doctors ask: Is he capable of sex with women? Where did he first get his fascination with clothes like those? Does he actually want to wear the clothes or only play with them, masturbate with them, and hoard them up in his drawers? Does he steal women's clothes? What does he do when he wears the clothes? Does he imagine he is female or does he pretend he is a man desiring the woman he sees in the mirror? What does he fantasize about? Throughout fifty years of analyses of transvestism, doctors echo a repeated desire to know more about the toilette of the men in question. Their analyses of female cross-dressers begin with the women's choice of garb as a given, and proceed to the women's other sexual and social propensities. How do we explain the psychiatrists' obsessions with women's clothes at the expense of men's wear?

Kaja Silverman, following J. C. Flugel, has implied that men's clothes just aren't very interesting. Since the "Great Renunciation" of the eighteenth century, when men shed their peacock apparel and took to staid, solemn, dark, proper clothing as a mark of their social seriousness and breeding, men's clothing has permitted few fantasmatic touches in style, color, or fabric.[18] Draping the body but rarely emphasizing its shape, and geared to the utilitarian, men's clothes have not been much fun. When women put them on, they become a disguise that masks all that is seen in the nineteenth century as feminine, attractive, and coquettish. Perhaps the doctors pay so much attention to the toilette of their male patients because they find the nuances of women's clothing more compelling?[19]

"We are all more or less fetishists," admits Emile Laurent in 1896. "Every woman whom a man loves in his heart is forcibly a little bit of a fetish" (FE, 4, 5). Paramount is the role of illusion in the workings of normal as well as pathological fetishism, for through the illusion of pleasure, men can be spurred on to the "self-sacrifice" of reproduction. Fashion creates illusions of remarkable power for lovers and pathologues alike, argues Laurent. Apparel "can advantageously serve a woman to bring out her good qualities or mask her defects. Such a woman,

18. See J. C. Flugel, The Psychology of Clothes (London: Hogarth, 1930). Silverman's "Fragments" relates his ideas to fetishism.

19. Or perhaps these doctors, like their patients, find an indelible appeal in the garments of women. Perhaps they are fascinated by men's appropriation of the private spheres of women's dressing rooms and by the private practices of women's primping. Perhaps the line between pathological fascination with women's clothing and the everyday obsessions of psychiatrists is a fine one indeed.

who would leave us absolutely cold with a simple attire, excites us strongly when she is well dressed" (FE, 68).[20]

What it meant for a woman to be "well dressed" became a central concern for doctors as they studied both male and female perversions at the turn of the century. Those analysts who saw women's cross-dressing as aberrant provide us with a unique aesthetics of the female body. Those who concerned themselves primarily with the aberrations of men's clothing obsessions became increasingly convinced of the decadence of the trappings with which women enveloped themselves. Those who remained ambivalent about the pathology of women's cross-dressing (and the very possibility of female fetishism) gave voice to a set of new concerns about the nature of women's relation to the garments and cloth out of which their bodies might be made.

"Woman, because of her physical makeup, is made to be draped, not to be molded," argued one late nineteenth-century opponent of men's wear for women. "Anything that deviates from the drape and approaches the tight-fitting, is antiartistic. In a man's suit, a woman is no longer a woman, and she is not a man: she is an [une] androgyne, which is to say she's something undefined, unsexual, less troubling than odious."[21] How do we explain the growing insistence that women's greatest appeal lay in what one did not see?

Beginning in 1800, police permission was legally required for all women wishing to wear pants into the Paris streets at any time other than carnival.[22] By the late nineteenth century, regular reports of scandals and arrests of women who flouted the law appeared in the press. Before the Third Republic, however, only a handful of women—among them Napoleon III's mistress Marguerite Bellanger and the painter Rosa Bonheur—actually requested these permits. To look at the documents collected at the Paris police archives, one would think that before the 1880s, no one much cared how women dressed as long as they avoided a scene.[23]

20. Small wonder that so many fin-de-siècle perverts are described as besotted with professionals of the spectacle: Moreau de Tours's "satyriast" is fixated upon actresses' legs (ASG, 237–39); Magnan's male "erotomaniac" chases an actress of the Opéra-Comique over half of France (AAPS, 23–24); Binet's favorite costume fetishist follows Italian models through the streets of Paris (FA, 164–65).

21. Emile Blavet, Le petit bleu, cited in John Grand-Carteret, La femme en culotte (Paris: Flammarion, n.d. [1899]), 383–84.

22. The original law dates from 7 November 1800 and underwent revisions in 1830, 1844, and 1857 (copies are in the Archives de la Préfecture de la police [APP], Dg58). Since disguises were forbidden during carnival time from the revolutionary period until 1836, women's male masquerades were doubtless frowned upon even at carnival until the July Monarchy years of the Opera Ball.

23. See APP, Dg58. The file consists of a few permits from the 1860s and an ever-

A commonplace argument about nineteenth-century women's transvestism holds that women assumed male dress either as a way of usurping the powers of male genius or as a way of challenging men's rightful superiority. Valerie Steele has argued that women's dress reform did *not* accompany the advance of women's rights.[24] In fact, Steele contends, women's attempts to improve their lot by transforming their costume, were met with ridicule, harassment, and legal action. Steele correctly identifies the results of *late* nineteenth-century women's appropriation of male dress, but she overlooks the extent to which these developments were the result of a changing view of women's cross-dressing. What had been acceptable, even titillating, in the July Monarchy came to be seen, during the Third Republic, as pathological, immoral, and threatening to the social order.

Three kinds of female masqueraders appear in the psychiatric and police annals of the nineteenth century. Two of them, asylum inmates and gender "frauds," proved worrisome well before the end of the century, for analysts believed these women endangered themselves and those around them with their sexual confusion. The third kind of masquerader, as we shall see, garnered her dangers from the psychiatric turn to perversion. And she, more than all the other perverts cataloged, attracted attention to her *social* as well as *sexual* role.

Crazy Masqueraders

In April 1845 a woman was brought to the Salpêtrière in a delirium: "She doesn't know her own sex," wrote the admitting doctor.[25] Another woman, in 1852, had manic delusions of being Napoleon.[26] The famous

increasing number of press clippings about cross-dressing women from the 1880s to the present. In the course of the twentieth century, clippings about male transvestites gradually come to outnumber those concerning women. Doubtless, no press reports were collected before the Third Republic, but even so, my research has turned up only rare commentaries on women's transvestism. Anxiety surrounding masquerades during the 1789 Revolution seems to have dissipated by the early nineteenth century. Théophile Gautier's *Mademoiselle de Maupin* (1835) joined winking appraisals of female "cavaliers" (cf. Boniface Xavier and Félix-Auguste Duvert, *Les cabinets particuliers: Folie-vaudeville en un acte* [Paris: Barba, 1832]), and images of cross-dressed carnival *débardeurs* in the July Monarchy. When press commentaries after 1830 took up scandals, they did so because the cross-dressed women had behaved in sexually provocative ways or because the women were perceived as prostitutes. An article in *Le charivari* before the first demonstrations of the Revolution (22 February 1848) addressed European fears of French female *débardeurs* as though the women promoted a particularly revolutionary zeal.

24. Steele, *Paris Fashion* (New York: Oxford University Press, 1988), 162.

25. *Archives de l'assistance publique* (hereafter abbreviated AAP), Salpêtrière, 6Q2–8, no. 14632.142, 10 April 1845.

26. AAP, Salpêtrière, 6R2–4, 28 May 1852.

aliéniste, Etienne Esquirol, described a woman whose frenzies were calmed by a change of habit:

> Madame M... was . . . very agitated, talking nonstop, insisting and re-
> peating heatedly that she was not a woman but a man. If someone
> speaking to her called her "Madame," she immediately became more
> agitated, swearing or indulging in violent behavior. [A superintendent]
> arranged with Doctor Pinel to get men's clothing for this woman: she
> put on these clothes with raptures of joy, and strolled ostentatiously
> among all her companions; she was calmer, more tranquil, and talked
> much less, but she got furiously excited if someone did not call her
> "Monsieur" or if someone called her "Madame."[27]

These three cases of female transvestism, the only ones I have encountered in French psychiatric studies before the 1880s, accede to the pathological through women's psychotic behavior. The *aliénistes*, in their
attempt to diagnose the women's manias, give a voice to the content of
their patients' desires. A woman's request to wear men's clothes would
not in itself constitute a rationale for her family or the police to bring her
to the Salpêtrière. A man, however, who aspired to emulate women in
his dress, hair, and walk, was confided into Esquirol's treatment by
family members.[28] For most of the century, in order to become a psychiatric case, a cross-dressing woman had to do far more than spend her
days primping, but a man's cross-dressing by itself seems to have been
enough to enlist an *aliéniste* in his case.[29]

By the fin de siècle, the conditions for becoming a psychiatric subject
had drastically changed: cross-dressed women began to enter psychiatric texts simply through their arrest by the police. Sexologists such as
Krafft-Ebing, Hirschfeld, and Moll report as "observations" cases culled

27. Esquirol, *Des maladies mentales* (Paris: Baillière, 1838), 1:52.

28. "M . . . was not talking irrationally," concluded Esquirol, who declared himself
unable to "return reason to this unfortunate man." Ibid., 52.

29. A similar example of a male cross-dresser without any kind of psychotic behavior appears in H. Fraenkel, *Journal de médecine* 22: 102, and concerns a Prussian
in the 1840s. Yannick Ripa, "Contribution à une histoire des femmes, des médecins, et
de la folie, 1838–1860" (Diss., Université de Paris VII, 1983), 1:156, refers to the
frequency of male asylum cases concerning men who believed they had become
women. I do not know whether these men were committed because they cross-dressed
or whether their beliefs were symptoms of other deliriums for which they were hospi-
talized. My hunch is that men recognized in the streets by the Paris police as cross-
dressed would quickly have found themselves in the police *dépôt* under psychiatric
surveillance. If their family lacked the influence to hush up the arrest, they would
have been transported to the men's public asylum, Bicêtre. Renaudin, the individual
in one such case, reported in AAP, Dg58 (to whom I shall return), must have been a cut
above the usual Bicêtre clientele.

from newspapers, police reports, foreign medical journals, and other doctors' studies—frequently also the results of police intervention. Whereas at midcentury Dr. Ulysse Trélat could claim to have witnessed nearly every one of the seventy-seven patients he included in his *Folie lucide*, doctors of the turn of the century exchanged patients' case studies like baseball cards: having an example of a type of obsessional emerged as more important than observing the type oneself. And every compendium of perversions needed its cases of female as well as male clothing obsessionals.

Gender Frauds

A popular actress was discovered to be male after "her" death. A ball queen was unveiled as male. Cross-dressers who had attempted to re-make their bodies recur, like these, in the annals of turn-of-the-century psychiatry.[30] The cases of women who lived as men left the doctors awestruck, even indignant. For the perpetrators to elude discovery beneath their chosen masks implied a breakdown in the ordering mechanisms upon which doctors and police depended. Most transvestites and fetishists in the archives of psychiatry did not succeed in fooling all the people all the time. Yet their attempts to appropriate the illusory powers of fashion tell a suggestive tale about the relationship of artifice and masquerade to fantasies of sexuality.

The first psychiatrists to study perversion cataloged men's cross-dressing with fetishism, regardless of the men's sexual preference.[31] Cases of female cross-dressers were frequently classified as homosexuality or inversion. In 1910 Hirschfeld coined the expression *Transvestiten* to extract all clothing obsessionals from the category of homosexuality. Havelock Ellis brought all those who try to live in the guise of the other sex under the rubric of "eonism." Ellis rejected in particular the descriptive category *Verkleidungstrieb*, or "impulse to disguise." "Far from seeking disguise by adopting the garments of the opposite sex," said Ellis, such a man "feels . . . he has thereby become emancipated from disguise and is at last really himself."[32] The doctors who studied cross-dressers all reflected upon the masquerades and the dis-

30. Masson, *LT*, 47, citing Taylor, *Medical Jurisprudence* 2 (1873), also reported in Moll, *Les perversions de l'instinct génital*, 86, and *LT*, 57, citing Krafft-Ebing, *Jahrbuch für sexuelle Zwischenstufen* 3 (1901): 63.
31. We have seen this in Charcot and Magnan, ISG (1882), Magnan, AAPS (1885), Binet, FA (1887), Garnier, *LF* (1896), and Laurent, *FE* (1905).
32. Ellis, "Eonism," 12.

guises adopted by their subjects. Whether they saw these "put-ons" as falsifying the patient's true sex or as revealing a true sex, they all commented upon the fact that the patient wore the *wrong* clothes. His or her perversion, although potentially inborn, derived from the incorrect relationship between the garments worn and the body being remade.

When the individuals managed to achieve unrecognizable disguises, doctors wondered at the implications for gender roles, sexual mores, and social propriety. In most of the observations from turn-of-the-century Europe, doctors emphasized the success of disguises: "An 'invert' dressed as a boy and pretending to be a young man, succeeded, through ardent fervors, in winning the love of a normal young girl, and became engaged to her. But shortly after, this woman crook was unmasked, arrested, and taken to an insane asylum for observation. There," Dr. Auguste Forel reported, "I had him dressed again in women's clothes."[33] Krafft-Ebing analyzed the case of another nearly successful impostor who swindled the father of her bride out of a sum of money. When Count Sandor was discovered to be "no man at all, but a woman in male attire," she was arrested and brought to trial. Acquitted as irresponsible for her acts and sent home, she "again gave herself out as Count Sandor" (PS, 357–64). Krafft-Ebing treated for her "viraginity" a charwoman who had engaged herself to a young girl "under the pretext that she was a man and belonged to an aristocratic family." Under his care, "she bewailed the fact that she was not born a man, as she hated feminine things and dress generally." Once he had exacted her promise "to conquer her perverse sexual inclinations," he dismissed her from the asylum (PS, 354– 55). Finally, Krafft-Ebing reported a case of a Wisconsin woman who "eloped in 1883 with a young girl, married her, and lived with her as husband undisturbed" (PS, 364–65)—presumably until it was discovered that the body she had remade did not correspond to social standards.

Masquerades of Convenience

Some women acknowledged they wore their masquerades to achieve parity with men. In 1889 the Parisian press reported a case of a woman brought before the Paris police commissioner for having passed herself off as a man for the preceding ten years: "She told . . . the judge that she had left Strasburg, where she left her husband because of 'incom-

---

33. Masson, LT, 71–72, from Auguste Forel, *La question sexuelle*, 5th rev. ed. (Paris: Masson, 1922).

patibility of temper,' and arrived in Paris [in 1878]. The man who carried her off had a printshop; soon she entered into partnership with her lover, and from then on she wore a man's suit, which, she said, allows women to devote themselves more freely to the tasks of business." What surprised everyone, from the police to the press, was that this woman had pursued her business affairs for ten years "without anyone ever noticing her counterfeit presence." When the judge explained to her that she was breaking the law, she apologized, explaining that she was unaware of the law, and expressed the desire to request the prefecture's permission henceforth to wear men's clothes.[34]

In 1882 a press report recorded that women caught dressing as men without permission had been tried and sentenced to imprisonment.[35] According to police records, at this time only ten women possessed police permits to cross-dress. Since the police required a doctor's testimony that male clothes were necessary to the woman's health, women who got permission must have appealed to their doctors' sympathy as well as expertise. Medical literature leaves us no clues to what anyone saw as a sufficient *cause de santé* to warrant male apparel.

The police were far more certain that "health reasons" did not warrant Jacques-François Renaudin's desire to wear women's clothes. In 1846, however, when they arrested him, they found no laws prohibiting his choice of costume. To avoid "public polemics," the police chief requested that his officers leave Renaudin alone "unless beneath the clothes of a woman he should commit a public outrage to modesty."[36] Despite the lack of laws contravening such choices, cases of cross-dressing men far outnumber those of women in French as well as German psychiatric studies of the fin de siècle. We know from Garnier's observations of the police prefecture that by the last decade of the century, men were regularly arrested for clothing obsessions: "One day they brought to the special infirmary a young butcher, Louis J., whose accouterments were among the most singular. Under a full coat he was wearing: a blouse made of black cloth, a corset bottom, a corset, a camisole, a collerette, a knit of light fabric, and finally a woman's blouse. He also wore fine stockings and garters." Louis had been collecting women's underwear for years—to the point that he had reduced himself to poverty by his expensive acquisitions. At the police infirmary, he begged Garnier to "authorize" him to wear women's clothing (*LF*, 62–64).

---

34. *Le temps*, 2 September 1889, APP, Dg58. Articles from *Le temps* and *La petite république française*, 11 April 1889, recount her previous police harrassment.
35. APP, Dg58. 19 September 1882 (probably from *La petite république française*).
36. APP, Dg58.

By 1896 the prefecture psychiatrist was *not* swayed by concerns over "public polemics."

Garnier's study reminds us of the power of fashion to entice men as well as women into its web. One man of letters followed prostitutes, seduced by the richness of the costume he was convinced lay beneath their outer garments. What enchanted him was "all that is fine, elegant, coquettish; it is the *envelope* of the woman that pleases him and not the woman herself" (*LF*, 54–55). Like the underwear fetishist, this man collected "the articles of women's toilette," "telling himself all the same that they were compromising and that they could make people think he had the tastes of pederasty" (*LF*, 55). Ironically, this clothing obsessional dreamed of penetrating the most private spaces of women's worlds, introducing *his* own "modesty" into *her* dressing room: "I would have wished, for the sake of modesty, to be ladies' maid to an elegant woman of the world, to help my mistress undergo four dress changes each day, or to undergo four for myself" (*LF*, 58).

Garnier appeals for help for these men whom he believes are doomed by their "degeneracy" to commit acts viewed as criminal by social norms. Like the kleptomaniac who steals nightcaps because he desires their odor (*LF*, 36–37), the women's shirt fetishist who breaks into homes to steal the women's underwear he applies to his genitals (*LF*, 45), and the silk fetishist who can't prevent himself from stroking women wearing the fabric he desires (*LF*, 47–48), Garnier's cross-dressers are "fetishistic obsessionals," irresistibly pushed toward cloth and clothing out of a desire for a "contact which sums up for [them] sensual beatitude" (*LF*, 48). The "envelopes" of women, which so please them, belong to the domain of artifice, illusion, and coquetry. They have been enticed into the theater of illusion their psychiatrist believed necessary to sexual reproduction and have found the masquerades of women to their liking.[37]

The cases of female clothing obsessionals cataloged between the 1870s and 1930s belong to three categories. Women of the first group like the case we saw in Esquirol, enter the asylum because of severely agitated behavior and are discovered to suffer from gender identity confusion as well.[38] Women of the second group have tried to transform their lives completely into those of men. Some have succeeded; some have

37. "But am I not a woman?" asks the aging lawyer described by Laurent. Enclosing himself with a woman who shares his pleasure in dressing up, he drapes himself from head to foot in the best lingerie, the finest skirts. *Les bisexués*, 76. Laurent sees this man as two people in one.

38. Two such cases are recorded by Laurent in 1894 (*Les bisexués*, 190) and by Petit in 1933 (cited in Masson, *LT*, 92–93).

been unmasked. All have left all social expectations behind to confront the confusion of doctors who can't see why anyone would want to give up all that "coquetry," "indiscretion," "capriciousness," "vanity," and "hysteria," for a life in a man's shoes.[39]

Women of the third group assume male clothing for what they claim is their convenience. They have often rejected female social roles, sought police permission to cross-dress, or been arrested for their failure to obtain permission.[40] One woman declared she dressed as a man to double her daily earnings.[41] The painter Rosa Bonheur got a doctor to claim her health warranted a police *permission de travestissement*.[42] Some members of this group prefer women; others prefer men. Psychiatrists repeatedly emphasize their rejection of feminine toys, tastes, style, and expectations. The doctors tell us little of what replaced these. What the women nevertheless seem to share are aspirations to an easier life.[43]

"Fashion constructs female subjectivity and female sexuality," Kaja Silverman reminds us.[44] In rejecting nineteenth-century fashion dictates, these women chose to construct their own subjectivity and sexuality within an order they found acceptable for their goals and desires. Most striking in the discussions of these women's choices, however, is that we never learn *how* they reappropriated the fashion of their new roles. Can their masquerades have been that boring? Have the doctors simply chosen to fix their gaze elsewhere? Or as Silverman also suggests, have these women appropriated disguises "potentially disruptive of gender and the symbolic order" (148), which, although resembling male garments, nevertheless left something to be desired?

39. These words recur in psychiatric descriptions of female nature. See Julien Joseph Virey, *De la femme*, 2d ed. (Paris: Crochard, 1925); Jules Falret, "De la folie raisonnante," *Annales médico-pathologiques* (1866): 406–7; Henri Huchard, "Caractère, moeurs, état mental des hystériques," *Archives de neurologie* 3 (February 1882): 187–211.

40. Police permission was necessary in Germany as well as in Paris. Hirschfeld, *Die Transvestiten*, 116–27. Wilhelm Stekel records a case of a woman who has police permission to cross-dress. *Der Fetischismus dargestellt für Arzte und Kriminalogen*, 1923, discussed in Ellis, "Eonism," 18–19. Moll presents a case in Krafft-Ebing of a woman denied police permission to cross-dress (Masson, LT, 74).

41. See Laure-Paul Flobert, "La femme et le costume masculin," *Le vieux papier, Bulletin de la Société archéologique, historique, et artistique* 10, no. 67 (1911): 359–60. The woman in question claimed to have changed to men's clothes to raise her take from 2.50 to 4 francs per day!

42. See Albert Boime, "The Case of Rosa Bonheur: Why Should a Woman Want to Be More Like a Man?" *Art History* 4, no. 4 (1981): 384–95.

43. Curiously perhaps, while women cross-dressers usually attempted to increase their social status by assuming male guise, doctors noted that male cross-dressers frequently attempted to lower their status by appropriating the garb of servants, chambermaids, nurses, and prostitutes. See Hirschfeld, *APS*, 151.

44. Silverman, "Fragments," 148.

Reforged Bodies, Reforged Shrouds

"The greatest attraction of what we see, isn't it what we don't see?" asks a turn-of-the-century opponent of women's dress reform.[45] The veils of fashion mask as well as tempt. The disguises of *Verkleidungstrieb* bring out the shapes of forms just as successfully as they hide faults. The masquerade in male fashion gives women ways to show off as well as cover up. Gavarni's carnival lithographs remind us that female fashion in the first half of the nineteenth century could just as easily include the titillation of breeches and a loosely fitting shirt.[46] A six-hundred-page volume called *Le pantalon féminin* traces the erotic use of *les culottes* from the sixteenth century to the turn of the nineteenth, pausing to ogle "those ladies" whose various states of undress included bloomers carefully tailored for male fetishistic desire.[47] Two dozen erotic lithographs housed in the *enfer* of the Bibliothèque nationale depict men and women in varied states of cross-dressing engaging in sexual acts that, perhaps for the benefit of homophobes, ensure that viewers know that each partner has heterosexually appropriate organs.[48] In his *Salon de 1846* Charles Baudelaire used such an image by Nicolas Tassaert to call for a museum of love devoted to the images his contemporaries coveted, like fetish objects, in privacy and moral ambivalence.[49]

Novelist George Sand, actress Sarah Bernhardt, and traveler Isabelle Eberhardt appropriated the guise of men not to play at sexual appeal but simply to enjoy the ease of movement it afforded.[50] Like the ball dancers whose cancans were more daring for the pants that protected their bodies from penetrating gazes, the women who became known for dressing as they pleased offered no justifications for their choices.[51] None re-

45. Blavet, *Le petit bleu*, cited in Grand-Carteret, *La femme en culotte*, 384.
46. I discuss these lithographs in "Transvestite Lookers: Lithographic Jokes and Female Spectacles in Nineteenth-Century France," ms. See also Nancy Olson, *Gavarni: The Carnival Lithographs* (New Haven: Yale University Press, 1979).
47. Pierre Dufay, *Le pantalon féminin* (Paris: Carrington, 1916).
48. I discuss these images in a work-in-progress on censorship and aesthetics titled "Pornographic Masquerades: Sexual Liberties, Gender Politics, and Censorship in the Revolutions of 1789 and 1848."
49. See *Art in Paris, 1845–1862*, ed. and trans. Jonathan Mayne (New York: Phaidon, 1965), 68–70 and fig. 17.
50. See Sand, *Histoire de ma vie* (Paris: Gallimard, 1970); Bernhardt, *My Double Life* (London: Heinemann, c. 1907); and Eberhardt, *Lettres et journaliers*, ed. Eglal Errera (Paris: Actes du Sud, 1987).
51. Gavarni satirizes cancan dancers in his lithographs. Sand's autobiography explains that her mother also cross-dressed in the country and that she grew up wearing men's apparel to ride and hunt (*Histoire de ma vie*, 1: 1079). Her mother supposedly advised her to cross-dress when she found that in Paris she did not have enough clothes: her mother confided that as a young woman she too had dressed as a man to follow her husband and accompany him to the theater (2: 118).

quested police permission for her *travestissement*. None was ever arrested. Historians have suggested that women adopted male dress on a widespread basis throughout the nineteenth century, largely ignoring legal contraventions.[52] I believe women's transvestism was a common and accepted practice in certain circles until the last two decades of the century. Even then, as long as women were above the law, like Sand, Bernhardt, Eberhardt, or other women of the *haute bourgeoisie*, they could name their reasons for dressing as they pleased. For most of the century, other women needed rationales: hunting, riding, boating, theatrical events, balls, even simply "going out" into the filthy streets of Paris provided justifications for women to wear what they wanted— especially if their husbands accompanied them.[53] By the end of the Second Empire, for the middle classes, this situation had changed.

The Goncourts complained in 1864 in *Renée Maupérin* that women were becoming *garçonnière*.[54] Barbey d'Aurevilly's vicious attack on *Les bas bleus* in 1875 indicted women for trying to be men and did so by addressing their "masquerades" as well as their social aspirations.[55] Critics of the communist *pétroleuses* described them as hysterics in male garb, spreading gender confusion and savagery to a hitherto civilized land.[56] The Ligue d'affranchissement des femmes in 1886 demanded "liberty of dress" as well as liberty in the legal domain—and were greeted with ridicule and contempt.[57] A worker's paper noted that the police were circulating reminders to women about police prohibitions against cross-dressing: "It seems that for some time it has been classy, in a certain crowd, for women to dress as men. Was it to prove

52. See Bonnie Smith, *Changing Lives* (Lexington, Mass.: D. C. Heath, 1989), 200: "Both smoking and cross-dressing were fairly common among women who had practical or ideological reasons for breaking conventions about what women should do." Steele argues that "although women did not wear trousers or short skirts *as a general rule*, many women did occasionally adopt them under particular circumstances." *Paris Fashion*, 162. See also Marie-Jo Bonnet, *Un choix sans équivoque: Recherches historiques sur les relations amoureuses entre les femmes, XVIe–XXe siècle* (Paris: Denoël, 1981), 195–220.

53. See Flobert, "La femme," 288–89, 349–66; as well as Grand-Carteret, *La femme en culotte*.

54. Edmond and Jules Goncourt, *Renée Maupérin*, cited in Steele, *Paris Fashion*, 265.

55. Jules Barbey d'Aurevilly, "Les bas-bleus" (1875), reprinted in *La femme au 19e siècle*, ed. Nicole Priollaud (Paris: Liana Levi, 1983): "Men are women there and women are men. The sexes are reversed. It is masquerades in all spheres that the bluestockings want!" (96).

56. See Edith Thomas, *The Women Incendiaries*, trans. James and Starr Atkinson (New York: Braziller, 1966). Maxime Du Camp's description of the *pétroleuses* in *Les convulsions de Paris* (Paris: Hachette, 1880) is the most vitriolic, if not the most hysterical. Steele reproduces an American newspaper illustration of a Paris boulevard in March 1871: among the crowd is a cross-dressed woman (166).

57. See *La lanterne*, 9 November 1890; Grand-Carteret, *La femme en culotte*, 192.

that these women really wore the pants that they cross-dressed this way? It really wasn't worth the effort."[58]

Just as in earlier moments when women's rights were at stake, now women's increasingly forceful demands for divorce rights and legal self-determination brought indignant attacks on the activists' femininity. Feminists might as well have worn men's clothes for all the jeering about their dowdiness and lack of feminine graces. Ridicule of women's demands in 1848 had taken the form of caricatures of Vésuviennes that mocked female revolutionary participation through images of attractive women clad in military uniforms. At their most biting, Edouard de Beaumont's images taunted women for their abandonment of domestic responsibilities and hinted that the "public" duties they had assumed included sexual freedom.[59] By the Third Republic, attacks on women's femininity had become far more widespread and yet more vitriolic.

"Qui culotte a, liberté a," runs an old proverb: "Who has the pants, has liberty."[60] In the 1880s, the freedoms associated with wearing pants suddenly became a terrifying specter for the French middle classes. It should come as no surprise that the psychiatric profession echoed their interests. What had changed? First, increasing pressure for improvements in women's legal and social status reminded conservatives what might be at stake in granting women unconditional bodily self-determination.[61] Second, the ever-lowering birth rate in France upped the ante on women's feminine and maternal essence.[62] The Franco-Prussian War and the Commune left the French reeling from bloodshed, terrified that unless all good French men and women got down to duty, the next war might bring an end to the "French race." Doctors made

58. Le moniteur de syndicats ouvriers, 27 April–6 May 1886.
59. Le charivari (March–July 1848). I discuss these images in "Pornographic Masquerades." See also Laura Struminger, "The Vésuviennes: Images of Women Warriors in 1848 and Their Significance for French History," History of European Ideas 8, no. 4–5 (1987): 451–88.
60. Quoted in Flobert, "La femme," 349.
61. See Claire Moses, French Feminism in the Nineteenth Century (Albany: SUNY Press 1984); Steven C. Hause with Anne R. Kenney, Women's Suffrage and Social Politics in the French Third Republic (Princeton: Princeton University Press, 1984); Patrick Kay Bidelman, Pariahs Stand Up! The Founding of the Liberal Feminist Movement in France, 1858–1889 (Westport: Greenwood Press, 1982); and Karen Offen, "Liberty, Equality, and Justice for Women: The Theory and Practice of Feminism in Nineteenth-Century Europe," in Becoming Visible, ed. Renate Bridenthal, Claudia Koonz, and Susan Stuard, 2d ed. (New York: Houghton Mifflin, 1987), 335–74; Smith, Changing Lives.
62. See Offen, "Depopulation, Nationalism, and Feminism in Fin-de-Siècle France," American Historical Review 89 (June 1984): 648–76; Angus McLaren, Sexuality and the Social Order: The Debate over the Fertility of Women and Workers in France, 1770–1920 (New York: Holmes and Meier, 1983); Francis Ronsin, La grève des ventres (Paris: Denoël, 1980).

certain to note that women clothing obsessionals had abandoned husbands and even children, pathologizing them by demonstrating their lack of commitment to reproduction.[63] Third, the specter of syphilitic prostitution with its authorization of erotic cross-dressing increasingly struck terror into bourgeois hearts.[64] Fourth, fears about homosexuality incited concerns over degeneracy and reproduction. Scandals surrounding literature about clothing obsessionals brought public attention to the pathological behavior psychiatrists attributed to cross-dressers.[65] Fifth, male cross-dressing, already pathologized as part of the psychiatric exploration of perversion, projected a new context in which the public might read female cross-dressing. Transvestite men are the most horrible of women, Dr. Louis Reuss declared in 1886: "The male invert gathers in himself the worst faults of women."[66] Certainly it was bad enough that male cross-dressers, perverts, and homosexuals were seen as monstrous. When male monstrosity began to be associated with essential femaleness, all female aberrations gained even more teratological dimensions.

Clothes might remake desires, worried doctors and moralists. The "theater of gender"[67] into which psychiatry needed to cast women increasingly depended upon their participation in masquerades designed for heterosexual excitement. As Thomas W. Laqueur has shown, psychiatry required "man-made" sexual distinctions that allowed no tinkering: "The power of culture thus represents itself in bodies, and forges them,

63. For an overview of this tendency, see Masson, LT.

64. Even erotic imagery turned away from cross-dressing at the turn of the century. This change bears out Steele's argument that trousers were seen as either immoral because prostitutes wore them or shabby because the working classes wore them (164). Just as prostitutes had influenced bourgeois women's fashions throughout the century, however, by the Third Republic their clothing—even pants—was unlikely to shock anyone. See Steele, Paris Fashion, 6–7, 169–70; and Susan Hollis Clayson, "Representations of Prostitution in Early Third-Republic France" (Ph.D. diss., UCLA, 1984). The eroticized framework for cross-dressing may have been increased as much by maisons de passe as by prints sold near the Palais Royal—but was itself threatened by syphilis in the Third Republic. See Alain Corbin, "La grande peur de la syphilis," in Peurs et terreurs face à la contagion, ed. Jean-Pierre Bardet et al. (Paris: Fayard, 1988).

65. Victor Marguerite's 1922 novel La garçonne refueled the fires left burning by Rachilde's 1889 Monsieur Vénus. See Bonnet, Changing Lives, 204, 211–12. On the discourse about homosexuality, see David Greenberg, The Construction of Homosexuality (Chicago: University of Chicago Press, 1988); George Mosse, Nationalism and Sexuality (Madison: University of Wisconsin Press, 1988); Lawrence Birken, Consuming Desire: Sexual Science and the Emergence of the Culture of Abundance, 1871–1914 (Ithaca: Cornell University Press, 1988); Jeffrey Weeks, Sexuality and Its Discontents (London: Routledge, 1985).

66. Dr. Louis Reuss, "Des aberrations du sens génésique chez l'homme," Annales d'hygiène publique, 3d ser., 16 (1886): 131.

67. See Thomas W. Laqueur, "Amor Veneris, vel Dulcedo Appeletur," in Fragments for a History of the Human Body, Part III, Zone 5, ed. Michel Feher (New York: Zone, 1989), 102.

as on an anvil."[68] In nineteenth-century France the power of culture represented itself as well in the shrouds that enveloped bodies, forging them in ways that might control the bodies within.

Female Spectacles, Feminine Fetishes

"To avoid being noticed when dressed as a man, one must already be accustomed to avoiding notice when dressed as a woman," wrote George Sand.[69] Whereas thinkers of the early nineteenth century counseled women to avoid making spectacles of themselves, by the Third Republic, doctors as well as journalists encouraged women to make sure their femininity would be noticed.[70] Although women's excessive vanity incurred criticism throughout the nineteenth century, by the last decades of the century, doctors and moralists seem to have given up the fight. So what if bourgeois women had learned their fashion tricks from prostitutes? Who cared if working-class women put on airs?[71] As long as women kept their hands where they "belonged," engaged in their conjugal duties, and behaved themselves in public, they might appropriate any female fashion they saw fit.[72]

Just as women began to gain control over female fashion, psychiatrists sounded new alarms: Women had started to shoplift, and the number of

68. Ibid., 90–131, especially 102–3.
69. Sand, Histoire de ma vie, 2:118.
70. See David Kunzle, Fashion and Fetishism (Totowa, N.J.: Rowman and Littlefield, 1982); Valerie Steele, Fashion and Eroticism (Oxford: Oxford University Press, 1985); Steele, Paris Fashion; and Philippe Perrot, Le travail des apparences, ou les transformations du corps féminin, XVIII–XIXe siècle (Paris: Seuil, 1984).
71. On fashion and prostitution, see Clayson, "Representations of Prostitution"; Alain Corbin, Les filles de noce (Paris: Aubier, 1978); as well as Marina Valverde, "The Love of Finery: Fashion and the Fallen Woman in Nineteenth-Century Social Discourse," Victorian Studies (Winter 1989): 168–88. Alexandre Parent-Duchâtelet attributed women's fall into prostitution in part to their love of finery and desire for an appearance above their working-class station (De la prostitution dans la ville de Paris [Paris: Baillière, 1836]). His views are echoed in particular by Joséphine Mallet, La femme en prison (Paris: Moulins, 1840), 70–71. On nineteenth-century consumer society and women's desires, see Michael B. Miller, The Bon Marché (Princeton: Princeton University Press, 1981); Rosalind Williams, Dream Worlds (Berkeley: University of California Press, 1982); and Rachel Bowlby, Just Looking: Consumer Culture in Dreiser, Gissing, and Zola (New York: Methuen, 1985).
72. Octave Uzanne's studies of female fashion along with the mushrooming imagery of women's fashion in the fin-de-siècle expositions all reflected a growing excitement about women's fashion. Debora Silverman relates the stylization of woman in fashion and furnishings to women's growing political power. Art Nouveau in Fin-de-Siècle France (Berkeley: University of California Press, 1989).

kleptomaniacs was sharply increasing. In a series of works analyzed by Patricia O'Brien and Ann-Louise Shapiro, doctors insisted that kleptomania was related to menstrual syndromes and menopause.[73] Some doctors attributed the rash of department store thefts to the capriciousness of hysterics, their criminal nature, and their coquettish instincts.[74] Others theorized that department stores "contain and spread out before desirous gazes the richest of materials, the most luxurious items of dress, and the most seductive inessentials." What woman could resist these temptations, Legrand du Saulle asked: "Women of all circumstances— attracted into these elegant surroundings by the natural instincts of their sex, fascinated by so many foolhardy provocations, dazzled by the abundance of lace and trinkets—find themselves overtaken by a sudden incitement, not premeditated, but almost savage: they put a clumsy yet furtive hand on one of those displayed items, and there they are, improvising as thieves" (LH, 437). Like Ulysse Trélat's "lucid madwomen," whose passion for luxurious objects drives their husbands to bankruptcy, these fashion obsessionals suffer from excessive vanity and "an excessive taste for chiffons, ribbons, and hats."[75] Like the kleptomaniac cataloged by Trélat two decades before les voleuses aux étalages (display thieves) began ravaging the Bon Marché, these women wanted to wear the most beautiful fabrics (LH, 263).

Although cross-dressers seem to enter French psychiatric literature only very late in the nineteenth century, female clothes and cloth obsessionals like these had been commonplace from early in the century. Some shared the taste of the male silk fetishist examined by Garnier in 1892, who "from age six . . . fingered with intoxication this fabric and experienced at its touch the most supreme pleasures."[76] Others, like the underwear fetishist described by Garnier, refused to content themselves with their own wardrobe and stole cloth to make new dresses.[77] Others,

73. See Patricia O'Brien, "The Kleptomania Diagnosis: Bourgeois Women and Theft in Late Nineteenth-Century France," Journal of Social History (Fall 1983): 65–77; and Ann-Louise Shapiro, "Disordered Bodies/Disorderly Acts: Medical Discourse and the Female Criminal in Nineteenth-Century Paris," Genders 4 (Spring 1989): 68–86.

74. See Legrand du Saulle, LH, 421–56, 464–65, 483–88; and O'Brien, "The Kleptomania Diagnosis," 65–68.

75. See Ulysse Trélat, La folie lucide (Paris: Delahaye, 1861), 122.

76. Garnier, LF, 46–47.

77. Legrand du Saulle, LH, 427. She already had five or six dresses—enough as far as her doctor was concerned. The fact that she did not need the clothes convinced the doctor of her lack of control over her behavior—and proved her legal irresponsibility. Legrand du Saulle contrasts the case of a woman who stole and sold embroidery and lace (485–86). This woman needed the money enough to convince the doctor that her minimal hysteria had not led to uncontrollable impulsions. She was a "professional" and not a "pathological thief" (452).

like the man who told Garnier of his dreams of becoming an aristocratic woman's private dresser, had illusions of becoming what they are not. "Deprived of beauty, but full of pride," wrote Trélat of one of these "arrogant madwomen," "she put on ridiculous airs to go to the ball, despite her minimal success" (LF, 210).[78] If we are to believe the analysts of the midcentury, the spectacles of madwomen entail femininity as stunningly as do the objects of their masquerades.

Legrand du Saulle tells of a woman detained at Saint-Lazare Prison whose elegance as well as a "certain coquetry in her dress and in her bearing" make him suspicious that she is only faking mental problems. His closer examination of the case convinces him that her coquetry belongs to a complicated set of symptoms of hysteria and degeneracy: "She has no needs, since her living and that of her child are amply secured, and yet she manages her expenditures so badly that she is always short of money. . . . She can never resist the temptation to buy what pleases her, even when she can't use it. This is why one finds at her house nine shawls, lace, chiffons, and all sorts of other objects buried and forgotten in her drawers" (LH, 446–47). Like male clothing obsessionals described by late nineteenth-century psychiatrists under the heading of fetishism, this woman has been driven mad by the objects of female vanity. Because she does not need the objects she steals, the aliéniste rules that she cannot possibly be legally responsible for her acts. Yet the doctors who record these proliferating cases of female kleptomania seem to forget that one can never have enough of illusion. Just as there are endless ways to mask faults or to ornament forms in search of the illusions that will tempt men to reproduction, one could find in any department store enough fabric, furs, lace, jewels, ribbons, and makeup to drive desiring women to distraction. Doctors had long applauded the successful artifices women use to ornament their beauty. Women of the fin de siècle found that the objects of their masquerades could lead them, like men, to excesses.

Nineteenth-century gender relations took place in a theatrical realm in which all desire was mediated by the trappings of consumer culture. In such a realm, the female body was commodified not only through social relations but through the artifices and signs that marked those relations. Women's apparel, lingerie, jewels, and makeup signaled their value as

78. Pride is a problem in particular for those "less favored," remarks Trélat. Their dreams of richness lead them into expenditures they can scarcely afford. Immoderate vanity drives even bourgeoises to dangerous financial extremes, however. Trélat's Mme., for example, spends a fortune on furs, fabrics, and furnishings. La folie lucide, 172–74.

well as their availability for exchange. In such a "theater of gender," the clothes that "made" a woman's body might generate female as well as male fantasies. Her excessive belief in those fantasies could lead her to kleptomania, but with the help of *aliénistes*, there, at least, she could be exonerated. Her deviations from those fantasies, her rejection of the masquerades of femininity, however, marked her as perverse. She had not dressed for her part.

A woman's refusal to wear the garb of nineteenth-century femininity must then be read in a context radically different from that of a man's appropriation of women's clothing. Pathologized only late in the century, illegal yet largely tolerated, generating fewer scandals because already embedded in a tradition of carnival, eroticism, and social protest, women's late nineteenth-century transvestism nevertheless came to challenge social, moral, and psychiatric norms. Men who cross-dressed in this era were read as perversely wanting to share in the masquerades of commodified femininity. Medical fascination particularly dwelled on those who walked the line between representing femininity and worshiping it. The most monstrous of men, doctors argued, were those who said they wanted to be female, because the assumption was that no one in his right mind would have such an aspiration. Women who cross-dressed, however, were read simply as wanting to be men. No one seemed to understand why they would abandon put-ons for a disguise that defied display.

The nineteenth century defined two kinds of cross-dressing for men and women, and divided them across gender lines. Masquerade— putting on an extra layer of display—ultimately became the realm of women in this theater of gender. Disguise—the art of the cover-up— though it might seem a logical extension of masquerade, nevertheless came to define the pathologized form of female transvestism. Male masquerades were seen as problematic, but male disguises emerged as the cornerstone of both nineteenth-century fashion and moral behavior. The man was not allowed to put on a show, but he could put one over on anyone he liked. Double identity, double entendres, even double lives were acceptable to any who could master their challenges. His duplicity depended, in fact, on his ability to bring the masquerades of others into his service. Woe to the nineteenth-century woman who tried to live a double life. She would be better served by ripping off fine dresses from department stores: at least she could always say she did not need the second skin they might have afforded her. As for the nineteenth-century woman caught trying to live duplicitously, even her masquerades would not save her from the police, doctors, and public opinion.

Female transvestism, unlike the male fetishism to which it is compared, does not engage in a commodification of the female body. It does not depend on the overdetermined objects of sexual disguise. If it covers up, it does so by denying those very body parts sought out and fantasized about by male fetishists. It holds out on male fetishism of both "pathological" and "normal" types. But female transvestism does not always just cover up. Transvestism is, after all, dressing across gender boundaries, not just disguise (*Verkleidung*). In its most subversive moments, female cross-dressing *plays* on the boundaries between gender, translating the lines that divide into the sources of excitement, teasing difference into desire.

Why then does female fetishism threaten doctors so much? Because it suggests that male bodies might also be commodified? Because it signals an objectification of the trappings of maleness? Because it demonstrates that women, too, can invest the female body and its trappings with eroticized meaning? Because it affronts the fantasy of feminine *modesty* that the objects of fetishism are purported to protect and advance?[79] Because a woman's appropriation of a fetish confronts men with the realities nineteenth-century Europe ensured she lacked?

The fetish has traditionally been seen as an object that allows its believer to maintain a fantasy of *presence* even when all signs point to absence. The fetish magically procures illusions that nothing is amiss even when no power remains for belief. The nineteenth-century fantasy of women's inability to fetishize almost magically preserves a gender line between the sexes that would be seen to *distribute* resources, jobs, education, knowledge, and even desire. The fantasy of the inadequate female fetishist magically procures an illusion that if everyone wears his or her proper guise, the power necessary to fantasy will be recharged. Female fetishists threaten for the same reasons female cross-dressers come to scandalize: because they subvert the values that insist the lines between gender tell an indelible, magical story of primal difference. Most of all, female fetishists threaten, as Clérambault's study shows, because they invest clothes, objects, and even knowledge with desires that can be pirated only with their consent.

Pilfered Longings

If it is a man who rubs a fetish object against his genitals, Clérambault calls the act coitus. If it is a woman, Clérambault labels her act masturba-

---

79. Cf. Kofman on female weavings that cover women up so men don't have to see their flaws. (*The Enigma of Woman*).

tion. The man's act puts in motion "all the physical and moral factors of male love while the woman's . . . is far from putting into play all the elements of sensuality" (PE, 698). Male fetishists have a remarkable arsenal of tricks, Clérambault believes. They engage in debauchery of the imagination, celebrating their acts in writings and drawings. They summon "splendid" imaginary scenes during masturbation and coitus, "transforming reality in their thoughts, enriching it and ennobling it" (PE, 699). The three female cloth obsessionals whom Clérambault analyzed in 1908 achieve none of the splendor, richness, and nobility of the male pervert. The doctor dismisses their actions as pale imitations: "They masturbate with the silk without any more reverie than a solitary epicure savoring a fine wine; in the absence of any pieces of silk, they do not dream of sumptuous silks; to help them masturbate they do not supplement the touch of the silk with visions of people dressed in silk, nor do they imagine themselves jumping wantonly into an abundance of various silks." For these three women, silk has "purely" tactile appeals (PE, 699). Its "aesthetic qualities" leave Clérambault unimpressed.[80] For a man, Clérambault believes, the fetish object is "all of a person." For women, the object is just a thing for rubbing.

To read Clérambault's contemptuous portrait of female cloth obsessionals, one might think that being a male fetishist was a feat to attain. One is reminded of nineteenth-century debates about whether women can be geniuses and of eighteenth-century polemics on women's lack of *sensibilité*. Women's relationship to their pseudofetish object is a barren one indeed: "In their contact with the silk, they are passive; their personality is closed to the outer world, stripped of vision, stripped of desire; the opposite sex does not exist anymore; their orgasm is indeed genital, but it satisfies so much for itself that one could call it asexual" (PE, 704). Clérambault's women—all diagnosed as hysterical and all driven to masturbate with cloth they steal—are not fetishists, we are told, but rather cases that deserve to be placed "next to fetishism and in its shadow." Their perversion has a particular "feminine quality" about it— "well adapted to a female temperament." This "shadow form of fetishism" Clérambault finds "less paradoxical, less complex, and less picturesque" than the perversions of men.

What Clérambault rejected as inferior about his female "fetishists" was the *quality* of their fantasies. Yet he describes all these women as having an unusual propensity for "the most fantastical reveries."[81] What then

---

80. "They seem quite minimal and quite schematic next to the complex set of sensorial, aesthetic, and moral evocations which the fetish evokes for men" (PE, 699). Clues to what cloth fetishes evoked for Clérambault *himself* may be found in Joan Copjec, "The Sartorial Superego," *October* 50 (Fall 1989): 57–96.
81. This remark participates in a large network of late nineteenth-century psychi-

makes this doctor so convinced of the inferiority of women's fetishistic practices? Quite simply that the women's fantasies have *nothing to do* with the piece of silk.[82] It hasn't been anywhere the women care about or belonged to anyone they desire. It has no past, no future. It evokes no associations. It tells no stories. It leaves the doctor without a clue about the imaginations of women. It withholds from him the fantasies he would plunder and the desires he would believe he knew.

"All women are clothes fetishists," proclaimed Freud in 1909, making an observation that might seem a relief from the bitter misogyny of Clérambault.[83] For it is precisely women's *style* to which feminist critics have appealed in their attempt to rethink women's exclusion from fetishism. Sarah Kofman has suggested that feminist theorists steal back fetishism as a prerogative of female narcissism. Naomi Schor has posited irony as the trope of feminist fetishism, insisting on the power of women's appropriations of *female*, not male, masquerades. Kaja Silverman has called for the return to vintage feminine dress as an ironic way of "salvaging the images that have traditionally sustained female subjectivity" yet at the same time challenging the identities women have been given through those clothes.[84] Renegotiating through spectacle the en-

---

atric condemnations of female fantasy. Like other hysterics, these women are perceived to have a lying, romanesque nature, a wild imagination, and a remarkable capacity for theater. See Huchard, "Caractère," 187–211; Legrand du Saulle, *LH*, 71; and Falret, "De la folie," 406–7. One can expect nearly anything from them, including shameless prostitution and cross-dressing. Krafft-Ebing, *PS*, 409. When "Vénus" attaches itself to her prey, female perverts remain incorrigible. Their imaginations, so trivialized by Clérambault, know no bounds. Cf. Moreau de Tours, *ASG*, 189–91, 195.

82. "Our cases are characterized by the search for contact with certain fabrics, the orgasm caused by cutaneous contact alone. Their preference is for this type of aphrodisiac above others, but without absolute exclusivity; they are indifferent to the form, to the past, and to the evocative value of the fragment of fabric put into play. These cases are further characterized by a lack of attachment to the object after its use, a lack of ordinary evocation of the opposite sex, preferences for silk, the association with kleptomania, and finally the occurrence of this entire scene only in women" (PE, 720).

83. Freud's description of female fetishism stops short of the pathological: "Even the most intelligent women behave defenselessly against the demands of fashion." Women's "fetishism" becomes problematic for Freud when they follow "the demands of fashion" to wear "pieces of clothing which do not show them to their best advantage, which do not suit them." Freud's description of women's fetishistic use of clothing betrays the turn-of-the-century fascination with both masquerade and disguise. It equally embraces recurrent questions in this era's analyses of "perversion": Are women as prone to perversions as men? Are women perverts like male perverts? Or are all male perverts simply like women? Freud stops short of modeling the reading of perversion on the fetishism he attributes to all women, however. His female fetishists are here to put men's fashion taste on display. See "Freud and Fetishism: Previously Unpublished Minutes of the Vienna Psychoanalytic Society," ed. and trans. Louis Rose, *Psychoanalytic Quarterly* 57 (1988), 147–66.

84. Silverman, "Fragments," 149.

velopes that contain both body and ego,[85] Kofman, Schor, and Silverman would redraw the map of women's subjectivity.[86]

Kleptomaniacs are the female equivalents of male fetishists, some psychiatrists argued at the end of the nineteenth century.[87] Embracing what Michael Miller calls the "irresistible cult of consumption,"[88] they succumbed to the desires for masquerade, spectacle, and theater which increasingly surrounded women at the turn of the century. They were seduced into collecting the objects that even *they* knew could not disguise what they lacked.

I would not call for us to resuscitate female fetishism, or even female narcissism, but rather for us to reclaim the longings of kleptomaniacs. I would ask that we use our hard-won ironic distance to write a new aesthetics of the female body, its spectacles, and its masquerades. Such an aesthetics must begin with a kind of fetishism—of the archival sort. We must become *collectionneuses* of our pasts, arbitrators of the details of psychiatric history, articulators of the differences doctors have invested in gender. By reclaiming the longings of kleptomaniacs, we can usurp what has long floated seductively beyond women's reach. Only then can we know what is at stake in fetishized bodies. Only then can we begin to understand what is hidden in the shrouds forged around them.

85. Jean Laplanche, cited ibid., 147.

86. See Silverman, "Fragments," 149: "If clothing not only draws the body so that it can be seen, but also maps out the shape of the ego, then every transformation within a society's vestimentary code implies some kind of shift within its ways of articulating subjectivity."

87. See O'Brien, "The Kleptomania Diagnosis," 68. Stekel linked fetishism and kleptomania in "The Psychology of Kleptomania," in *Twelve Essays on Sex and Psychoanalysis*, ed. and trans. S. A. Tannenbaum (New York: Eugenics, 1932).

88. Miller, *The Bon Marché*, 178.

Fetishism and Decadence:
Salome's Severed Heads

Charles Bernheimer

No concept in the Freudian arsenal has been subjected to fiercer critique, and none has endured more obstinately, than castration. The tenacity of castration, its refusal, as it were, to go away and leave us alone, reflects its power as a theoretical tool. Articulating the field of difference in terms of presence and absence, wholeness and lack, masculine and feminine, desire and the Law, the castration complex is rich in speculative implications. In fact, one could argue that the fantasy of castration forms the core of psychoanalytic theory: without castration, psychoanalysis would lack its oedipal key to differential structures in the psyche, the family, and society.

The universality of the castration complex was a discovery necessary to engendering Freud's science of unconscious fantasy. But precisely this claim to universality may be the most historically determined of all Freud's major theoretical premises. Castration, I will argue in this essay, is the seminal fantasy of the decadent imagination. By reading sexual difference through this fantasmatic complex, Freud is offering as scientific fact an interpretation of gender rooted in the misogynist fears of his fin de siècle. I make the connection between the construction of Freudian theory and literary representations of Salome through their common historical genesis in these fearful fantasies of feminine difference. In my reading, the priority attributed to castration within psychoanalysis has much the same function as the priority attributed to art within decadent aesthetics.

I would like to thank Professors Emily Apter and Thaïs Morgan for their careful critiques of an earlier version of this essay.

Etymologically, the fetish is a decadent object. The word comes from the Portuguese *feitiço*, "artificial, skillfully contrived," which in turn derives from the Latin *facticius*, "made by art." The sense of human fabrication as opposed to biological origin, of cultural signs replacing natural substance, is at the basis of other words in the Romance languages deriving from the same Latin root: Spanish *afeitar*, "to make up, adorn, embellish," and *afeite*, "dress, ornament, cosmetics"; French *feint*, "feigned, simulated." Furthermore, the French word *maquillage*, "makeup," is semantically connected to "fetish" through the Germanic root *maken*, "to make." As a verb, *maquiller*, like the words deriving from *facticius*, suggests not just painting one's face but also to fake, disguise, mask.

I hardly need stress the importance to decadent aesthetics of ideas such as the primacy of artifice over nature, the value of cosmetic ornament, the sense of art as an enchanting fakery, a surface play of masks and disguises. Such ideas are implicitly encoded by gender. One of the earliest and most influential proclamations of this position, Baudelaire's "Eloge du maquillage," clearly exposes the gender dynamics that will later become the focus of the psychoanalytic explanation of the fetish. "Woman performs a kind of duty," writes Baudelaire in 1863, "when she endeavors to appear magical and supernatural: she should dazzle men and charm them, she is an idol who should cover herself with gold so as to be adored. She should therefore borrow from all the arts the means of rising above nature so as to better subjugate the hearts and impress the minds of men."[1] Baudelaire praises makeup because it permits woman to construct herself as a fetish, as a dazzling, shiny surface that covers over and obscures the corrupt sexual nature beneath. "Woman is *natural*, that is, abominable," Baudelaire noted in "Mon coeur mis à nu" (*BOC*, 1272). Hence he praises fashion for its idealizing impulse to achieve "a sublime deformation of nature" (*BOC*, 1184). Although woman applies makeup to herself—the mirror, as we shall see, is a crucial instrument of fetishistic ritual—it is man who prescribes this artificial cover-up as a duty. The self-regarding female idol rises above her gross, unclean nature at the behest of male artists eager to keep her at an impressive distance.

Although not spelled out as explicitly, a similar attitude toward female sexuality subtends Wilde's decadent aesthetics. Indeed, Wilde praises lying in "The Decay of Lying" in much the same spirit as Baudelaire praises makeup in "Éloge du maquillage." To lie about Nature, Wilde

1. Charles Baudelaire, *Le peintre de la vie moderne*, in *Oeuvres complètes* (Paris: Gallimard, 1961), 1184, hereafter abbreviated *BOC*. All translations in this essay are my own.

argues, is to make it (her) up, thereby creating Art as a self-reflective idol. "Art takes life as part of her rough material, recreates it, and refashions it in fresh forms, is absolutely indifferent to fact, invents, imagines, dreams, and keeps between herself and reality the impenetrable barrier of beautiful style, of decorative or ideal treatment."[2] The decorative barrier needs to be impenetrable (the sexual connotation is evident) so as to protect the (male) artist from the "vulgarity" of (female) nature, which "hates mind" (*AD*, 169) and threatens to destroy his carefully cultivated individuality. Art is woman as corrected through male invention, "our spirited protest, our gallant attempt to teach Nature her proper place" (*AD*, 168). Masculine protest motivates the fetishization of art by denying its mimetic reference to nature: "Art finds her own perfection within, and not outside of, herself. She is not to be judged by any external standard of resemblance. She is a veil rather than a mirror" (*AD*, 184).

The decadent refusal of mimesis (which is not total, for "art takes life as part of her rough material") corresponds in Freud's theory of fetishism to the denial of castration. The fetish, according to Freud, acts as a veil covering over the male child's perception that his mother lacks a phallus. He determines, unconsciously of course, not to judge her by any external standard of resemblance, such as that of his own bodily integrity, for to do so would suggest not only her lack but his own possible mutilation. Instead, he maintains the fiction of her perfection through the artifice of a magical object, often a shiny, reflective one, that acts as an impenetrable barrier to the perception of female castration while it remains as a kind of permanent "memorial"[3] to that perception. The fetish serves, in fantasy, to make woman up, to veil the unwelcome gap in the place of her imagined phallus, to disguise through artifice the discovery of the horrifying mutilation that defines her "natural" difference.

Such, in any case, is a reading of Freud that suggests his sympathy with certain key assumptions of the decadent imagination.[4] It is not just that Freud's theory of fetishism serves to label decadent aesthetics as fetishistic, which of course it does. My point is that Freud's theory participates in the ideology of decadence insofar as that ideology veils the purely constructed quality of the identification of female nature with

2. Oscar Wilde, "The Decay of Lying," in *Aesthetes and Decadents of the 1890s,* ed. Karl Beckson (Chicago: Academy, 1981), 179, hereafter abbreviated *AD*.
3. Sigmund Freud, "Fetishism," in *Standard Edition,* 21:154, hereafter abbreviated *SE*.
4. For a more detailed discussion of Freud's theory, see my article "'Castration' as Fetish," *Paragraph* 14 (1991): 1–9.

castration. Over and over again Freud refers to "the fact of castration" as something the little girl must "acknowledge" to be the truth of her sexuality and the little boy must confront as a threat to his sexual identity. The imperative here carries some of the force of Wilde's insistence that Nature must be taught her proper place. Psychoanalysis naturalizes castration as the proper definition of woman's difference. Or rather, it does so at those decadent moments in Freud's text when he appears to sustain that great lie, to use Wilde's term, of the woman's penis, artifice if there ever was one, nonmimetic fantasy, cosmetic embellishment. Even after it is revealed to be a false front, this construct continues to determine a central truth of psychoanalysis, the truth of castration. But this truth is of course a phallocentric deceit: woman cannot be deprived of an organ that was never hers in the first place. In terms of the criterion of factual reality that Freud himself introduces in this context, the unmasking of sexual difference reveals that woman is uncastratable, not that she is castrated. When psychoanalysis attributes to woman a sexual nature that is lacking, wounded, incomplete, it is duplicating the revelation that Wilde attributes to Art: "Nature's lack of design . . . her absolutely unfinished condition" (AD, 168).

Castration, I am arguing, is as decadent an interpretation of sexual difference as is the defense mechanism it motivates, fetishism. The failure of this defense confronts the decadent imagination with a horrifying picture of biological origin, the mother's castrated genitals. The mythological figure that represents this repulsive horror, Freud argues, is the decapitated head of Medusa. Associating this representation with Greek art, Freud says nothing about its proliferation in the painting, sculpture, and literature of his own fin de siècle. This proliferation, of which Freud's text is a symptom, is the consequence of the widespread decadent fantasy of the castrated (m)other.

In Freud's interpretation, Medusa is castration seen head on.[5] The severed head looks back at the spectator, giving him, as it were, the evil eye. As analyzed by Jean Clair in a suggestive book, Medusa is the (male) look fascinated by its (female) otherness in the mirror.[6] It is the emblem of the failure of Narcissus's specular self-love, suggesting that his identity is monstrously mutilated. But this terror that castration might inhabit the male imago has a compensation for the spectator. This, in any case, is the claim Freud makes, in what appears as a rather desperate interpretive move: Medusa's spectator, as Freud sees him, though petrified with fear, is reassured by his very stiffness that he is still in possession of

5. See "Medusa's Head," in SE, 18:273–74, hereafter abbreviated MH.
6. Jean Clair, Méduse (Paris: Gallimard, 1989), especially 48–53.

a penis. Freud here seems to fantasize a kind of salvation through petri-
fication, through the hardness of inanimate matter, as if Narcissus were
to become frozen in the mirror of his phallic consolation. In theory, the
fear of castration arouses sexual excitement. This self-stimulation is of a
fetishistic nature. As an interpretive gesture, the stiffness of Medusa's
viewer is, as Freud says of the fetish, "a token of triumph over the threat
of castration and a protection against it" (MH, 154). The mechanism of
"transformation of affect" (MH, 273), which Freud offers as an explanation for the spectator's reassurance, is a tool of masculine protest. The
fetishistic function of Freud's own text is revealed in this decadent moment of theoretical stiffening.

Castration, fetishism, decadence, the mirror of Medusa—the single
fin-de-siècle figure who served to focus the interplay of these factors
most dramatically was Salome. There were literally hundreds of versions of Salome painted in Europe between 1870 and 1910.[7] The most
influential for the literary evocations that are my central concern in this
essay were two by Gustave Moreau, *Salome Dancing*, in oils, and *The
Apparition*, in watercolor, both first shown at the Salon of 1876, both
described at great length by Huysmans in his breviary of the decadent
spirit, *A rebours* (1884). Huysmans, or rather his protagonist, Des Esseintes, notes that the biblical descriptions of Mark and Matthew draw a
veil over "the maddening charms, the potent depravity of the dancer."[8]
Indeed, both texts say only that Herodias's daughter danced at Herod's
birthday banquet and that he was "so delighted" that he promised her
anything she might want. The girl, unnamed in the texts, then asks her
mother what she should request and Herodias, to revenge herself against
John the Baptist for having condemned her marriage to her first husband's brother, tells her daughter to demand John's head. This she does,
requesting that the severed head be brought to her "on a platter." When
it is, she carries it over to her mother.

The story stresses above all Salome's function as an obedient agent of
her mother's vengeful desire.[9] Salome's dance is not visualized at all;
there is no indication that there was anything sensuous or depraved
about it. Nor is it clear from the biblical stories that the source of Herod's

7. For an account of many of these paintings, see Bram Dijkstra, *Idols of Perversity*
(New York: Oxford University Press, 1986), 379–98.

8. Joris-Karl Huysmans, *A rebours* (Paris: Gallimard, 1977), 148, hereafter abbreviated AR.

9. For an interpretation that stresses the mimetic quality of this desire, see René
Girard, "Scandal and the Dance: Salome in the Gospel of Mark," *New Literary History*
15 (Winter 1984): 311–24, and the cogent response to his reading by Françoise
Meltzer, which follows on 325–32.

"delight" was raging incestuous lust. The decadent vision of Salome as vicious femme fatále, representing "undying lust, the Goddess of immortal Hysteria . . . the monstrous Beast, indifferent, irresponsible, insensible" (AR, 149) was conceived, says Huysmans, "apart from any data given in the New Testament" (AR, 148). While this assessment may be true in terms of the visual content of decadent art and literature, it neglects the impact on the decadent imagination of the mother-daughter relationship. Salome in the Gospels is the vehicle of her mother's homicidal desire. The princess wants the same beheading as the queen. Indeed, the daughter seems to enter so wholeheartedly into the mother's murderous scheme that she thoughtfully asks for John's head on a platter, apparently the better to offer it up to Herodias. Thus, it is entirely in the spirit of the gospel story that Flaubert has the narrator of his tale "Hérodias" remark, when Salome removes her veil before dancing, "It was Hérodias, as she had been in her youth."[10] Adding to the sense of continuity between mother and daughter is the fact that in the Middle Ages Salome's name became confused with that of Herodias—a confusion that may underlie Mallarmé's name for his Salome figure: Hérodiade.[11] In short, for the kind of imaginations that Huysmans defines as capable of giving body to the shadowy figure of Salome, "unhinged minds, sharpened and rendered visionary by neurosis" (AR, 148), the biblical story shows that what is fundamental to female desire, what is passed on from generation to generation, from mother to daughter, is the urge to behead men.

The decadent visionary accepts Freud's fantasmatic equation "to decapitate = to castrate" (MH, 273) and sees women as agents of male dismemberment. Salome signifies this desire to castrate, which her dance celebrates, but she also signifies the motive for her desire, the "natural" condition of women from the point of view of decadent male neurosis, her castration. Herodias-Salome wants what she lacks. In Des Esseintes's fantasy about the meaning of Moreau's Salome Dancing, he dwells on the possible symbolism of the lotus scepter Salome is carrying. He imagines that it has a "phallic significance" and that the painter may have remembered the Egyptian embalming rite of inserting lotus petals into the sexual organs of a female corpse "in order to purify them" (AR, 150). Equating the dancer with "mortal woman, a soiled vessel,

10. Gustave Flaubert, Trois contes (Paris: Gallimard, 1973), 134.
11. For an overview of treatments of the Salome story, see Helen Grace Zagona, The Legend of Salome and the Principle of Art for Art's Sake (Geneva: Droz, 1960). Françoise Meltzer does an interesting analysis both of the Salome legend and of Huysmans's reading of Moreau in Salome and the Dance of Writing (Chicago: University of Chicago Press, 1986). Meltzer's Derridean perspective leads her to stress quite different interpretive problems from those I discuss here.

ultimate cause of all sins and all crimes," Huysmans fantasizes Salome as a function of her "impure wound" (AR, 150): she must mutilate the other in order to complete herself. Yet that completion, Huysmans implies, can come only in death and only through the artifices of male ritual, which empty the female body of its internal organs (the brain is pulled out through the nostrils, the entrails through an incision in the side) and make it up as a shiny surface, with gilded nails and teeth.

The fetishistic implications of this embalming fantasy, clearly a defensive and punishing response to the evocation of Salome as castrating and castrated, are brought out in Huysmans's description of the second Moreau work owned by Des Esseintes, The Apparition. In this watercolor Salome is depicted "petrified, hypnotized by horror" (AR, 152). She is transfixed by the terrifying vision of John's severed head, which she sees before her, risen from the plate on the floor and "gazing, livid, the colorless lips parted, the crimson neck dripping tears of blood" (AR, 151). Frozen by her vision of the risen head, Salome is transfixed in return by its eyes, which "appear to be fixated, as if in agonized concentration, on the dancer" (AR, 151). John's head is a version of Medusa's. In this paradigmatic decadent image, what Salome is seeing head on is her own castration mirrored back to her. Her specular identification with the head's decapitation is further suggested in the painting, as Huysmans describes it, by the only movement of her otherwise paralyzed body: "Her hand claws convulsively at her throat" (AR, 151). In this decadent interpretation, The Apparition shows a guilty, terrified Salome, incapable of annexing the power represented by John's head, the desired phallus. She can read only her own mutilation in John's eyes.[12]

But Huysmans is not satisfied to decapitate Salome in the mirror of Medusa. Foreshadowing Freud, he offers himself the consolation of constructing the petrified Salome as a gleaming, brilliant fetish. Her body, in his description of Moreau's watercolor, is nothing but an artificial surface covered with "wrought metals and translucent gems" (AR, 151). Molded and constrained by a corset and a girdle, she is like a highly ornamented sculpture, beautiful but lifeless. What animation she has proceeds from the burning rays of John's aureole, which, reflected by Salome's jewels, transform her body into a play of incandescent sparks. These "prick her on the neck, legs, and arms with points of fire, vermillion like coal, violet like jets of gas, blue like alcohol flames, white like astral rays" (AR, 152). These points of fire constitute "the impenetra-

12. Although I find Huysmans's interpretation of the painting persuasive, it is by no means the only possible one. Bram Dijkstra, Idols of Perversity, 382, claims that "in fact" Moreau's Salome is eagerly reaching out in "ecstatic hunger" for the severed head. As we shall see, this is a rather Wildean reading of Moreau.

ble barrier of beautiful style, of decorative or ideal treatment" that Wilde recommends putting between art and reality. The mimetic reference to (female) nature is abolished, or nearly so, and masculine power, emanating from the severed head, produces in the place of woman an arbitrary set of metaphorical substitutions.

The decapitated head gives life to jewels, but this life is in reality an afterlife, like the survival of an embalmed corpse. It is the enchanted life of the fetish.[13] The perspective of such an afterlife is like that one might attribute to John's severed head. Looking at Salome, John's vision becomes reflexive: He sees the brilliant reflections of his own disembodied light. Only a highly mobile metaphorical language can trace these dazzling surface effects. Decapitation thus becomes the bodily metaphor for an impersonal, nonmimetic language, "not to be judged by any external standard of resemblance." Such a language would be like the one Mallarmé evokes in his famous description of pure poetry, which might have been conceived by the head of John the Baptist as he (it) stared at Salome: "The pure work implies the disappearance of the speaking poet, who yields his initiative to words, mobilized by the shock of their differences; they light up with reciprocal reflections like a virtual trail of sparks over jewels, replacing the breath perceptible in the old lyric impulse or the enthusiastic personal shaping of the sentence."[14] Huysmans's descriptive style is obviously far from having the purity and autonomy Mallarmé imagines here: too strong and too neurotic a lyrical impulse animates the novelist's evocation of Salome's jewel-covered body. Huysmans is too passionately involved in extolling, through "the enthusiastic personal shaping of the sentence," the beauty of the female body's translation into male artifice. Yet this translation constitutes the first step toward "the pure work."

Mallarmé, more detached and sophisticated, makes this translation, or, to use his term, transposition, the explicit subject of his poem *Hérodiade*. The name purposely blurs the distinction between the princess Salome and her mother Herodias. Mallarmé portrays Hérodiade not as a bloodthirsty femme fatale but as a narcissist who wants to become one with the fetishized surface of her body. Through the very articulation of that wish, however, she realizes her difference from the ornamentalized

13. Toward the end of her chapter on fetishism in *Creativity and Perversion* (New York: Norton, 1984), Janine Chasseguet-Smirgel remarks: "The practice of embalming, by the Egyptians in particular, exactly produces a fetish. Make-up is applied to the putrefying body, which is then decorated with jewels, dressed up with a golden mask, and made into a god" (87–88).
14. Stéphane Mallarmé, "Variations sur un sujet," *Oeuvres complètes* (Paris: Gallimard, 1945), 366, hereafter abbreviated *MOC*.

surface she seeks to capture in the mirror. Hérodiade figures a fundamental desire of Mallarméan poetry: to see itself as a hard, reflective
surface without organic or psychological depth. But Hérodiade is also a
woman speaking and thinking, a consciousness striving for self-
possession and struggling with sexuality. This tension is at the heart of
the poem.

Hérodiade's project is to construct herself as a solitary, virgin idol
whose sole other is her specular reflection. She sees herself as constituted of metallic gleams, radiating from her golden hair, and effulgent
flashes, blazing from her jewellike eyes. Her cold sterility, her fear of
being touched—these apparently psychological traits are metaphors for
a poetic language that wishes to cut itself off from "la chair inutile" ("the
useless flesh") (MOC, 47), from any reference to bodies, to organic origin, to sexual difference. Hérodiade's goal seems to be the evacuation of
her biological and psychic interiority, her mummification as a glittering
fetish.

But Hérodiade's resistance to her death wish echoes throughout the
poem in the words conveying the princess's affective response to her
self-paralyzing desire. The brilliance of her hair is "cruel"; her cherished
virginity is also a "horror"; her chastity makes her comparable to an
"inviolate reptile." It is as if Hérodiade had caught a glimpse of Medusa
in the mirror and realized the monstrous consequence of her immobiliz-
ing dream: "Mais, horreur! des soirs, dans ta sévère fontaine / J'ai de mon
rêve épars connu la nudité" ("But, how dreadful! Some evenings, in your
unsparing fountain, I perceived the nakedness of my scattered dream")
(MOC, 45).

Hérodiade's speech juxtaposes contradictory perspectives: In one line
she declares that her desire has nothing human about it and that she is a
sculpture crafted by art alone; in the next she imagines paradise in terms
of the milk she drank at her nurse's breast. Hérodiade's nostalgia returns
her to an organic origin, to a breast rather than to a mechanical device. It
is as if the Medusa head in the mirror were the reflection of the violence
done to the mother by the attempt to fetishize the self in her image. At
the end of the poem Hérodiade seems almost willing to abandon her
cosmetic enterprise. She admits that her bravura claims to aesthetic self-
sufficiency have been a lie and that she is waiting for "something unknown" to come and "finally make these cold jewels part [se séparer]"
(MOC, 48). This readiness to have her fetishized armor pulled apart
suggests a desire for sexual initiation. Hérodiade, finally, is too much a
desiring woman to remain trapped in "the idolatry of a mirror" (MOC,
48). Therefore, she fails as a figure of poetry's narcissistic absorption in
verbal reflexivity.

Section 3 of *Hérodiade*, "Cantique de Saint Jean" (*MOC*, 49), abandons the princess and actually adopts the voice of John the Baptist's severed head. As it arches through the air, John's head celebrates its "clean break" with "les anciens désaccords / Avec le corps" ("the old dissensions with the body"). Expressing none of Hérodiade's ambivalence about cutting herself off from her sexual body, John's head experiences the loss of its body as a liberation from the dualistic world of desire. Decapitation facilitates John's union with the very principle of poetic creation.[15] Now he is "illuminated by the same principle that elected me." Decapitation is the price joyfully paid for the afterlife of the head that "surges up" with new creative potency and, from its solitary lookout, sociably "bows a salutation" down to earth. This fantastic talking head is the poet's fetish. Its "triumphant flights" defeat the fundamental female desire to behead/castrate. Indeed, the head's "pure gaze" does not even encompass Salome, who is now no more than an instrument of poetry's triumphant erection.

Wilde's version of Salome is self-consciously belated and self-consciously French. Although he may first have thought of writing about Salome in England in 1890, all the details of the project were worked out, and most of it written (in French), in Paris during the fall of 1891. Wilde involved most of his many French literary friends and acquaintances in the gestation of his subject, obsessively testing out ideas on people such as Jean Lorrain, Marcel Schwob, and Pierre Louÿs, writers of a strong decadent persuasion. He had a broad knowledge of the Salome iconography, going back to Rubens, Leonardo, and Dürer, but, notes Richard Ellmann in his biography, "Only Moreau satisfied him, and he liked to quote Huysmans's description of the Moreau paintings."[16] The passage from *Hérodiade* printed in *A rebours*, a passage that Des Esseintes liked to recite as he contemplated his Moreau pictures, also had an immense impact on Wilde. How much more of this poem Wilde may have read is impossible to establish, but his friendship with writers in Mallarmé's close entourage suggests that he would probably have seen additional parts of this work that Ellmann calls "the best-known unfinished poem since Kubla Khan" (*OW*, 339). Despite his admiration for Mallarmé and the latter's praise of *Dorian Gray*, Wilde attended only a few of the famous *mardis*. Ellmann supposes that this diffidence was due to Wilde's awareness that he was engaged in a deliberate trespass on

15. For a different but complementary reading of this poem, see Leo Bersani, *The Death of Stéphane Mallarmé* (Cambridge: Cambridge University Press, 1982), 78–81.
16. Richard Ellmann, *Oscar Wilde* (New York: Vintage, 1987), 342, hereafter abbreviated *OW*.

the *maître's* poetic terrain. However this may be, it is clear that Wilde intended to challenge his literary forebears. Responding to a criticism that the play was reminiscent of Flaubert's "Hérodias," he replied: "Remember, dans la littérature il faut tuer son père" (*OW*, 375).

Wilde's project is to kill his French fathers using their mother tongue. He stages his filial belatedness not only by deliberately echoing prior versions of the Judean princess by Flaubert, Huysmans, and Mallarmé but also by evoking, in ways that I cannot detail here, the whole style of aesthetic decadence associated with such writers as Théophile Gautier, Maurice Maeterlinck, and Anatole France. These authors were all mentioned by the most perceptive reviewer of the play's text when it was published in England in 1893. But this anonymous critic interprets Wilde's tactical recognition of belatedness as a failure of creative verve. *Salomé*, he complains in the *Pall Mall Gazette*, is "the daughter of too many fathers. She is a victim of heredity."[17] But this is precisely Wilde's point. Salomé has no singular inheritance; no father can claim her. She is indeed what the reviewer calls her disparagingly, "a handbook to a library . . . the quintessence of a school of writing."[18] Salomé is a victim of her literary heredity only to the extent that one maintains that art should copy life. But if one adopts Wilde's maxim "Art never expresses anything but itself" (*AD*, 191), then the pollution the *Gazette* reviewer found in Salomé's blood is no more than the symptom of literature's artificial genesis, of its fetishistic displacement of organic interiority.

This displacement is the fundamental subject of Wilde's play. Salomé is a figure of decadent belatedness whose "life" reflects the unnaturalness of literature. A central issue in the play is what it means to contemplate this reflection.

The theme of the gaze is introduced in the opening scene when Herodias's page tries to persuade the young Syrian, whom he loves, to look away from Salomé: "Look at the moon. How strange the moon seems. She is like a woman rising from a tomb. She is like a dead woman. One might fancy she was looking for dead things" (*AD*, 195). This speech is characteristic of many others in *Salomé*. The sentences are short. There

17. *Pall Mall Gazette*, 27 February 1893, 3, reprinted in *Oscar Wilde: The Critical Heritage*, ed. Karl Beckson (London: Routledge and Kegan Paul, 1970), 136.
18. Ibid., 137. It could be argued that Wilde is belated even in adopting the perspective of belatedness: Jules Laforgue's 1886 "Salomé," the fourth of the *Moralités légendaires*, treats the princess as an excuse for an intertextual carnival that outrageously parodies Flaubert's "Hérodias" while it produces an anarchic effect of parasitical citationality. But Wilde may not have known Laforgue's nearly unreadable story, and his technique has none of the brashness of Laforgue's burlesque patchwork of mostly enigmatic references. For an excellent discussion of Laforgue, see Daniel Grojnowski, *Jules Laforgue et "l'originalité"* (Neuchâtel: A la Baconnière, 1988).

are no connectives between them to indicate logical relation. Each paratactic sentence has a kind of declarative autonomy, as if it were a talking head without a body. The effect is typical of a decadent style as defined by Paul Bourget, "where the unity of the book decomposes to give way to the independence of the page, where the page decomposes to give way to the independence of the sentence, and the sentence decomposes to give way to the independence of the word."[19] Individual words are foregrounded through their recurrence from sentence to sentence, producing a rhythmic, incantatory effect. In the quoted passage, "moon" occurs in sentences 1 and 2, "woman" and "like" in sentences 3 and 4, "dead" in sentences 4 and 5, "look" in sentence 1 and "looking" in sentence 5. The semantic counterpart to this rhythmic suspension of linear syntax and atomistic decomposition of textual wholeness is focused here, as elsewhere in the play, on the meaning of the look. The page suggests that to look is to see not what is but what seems. The look discovers the strangeness of things, how they are like other things, how, one might say, they are constitutive of a rhythm. The vehicle of the look's apprehension of strangeness is metaphor, which functions through verbal displacements and substitutions. The passage associates this process with a dead woman and the reanimation of her corpse. Male fancy recreates woman's strangeness and attributes to it a necrophilic drive. Originating in a metaphor, this drive is energized by rhetorical rather than psychic force.

Admittedly, this reading pushes interpretation to what may seem like an exaggerated extreme. This extremity is, however, the necessary point of analytic departure if one takes seriously Wilde's claim that "the primary aesthetic impression of a work of art borrows nothing from recognition or resemblance."[20] The verbal repetitions in Wilde's sentences create a sense of ritualized artifice, as if talking were a mode of reciting. Likewise, looking becomes a veil over the seen, a vehicle of productive nonrecognition rather than of mimetic apprehension. To pull a veil of metaphor over the object of sight is, so to speak, to suspend its life, but also to prolong that life in the shimmering folds of the veil's unfurling.

Wilde contrasts this aesthetic form of the look's mortifying power with its naturalistic form, the look as the agent of a desire to possess so urgent that it risks destroying its object. This urgency provides Wilde with the "rough material" for his story, its mimetic connection to "that dreadful universal thing called human nature" (AD, 175). The Syrian captain and Herod both want (to look at) Salomé, whereas the page and Herodias,

19. Paul Bourget, Essais de psychologie contemporaine, vol. 1 (Paris: Plon, 1912), 20.

20. Letter to the editor of the Speaker, December 1891, in Letters of Oscar Wilde, ed. Rupert Hart-Davis (London: Rupert Hart-Davis, 1962), 299.

jealous, warn them not to; Salomé desires (to look at) Jokanaan, who refuses to return her gaze and has eyes only for God. Desire never coincides with its object—this is the tragic psychological truth of the play. Desire never sees straight—this is closer to its literary truth, the deviation being due to literature's decadent desire to fetishize itself.

Salomé's description of what she sees when she looks at Jokanaan is the most striking example of the gaze's metaphoric displacement of its object. Salomé begins by associating Jokanaan with death and negation: the "black hole" of his prison is "like a tomb," his eyes are "like black holes," he is "wasted" (AD, 206). He represents for her the denial of the body and of sexuality: "I am sure he is as chaste as the moon is" (AD, 206). As chaste also as Salomé herself, who identifies with the moon, praising its cold virginity. As chaste also as Mallarmé's Hérodiade, who likes to confirm her mineral sterility in the mirror. Chastity is here an essentially literary condition: Salomé recognizes in Jokanaan not a desirable sexual being but a desirable mirror of her own literary constitution. This is the meaning of her evocation of Jokanaan's physical attractions in terms borrowed from the Song of Songs: his white body is like hers, is "like the lilies of the field," is "like the snows in the mountains of Judaea" (AD, 208), and so forth. The "likes" proliferate as Salomé plunders the language of erotic psalmody to describe Jokanaan's incomparable eyes, body, mouth, and hair (at once like clusters of grapes and like great cedars of Lebanon!). As Gail Finney points out, this part-by-part praise of the beloved's physical attributes derives from a standard Petrarchan convention, elaborated during the Renaissance in the blason tradition, which makes individual anatomical features the occasions for extravagant rhetorical celebration. The fact that this tradition firmly establishes the male poet as the subject of the gaze and a desirable woman as its object leads Finney to conclude that Salomé is, "on a disguised, symbolic level,"[21] a man. It is in a male role, Finney argues, that Salomé fetishizes Jokanaan's bodily parts, her ornamental dismemberment of his physical integrity being an attempt to gain control over the forbidden object of homosexual desire. I would take this quite plausible interpretation a step further, to suggest the connection between homosexuality in Wilde's fantasy and a kind of "chaste" displacement of the body into the domain of rhetoric, where issues of sexual difference are dissolved in the murmur of (derivative) metaphoric elaboration. It is just such a displacement that the homosexual page, in the play's opening scene, is trying to induce in the gaze of the man he loves.

21. Gail Finney, Women in Modern Drama (Ithaca: Cornell University Press, 1989), 62.

But Jokanaan refuses to be assimilated into Salomé's rhetoric. Sexual difference is for him the bedrock of the spiritual life. Suggesting the closeness of the decadent perspective on woman to the Christian view, Jokanaan identifies Salomé with her mother and with the essential perversity and unbridled sexuality of female nature. Salomé's response to this vituperative condemnation is simply to switch metaphoric registers, turning from the positive context of Narcissus to the negative one of Medusa. Having first compared Jokanaan's hair both to clusters of grapes and to cedars of Lebanon, in an incongruous pairing that suggests how dissociated rhetorical display is from its object, she sees his hair after his rebuff as "a knot of serpents coiled round [his] neck" (AD, 208). In naturalistic psychological terms this switch reflects Salomé's childish petulance; in aesthetic terms it exhibits the decomposed parts of a belated poetic creation. Salomé as Jokanaan, Salomé as Narcissus, Salomé as Medusa—this substitution of masks produces the "strange music" that the princess claims to hear when she "look[s] on" Jokanaan (AD, 236). Salomé, it seems, has learned the lesson that Herod applies to himself: "One should not look at anything. Neither at things, nor at people should one look. Only in mirrors is it well to look, for mirrors do but show us masks" (AD, 229).

To displace desire from the world into art sounds like Freud's definition of sublimation. Through sublimation libido transferred from sexual objects is made available for original artistic creativity. In decadence, however, this creative energy finds itself framed in a mirror of reflection and repetition. The mirror is full of already painted masks; the artist's belatedness stares him in the face like the knot of serpents swarming around Medusa's head. The decadent solution is to embrace paralysis as creative potential, to make of the petrifying head the vehicle of one's originality. Sublimation thereby becomes fetishistic. Libido is discontinuously displaced among bodiless masks. The apogee of this displacement is the strange music Mallarmé puts into the mouth of John's severed head as it surges forth in triumphant flight.

Does Wilde serve (up) John's head otherwise? The answer would at first appear to be yes. The prophet's pate is the decadent emblem of woman as castrated and castrating. Salomé is not content to "look on" Jokanaan: she wants to touch the prophet's body and to kiss his mouth. Her desire violates the shared bond of chastity that initially attracted her to Jokanaan. Insofar as this bond generates a literary play of masks, Salomé's desire for the male's sensuous presence appears to violate her specular self-constructions. But her carnal lust is a mask already made up in the mirror. It is to be found, for instance, in Huysmans's "symbolic deity of undying Lust, [which] poisons everything that comes close to it, everything that sees it, everything it touches" (AR, 149). We are dealing here with two different levels of literary self-consciousness: Salomé expresses the literariness of her gaze, Wilde expresses the literariness of her desire to possess its object. Wilde, it could be said, "looks on" Salomé in the same way as Salomé "looks on" Jokanaan.

Wilde's gaze, cultivated in the library like a decadent plant in the hothouse, exaggerates to the point of comic absurdity the characteristic traits of the femme fatale. She wants to kill men, specifically, to dismember them: "Well, I tell thee, there are not dead men enough" (AD, 234). She gets erotic pleasure from cannibalizing male corpses: "I will bite [thy mouth] with my teeth as one bites a ripe fruit" (AD, 234), she says to Jokanaan's taciturn head. She loves revenge and delights in perverse cruelty: "Well, I still live, but thou art dead, and thy head belongs to me. I can do with it what I will. I can throw it to the dogs and the birds of the air" (AD, 234). Her lust knows no bounds: "Neither the floods nor the great waters can quench my passion" (AD, 236). Salomé's castrating desire is in effect a parodic collage of desire's decadent articulations. If, as Ellmann writes, Salomé "dies into a parable of self-consuming passion" (OW, 345), the point to stress is that the parable preexisted Wilde's belated retelling and that her passion has already been consumed by its representations. Wilde's princess is as artificial, made up, and ornamental when she yearns for male flesh as when she rhapsodizes about the lilies of the field. These attitudes are juxtaposed masks, bodiless rhetorical postures.[22] It is as if Salomé's life as a figure for woman's "natural" desire to decapitate the male had been truncated and she were now enjoying the afterlife afforded by her own beheading. *The Decapitation of Salomé*—this was Wilde's first title for the play.

The fetishized female body was not, however, the primary focus of Wilde's gaze, as is revealed by Aubrey Beardsley's illustrations. Recent interpreters agree that these pictures provide a kind of witty commentary on the plot, obliquely displaying vectors of desire and erotic associations that are disguised in the text.[23] The instability of gender in the

22. My reading here diverges significantly from that of Elliot Gilbert, "'Tumult of Images': Wilde, Beardsley, and Salomé," *Victorian Studies* 26 (Winter 1983). Gilbert stresses the "unmediated" and "natural" quality of Salomé's passionate challenge to patriarchal art and culture. I would also argue that any resemblance between Salomé and the New Woman of the 1890s should be appreciated in a parodic mode.

23. This point of view was first argued by Elliot Gilbert, "'Tumult of Images.'" In *Sexual Anarchy: Gender and Culture at the Fin de Siècle* (New York: Viking, 1990), Elaine Showalter goes so far as to claim that "the Beardsley drawings all depict scenes or moments described in the play" (151). Richard Dellamora offers a number of provocative readings of the illustrations in "Traversing the Feminine in Oscar Wilde's *Salomé*," in *Men Writing the Feminine*, ed. Thaïs Morgan (forthcoming from Illinois University Press).

veiled play of homoerotic vision is suggested by Beardsley's having changed the title of his first drawing of Wilde's lunar countenance from "The Man in the Moon" to "The Woman in the Moon." One of the figures androgynous Wilde observes is a naked male, the other a clothed figure of uncertain sex. The identities of these figures are left so unmarked that one astute critic, Richard Dellamora, can interpret them as Jokanaan and Salomé, while another astute critic, Elaine Showalter, sees them as the page of Herodias and the young Syrian. According to Dellamora, Beardsley is playing with the viewer's gender assumptions by having Jokanaan appear to shield Salomé from Wilde's lustful gaze, while, for those in the know, the image reveals the true homosexual object of that gaze.[24] According to Showalter, the page and Syrian are gay lovers over whose immanent expulsion from paradise a dreamily fantasizing Wilde-Jehovah presides.[25] I would argue that the identities of these figures cannot be fixed and that this mobility of gender and desire illustrates a gaze liberated from the defenses of specular reflection. The lunar face of Wilde is itself subject to this figurative mobility, for the moon, from the outset of the play, is most often associated with Salomé, who, in other drawings, resembles Jokanaan.

Beardsley's drawing of Salomé floating in air as she holds the severed head of Jokanaan before her was the artist's tribute to Wilde's play and earned him the commission to illustrate the English version. One of the ways this tribute is Wildean is in its being Huysmanian, Moreauesque, and Mallarméan as well. Beardsley's Salomé is staring at her own image as Medusa. The twisting black locks of her hair are a version of his snakelike tresses. But this Salomé, unlike Huysmans's, is not petrified by fear. On the contrary, she is uplifted in an ecstasy that resembles that of John's head in Mallarmé's "Cantique." Salomé appears here in a "triumphant flight" that frees her from "les anciens désaccords avec le corps." Beardsley and Wilde, however, move away from old bodily discords not in order to create a higher, sublimated harmony but in order to invent new bodily disharmonies and play perversely with genders and sexualities. This perversity is exhibited in the many suggestions of deviant sexual practices that suffuse the image. There is the suggestion of same-sex love in the visual similarity of the two heads—but is the implication homosexual or lesbian? There are the phallic images of the flower erect on its stalk and of the head erect on a rhyming, albeit fragmented, lance of blood. Is Salomé, then, a cross-dressed male about to engage in fellatio, as Dellamora suggests? Support for such a reading is offered by the

24. Dellamora, "Traversing the Feminine," 15.
25. Showalter, *Sexual Anarchy*, 144.

Aubrey Beardsley. "The Woman in the Moon." 1894. Illustration for *Salomé,* by Oscar Wilde. Harvard College Library.

Aubrey Beardsley. "J'ai Baisé ta Bouche Iokanaan." 1893.
Drawing from *The Studio*. no. 1. Harvard College Library.

French inscription "J'ai baisé ta bouche," which brings the slang meaning of *baiser* together with the buccal orifice. Should one further broaden the field of sexual imagery to include the peacock feathers, which Elliot Gilbert tells us have "vulval eyes"?[26] Beardsley's drawing, titled "The Climax" in its second version, invites its viewer to fantasize a number of different erotic climaxes, this plurality being the artist's illustrative point. Medusa imagery thus becomes, for both Beardsley and Wilde, a stimulus to sexual inversion, confusion, and parody, rather than a horrifying symbol of emasculation.

The violence produced by reductive symbolic interpretation is brought out clearly in the drama's final moment. As Herod is about to retreat into his palace, he turns around, sees Salomé embracing Jokanaan's severed head, and orders her to be killed. His gaze is in direct violation of his own taboo against looking at anything other than mirrors. Indeed, his assertion of power and moral outrage (he calls Salomé "monstrous") is actually a gesture of weakness in his own terms, since it confirms his inability to be satisfied by specular imagery and rhetoric. Identifying Salomé with the defeat of his phallic desire, Herod's "turn" symbolically reinstates castration as a threat directed specifically against patriarchal privilege. Earlier, he had warned against making such naturalizing symbolic equations: "How red those petals are! They are like stains of blood on the cloth. That does not matter. It is not wise to find symbols in everything that one sees. It makes life too full of terrors. It were better to say that stains of blood are as lovely as rose petals" (*AD*, 225). It is precisely this fetishizing wisdom that fails the tetrarch at the end. He finds symbolic "matter" in Salomé's dismissal of the "matter" of whether or not she has tasted blood on Jokanaan's lips: "But what matter? what matter? I have kissed thy mouth" (*AD*, 233). For Herod, this blood symbolizes the mutilation of his official authority, Salomé having exploited the symbolic value of his kingly word to fulfill her desire against his. His order of execution sets to rights the patriarchal order of nature: women are not as lovely as petals; the fact of the matter is that they stain cloths with blood.

"The fact of castration"—this, we remember, is Freud's curious phrase. I want to return in conclusion to Freud's theoretical codification of the central decadent fantasy identifying woman with castration. In this context, castration's "factuality" can obviously be nothing other than symbolic. Freud is much like Herod, to whom Wilde attributes the Romantic notion that symbols have an organic basis in nature. The sym-

26. Gilbert, "'Tumult of Images,'" 153.

bol, writes Coleridge, "always partakes of the reality which it renders intelligible; and while it enunciates the whole, abides itself as a living part in that unity of which it is the representative."[27] Castration symbolizes the "reality" that lies naturally beneath the surface—organic interiority, maternal origin, a primary unity of being. It "partakes of" this reality in the mode of loss. Freud images castration as that which the male child "sees" when he catches a glimpse of what is under the mother's underlinen. This sight reveals the falsity of an original hypothesis about sexuality, that all humans have a penis. This enlightenment does not, however, prompt the child to abandon his narcissistically flattering theory. He does not conclude that there is an anatomical difference but that a mutilation has occurred. His allegiance to the truth of his theory is so powerful that he cannot see the female genitals for what they are, that is, different. For him, they exist only insofar as they symbolize the absence of a theorized presence. The presence is the monosexual whole of which castration is a living part. Hence arises the characteristically decadent move in interpretation: woman is symbolized as mutilated man; to discover her "nature" is to uncover her lack.

The Freudian male child invents castration as a theoretical veil that obscures woman's difference while apparently giving access to its knowledge. With a slight but crucial adjustment, Freud's description of the normal boy's strategy for dealing with sexual difference corresponds to his analysis of fetishistic perversion. The adjustment concerns the object of the fetishist's denial. Freud claims that the fetishist denies castration while recognizing its reality, but it would be more accurate to say that the fetishist embraces castration as a defense against what he finds still more "uncanny and intolerable"[28]—that is, woman's otherness, her specific difference. It is this difference that his fetish at once obscures and reveals, not the "fact" of female mutilation. The fetishist is characterized not by his incapacity to accept woman's lack but rather by his incapacity not to see woman as lacking. This is precisely the negative interpretation of woman's sexual nature that Freud insists *all* men must accept as their own. They must acknowledge, he says in the essay "Fetishism," "the unwelcome fact of women's castration" (SE, 21:156) and master the typical accompanying reactions he elsewhere identifies, "horror of the mutilated creature or triumphant contempt for her."[29]

27. Samuel Taylor Coleridge, *The Statesman's Manual*, ed. W. G. T. Shedd (New York: Harper and Brothers, 1875), 437–38.

28. Sigmund Freud, "Leonardo Da Vinci and a Memory of His Childhood" (1910), in *Standard Edition*, 11:95.

29. Freud, *Some Psychical Consequences of the Anatomical Distinction between the Sexes* (1925), in *SE*, 19:252.

Freud's analysis of female maturation reinforces his theory's veiling of woman's difference. Incapable of accepting her sexual organs as valuable in themselves, Freud's little girl, when confronted with the anatomical distinction between the sexes, instantaneously interprets herself as castrated. To fail to do so, Freud suggests, would be to risk a loss of reality that "in an adult would mean the beginning of psychosis" (SE, 19:253). Madness will be the consequence if a girl refuses to accept as real the perfectly unreal "fact" of her castration. Yet it is not clear just what narcissistic reward she obtains through her swift and unquestioning assumption of her inferiority. As I see it, the reward is entirely theoretical: by accepting the ontological truth of her lack, the girl becomes the perfect object of male fetishism. She collaborates in transposing the seen, her own difference, into a theoretical framework that defines the seeable.

This framework delimits the scene of decadence. For Wilde, the qualifying term is *beauty*. "One does not see anything until one sees its beauty," he says. "Then and only then does it come into existence" (AD, 189). The fetish returns the gaze from the depths of symbolic meaning to the glittering details of the aesthetic surface.[30] In Freud's famous example, it returns the gaze from the symbolic significance of the nose as mother's phallus to the brilliant shine on the nose, the *Glanz auf der Nase*. The shiny surface is like a mirror, perhaps the most widespread of decadent fetishes. The mirror is the agent of alienating falsity, the magical medium in which the male self can theorize itself as being the other as well, where sameness can overtake separation and sexual difference. The mirror presents (female) depth as an illusion; it offers, in Wilde's phrase, the truth of masks.

This truth has a great appeal in our own fin de siècle, when gender is once more in crisis, sexually transmitted disease is again an obsession, and a critique of biological essentialism performs a necessary first step in the subversion of patriarchal ideology.[31] In this regard my essay sounds a cautionary note: the playful truth of masks may not be as liberating as it first appears. It may be linked in a reactionary mode to a reductive definition of gender based on the "fact" of castration. At issue is whether or not the play of sexualities is being fetishized, whether or not the play is masking a fundamental repulsion from female sexuality, whether or not, in the terms of my argument here, the play is decadent.

30. Wilde declares in the preface to *Dorian Gray* that "all art is at once surface and symbol." Then he goes on to warn that "those who go beneath the surface do so at their peril." *The Picture of Dorian Gray and Other Writings* (New York: Bantam, 1982), 3.

31. For a stimulating discussion of these analogies from a literary and cultural perspective, see Elaine Showalter, *Sexual Anarchy*.

This question is often extremely hard to resolve. I have presented Oscar Wilde both as a Herod figure, whose ideal of specular detachment is fetishistically bound to his castration fears, and as a Beardsley figure, for whom desire and gender offer unbounded access to multiple erotic and rhetorical possibilities. In this as in most other aspects of his creativity, Wilde is divided. On the one hand, he remains enclosed within the decadent castration-fetishism structure; on the other, he breaks free of the symbolic bond of reaction and opens the representational field to ludic transpositions and gay disguises.

Theory continues to be particularly susceptible to the decadent lure of the gender dynamics set in motion by the castration-fetishism machinery. The major, and all too obvious, reason for this appeal is that castration is a bulwark of phallocentric ideology. The massive authority of Freud's thought (whose historical roots in the decadent soil of the fin de siècle are too often overlooked), the close link between decadent aesthetics and modernism, the systematic fetishism that underpins our consumer culture—these are other important factors. But there is also the fact, not to be neglected, that castration appeals to theory because it privileges the theoretical. Indeed it could be said that castration *produces* female sexuality out of (male) theory. Woman lacks because theory is full, woman is mutilated because theory holds to its erection despite evidence of the monument's collapse. Castration is theory's decadent fetish. It is high time to discard it on the compost heap of history.

Remy de Gourmont with Freud: Fetishism and Patriotism

Jeffrey Mehlman

On the genealogical path bringing the term *fetishism* from the realm of "primitive" religion to that of (all too) "sophisticated" sexuality, an odd reversal took place. The psychologist Alfred Binet, whose twin legacies to the twentieth century were "fetishism" and the IQ test, observed (against what might have been expected from a reading of Comte) that fetishism as an amorous practice, rather than harking back to the traditions of polytheism, was in fact similar to monotheism (in its opposition to the more polymorphous—that is, tendentially polytheistic—orientation of mature sexuality).[1] The secularization of religion or the sacralization of sex marked by the term *fetishism* would thus be concomitant with a move from the polytheistic to the monotheistic. *Monotheism*: fetishism, in fetishizing, is a *stabilizer* of libido and to that extent would appear to be almost an ego function. And indeed the psychic crisis occasioned by the fetish is entirely (and surprisingly) intra-egological: *Ichspaltung*. On the one hand, then, fetishism, for Freud, partakes of the split within the ego and to that extent is part of a conceptual and terminological series that takes us from fetish to narcissism (the predicament of an ego *essentially* split) and psychosis. On the other

This paper was originally delivered at a session of the 1987 MLA convention devoted to literature and fetishism and organized by Emily Apter.

1. Alfred Binet, "Le fétichisme dans l'amour: Etude de psychologie morbide," *Revue philosophique* 24 (1887): 263. Jean-Baptiste Pontalis, in his introduction to the issue of *Nouvelle revue de psychanalyse* (2 [Autumn 1970]: 5–15) dedicated to "objects of fetishism" (197), describes Binet's reversal as "delectable" (6). For Binet's seminal contribution to IQ testing, see Stephen Jay Gould, *The Mismeasure of Man* (New York: Norton, 1981), 148–54.

hand, fetishism extends benignly in the direction of the most normal of functions: object choice. As Freud put it, "A certain measure of fetishism is found in normal love."[2]

In the annals of the secularization of religion, there is another tendentially monotheistic formation, a more familiar and even *transparent* case that I would like to play off against fetishism. It is that of late nineteenth-century nationalism, or as it came to be called in France, *le patriotisme*. Like fetishism—which extends in the directions of normality (object choice) and madness, which it might be provocative to construe as normal madness—late nineteenth-century French nationalism was the normal madness of the day. But the parallel is stranger still. For Freud's fetishist is the male unresigned to the imagined amputation of the mother's phallus; he would deny it, affirm the maleness of what he nevertheless accepts to be his female parent. The cult of *la patrie* entails a similar denial of sexual difference: morphologically, we are served up a female father, a *pater* of feminine gender. Nationalism, or *patriotisme*, that is, before being a *transparent* good of late nineteenth-century France, was *trans-parental*: the cult of the female *pater*.[3] Furthermore, fin-de-siècle patriotism was similarly obsessed with a denial of amputation. The cult of *la patrie* was predicated on the denial of that "open wound," the lost province of Alsace-Lorraine.[4] Third Republican patriotism and fetishism, in this perspective, begin seeming oddly cognate; indeed, one could almost transcribe the title of Remy de Gourmont's polemic against the fetishization of Alsace-Lorraine, *Le joujou patriotisme* (1891), as the fetish (*joujou*) fetishism (*patriotisme*).[5]

My focus in these remarks is Remy de Gourmont and his critique of the fetishization of Alsace-Lorraine. But first a word about Gourmont himself; then two comments on the cult of Alsace-Lorraine.

On Gourmont: For the high-modernist generation of Eliot and Pound, Gourmont was, of course, the French intellectual par excellence.[6]

2. Freud, *Three Essays on the Theory of Sexuality*, in *Standard Edition*, 7:154.

3. I adopt the term from Eric Cheyfitz's study of "sexual politics" in the language of Emerson, *The Trans-Parent* (Baltimore: Johns Hopkins University Press, 1981).

4. For the thematic of the "open wound," see the selection from Georges Ducocq, *Les provinces inébranlables* (1913), "La blessure toujours ouverte," anthologized by Raoul Girardet in *Le nationalisme français, 1871–1914* (Paris: Armand Colin, 1966), 246–49. In *L'autorité* of 21 February 1871, Paul de Cassagnac could write: "We have in our loins a bleeding wound, a wound that shall never heal."

5. "Le joujou patriotisme" originally appeared in the *Mercure de France* issue of April 1891. Page references in the text are to Jean-Pierre Rioux's annotated edition (Paris: Pauvert, 1967), hereafter abbreviated *JJP*.

6. Pound thought Gourmont's works to be "the best portrait available, the best record, that is, of the civilized mind from 1885 to 1915." For Eliot, he had "the intelligence of an Aristotle." Quoted in Glenn S. Burne, *Remy de Gourmont: His Ideas*

Whereas Lacan, in our own fin de siècle, I would suggest, at times seems to hark back to the outrageous Léon Bloy, part religious mystic and part stand-up comic, Remy de Gourmont, Bloy's contemporary, appears in retrospect to have been something of a Michel Foucault before the fact.[7] Specifically, what the sometime employee of the Bibliothèque nationale shared with his latter-day incarnation were (1) vast erudition; (2) a Nietzschean propensity for the genre of institutional genealogy; (3) an iconoclastic libertarianism that in matters sexual flirted with the salacious; (4) an exquisitely aristocratic sense of French prose. Those four dimensions are amply apparent in what is perhaps his best book, *La culture des idées* (1900).[8] The volume's centerpiece is the essay "La dissociation des idées," to which we shall return. Suffice it for the moment to observe that Gourmont scholars are in agreement that the first "idea" to be "dissociated" by the author was "patriotism," the first textual exercise in Gourmont's vaunted method, *Le joujou patriotisme.*[9] Whereby, we return to the fetishization of Alsace.

Two comments on Alsace-Lorraine:

1. Third Republican French patriotism, to the extent that it centered on the denial of the loss (or "amputation") of the "lost provinces," was a meditation on and a refusal of (the concept of) the unconscious. The key texts here are Numa-Denis Fustel de Coulanges's response to Theodor Mommsen (1870) and Ernest Renan's "Qu'est-ce qu'une nation?" (1882).[10] For Fustel de Coulanges the problem is posed as follows: Alsace may be German by its race and its language (i.e., by its unconscious); it remains French by the (conscious) will of its inhabitants.[11] Similarly Renan, after being a leading ideologue of (unconscious) racial

---

and Influence in England and America (Carbondale: Southern Illinois University Press, 1963), 5 and 112. See also Richard Sieburth, *Instigations: Ezra Pound and Remy de Gourmont* (Cambridge: Harvard University Press, 1978).

7. For the Lacan-Bloy link, see my "Future of an Allusion: Lacan with Léon Bloy," in *Legacies of Anti-Semitism in France* (Minneapolis: University of Minnesota Press, 1983), 23–33, as well as "The Paranoid Style in French Prose: Bloy, Céline, Lacan," in *Oxford Literary Review* 12, nos. 1–2 (1990): 139–54.

8. Page references are to *La culture des idées* (Paris: Mercure de France, 1983), hereafter abbreviated *CI.* For the Gourmont-Foucault connection, see, among many other examples, "La morale de l'amour," 209: "The works of these eminent physicians of love have taken the place, as clandestine reading, of outmoded confessors' manuals and the piquant dissertations *in sexto* which so delighted many a school boy."

9. The point is made by Herbert Juin in his preface to *La culture des idées*, 8, and by Jean-Pierre Rioux in his introduction to *Le joujou patriotisme*, 22.

10. The relevant texts from Fustel de Coulanges, "L'Alsace est-elle allemande ou française?" and Renan, "Qu'est-ce qu'une nation?" are assembled in Girardet, *Le nationalisme français*, 62–67, and are commented on provocatively by Alain Finkelkraut in *La défaite de la pensée* (Paris: Gallimard, 1987).

11. See Girardet, *Le nationalisme français*, 64.

identity was to do an about-face when confronted by the case of Alsace-Lorraine. A nation, he suggested, is a daily plebiscite.[12] So that the irredentist ideology of denying the loss of the two provinces, a loss that in the binary world of Franco-German relations seemed castratory in the extreme, was an ideology intent on disenfranchising the supremacy of (the concept of) the unconscious: the passivity of language, race, etc. Transposed into Freudian terms, the transition is from denial (Verleugnung) of loss to foreclosure (Verwerfung) of the linguistic cornerstone of the unconscious, from fetishism to psychosis. . . .

2. One of the most influential channels through which the cult of la patrie was sustained in Third Republican France was the children's school manual Le tour de France par deux enfants by the pseudonymous G. Bruno.[13] It is the story of two children of Lorraine, who, after the defeat, slip into France, and come to know the entirety of their homeland, "la mère commune," in the course of their journeys.[14] The book's influence was so widespread that recent historians have dubbed it the "Little Red Book" of the Third Republic. In the context of our speculations on fetishism, the point to be registered is that the framing conceit of the Tour is the agonizing migration from the boys' native city in Lorraine. For its name is Phalsbourg. Our scenario then is mother France, never more herself, never more a mother—that is, a patrie, a feminized father—than in the movement that inspires her children to refuse to admit the loss of her . . . Phalsbourg.

Consider now Gourmont's "dissociation of ideas." As a practice it was a school of defetishization, of psychical mobility. Against the forces of inertia that would allow random associations to congeal into what was called truth, it was a call to dismantle truths and effect the "equivocal and fragile formation of new connections" (CI, 81): such flimsy but salutary links as the ones we are weaving between Freud's fetishism and Gourmont's patriotism. In psychoanalytic terms it was an affirmation of the bizarre connections effected by the primary process in opposition to the stable—and idealized—formations of the secondary ones. (But Gourmont, a self-conscious ideologue of the unconscious, himself talked of "dissociation" as "analysis" [CI, 88], and the whole history of philosophy has established the affinity between "psyche" and idea," so that the transition between psychoanalysis and the dissociation of ideas was perhaps always already in effect.)

Turn now to Gourmont's first exercise in dissociation: Le joujou patriotisme. The text begins with arch-nationalist Paul Déroulède referring

12. Ibid., 66.
13. Paris: Belin, 1981.
14. Quoted in Girardet, Le nationalisme français, 74.

to a sentimental portrait of an Alsatian nursemaid, "and bending over toward France, who is far from deaf." He nevertheless shouts in her ear: "Don't cry, grandma, we'll get her back for you, *ta symbolique nounou!*" (*JJP*, 58). *Nounou* (nurse) rhymes with the title word *joujou*: *ton symbolique joujou . . . ton joujou le symbolique* (the possibilities are numerous). To which Mother France responds: "Frankly, I'd really rather you tell me a few different secrets." As for the dandy Gourmont, he too equates (or refuses to) the amputated lands with a bodily part: "Personally, I would not give, in exchange for those forgotten lands, either the pinky of my right hand, since it offers support when I write, or the pinky of my left hand, since it helps me flick the ashes from my cigarette" (*JJP*, 58). From the Wolf Man to Gourmont, the amputated finger can serve as an equivalent of the phallus (Freud) or the lost provinces (Gourmont).

Gourmont's attack against the fetishization of Alsace-Lorraine next turns to the myriad and polymorphous options for national self-assertion that have been sacrificed to the binary logic of Franco-German rivalry: "And then, I would ask you, out of sheer curiosity, what share of your precious hide you would be willing to give up in order to join to France either Belgian Wallonia or the Lausanne Valley—regions, it seems to me, a bit more French in language and race than the banks of the Rhine. No one barks against the British, who hold the Channel Islands and distant, but plainly French, Canada, an overseas province, but as much a province of France as Charentes or Picardy" (*JJP*, 59). Gourmont's patriotism, that is, exactly like Freud's fetishism, (as interpreted by Jean-Baptiste Pontalis) is tendentially monotheistic, and Gourmont's therapy is a wry polymorphism: Why not Belgium, Switzerland, or Guernsey? The affirmation of polymorphism here is no doubt ironic, but elsewhere—in "Le paganisme éternel," Gourmont's affirmation of the perennial pagan or polytheistic substrate sustaining and corroding Catholic monotheism from within—the argument is structurally identical and proffered without irony.[15] And patriotism, as we know, was for Gourmont one of the sadder vicissitudes of religion. In his words: "Deprive them of all religion, of any ideal, and to think that they then throw themselves, starved, onto patriotism! No, it's really too dumb" (*JJP*, 67).

So much for patriotism, the first idea dissociated by Gourmont. I turn now to the last, or at the least the final example in "La dissociation des idées": "Beauty is a woman" (*CI*, 108). To dissociate, that is, is to demonstrate that given the difference between male and female, "that distinction is almost always in favor of the man" (*CI*, 109). It is, in Freud's

15. See "Le paganisme éternel," *CI*, 141–81.

terms, to defetishize the woman, to reaffirm her fundamental "imperfection" (Gourmont). With results perhaps best captured in the supremely phallic prose of Gourmont at his best. Consider, for example, this image for the relative transiency of great literature in light of the fundamental historical instability of language itself over long periods of time: "Languages [or tongues] swell and flake like cement; or rather they are like plane trees, which can live only by constantly changing their bark, and which, early each spring, shed on the moss at their feet the lovers' names graven in their very flesh" (CI, 34). Writing as a fundamental falling off concomitant with the vertical growth or "swelling" of an organ. Writing, that is, or "castration."[16]

Where does this leave us? We began with an improbable linkage between Freud's "fetishism" and Gourmont's "patriotisme": Alsace as fetish, a notion as uninviting perhaps as recommending choucroute as an aphrodisiac. As connections ramified—the morphological peculiarity of la patrie; the denial of amputation; Fustel's polemic against Mommsen and the primacy of the linguistic unconscious; the Third Republican cult of Phalsbourg; the binarization of French foreign policy; the bond between the relinquishing of the lost provinces, Gourmont's first dissociation, and the decoupling of the essentially "imperfect" female body from the ideal of Beauty, his last—our exercise on Gourmont and Freud, which is as well an exercise in Gourmont and Freud, has taken on a certain air of inevitability.

Three final reflections:

1. Le joujou patriotisme, Gourmont's first exercise in the dissociation of ideas, should be in theory—at some level—a wellspring for the Anglo-American generation that swore by Gourmont, in whom Eliot and Pound saw the French intellectual par excellence. To see that text simul-

---

16. The image recurs in masked form at a key juncture in "La dissociation des idées." Gourmont's subject is how abstract notions, such as injustice, tend to fuse, however imperfectly, with concrete images: "An amusing example of the way in which ideas are thus deflected was recently given by the corporation of house-painters, at the ceremony called the 'Triumph of the Republic.' These workmen carried a banner on which their demands for social justice were summed up in the cry: 'Down with Ripolin.' The reader should know that Ripolin is a prepared paint which anyone can apply in order to understand the full sincerity of this slogan as well as its artlessness. Ripolin here represents injustice and oppression. It is the enemy. . . . We all have our Ripolin with which we color, according to our needs, the abstract ideas which otherwise would be of no personal use to us" (CI, 107). To "dissociate" would be to remove—or tear down—the Ripolin from every (abstract) surface: precisely the program of those who effected the initial association. In this image the raised banner and the call to tear down the paint repeat the swelling tongue (or growing plane tree) and flaking cement (or falling bark) in the castratory image quoted in the text. But the Ripolin image adds an aporetic (or castratory) dimension all its own.

taneously as a bridge to Freud's metapsychology would be to reopen the debate about the relation between modernism and postmodernism.

2. Le joujou patriotisme, which cost Gourmont his job at the Bibliothèque nationale and became a cause célèbre among the Parisian intelligentsia, can be read as a breviary of collaboration with Germany victorious. It would be possible to line up passages from Le joujou that were all but cited by French literary collaborators (Henry de Montherlant, Robert Brasillach), near collaborators (Jean Giraudoux), and after-the-fact apologists for collaboration (Jean Paulhan) with the Nazis in 1940. In these years when many are pondering the wartime texts of Paul de Man, Gourmont's essay (and the reaction of Mallarmé, among others, to it) is no doubt worthy of scrutiny.[17]

3. Finally, the technique of "dissociation" advocated by Gourmont finds itself reinscribed, writ large, as it were, as the great cultural disaster lamented by Gourmont throughout the essays of La culture des idées. I refer to that major split or dissociation effected in the Renaissance whereby reformers (Luther, Calvin) disembedded Christianity from the finite and humanists purged mythology of its attachment to the infinite. The (defetishizing) dissociation of ideas was to decouple a concrete from an abstract element. And yet historically such activity was recommended as an antidote against a historical pass in which the finite (or pagan) had become woefully dissociated from the infinite (or Christian). It was a split, Gourmont hoped, to which the Catholic renewal of Chateaubriand, Hugo, and Huysmans might put an end.[18]

But might not the relation between the (defetishizing) dissociation of ideas and the (fetishized) split or dissociation that seems its sinister shadow have repercussions within Freud's oeuvre as well? Consider the relation between "castration" and fetishism: the fetishist maintains the female phallus on the mode of its inexistence; but to the extent that "castration" itself would lose the phallus in its differential inscription, positing the phallus's (as opposed to the penis's) insistence or "inexistence," the difference between the two is unsettled. Similarly, the splitting of the ego concomitant with fetishism might well be seen as a *fundamental* characteristic of an ego construed to be narcissistic (i.e.,

17. After Gourmont was dismissed from his position at the Bibliothèque nationale, Mallarmé (in the Mercure de France of April 1891) signed a letter in support of his attack against "false patriotism." It is reproduced in Le joujou patriotisme, 79.

For Rioux, the Resistance in contemporary France is a taboo notion that has taken the place of what was in Gourmont's day called "la Revanche." For further observations on the de Man case, see my "Perspectives: On de Man and Le Soir" in Responses, ed. Werner Hamacher, Neil Hertz, and Thomas Keenan (Lincoln: University of Nebraska Press, 1989), 324–33, as well as my "Prosopopeia Revisited," Romantic Review 81, no. 1 (1990): 137–43.

18. See "Le paganisme éternel," CI, 152.

split) in its essence. But then the question arises of whether "castration" itself, assumed to be the bedrock of the repressed, might not, in its bound and binding essence, be part and parcel of the forces of repression.[19] As though castration itself were always already contaminated by its seeming egological parody, fetishism. As though "castration" might itself ultimately merit reading as a fetishized formation within Freud's text. Just as the dissociation of ideas—of the concrete from the abstract—was perhaps never free of the taint of the congealed dissociation of the finite from the infinite in Protestant Europe. . . .

Toward the end of *La culture des idées*, Gourmont meditates on the transitoriness of national languages and quotes Victor Hugo, a predecessor, he claims, of Nietzsche, on the day when "Europe would know only Europeans, and no longer Frenchmen, Germans, and Russians" (*CI*, 305). Rarely will the self-proclaimed prophet have seemed more prescient. Now in the course of issuing his prophecy, almost inadvertently, Hugo, in 1867, simultaneously sowed the seed of our own argument, for three years prior to the first German annexation of Alsace-Lorraine, the poet asked rhetorically in support of his pan-European vision: "Est-ce que les Allemands ont une queue?" ("Do the Germans indeed have a tail?") (*CI*, 305). The implied response was, of course, negative: the Germans are as human as we, and there can be no basis for any European *Spaltung* the length of the Rhine. French history, however, was to spend a century attempting to give the lie to Hugo's rhetorical query. Not only were the Germans to have a *queue*, alas, but it was one—centered, say, on Phalsbourg—that had been amputated from (and must be restored to) the glorious "trans-parent," *la patrie*.

Unless, of course, Hugo himself, as quoted by Gourmont, was wiser than his own rhetorical question. Earlier we read Gourmont's image of a tongue (*langue*) swelling phallic and observed that his prose was in important ways written under the sign of castration. No sooner has Gourmont's Hugo established the "tailless" humanity of the Germans, than he moves on to the subject of European linguistic integration: "The Babel of languages (*langues*) will come to an end: a single one will suffice." With German consonants too harsh for the peoples of the south, and with Italian too mellow for the Germans themselves, French emerges as the ideal—and only—future European language. But with the Germans shorn of their *queue* and the French *patrie* endowed with a supreme(ly phallic) tongue, the Hugo text footnoted by Gourmont appears to be subliminally offering precisely the kind of fetishized solution that Gourmont would later attempt to analyze and dissociate into oblivion.

19. I have argued this point, drawing on analyses of Jean Laplanche, in *Revolution and Repetition* (Berkeley: University of California Press, 1977), 95–104.

Fetishism and Its Ironies

Naomi Schor

The fetishization of irony runs unchallenged through both high modernism and postmodernism; even in the face of the major cultural mutation of the second half of the twentieth century, irony remains the indelible marker of the elite, whether it be in literature, theory, or the arts. On the other side of irony stand pathos, literalism, immediacy, none of which have been either identified with or promoted by postmodernism, an aesthetic marked rather by what Fredric Jameson has called the "waning of affect" and the triumph of pastiche.[1] Thus it is that Flaubert, the totem figure of modern ironists, has been effortlessly recycled by many (including myself) as the patron saint of postmodernism. Commenting on Barthes's celebrated characterization of Flaubert's irony in S/Z as "impregnated with uncertainty," Jonathan Culler writes: "It is as if Barthes were saying: with Flaubert 'the code of postmodernism had been written.'"[2] At the same time fetishism, the perversion par excellence of the age of mechanical reproduction and late capitalist commodification, has not escaped ironization. When, for example, in the celebrated penultimate chapter of L'éducation sentimentale, Frédéric Moreau says to his beloved Mme Arnoux, "the sight of your foot disturbs

This essay has benefited from the readings of Elizabeth Weed, Nancy Miller, and Susan Rubin Suleiman. I also thank Emily Apter for her invitation to present this text at the 1987 MLA special session on fetishism.

1. Fredric Jameson, "Postmodernism, or The Cultural Logic of Late Capitalism," New Left Review 146 (1984): 61–62.

2. Jonathan Culler, "The Uses of Madame Bovary," in Flaubert and Postmodernism, ed. Naomi Schor and Henry Majewski (Lincoln: University of Nebraska Press, 1984), 5.

me,"[3] that expression of fetishistic eroticism comes under the sway of the corrosive irony of that belated love scene. But to speak as loosely as I have just done of the fetishization of irony and the ironization of fetishism does not begin to exhaust the intricacies of their mutual interrelationship. In what follows, I want to consider a quite different modality of the imbrication of irony and fetishism as they are emblematically inscribed in Flaubert, and, further, as they intersect with feminism. Taking as my starting point a detailed reading of Flaubert's first novel, Mémoires d'un fou, I want to speculate briefly on the implications for late twentieth-century feminism of the fetishism-irony linkage bequeathed us by the nineteenth century, notably via Flaubert.

In her brilliant reading of the text, Shoshana Felman writes: "The Memoirs of a Madman is then perhaps the madness of memories, or of memory itself."[4] She then goes on to speak exclusively of the madness in and of the text, leaving tantalizingly unexplored the other part of the title and the text, precisely the one that pertains to memory. And yet memory and its operations are arguably as central to this curious case history as is madness, for the progression of the narrative is explicitly determined by the logic of memory, and that progression is famously chaotic, maddeningly fitful, a perfect mimesis of the narrator's unstable mental state. Indeed, as Michal Peled Ginsburg has shown, Flaubert's chronic difficulty in both generating and "sustaining a narrative"[5] begins with Mémoires d'un fou. According to Ginsburg the narrative breakdowns that constantly threaten to stall the forward movement of Flaubert's plots result here and throughout his oeuvre from the disabling tension between the imperatives of representation and those of narcissism; in Mémoires, I contend, the fitful starts and stops of the autobiographical narrative are overdetermined by the play of memory, the interplay of the plural memories inscribed in the title.

From the outset the narrator informs us that the organizing principle of his memoirs will be antilinear, thus, by the same token, antiliterary: "This is neither a novel nor a play with a fixed outline, nor a single premeditated idea with pickets to make thought wend down perfectly straight paths."[6] Rather than follow a preestablished plan, a constraining

3. "La vue de votre pied me trouble." Gustave Flaubert, L'éducation sentimentale (Paris: Garnier-Flammarion, 1969), 440; idem, Sentimental Education, trans. Robert Baldick (Harmondsworth, Eng.: Penguin, 1964), 414.

4. Shoshana Felman, Writing and Madness: (Literature/Philosophy/Psychoanalysis), trans. Martha Noel Evans (Ithaca: Cornell University Press, 1985), 81.

5. Michal Peled Ginsburg, Flaubert Writing: A Study in Narrative Strategies (Stanford: Stanford University Press, 1986), 1.

6. "Ce n'est point un roman ni un drame avec un plan fixe, ou une seule idée préméditée, avec des jalons pour faire serpenter la pensée dans des allées tirées au

outline, the narrator will obey another narrative logic, the errant logic of free association: "I am going to put down on paper everything that will come into my head, my ideas along with my memories, my impressions, my dreams, my whims, everything that goes through my head and soul."[7] The narrative rule of *Mémoires* is then the cardinal rule of psychoanalysis, which commands the analysand to verbalize all her thoughts, no matter how trivial or embarrassing they may seem. Designed to circumvent the workings of censorship, the analytic contract produces as a side effect a narrative contract ruled by the unconscious.

After various preliminaries, which all have the effect of delaying the beginning of the promised memoirs, in the section numbered 3 the narrator at last seems ready to get on with his narrative: "I am therefore going to write the story of my life" ("Je vais donc écrire l'histoire de ma vie" [*MF*, 230]). The reluctance one detects in this opening statement is immediately amplified in the following, which works to arrest the narrative at the very moment when it seems at last to be on its way: "What a life! But have I lived?" ("Quelle vie! Mais ai-je vécu?"). The existential, not to say ontological, doubt of the narrator is resolved when he determines that he has lived, though not a life rich in events; his is a life of the mind. The memoirs of a madman will then recount not the usual stuff of memoirs—significant lives played out on the world-historical stage—but rather the personal "impressions" of a thinker. From that point on, the narration gets under way with a rambling account of the narrator's days at boarding school and his failed initiation into society. The forward progression of the plot line, such as it is, is anything but smooth. Ellipses punctuate the text, and twice the diegesis is broken off: first (and we shall return to this in a moment) when, after a three-week interruption, the enunciation resumes with the words: "Here is where my story *truly* begins" ("Ici commence *vraiment* mon histoire" [*MF*, 236, emphasis added]); once again, when in the midst of recounting his youthful loves, the narrator interpolates a fragment whose writing is said to predate that of the memoirs.

What then separates the false beginning from the "real" one? A memory, of course. A bizarre, inexplicable memory whose content is insistently dismissed as insignificant and yet whose effect is emphatically described as indelible: "There are insignificant things that have struck

---

cordeau." Gustave Flaubert, *Mémoires d'un fou*, in *Oeuvres complètes*, vol. 1 (Paris: Seuil 1964), 230, hereafter abbreviated *MF*.

7. "Je vais mettre sur le papier tout ce qui me viendra à la tête, mes idées avec mes souvenirs, mes impressions, mes rêves, mes caprices, tout ce qui passe dans la pensée et dans l'âme." Ibid.

me deeply and whose impression I will bear forever like the mark of a branding iron, though they are banal and inane."[8] What we have here, then, is a particular type of memory, what Freud terms a screen memory, distinguished from an ordinary memory precisely by the trivial, seemingly insignificant nature of its content.[9] Accurate in every detail, screen memories paradoxically conserve apparently indifferent events, while contemporaneous events of great importance in the subject's life go seemingly unremembered, unrecorded. And yet, as Freud demonstrates, there is a relationship between the hyperclear screen memory, with its insignificant content, and the screened-off traumatic memory, whose content is anything but insignificant. And that relationship is often metonymic, involving the spatial contiguity of the screen and the screened off, the representable and the unrepresentable. Let us now turn to the madman's screen memory in order to see what if any other memory it might be serving to screen off from the reader's as well as the narrator's scrutiny.

The memory involves a neighboring chateau the narrator used to visit in his youth with his family, a melancholy place where nothing has changed since the eighteenth century, including its sole occupant, an aged noblewoman. On the face of it the description of the chateau and its surrounding park does indeed seem insignificant, banal. And yet the memory of his childhood visits to this fairy-tale castle is branded red hot on the narrator's mind. The recounting of this memory is subject to a double cut, an internal ellipsis that breaks up the account of the memory and an external ellipsis followed by a heading in capital letters marking a three-week interruption in the narration. It is only after these twin ellipses and this temporal disjunction that the story is said to *really* begin. What then is being screened off by this elaborate staging? What is the nature of the unrepresentable traumatic memory? What is the relationship between the screened-off memory and the recollected events that are said to constitute the real beginning of the madman's story? This then is the screen memory:

> Often we extended our visits until quite late in the evening, gathered around the old mistress, in a great room paved with white flagstones, in front of a large marble fireplace. I can still see her golden snuff-box filled with the best Spanish tobacco, her white long-haired pug, and her

8. "Il y a des choses insignifiantes qui m'ont frappé fortement et que je garderai toujours comme l'empreinte d'un fer rouge, quoiqu'elles soient banales et niaises" (*MF*, 235).

9. On Freud's screen memories, see chapter 4 in Naomi Schor, *Reading in Detail: Aesthetics and the Feminine* (New York: Methuen, 1987), 65–78.

dainty little foot encased in a pretty high-heeled shoe adorned with a black rose.[10]

It is then the recollected sight of a dainty foot shod in a high-heeled shoe decorated with a single black rose that causes the text to break off, to blink as it were. For an elegiac postscript follows the first ellipsis: "It's all so long ago! The mistress is dead, her pugs too, her snuff-box is in the notary's pocket; the castle is a factory and the poor little shoe has been thrown into the river."[11]

The screen memory hides a primal, perhaps even *the* primal scriptural scene of fetishism in Flaubert, a scene that will be repeated with variations throughout his oeuvre. The fetish might indeed be viewed as a permanent screen object destined both to screen off and to gesture toward the unrepresentable memory of the actual sighting of the mother's genitals. The black rose—rather than the shoe—is the node in this scene of fetishism, for it is the metaphor for the female sexual organ which will be disseminated throughout Flaubert's writings. What I will call Flaubert's fetish issues directly from this ornament. And that fetish is a shawl. Indeed, in the memory ushered in by this screen memory, the sacred memory of the narrator's encounter with the reassuringly maternal and phallic Maria—her downy upper lip and her great milk-swollen breasts are among her most eroticized features—on the beaches of Flanders, a curiously striped shawl is featured. It is as though the decorated shoe, which had been cast away into the river, had washed up on the shore and the concentric black rose had been reconfigured in the vertical: "That day a charming red pelisse with black stripes had remained on the shore. The tide was rising, the shore was festooned with foam; already a more powerful wave had wet the silk fringes of this mantle. I removed it to a higher place; the material was soft and light, it was a woman's mantle."[12] Some thirty years later, Maria's striped, fringed shawl reappears, when on the boat carrying Frédéric Moreau home, he

10. "Nous prolongions souvent nos visites assez tard le soir, réunis autour de la vieille maîtresse, dans une grande salle couverte de dalles blanches, devant une vaste cheminée en marbre. Je vois encore sa tabatière d'or pleine du meilleur tabac d'Espagne, son carlin aux longs poils blancs, et son petit pied mignon, enveloppé dans un joli soulier à haut talon orné d'une rose noire" (*MF*, 236).

11. "Qu'il y a longtemps de tout cela! La maîtresse est morte, ses carlins aussi, sa tabatière est dans la poche du notaire; le château sert de fabrique, et le pauvre soulier a été jeté à la rivière" (*MF*, 236).

12. "Ce jour-là, une charmante pelisse rouge avec des raies noires était restée sur le rivage. La marée montait, le rivage était festonné d'écume; déjà un flot plus fort avait mouillé les franges de soie de ce manteau. Je l'ôtais pour le placer au loin; l'étoffe était moelleuse et légère, c'était un manteau de femme" (*MF*, 236).

meets Maria's final avatar, Marie Arnoux: "There was a long stole with purple stripes hanging over the brass rail behind her. How many times, out at sea, on damp evenings, she must have wrapped it around her body, covered her feet with it, or slept in it! Now the fringe was pulling it down, and it was on the point of falling into the water when Frédéric leapt forward and caught it."[13]

Fetishism defines the limits of realist description, for the fetishist cannot describe that which he would deny: woman's genitals and the threat they represent. Under the linguistic regime of fetishism the dreaded female genitals can be represented only figuratively, in the guise of a singularly apt metaphor, a black rose. For as Susan Suleiman has shown in her reading of George Bataille's pornographic *Histoire de l'oeil*, pink and black recur in periphrases for woman's genitals.[14] Fetishism necessarily speaks in tropes, but if it does, irony and not metaphor is the trope of fetishism. We return here to the question of the relationship of fetishism and irony, but this time it is necessary to define our terms as carefully as possible. There are, of course, as many definitions of irony as there are rhetoricians and philosophers writing on the subject. As the author of one guide to irony notes, quoting Nietzsche: "Only that which has no history can be defined," and irony, like fetishism, I argue, does have a history.[15] I take as my guiding definition the very apt one provided by Rainer Warning in his suggestive analysis of Flaubertian irony: "Our thesis will be that this 'order' of ironic discourse consists essentially in the citation of reference discourses and that this act of citation is to be understood in light of an ambivalent relationship of deceptive illusion and repetition, of critique and redemption, of deceptive illusion and aesthetic resemblance."[16] The cited discourse, in this instance the clichéd discourse of Romanticism, which is so often ironized in Flaubert, is then both rejected and introjected, negated and preserved through the use of irony. Irony in Flaubert functions as a strategy for sublation, enabling Flaubert to distance himself from Romanticism, "reactualizing" it all the while. The homology between irony

13. "Un long châle à bandes violettes était placé derrière son dos, sur le bordage de cuivre. Elle avait dû, bien des fois, au milieu de la mer, durant les soirs humides, en envelopper sa taille, s'en couvrir les pieds, dormir dedans! Mais, entraîné par les franges, il glissait peu à peu, il allait tomber dans l'eau; Frédéric fit un bond et le rattrapa" (*MF*, 236).

14. Susan Rubin Suleiman, "Pornography, Transgression, and the Avant-Garde: Bataille's Story of the Eye," in *The Poetics of Gender*, ed. Nancy K. Miller (New York: Columbia University Press, 1986), 126–27.

15. D. C. Muecke, *Irony and the Ironic* (London: Methuen, 1970), 7.

16. Rainer Warning, "Irony and the 'Order of Discourse' in Flaubert," *New Literary History* 13 (1982): 255.

and fetishism should then be quite clear: just as the fetish enables the fetishist simultaneously to recognize and to deny woman's castration, irony allows the ironist both to reject and to reappropriate the discourse of reference, Romanticism in the case of Flaubert. Surely it is of more than passing interest that the discourse of Romanticism occupies in this homology the same position as woman's castration. The discreditation of Romanticism is shown to be bound up with its association of the feminine, while femininity appears to inspire dread because of its association with a discourse of imaginary immediacy and plenitude. Flaubert's irony and Flaubert's fetishism are two aspects of the same phenomenon. In Flaubert rhetorical undecidability is aligned with the sexual; the oscillations of the fetishist are figured by the uncertainties of the ironist. The uses of uncertainty in Flaubert are, to paraphrase Barthes, to keep the reader from ever being able to answer the question: Is woman castrated?

If the connection between fetishism and irony has been made—and I am not aware that it has been, inasmuch as rhetoricians and psychoanalytic critics rarely speak the same language—then the consequences of this connection have yet to be drawn, notably as they affect women, that is, precisely those whose otherness the fetish is enlisted to block off, deny. If irony is the trope of fetishism and if female fetishism is a rare, if not nonexistent, perversion, then it would seem to follow that irony is a trope absent from women's writing. And indeed it is generally acknowledged that with the spectacular exception of Jane Austen, irony does not feature prominently in the history of women's fiction. The ironist in Western discourse has until recently almost always been male.

Some years ago in a piece titled "Female Fetishism" I called for the strategic appropriation of the undecidability of fetishism by women.[17] I now want to revise or update that formulation. For it appears to me now that what I was obscurely groping toward in that piece, though I didn't know it at the time, was in fact irony. What needs to be appropriated by women is irony, but an irony peeled off from fetishism, a feminist irony that would divorce the uncertainty of the ironist from the oscillations of the fetishist, an irony that would stand, in short, at the antipodes of the "irresponsible" (Barthes) model of Flaubertian irony.[18] In calling for a

17. Naomi Schor, "Female Fetishism: The Case of George Sand," in *The Female Body in Western Culture: Contemporary Perspectives*, ed. Susan Rubin Suleiman (Cambridge: Harvard University Press, 1986), 363–72.

18. The responsible feminist irony I am calling for here would seem to bear some sort of resemblance to what Wayne Booth has termed "stable irony," a form of irony whose ultimate meaning—in contrast to that of the unstable irony of modernity—can be reconstructed. *A Rhetoric of Irony* (Chicago: University of Chicago Press, 1974).

feminist appropriation of irony I am echoing, among others, Donna Haraway whose widely read "Manifesto for Cyborgs" is a call for "an ironic political myth faithful to feminism, socialism, and materialism." "Irony," writes Haraway in the opening paragraph of her text, "is . . . about the tension of holding incompatible things together because both or all are necessary and true. . . . It is also a rhetorical strategy and political method, one I would like to see more honored within socialist feminism."[19] While I share Haraway's and other feminists' sense that, in Nancy Miller's words, "it may be worth the risk of trying out this kind of duplicity on the road,"[20] I fear that until irony is divorced from fetishism, the risk of irony must be taken with extreme care lest the feminist ironist find herself playing straight into the hands of the male fetishist from whose perverse images of women she sets out to distance herself.

The appropriation by feminism of an irony that does not turn on castration entails the historicization of both irony and fetishism. Breaking with high structuralism's insistence on the timelessness of tropes, Warning insists on the historicity of Flaubertian irony: "Irony has its historical position in times of transition between the old that has already passed on and the new that cannot yet be made out."[21] If for Warning irony is the trope of choice in transitional historical periods, D. C. Muecke notes the "almost cancerous growth of the concept of irony since the 1790s."[22] Similar arguments could and have been made (by Stephen Heath) regarding the rise of fetishism as a widespread perversion in the age of commodification and the sexual fix. Hence the remark-

---

This resemblance is, however, at best only partial: Booth's agenda in promoting stable irony is fundamentally conservative (see Susan Suleiman, "Interpreting Ironies," *Diacritics* 6 [Summer 1976]: 15–21), and mine is not. Politically engaged feminist irony would retain the destabilizing effects of modernist irony while rejecting its misogynistic libidinal economy. Arguing for a radical discontinuity between modernist and postmodernist texts, in *Irony/Humor: Critical Paradigms* (Baltimore: Johns Hopkins University Press, 1988), Candace Lang reserves the term *irony* for the (relatively) stable irony of modernism and rebaptizes what is (mistakenly) referred to as postmodernist irony, humor. Lang would then contest my initial assumption that modernist irony persists in postmodernism; however, as she wryly concedes: "I rather doubt if my proposal for a less misleading terminology will have the slightest effect on general usage" (4). I shall then stick to general usage while recognizing that part of the problem in defining feminist irony (as well as female fetishism) is the inadequacy of an ancient terminology when applied to new cultural phenomena.

19. Donna Haraway, "A Manifesto for Cyborgs: Science, Technology, and Socialist Feminism in the 1980s," *Socialist Review* 80 (March–April 1985): 65.

20. Nancy Miller, "Changing the Subject: Authorship, Writing, and the Reader," in *Feminist Studies/Critical Studies*, ed. Teresa de Lauretis (Bloomington: Indiana University Press, 1986), 119 n. 18, and see 114.

21. Warning, "Irony," 264–65.

22. Muecke, *Irony*, 33.

able coalescence of irony and fetishism in Flaubert's fiction is neither an accident nor an idiopathic fluke; rather, it is the product of the convergence of a number of factors, among them, the heightened interest in irony brought about by German Romanticism, the passage from one socioeconomic order to another, the invention of sexuality and the pinning down of sexual difference. Today, in the age of the simulacrum, which has also been described with tremendous overoptimism as postfeminist, the conditions for the undoing of the mid-nineteenth-century concatenation of irony and fetishism are at hand. The withering away of ironic fetishism and fetishistic irony may well be a utopian scenario, rather like the one Luce Irigaray evokes in *This Sex Which Is Not One*, where she speculates on what it would be like if the "gods got together" and refused to go to market, if women refused to participate in the homosexual system of exchange. On the other hand, we cannot hope to liquidate modernism in its earliest and latest manifestations without unhooking the venerable trope of irony from the exclusively male perversion that is fetishism. We shall continue, of course, to read Flaubert but otherwise: less as an ironist and more for the pathos that is perhaps the mode of post-postmodernism.

Lesbian Fetishism?

Elizabeth Grosz

At first sight it seems rather odd that some human subjects gain sexual gratification from a piece of cloth, a shoe, long hair, or jewelry, from wearing certain clothing or from dressing up another person in a particular way. This sense of oddity diminishes a little, though not entirely, when we realize that fetishism is not really a *human* perversion at all but a uniquely male one (as is exhibitionism; kleptomania is an equivalently feminine perversion). With very few exceptions, psychoanalytic literature has pretty well agreed that fetishism is a male perversion, and its existence in women is assumed to be impossible. In one sense, I do not want to disagree with this claim; in psychoanalytic terms it makes no sense for women to be fetishists, and it is unimaginable that women would get sexual gratification from the use of inanimate objects or mere partial objects *alone*.[1] In another, more strategic and political sense, it seems plausible to suggest, as Naomi Schor does in her analysis of George Sand,[2] that there *can* be a form of female fetishism and to claim, further, that lesbianism provides its most manifest and tangible expression.

This paper was delivered at the "Queer Theory" Conference, February 10–11, 1990, at the University of California at Santa Cruz. My thanks to Teresa de Lauretis.

1. This is analogous to the claim that pornography, like fetishism, is a male preserve; in itself it remains inadequate as a form of sexual satisfaction for it reduces women to the position of (voyeuristic/fetishistic) objects, not subjects.

2. Naomi Schor, "Female Fetishism: The Case of George Sand," in *The Female Body in Western Culture: Contemporary Perspectives*, ed. Susan R. Suleiman (Cambridge: Harvard University Press, 1986), 363–72.

Like the fetishist, I want to have it both ways. On the one hand, I agree with the psychoanalytic orthodoxy that female fetishism is psychically inconceivable; on the other hand, I also claim that both "normal" (i.e., heterosexual) femininity and female homosexuality can be seen—in sociopolitical terms—to be in excess of their psychoanalytic descriptions as a form of fetishism (in the same way that, I would claim, feminism can be seen as a form of mass or collective psychosis, a political disavowal of women's social reality as oppressed). My essay is devoted to an exploration of how lesbianism may be understood in this way. I do not deal specifically with any quasi-fetishistic variations of lesbianism (sadomasochism, transvestism, the use of sexual paraphernalia, implements, or even prosthesis). Fascinating as these may be, they cannot be regarded as fetishes until it can first be shown that female fetishism is possible.

This essay is divided into two parts (as fetishism itself is divided): in the first part I examine orthodox psychoanalytic theorists, outlining Freud's and Lacan's notions; and in the second part, I play with these orthodox views, stretching them beyond the limits of their tolerance (play, if you recall, is a form of mastery, a conversion of passivity into activity, as well as a technique for the production of pleasure). Half serious, then, but also half playful, this is not only a reading of psychoanalytic concepts and methods but also an examination of how feminist theory may utilize precisely those discourses it wishes—and needs—to subvert in order to secure its own purposes, using them as strategic tools in its own struggles. This essay is both substantive and methodological, an analysis of the usefulness of psychoanalytic concepts and an illustration of how feminists may read patriarchal texts against the grain, so that they may be actively worked upon and strategically harnessed for purposes for which they were not intended.

Psychoanalysis and Fetishism

What then are the salient features of Freud's account of fetishism? Freud raised the question of fetishism early in his career (in the original 1905 edition of *The Three Essays*)[3] and returned to it again in one of the final papers of his life, "Splitting of the Ego in the Process of Defence" (1938). He turned to the topic every few years, in *Jensen's Gradiva*, in his case study of the Rat Man, in his study of Leonardo, and in the paper "Negation," focusing on it in "Fetishism."

3. Sigmund Freud, *Three Essays on the Theory of Sexuality* (1905), in *Standard Edition*, 7:130–243.

In the first of *The Three Essays*, Freud distinguished two types of sexual aberration, those in which there is a deviation in the sexual object (he mentions homosexuality, pedophilia, and bestiality), and those in which there is a deviation in the sexual aim (transvestism, voyeurism, exhibitionism). He includes fetishism in the second category (although he claimed that it could also be included in the first) because its main characteristic is a sexual overvaluation of a part of the body or an inanimate object. Overvaluation, a characteristic of anaclitic or masculine forms of loving[4] creates the fetish as such, the fetishistic object's attainment being sufficient in itself to bring about orgasmic gratification. Freud regarded the perversions as the opposite of neuroses. They are positive and negative sides of the same coin. The perversions avoid the repression that characterizes the neuroses. The pervert expresses precisely what it is that the neurotic represses. That is, the pervert does what the neurotic subject would like to do but is unable to because the expression of a perverse impulse yields more unpleasure than pleasure.[5] Insofar as sexual "normality" has any meaning for Freud (it is quite clear that he uses the term descriptively, not normatively, and that he seriously destabilized the term), it is defined in social terms as copulative, nonincestual heterosexuality.[6] Lesbianism, like male homosexuality, is classified as a perversion.

There are several ingredients necessary to understand Freud's correlation of fetishism with the paths open to masculine development. I will try to simplify and explain as clearly as I can why Freud believes only males can be fetishists. The fetishist, it seems, undergoes the Oedipus complex with one major element that differentiates his position from that of the eventual homosexual or heterosexual. In the latter cases, the boy witnesses the sight of female genitals and is threatened with castration at two different moments.[7] But "it is different if both factors *occur*

4. See Freud, "Contributions to the Psychology of Love" (1911), in *Standard Edition*, 11:165–75.

5. Incidentally, Freud quite dramatically changed his mind about the negative and positive roles of the perversions and neuroses in 1919 with his paper "A Child Is Being Beaten: A Contribution to the Study of the Origin of Perversions," *Standard Edition*, 17: 179–204, where he claims that even perversions are the result of repression.

6. Interestingly, Lacan claims that fetishism is the only perversion for which there is no corresponding neurosis. See Jacques Lacan and Wladimir Granoff, "Fetishism: The Symbolic, the Imaginary, and the Real," in *Perversions, Psychodynamics, and Therapy*, ed. Sandor Lorand (London: Tavistock, 1956), 265.

7. Freud claims that there is a period of time in which the boy is able to disavow one or the other (depending on which occurs first). In "Analysis of a Phobia in a Five-Year-Old Boy" (*Standard Edition*, 10:5–149), Little Hans provides the perfect illustration, with the birth of his sister Hanna; he disavows what he sees when the baby girl's diaper is removed. He exclaims to his mother "but she's got no teeth" (!)—a displacement, Freud suggests, from his perception of her castration. He cannot readily admit

simultaneously. In that case the threat revives the memory of the perception which had hitherto been regarded as harmless and finds in that
memory a dreaded affirmation."[8]

Here Freud claims that if the boy experiences the sight of the female's
castrated condition simultaneously with the threat of castration, he can
no longer disavow his perception, nor yet can he accept the implications
of the castration threat, which means the abandonment of his pleasure-
seeking sexual impulses and his submission to the oedipal interdict:

> He replies to the conflict with two contrary reactions, both of which are
> valid and effective. On the one hand, with the help of certain mecha-
> nisms, he rejects reality and refuses to accept any prohibition; on the
> other hand, in the same breath he recognizes the danger of reality, takes
> over the fear of that danger as a pathological symptom and tries subse-
> quently to divest himself of the fear. . . . the instinct is allowed to retain
> its satisfaction and proper respect is shown to reality. But everything
> has to be paid for in one way or another, and this success is achieved at
> the price of a rift in the ego which never heals but which increases as
> time goes on. The two contrary reactions to the conflict persist as the
> centre-piece of a splitting of the ego."[9]

I will return to this notion of the splitting of the ego later, but for the
moment, what is crucial is the oedipal configuration of the fetishist's
etiology. The fetishist is the boy/child who, for some reason, whether
these two events occur simultaneously or not, is unable to resolve the
oedipal conflict in its various alternatives. He is unable or unwilling to
abandon the mother as love object and accept the postoedipal restraints
on his sexual impulses; nor can he, like the homosexual son, accept
symbolic castration in order to take on the "feminine" position and
adopt a passive sexual role in relation to his father. Unlike either the
heterosexual or the homosexual, the fetishist wants to have his cake and

---

to himself that she has no penis (to do so would imperil the security of his own
possession of the organ) so he displaces his perception of what is missing from the
genitals to the teeth. At a later time moreover, the boy is directly threatened with
castration by his mother for his masturbation. She threatens to call the doctor, who
will remove his "widdler." Once again, he disavows the threat and brazenly pro-
claims: "So what? I'll widdle with my bottom." This kind of disavowal is a "normal"
psychic defense mechanism available to children of both sexes and it operates primarily with respect to the threat (for boys) or its symbolic actuality (for girls) of
castration.

8. Freud, "Splitting of the Ego in the Process of Defence" (1938), *Standard Edition*,
23:276, emphasis added.

9. Ibid., 275–76.

eat it too. He is not prepared to "pay" for his desire by facing the oedipal prohibition, that prohibition which gives the boy the ghastly choice—give up the mother or lose the penis. The fetish "remains a token of triumph over the threat of castration and a protection against it. It also saves the fetishist from becoming a homosexual, by endowing women with the characteristic which makes them tolerable as sexual objects. . . . what other men have to woo and make exertions for can be had by the fetishist with no trouble at all."[10]

The fetish is thus a substitute for, a talisman of, the phallus, but not just any old phallus. For the preoedipal boy, the most valued of all phalluses is not his own (for the penis is not yet elevated to the function of the phallus) but his mother's—the phallus, that is, that endows her with power and authority. He must disavow maternal castration if he is to protect himself against the possibility of his own castration. The fetish is his homage to the missing maternal phallus, his way of both preserving his belief in it and at the same time accepting her castration and the possibility of his own:

> Yes, in his mind the woman *has* got a penis, in spite of everything; but this penis is no longer the same as it was before. Something else has taken its place, has been appointed its substitute . . . and it now inherits the interest which was formerly directed to its predecessor. But this interest suffers an extraordinary increase as well, because the horror of castration has set up a memorial to itself in the creation of this substitute.[11]

The fetish cannot simply be equivalent to the maternal or female penis, for it both affirms and denies women's castration. There is no symbolic equation between the fetish and the penis, because, as Lacan so cogently argues, the phallus is not the equivalent of the penis (this is why the mother's phallus is the most significant one in the child's erotic life). The relation between phallus and fetish is already entirely bound up with the order of signifiers. The penis (as real organ) can take on the role of the phallus only because it is *missing*, that is, because women are castrated. (The two terms affirmed and denied as equivalent are both signifiers. At no point does the real enter the equation.) Lacan suggests that Freud's example in "Fetishism," the case of the young man with a fetish for shiny noses, can be explained only in terms of a displacement

10. Freud, "Fetishism" (1927), *Standard Edition*, 21:154.
11. Ibid.

initiated in language, a shift from the English "glance at the nose" to the German *Glanz auf der Nase*:

> We are now in a dimension where meaning seems lost, the dimension where is to be found, apparently, the fetishist perversion, the taste for shiny noses. And, if there were no elaboration upon the nose or the amputated lock of hair, this would be as impossible to analyze as a true perverse fixation. Indeed, if a slipper were, strictly speaking, the displacement of the female organ and no other elements were present to elaborate primary data, we would consider ourselves faced with a primitive perversion completely beyond the reach of analysis.[12]

The fetish is heir to all the ambivalences and the undecidability of the boy's attitude to maternal castration. Sandor Lorand's famous case study of the fetishist Little Harry shows that Harry caresses the shoes of his mother and of Lorand, while he also exhibits impulses to cut them. His whole symptomatology is marked with the same ambivalence that characterizes his relation to the mother's phallus. The boy has ample preoedipal access to the mother's body, having slept with her in the same bed until he was over three.[13] He knows that her sexual organ is not the same as his own. Yet he disavows any knowledge of genital differences in order to stave off the castration threat that he perceives being directed to his own organ. He not only caresses and cuts shoes, he develops a phobia about pendulum clocks (which remind him of the doctor's surgery where he had an operation for phimosis at the age of two); he obsessively cuts locks of his own hair without knowing why, and most particularly, he develops a mortal dread of amputees: "A relative came in to visit the family, a man with one leg amputated. Harry could not be induced to enter the room; the moment he had heard the voice of the

12. This quotation is worth reproducing in full: "The word is a gift of language and language is not immaterial. It is subtle matter but matter nonetheless. It can fecundate the hysterical woman, it can stand for the flow of urine or for excrement withheld. Words can also suffer symbolic wounds. We recall the 'Wespe' with a castrated W. when the wolf man realized the symbolic punishment which was inflicted upon him by Grouscha . . . The imaginary is decipherable only if it is rendered into symbols." Lacan and Granoff, "Fetishism," 268–69. In short, the fetish is interpretable, not because of any analogy or correspondence between the penis or vagina and the fetish, just as dreams are not interpretable based on visual resemblances. Psychoanalysis is the talking cure and as such it relies on the verbal elaboration of the symptom and its linguistic context, which is provided by the web of free associations. Fetishism emerges at the moment when the imaginary tilts into the symbolic, the preoedipal is transformed into the oedipal, or anxiety is transformed into guilt.

13. Sandor Lorand, "Fetishism in *Statu Nascendi*," *International Journal of Psychoanalysis* 11 (October 1930): 423.

man outside the door he ran screaming into the bedroom."[14] Harry both affirms and denies, both acknowledges and refuses to accept, the possibility of his own castration. Harry's preoccupation with shoes or Freud's patient's dependence on the shiny nose, then, functions as a sign by virtue of its reference not to the *penis* but only to the phallus.[15]

Freud attributes the peculiarities of fetishism to its reliance on the psychic defense mechanism of disavowal. Disavowal must be distinguished from three other major forms of psychic defense, repression (the mainspring of neurosis—which I will not discuss here), negation or denial, and repudiation or foreclosure (the major mechanism defining psychosis). In order to understand what is unique about fetishism and why Freud restricted it to masculine development, it is worth exploring these defense mechanisms in a little more detail.

Negation is a provisional "lifting of repression, though not of course an acceptance of what is repressed. . . . The outcome of this is a kind of intellectual acceptance of the repressed, while at the same time what is essential to the repression persists."[16] The repression is lifted on the condition that the repressed contents are verbally and affectively negated. In negation, there is an affirmation of what is repressed. (To negate or deny something one must have previously affirmed it.) Affirmation is the process of registering or fixing a drive to an ideational content, signifying the former by the latter. Affirmation is both the condition of signification and of repression (something must be signified

14. Ibid., 422.
15. The penis must already function as a signifier, an imaginary object, from the moment the boy attributes it to the mother. The fetish is not a representation of the penis any more than a pore of skin can represent the vagina. The child's perception of the mother's lack, and his symbolic utilization of the last object witnessed before he "sees" the lack, shoes, stockings, underwear, fur, etc., does not adequately explain fetishism, because the fetish is a substitute only for the phallus. The penis takes on the function of the phallus only because it is the mark or trace that excludes (at least) half the population. From being a real organ, the penis is transformed into an imaginary object dividing the sexes according to its presence or absence, possessed by some and desired by others. Only then can it function as a symbolic object (an object of union/exchange) between the sexes. The phallus distributes access to the social categories invested with various power relations.

The phallus is the "signifier of signifiers," the term that defines each subject's access to the symbolic order. It is emblematic of the structure of language, the gap dividing language from the real, which enables the signifier to slide over the signified and makes the polyvalence and play of language possible. This gap is the founding trace constituting the unconscious as such through repression of the signifier of incestuous desire. When the veil is lifted there is only the Medusa, women's castrated genitals, lacking, incomplete, horrifying (for men). Salome's dance, like striptease, can seduce only when at least one veil remains, alluring yet hiding the *nothing* of women's sex. The fetish thus plays the role of the veil, both outlining and yet covering over women's castration.

16. Freud, "Negation" (1925), in *Standard Edition*, 19:236.

before it can be relegated to the unconscious) and the return of the repressed. By simply adding a "no" to the affirmation, negation allows a conscious registration of the repressed content and avoids censorship. It is a very economical mode of psychic defense, accepting unconscious contents on the condition that they are denied.

Repudiation involves the rejection of an idea that emanates from external reality rather than from the id. It is a failure to register an impression, involving a rejection of or detachment from a piece of reality. The psychotic's hallucination is not the return of the repressed—that is, the return of a signifier—but the return of the real that has never been signified, a foreclosed or scotomized perception, something falling on the subject's psychic blind spot. The subject's perception is not projected outward onto the external world. Rather, what is internally obliterated reappears for the subject as if it emanates from the Real, in hallucinatory rather than projective form. It confronts the subject from an independent, outside position. Disavowal exists somewhere midway between these psychic defenses. Like repression and negation, it involves the psychic registration of an impulse, most notably the oedipal impulse; but like foreclosure or repudiation, it refuses the contents of a perception or piece of reality. It does not rely upon or utilize the unconscious. It predates the establishment of the unconscious and, like repudiation, involves a split in the ego. Unlike psychosis, however, it does not involve a failure of representation but is remarkably prolific in representational means.

The fetishist maintains two attitudes: the *disavowal* (affirmation and denial) of women's lack and its recognition and acceptance. The two attitudes "persist side by side throughout their lives without influencing each other. Here is what may rightly be called a splitting of the ego."[17] Unlike repression, where the ego represses a representative of the id, in disavowal two parts of the ego utilize contradictory forms of defense. In this way the fetish, as a substitute for the maternal phallus, affirms *and* denies women's castration. The fetishist is midway between neurosis and psychosis; he preserves himself from psychosis by representing the maternal phallus through fetishistic substitution, yet he is saved from neurosis by his repression of the castration threat. It is as if one part of the ego (which accepts castration) is neurotic, and the other part (which repudiates castration) is psychotic.

What is the major difference between the psychotic and the fetishist if both share disavowal and a rejection of a piece of reality? The difference

---

17. Freud, "Splitting of the Ego," 276.

seems to lie in opposition between hallucination and substitution. The fetishist "did not simply contradict his perceptions and hallucinate a penis where there was none to be seen, he effected no more than a displacement of value—he transferred the importance of the penis to another part of the body."[18] This displacement of value from the penis to another part of the body or onto an inanimate object is crucial to my discussion of the possibility of female fetishism and lesbian fetishism in particular.

Fetishism and Femininity

Why is female fetishism an oxymoron?[19] On Freud's account, female fetishism is not possible because there is no reason for the girl to disavow the mother's castration. Disavowal will not protect her against the acknowledgment of her own castration. Unlike the boy, threatened by possible castration, the girl has already been castrated and her task is the passive one of accepting her status. Disavowal in girls is by no means uncommon, but it makes no sense for a girl to disavow the *mother's* castration. Rather, she tends to disavow her own castration.

Freud's position is generally accepted by contemporary psychoanalytic theorists, despite reported cases of female fetishism. For example, Juliet Hopkins describes the case of a six-year-old girl who developed a foot and shoe fetish. The girl had a particular fetish object, a tobacco tin, which "she used exclusively for sexual purposes . . . when she masturbated."[20] Underlying the girl's fetishism, however, and perhaps explaining it, was a form of psychosis in which "the girl believed herself to be a boy." Hopkins refers to Greenacre's claim that the "symptoms of fetishism only develop in females in whom the illusionary phallus has gained such strength as to approach the delusional."[21] That is to say, fetishism is possible in females who believe themselves to be male. Naomi Schor also cites four cases of female fetishism, but all, similarly, seem to exhibit a strong identification of the girl with the phallic position of masculinity. These girls border on psychotic because they repudiate rather

18. Freud, "Splitting of the Ego," 277.
19. Cf. Schor, "Female Fetishism," 365.
20. Juliet Hopkins, "The Probable Role of Trauma in a Case of Foot and Shoe Fetishism: Aspects of the Psychotherapy of a Six Year Old Girl," *International Review of Psychoanalysis* 11 (1984): 79–91.
21. Phyllis Greenacre, "Fetishism," in *Sexual Deviations*, ed. Ismond Rosen, 2d ed. (Oxford: Oxford University Press, 1979), 191–207.

than disavow the psychic reality of castration. They refuse their castrated condition and continue to believe in their own phallic position.
They do not exhibit the ambivalence, the duplicity of the fetishist's
disavowal, the simultaneous affirmation and denial of the kind that
saves the fetishist from psychosis.

In order to understand why Freud considered it impossible for women
to be fetishists, and yet to understand that lesbianism *could* be seen as a
form of female fetishism, we need to explore the operations of disavowal
and their effects on feminine development. There are three distinctive
paths that may result from the girl's disavowal of her own castration:
heterosexual (secondary) narcissism, hysteria, and the masculinity complex.

In his paper "On Narcissism: An Introduction" Freud outlines a series
of object choices open to the feminine or what he calls the "narcissistic"
type. Here the feminine subject (whether male or female) loves an object
according to its resemblance to, identity or connection with the self.
Indeed, Freud claims that as a kind of compensation for her recognition
of her inferiority, the girl may develop a narcissistic investment in her
own body, treating it as the corresponding male would an external love
object. She pampers her body, treats it with loving care; it becomes her
greatest asset; it is her means of ensuring that she is loved, and thus of
giving her some notion of her own self-worth. Freud suggests that what
she does is to phallicize her whole body, treating it as if it were the
phallus: If man believes he *has* the phallus (the object of desire) then
woman believes she *is* the phallus. The man's penis and the whole of the
woman's body are rendered psychically equivalent.[22] He *has* the object
of desire while she *is* the object of desire.

In the process of making herself the object of desire, the narcissistic
woman displaces the value of the phallus onto her own body, taken as a
whole. She *has* the phallus, then, only insofar as she *is* the phallus (for
someone who loves or desires her). This so-called normal path of femininity, the compensation for (and thus acceptance of) her castration,
involves the phallicization of her body. In this sense, the narcissistic
woman is an effect of the function of the phallus in the constitution of
sexual identity. The narcissistic woman, contrary to Sarah Kofman's
characterization, is far from independent and autonomous. She strives to
retain her position as the object of the other's desire through artifice,
appearance, or dissimulation. Illusion, travesty, makeup, the veil become the techniques she relies on both to cover over and to make visible

22. See Otto Fenichel, "The Symbolic Equation: Girl = Phallus" (1936), trans. Henry Alden Bunker, *Psychoanalytic Quarterly* 18 (1949): 303–24.

her "essential assets." They are her means of seducing or enticing the masculine or anaclitic lover, becoming a love object for him. While thus concealing her "deficiency" by these means, she secures a mode of access to the phallic. Ironically, in this aim of becoming the phallus, the object of the other's desire, she is revealed as the site of rupture, lack, or castration, both idealized and debased, bound up with the masquerade of femininity, the site of both excess and deficiency: "Paradoxical as this formulation may seem," writes Lacan, "I am saying that it is in order to be the phallus, that is to say, the signifier of the desire of the Other, that a woman will reject an essential part of femininity, namely, all her attributes in the masquerade."[23]

The narcissistic woman strives to make her body into the phallus. She devotes loving time and energy to the image she has for others. She paints/shaves/plucks/dyes/diets/exercises her body, and clearly derives pleasure from compliments about her looks. Her whole body becomes the phallus to compensate for her genital deficiency, which she is able to disavow through her narcissistic self-investment. She can utilize these techniques to mask or cover over this "secret" insufficiency.

If the narcissistic woman effects a phallicization of the whole of her body, then, in a sense she takes to an extreme the strategies utilized by the hysteric. Hysteria is a specifically feminine neurosis in which, through the somatic compliance of a part of the body, the hysterogenic zone, the subject's sexuality is able to be displaced. Like the narcissistic woman, the hysteric accepts her castrated position, but unlike the narcissist, her investment is not in a phallic subject who, through his desire, can bestow on her the position of being the phallic object. The hysteric eschews masculine desire, preferring instead the now lost preoedipal attachment to her mother (or mother substitutes). In rebelling against the passivity usually associated with femininity, she hystericizes, that is to say, phallicizes, not the whole of her body but a hysterical zone. Let us take Dora as an example. Dora displaces genital pleasure into a form of hysterical choking. Through a series of infantile identifications (which Freud seems rather confused about) she phallicizes her throat and uses it to signal her disgust at Herr K's sexual advances. She hystericized part of her body as a form of nostalgia, a monument to her maternal prehistory, one she must (but refuses to) abandon in exchange for the father's law. She does not retain the clitoris (as in the masculinity complex) or transfer sexual intensity to the vagina (as occurs in "normal," i.e., heterosexual femininity); her libido is now invested in a nongenital zone. The

23. Jacques Lacan, "The Signification of the Phallus," in *Ecrits: A Selection*, trans. Alan Sheridan (London: Tavistock, 1977), 290.

difference between the hysteric and the narcissist is the difference between the displacement of the phallus onto a part or onto the whole of the subject's own body (perhaps a difference of degree rather than kind?). Whereas the narcissist's whole body is the phallus (and thus she requires an external love object to bestow on her the status of the object of desire, thus accounting for her reliance on an anaclitic lover, whether heterosexual or homosexual), the hysteric gains a self-defined status as phallic. A part of her own body takes on the function of the phallus (confirming her objectlike status in patriarchy) while her subjectivity remains in an active position (one which takes her own body as its object).

Disavowal then is by no means unique to men; it is a defense mechanism open and available to women. Its operations do not necessarily signal psychosis but function as a form of protection, not, as in the case of boys, against potential loss but against personal debasement and the transformation of the woman's status. It is a strategy of self-protection, even if it implies a certain mode of detachment from sociosymbolic "reality."

The third distinctive effect of the girl's disavowal of her castration is what Freud calls the masculinity complex. The girl "suffering" from such a complex refuses to accept her secondary and subordinated status; she aspires to be treated like and to act the same as men. Freud suggests that although the masculinity complex may not necessarily imply lesbianism, nevertheless, many lesbians can be classified under this label. Whereas the so-called normal path to femininity involves accepting her castration and transferring her libidinal cathexes from the mother to the father (via penis envy), with the accompanying transformation of her leading sexual organ from the clitoris to the vagina (with its associated position of passivity), the woman suffering from the masculinity complex retains the clitoris as her leading sexual organ and the position of activity it implies. She may also retain the maternal figure as the model on which to base her later object attachments, in which case she will continue to love a female mother substitute. "Thus," Freud remarks, "the girl may refuse to accept the fact of being castrated, may harden herself in the conviction that she *does* possess a penis and may subsequently be compelled to behave as though she were a man."[24] Indeed, this is how Freud explains female homosexuality in those rare passages and texts when he refers to lesbianism at all. In the case of an unnamed female homosexual, he describes her as behaving like a chivalrous male lover,

24. Freud, "Some Psychical Consequences of the Anatomical Distinction between the Sexes" (1925), *Standard Edition*, 19:248–58.

displaying many of the characteristics attributed to the anaclitic or masculine type. She loves "like a man." Although we may dispute the appropriateness of this description to all kinds of lesbian love relations, it seems clear that it certainly describes at least one kind of lesbian relationship, that in which there is a form of reproduction of typical heterosexually coded relations between narcissistic (feminine) and anaclitic (masculine) lovers. In this case the "masculine" lover disavows her castration while the feminine lover accepts her castration but refuses to convert her love object from maternal to paternal.

As with male homosexuality, for psychoanalysis female homosexuality generally takes on one of two forms based on one or the other path of infantile development. The first path produces the masculinity complex. In this case, there is a disavowal of women's castration and a refusal to acknowledge the socially sanctioned meanings of sexual difference. The girl will continue to identify with the phallic mother and may even see the father as simply another embodiment of the phallic status of the mother (it is significant that this is the fate of the male fetishist as well). In refusing to acknowledge her difference from the phallic position, she retains the masculinity of her preoedipal position and the mother as a love object. The other path of female homosexuality involves an acceptance of her castrated status and the temporary taking on of the father as a love object as in "normal" femininity; but instead of transferring her attachment from the father to a suitable male father substitute, the girl seeks out a "phallic" woman, a woman precisely, one may suspect, with a masculinity complex. The latter seeks a feminine love object (as men do) while the former seeks a masculine love object (whether male or female). This pattern could be described as the homosexual equivalent of the complementary heterosexual association between anaclitic and narcissistic love objects.

But what relation does lesbianism have to female fetishism? Well, in the one case, that of the girl who has accepted her castration complex, there seems little or no relation. But in the case of the woman suffering from the masculinity complex, it may be possible to suggest some connection. Like the fetishist, she disavows women's castration, but this castration is her own, not that of the phallic mother. And like the fetishist, she takes on a substitute for the phallus, an object outside her own body. It is this which differentiates her from the narcissist and the hysteric, both of whom phallicize or fetishize their *own* bodies, thus not really preserving the fetishist structure of the displacement of phallic value from the mother's body to an object outside of oneself. By contrast, the masculine woman takes an external love object—another woman—and through this love object is able to function as if she *has* rather than *is* the phallus. As in fetishism, this behavior implies a splitting of the ego instead of the creation of the unconscious through repression. It is this splitting that, I would argue, inclines the masculine woman to feminism itself, insofar as feminism, or any oppositional political movement, involves a disavowal of social reality so that change becomes conceivable and possible. Yet whereas the fetishist remains the most satisfied and contented of all perverts (the fetishist rarely if ever seeks analysis for fetishistic behavior—the fetish never complains!), the masculine woman remains the least contented. The more she feels equal or superior to men, the greater is the disparity with her socially acknowledged position, the validation of her convictions by others, and presumably the more she is socially ostracized. She displaces phallic value onto an object outside the mother's (or her own) phallus, but in contrast to the fetishist's, her love object is not an inanimate or partial object but another subject. Her "fetish" is the result of not a fear of femininity but a love of it; it does not protect her from potential danger, for it introduces her to the effects of a widespread social homophobia.

What is to be gained by describing this form of female homosexuality as fetishistic is not entirely clear to me, and it is for this reason that my answer must remain strategic. I want to say that the masculine woman, like the fetishist, is or could be seen in terms of fetishism and also, at the same time, that she is not. At stake for me here in this wavering and ambivalence is the very status of psychoanalysis itself. Insofar as psychoanalysis may be said to offer real insights about women in patriarchal society, we need to stretch Freud's terms in order to show that in themselves they do not exclude or discriminate against women—that women are treated with historical accuracy to women's social positions. But insofar as psychoanalysis can be seen as an active participant in patriarchal social values, we need to show how its terms do not adequately accommodate women's specificities and differences from men. The categories that Freud proposes as universally relevant—the function of the phallus, the Oedipus complex, the ubiquity of the castration threat and women's status as passive—surely need to be contested in order that social relations themselves can be transformed. The choice available to feminist theorists is to accept psychoanalysis more or less wholesale (which implies bracketing off political questions raised by patriarchal power relations) or to reject it in its entirety (in which case one is left without an account of psychic and fantasy life) or to do a little of both (the "fetishist's" solution), specifically selecting a notion that is de ned impossible or is foreclosed by the theory to show how it may not be as implausible as it seems if the terms themselves are stretched beyond their normal confines—in short, developing paradoxes and contradictions to see how the theory itself copes (or does not cope) with its own unspoken assumptions or unacknowledged implications. I prefer to have it both ways: psychoanalysis does indeed describe patriarchal power relations and their adoption and internalization in both sexes; yet it is also limited in its historical and sociogeographical specificity. It does not adequately describe cultures not based on the nuclear family, nor does it describe the potential transmutations and revolutionary upheavals feminism hopes to effect. But if I like to have it both ways, it is less in the mode of the fetishist (who never "pays" for his pleasures) than in the mode of the lesbian (who always pays).

MAGIC CAPITAL

Fetishism and Materialism:
The Limits of Theory in Marx

William Pietz

Poststructuralism has made for real theoretical advances in many areas, but it has not helped us read Marx. Indeed its principal contribution has been a certain semiological reading of Marxian theory that impedes any fruitful engagement with Marx's writing. The notion of fetishism has figured prominently in this poststructuralist revision of Marx since it is the locus within Marxian discourse for questions about the relations of science, ideology, consciousness, and the cultural construction of social reality—questions that have come to the fore in efforts to theorize the radical potential of non-proletarian identities, new social movements, and cultural politics. The problem with the semiological reading of fetishism that seems to have won the day among left cultural critics—whether in its Baudrillardian, Derridean, or Lacanian variants— is that it eliminates from Marxian analysis that materialism which most distinguishes it and which is, in my opinion, its greatest asset as a critical method. Marx's materialist method is better comprehended through the very approaches—existential phenomenology, dialectical analysis, quantitative social science—that poststructuralist semiology rejects. For this reason, it seems worth prefacing this exposition of Marx's appropriation of the nineteenth-century discourse about fetishism with a discussion of the interpretation that I intend to oppose.

For various references, ideas, and encouragement related to this essay, I am grateful to Francesco Pellizzi, Bruce Robbins, Andrew Ross, Gayatri Spivak, Katie King, and Michael Taussig. For any number of decisive theoretical conversations, I thank Vivian Sobchack, Robert Meister, and Norman O. Brown.

The Semiological Reading of Marx

One can trace the semiological interpretation of Marx, not surprisingly, to the discussions in Ferdinand de Saussure's *Course in General Linguistics*, in which linguistics and economics are identified as kindred sciences, sciences of "value."[1] But it was in the context of 1950s anti-Stalinism and in the wake of Claude Lévi-Strauss's famous essay "The Structural Study of Myth" that Roland Barthes wrote what might be termed the "History and Class Consciousness" of the semiological reading of Marx, his 1957 essay "Myth Today." Lévi-Strauss had concluded his own essay with the claim that "the same logical processes operate in myth as in science."[2] Mythical thought (what used to be called the "primitive mind") and scientific reason obey the same laws, laws that also structure social organizations such as kinship systems. Different social structures, be they communicational systems like languages or concrete institutions, reflect the fundamental organizational structures of a given society like so many mirrors positioned around the walls of a room, each reflecting the same furniture from different angles with a "timelessness" that poststructuralism will identify with the timelessness Freud attributed to the "unconscious."[3] The "furniture" in Lévi-Strauss's image is not, of course, real furniture existing in the phenomenal space of lived experience and embodied movement but rather the general rules—the mental furniture—that inform a particular mode of social organization without themselves being objects of consciousness (people speak and marry without knowing the linguistic or kinship rules they use in performing these actions: hence such structures constitute a social unconscious shared by all members of a given culture). Dialectic, according to Lévi-Strauss, is simply the unlimited capacity of these mirrors to totalize all aspects of social experience through representation

1. Ferdinand de Saussure, *Course in General Linguistics*, trans. Wade Baskin (New York: McGraw-Hill, 1966), 79–81, 110–22. The idea is that any finite continuous sensible field—the continuum of heard phonic sound or of some quantifiable monetary substance—which may be arbitrarily divided within itself (e.g., the differentiation of voiced sound into phonemes, of gold into coins of a certain normative weight) can have an infinite capacity to represent objects of a different order of being, for example, a word for a "thing," a dollar for a commodity. An idealist theory, Saussure's example of a "value" is a chess knight, whose essence is the complex of paradigmatic and syntagmatic rules for its recognition and use within the game; the materiality of the piece itself is irrelevant: a pebble, a coin, any random token could have the value "knight" if it occupies the position and is moved correctly within the game.
2. Claude Lévi-Strauss, "The Structural Study of Myth," in *Structural Anthropology*, trans. Claire Jacobson and Brooke Grundfest Schoepf (Garden City, N.Y.: Doubleday, 1967), 227.
3. For the image of the hall of mirrors, see Lévi-Strauss, "The Structural Study of Myths," 214; and *The Savage Mind* (Chicago: University of Chicago Press, 1966), 263.

(an argument opposing Jean-Paul Sartre's privileging of the dialectical form of human temporality and historicity). But the metaplay with structures expressed in myths is really more combinatory and rhetorical than dialectical in any Marxian sense. Myths are likened to the dream-riddles decoded by Freud; indeed, structuralists identified the different processes of the "dreamwork" described by Freud with the different types of rhetorical figures, tropes, whose poetic operation had been classified in classical rhetoric. The psychic processes of the unconscious theorized by psychoanalysis were identified not only with the poetic structures theorized in linguistics but also with the performative rules of social organizations posited by structuralist social science. The result was a conception of general "cultural logics" whose rules were held to structure both social institutions and a collective ("political") unconscious. The poststructuralist critic of culture could then conceive a politics as a sort of radical analysis of these cultural logics analogous to Freud's psychoanalysis of individuals. This enormously flattering conception of the critical activity of intellectuals is theorized in the poststructuralist semiology inaugurated by Roland Barthes.

In the essay that Barthes himself claimed initiated semiological analysis, he identifies the structural dynamic of premodern myths theorized by Lévi-Strauss as also that of modern ideologies, and he understands ideology as language whose terms are mere images that have been "depoliticized" through their removal from the context of their praxis.[4] Barthes thereby rereads The German Ideology through Lévi-Strauss in a manner that allows him to condemn Stalinist repression while preserving a mystical belief in "revolution," conceived as non-ideological action fusing productive activity and operational language:

> If I am a woodcutter and I am led to name the tree which I am felling, whatever the form of my sentence, I "speak the tree," I do not speak about it. This means that my language is operational, transitively linked to its object; between the tree and myself there is nothing but my labour, that is to say, an action. This is political language: it represents nature for me only inasmuch as I am going to transform it, it is a language thanks to which I "act the object"; the tree is not an image for me, it is simply the meaning of my action. But if I am not a woodcutter, I can no longer "speak the tree," I can only speak about it, on it. My language is no longer the instrument of an "acted-on tree," it is the "tree-celebrated" which becomes the instrument of my language . . . a

4. Roland Barthes, Mythologies, trans. Annette Lavers (New York: Hill and Wang, 1972), 9.

second-order language, a metalanguage in which I shall henceforth not "act the things" but "act their names." . . .

There is therefore one language which is not mythical, it is the language of man as producer: wherever man speaks in order to transform reality and not to preserve it as an image, wherever he links his language to the making of things, metalanguage is referred to a language-object, and myth is impossible. This is why revolutionary language cannot be mythical. Revolution is defined as a cathartic act meant to reveal the political load of the world: it makes the world; and its language, all of it, is functionally absorbed in its making. . . . The bourgeoisie hides the fact that it is the bourgeoisie and thereby produces myth; revolution announces itself openly as revolution and thereby abolishes myth.[5]

Among the many reasons why this passage has not aged well is the point, stated dryly by Jacques Rancière in another context, that "the idea of revolution is fairly ideological."[6] While subsequent semiology (Maoists aside) moved away from belief in the semantic transparency of revolutionary action, it never seriously questioned the assumptions that allowed Barthes's untheorized elision of politics with labor and of operational linguistics with the phenomenology of embodied action. Instead of opening the question of the relation between political representation and productive activity, and between semiosis and embodied experience,[7] poststructural semiology, in rejecting Jacobin revolutionism and the mystique of direct action, also rejected any conception of consequential action, use value, or material production as something usefully distinguished from sign exchange and communicative activity. In doing this, it failed to confront fetishism as a problem distinct from that of ideology.

One can distinguish three particularly influential semiological articulations of the theory of fetishism. One of these was Jean Baudrillard's 1970 essay "Fetishism and Ideology: The Semiological Reduction," which was written as part of his project to develop "the political economy of the sign" and abolish "the artificial distinction between the economic and the ideological."[8] His essential move—Fredric Jameson refers to it as "virtually the paradigm gesture of the new production

---

5. Ibid., 145–46.
6. Jacques Rancière, "How to Use Lire le Capital," trans. Tanya Asad, Economy and Society 5 (1976): 382.
7. This latter has been theorized by Vivian Sobchack in The Address of the Eye: A Phenomenology of Film Experience (Princeton: Princeton University Press, 1992).
8. In Jean Baudrillard, For a Critique of the Political Economy of the Sign, trans. Charles Levin (St. Louis: Telos Press, 1981), 143.

process"[9]—was to collapse the distinction between exchange value and use value, developed in the abstract discussion of the commodity form in *Capital's* opening pages, with Saussure's distinction between the signifier and the signified.[10] The logic of ideology thereby becomes the internal logic of the commodity and the sign alike. A material commodity's relation to its use is conceived as the paradigmatic relation in a sign wherein the phatic vehicle that is the sensible signifier refers to some "real thing" (the signified, an object outside the signifier's own coded medium). Exchange value is identified as the syntagmatic dimension wherein different commodity-signifiers circulate through exchange transactions that equate their economic value, rather the way words in a poetic text are substituted for each other through metaphorical equations of meaning. Such circulation itself produces novel value representations (meaning-effects) because the exchange values borne by commodities have a certain independence from their alleged use values (their "proper meanings"). Market value is viewed as a function of the structure of differential relations among commodities as exchange values, apart from any relation to use or labor values, just the way word meaning is internal to signifiers and distinct from their objective reference (their significance). Moreover, notions such as "need" and "use value"—and the concepts of labor power and production related to them—are, contrary to what Marx said, the most ideologically constructed notions of all.[11] The presumption of a realm of production distinct from that of exchange is the illusion of an essentialist anthropology that would ground both in an order of consumption composed of unchanging needs and the natural use values that satisfy them. Baudrillard thus arrives at the central claim of the semiological reading of Marx: the claim that the Marxian theory of labor value tried to anchor the exchange value of commodities in a primary order of material production in just the same way that structuralist linguistics tried to anchor the meaning-effects of signifiers in a foundational order of the signified. Poststructuralist semiology thereby completes both the critique of signs begun by the structuralist linguistics and the critique of political economy begun by Marxism by overcoming their essentialist objectivism and humanism. In doing this, it reveals capitalist fetishism to be nothing other than the semiologist's own fascination with signs:

> If fetishism exists it is thus not a fetishism of the signified, a fetishism of substances and values (called ideological), which the fetish object

9. Fredric Jameson, *Postmodernism, or The Cultural Logic of Late Capitalism* (Durham, N.C.: Duke University Press, 1991), 395.

10. Baudrillard, *For a Critique*, 144.

11. Jean Baudrillard, *The Mirror of Production*, trans. Mark Poster (St. Louis: Telos Press, 1975), 22–23. Also Baudrillard, *For a Critique*, 63–87.

would incarnate for the alienated subject. Behind this reinterpretation (which is truly ideological) is a *fetishism of the signifier*. That is to say that the subject is trapped in the factitious, differential, encoded, systematized aspect of the object. It is not the passion (whether of objects or subjects) for substances that speaks in fetishism, it is the passion for the code.[12]

According to Baudrillard, contemporary consumer society increasingly reveals—through the technological forms of its own self-spectacle—the degree to which commodities are no longer objects (those posited, but absent, signifieds) but rather image signifiers, "simulated" objects existing in a "hyperreal" social order that has been schizophrenically freed from all fixed investments of individual personality and particular desire. In postmodern society (so it is said), it is no longer the material use of products that is the object of our consumption so much as their commodified meaning—the content of their form, their exchange value—now revealed as autonomous forces in packaging and advertising. The post-Marxist theory of ideology suited to contemporary society is precisely that "semiology of images" proposed by Barthes, but now understood as the capitalist mode of production itself.

From the perspective of the history of theories of fetishism, Baudrillard's position is that of a postmodern Kantianism in which the free-acting subject's subordination to and reification by objective social forms is driven not by superstitious ignorance and fear, as in Kant's Enlightenment philosophy, but by fascination and the desire for pure formalism itself.[13] The other influential semiological versions of Marxian fetish theory are more Hegelian than Kantian.[14] Whereas Baudrillard

12. Baudrillard, *For a Critique*, 92. See also Julia Kristeva's treatment of fetishism as "an objectification of the pure signifier." "From One Identity to Another," in *Desire in Language: A Semiotic Approach to Literature and Art*, trans. Thomas Gora, Alice Jardine, and Leon S. Roudiez (New York: Columbia University Press, 1980), 139. All emphases in quotations cited in this essay are those of the original authors.
13. For Kant's mature conception of fetishism, see *Religion within the Limits of Reason Alone*, trans. Theodore M. Greene and Hoyt H. Hudson (New York: Harper and Row, 1960), 165–68.
14. In contrast to Kant, Hegel emphasized the importance of random association and contingency in fetishism, which he viewed as the first spiritual expression of human subjectivity per se, in the form of arbitrary caprice and particular desire, projected and objectified as power in some (any) material object—"the first stone they come across," as Hegel puts it in his discussion of fetish worship in his *Philosophy of Mind*, trans. A. V. Miller (Oxford: Clarendon Press, 1971), 42. The fetish's "objectivity is nothing other than the fancy of the individual projecting itself into space" ("Diese Gegenständlichkeit nichts anderes ist als die zur Selbstanschauung sich bringende individuelle Willkür"—more literally, "This objectivity is nothing other than the individual arbitrary will bringing itself into self-intuiting appearance"). *The Philosophy of History*, trans. J. Sibree (New York: Dover, 1956), 94.

would view fetishism in terms of the desire to inhabit self-contained formal codes that overcome all internal ambiguity and external materiality, Derridean post-Marxists would locate the fetish in semantic indeterminacy and the ambivalent oscillation (hence no dialectical resolution) between contrary determinations, a "space" where codes and their logics break down in a materiality that is conceived in terms of pure difference, contingency, and chance.[15]

More influential than deconstruction's fetish was the conception, developed from Louis Althusser's appropriation of Lacanian psychoanalysis, of the fetish as the ideological object itself. In this theory, ideology is premised on the impossibility of knowing the historical Real: since the larger historical and social world in which we live can never, as such, become an object of direct experience for individuals, we substitute for this unexperienceable and unrepresentable reality an imaginary representation of our relation to history and society—a picture of the "Whole Earth," say—just the way a child, at the moment when self-consciousness first dawns, unable to experience his or her own subjectivity perceptually, substitutes for it the representable image of the self he or she sees pictured when looking in a mirror. "Ideology", writes Althusser in the formulation that has become a postmodernist article of faith, "is a 'Representation' of the Imaginary Relationship of Individuals to their Real Conditions of Existence."[16] Moreover, "Ideology Interpellates Individuals as Subjects. . . . the category of the subject is constitutive of all ideology."[17] The Subject—that aggressively self-protective emptiness, always already traumatized and primally antagonistic to all definiteness of desire—can no more be the object of concrete experience than can the historical Real. In its absence, to console and defend us from the terror of our constitutive formlessness, we substitute personas, mirror selves, from our socially defined subject-positions. Both society

15. For the Derridean notion of the fetish, the main text is *Glas*: "The fetish's consistency, resistance, remnance, is in proportion to its undecidable bond to contraries. Thus the fetish—in general—begins to exist only insofar as it begins to bind itself to contraries. . . . The economy of the fetish is more powerful than that of the truth—decidable—of the thing itself or than a deciding discourse of castration (*pro aut contra*). The fetish is not opposable. It oscillates like the clapper of a truth that rings awry [*cloche*]." "The fetish no longer has any decidable status. *Glas* of phallogocentrism." *Glas*, trans. John P. Leavey, Jr., and Richard Rand (Lincoln: University of Nebraska Press, 1986), 227, 226. For Derrida's essentially Hegelian conception of matter as "radical heterogeneity" and his belief that such a view is actually an advance over Marxian "dialectical materialism," see *Positions*, trans. Alan Bass (Chicago: University of Chicago Press, 1981), 64–66, 94.

16. Louis Althusser, "Ideology and Ideological State Apparatuses," in *Lenin and Philosophy, and Other Essays*, trans. Ben Brewster (New York: Monthly Review Press, 1971), 162.

17. Ibid., 170–71.

and the self are, so this line of argument goes, imaginary totalizations, false universals that exist in the form of images, ideological signifiers of holistic closures we can never truly know or be, fetishes.

But there is a problem. How can the antidialectical poststructuralist avoid conceiving this process of false semiotic objectification as a Hegelian dialectic that traces the story of the self-representations of self-consciousness without at the same time turning it into what Althusser called Hegel's materialist "mirror image"—"economism and even tech-nologism"?[18] Either move constructs a vision of historical inevitability upon a teleological narrative. In the former, contradictions in ideological consciousness (in the ethico-political "superstructure") determine those of the economic base, and hence the historical process; in the latter, contradictions in the material infrastructure determine all ideological superstructures, along with the course of history. Either way, one accepts a reified dialectic whose monocausal explanations fail to account for the historical fact of heterogeneous social formations and "uneven" development. The solution is found in the concept of a historical movement whose determination is both multicausal and incomplete—partly determined by many economic, political, and ideological structures, yet still retaining a bit of contingent indeterminacy. This conception is articulated by Althusser in the notions of "overdetermination" and, in a timely footnote praising Antonio Gramsci, "hegemony."[19] For semiological post-Marxism, the notions of overdetermination and cultural hegemony resolve the fundamental contradiction in Marx's own argument: that between his historical determinism—his theory that the contradictions in the capitalist mode of production's own system must themselves drive it to dissolution—and the subjectivist voluntarism of his appeal to conscious class struggle in making the revolution.[20] Freed from the residual scientism of Althusser, Lacanian post-Marxists can affirm the presence, in the historical field of events and in ourselves as agents, of indeterminacy and contingency as the open horizon that makes possible radical action and social change. Ernesto Laclau and Slavoj Žižek have identified this "radical indeterminacy" as the ground of a "pure antagonism" able to challenge oppressive orders.[21] Yet, for all this, the Lacanian strand of post-Marxist semiology culminates in the announcement

18. Louis Althusser, "Contradiction and Overdetermination," in For Marx, trans. Ben Brewster (London: Verso, 1977), 108.

19. Ibid., 114.

20. Ernesto Laclau, New Reflections on the Revolution of Our Time (London: Verso, 1990), 5–17.

21. Ibid., 79; Slavoj Žižek, "Beyond Discourse-Analysis," in Laclau, New Reflections, 252.

of a return to dialectic and to Hegel as "the first post-Marxist."[22] In his recent book *The Sublime Object of Ideology*, Žižek maintains that "the most consistent model of such an acknowledgement of antagonism is offered by Hegelian dialectics,"[23] and he proposes "a kind of 'return to Hegel'—to reactualize Hegelian dialectics by giving it a new reading on the basis of Lacanian psychoanalysis. The current image of Hegel as an 'idealist-monist' is totally misleading: what we find in Hegel is the strongest affirmation yet of difference and contingency—absolute knowledge' itself is nothing but a name for the acknowledgement of a certain radical loss."[24] Žižek makes this argument by way of a rereading of the theory of fetishism in which the Hegelian dialectic is rediscovered in the movement whereby ideological universals are produced through a process that converts the experience of objects lacking adequacy as expressive signifiers into the experience of them as objective signifiers of that very lack, and therefore, in some less finite sense, sublimely adequate. This is, indeed, the true Hegelian move: materiality, exteriority, resistance, is always the same, always the necessary mediating otherness through which abstractly subjective concepts are actualized as Ideas in a process of reconciliation to existing reality which is their own process of historical becoming. Žižek's great contribution is to reveal semiological criticism and poststructuralist theory as, at best, a form of the sort of left Hegelianism that Marx began his own intellectual development by criticizing.

In these semiological readings of Marx, the concept of materiality is always either replaced altogether by a concept of objectified form, of the pure signifier, or else abstracted on a textualist model as sheer heterogeneity and contingency, as the "outside" of preexisting codes where semantic effects are produced by aleatory play among homologous structures and homophonic forms. In this way, all dualities between form and content, sign and referent, exchange value and use value, subject and object, difference and contradiction, are "overcome," as is the need for dialectic. Marx's text itself can then be read rhetorically, and the Marxian notion of fetishism can be interpreted as a rhetorician's theory of ideology.[25]

22. Slavoj Žižek, *The Sublime Object of Ideology* (London: Verso, 1989), 5.
23. Ibid., 5–6.
24. Ibid., 7.
25. For influential readings of Marx along these lines, which exemplify the postmodernist's magisterial incomprehension of what Marx was actually talking about, see Hayden White, "Marx: The Philosophical Defense of History in the Metonymical Mode," in *Metahistory: The Historical Imagination in Nineteenth-Century Europe* (Baltimore: Johns Hopkins University Press, 1973), 281–330; and W. J. T. Mitchell, "The Rhetoric of Iconoclasm: Marxism, Ideology, and Fetishism," in *Iconology: Image, Text, Ideology* (Chicago: University of Chicago Press, 1986), 151–208.

In opposition to such approaches, the present essay searches for a more Marxian, materialist theoretical perspective by examining Marx's conception of economic fetishism in the light of his appropriation of the learned discourse about religious fetishism that was part of the intellectual context of nineteenth-century European scholarship. In this regard, Etienne Balibar is simply wrong when he argues that the discourse about fetishism occurs in Marx only during the writing of *Capital* and that it should be understood in terms of the problematic of "ideology," with "fetishism" conceived as Marx's attempt "to think both the real and the imaginary within ideology."[26] On the contrary, the problem of fetishism was very much present in Marx's thought (and writing) for twenty-five years prior to the publication of the first volume of *Capital*. Moreover, "fetishism" expresses a problematic distinct from that of "ideology," one with its own historical and conceptual specificity, concerned with articulating a materialist conception of theory.[27] In contrast to semiological post-Marxism, it is the Marxian view that the production of theoretical discourse is always an attempt at once to make intelligible and to complete (in a functional sense) some already institutionalized social reality. Theory always arises as a supplement not to the logic of a text but to a particular social practice; its analysis is best pursued not through deconstructions of intertextuality and aleatory play but by articulating the contradictions between institutional practices and the theories by which they explain and justify themselves and each other.[28] Indeed,

26. Étienne Balibar, "The Vacillation of Ideology," trans. Andrew Ross and Constance Penley, in *Marxism and the Interpretation of Culture*, ed. Cary Nelson and Lawrence Grossberg (Urbana: University of Illinois Press, 1988), 168.

27. I am more in agreement with Jacques Rancière when he insists, against Balibar, that "fetishism is *not at all* a theory of ideology." "How to Use *Lire 'Le Capital*,'" 382. Perhaps because Rancière's contribution to the Althusserian ur-text, *Reading Capital*, was dropped from the second French edition of that work (as a result of his break with Althusser over the events of 1968) and was not included in the English translation, the fact that the principle Althusserian text on fetish theory was by Rancière has been largely ignored by Anglophone theorists. The main section of Rancière's essay was eventually translated as "The Concept of 'Critique' and the 'Critique of Political Economy' (from the *1844 Manuscript* to *Capital*)," trans. Ben Brewster, in *Economy and Society* 5 (1976): 352–76, followed by his own self-criticism, "How to Use *Lire 'Le Capital*,'" 377–84. For British responses of this time defending against any possible revival of interest in the problem of fetishism, see Ben Brewster, "Fetishism in *Capital* and *Reading Capital*," *Economy and Society* 5 (1976): 344–51; Terrell Carver, "Marx's Commodity Fetishism," *Inquiry* 18 (1975): 39–63; Norman Geras, "Essence and Appearance: Aspects of Fetishism in Marx's *Capital*," *New Left Review* 65 (1971): 69–85; Nikolas Rose, "Fetishism and Ideology," *Ideology and Consciousness* 2 (Autumn 1977): 27–54.

28. For this conception of Marxian method, see Robert Meister, *Political Identity: Thinking through Marx* (London: Basil Blackwell, 1990), a book to which I am greatly indebted.

such a materialist analysis of ideological theories is expressed in the notion of fetishism that Marx developed in the course of his writings: revisiting Marx's theory of fetishism is a way to reopen the question of materialist criticism. As Robert Meister has written, "Without the premise of materialism the Marxist critique of ideology would tend to portray the concrete social formation as a hall of mirrors [alluding to Lévi-Strauss's image]. All essences would be reduced to appearances, and all appearances to the mutual reflection of overlapping social practices or 'discourses.' A Marxism lacking a dynamic material process such as 'accumulation' could never explain why the patterns and outcomes of institutional overlap change over time. We would be left with a series of static pictures of the range of institutional contradictions that make political action possible at any given moment. Instead of showing a path of development, historical argument would consist of demonstrating the discontinuities between these pictures, suggesting always that particular outcomes are 'contingent' rather than necessary. . . . Materialism provided Marx with a path out of the hall of mirrors."[29]

Insofar as the present essay arrives at any sort of general conclusions, they are the following. The Marxian theory of fetishism may be described as a critical, materialist theory of social desire. It presents modern political economy as a real social metaphysics (an institutional objectification of human temporality in the form of labor-power, surplus value, and credit-money) and, at the same time, as a fantastically alien misrepresentation (an inhuman, doubly inverted vision of the collective life of individuals as "civil society"). Its method is that of a historicizing, dialectical phenomenology of social reality complementary to class analysis and giving concrete theoretical expression to what I believe Meister rightly terms Marx's *political materialism*.

Marx and the Discourse about Fetishism

In his mature thought, Marx understood "capital" to be a species of fetish. A factory machine, a wheat field, a pension fund, and other "things" reckoned as capital by accountants and political economists are fetishes, in Marx's view, not in their physical existence or concrete functions per se but in their reality as material forms ("part-objects") of a distinctive type of social system. The truth of capital, for Marx, is found in its social essence as an organizing principle, as the universal form for

29. Ibid., 243–44.

social processes aiming at the formation and accumulation of precisely this sort of materialized value: that odd type of "sensuous supersensuous thing" (sinnlich übersinnliches Ding)[30] called capital.

Fetishism is the term Marx used to characterize the capitalist social process *as a whole*. At the very least, his employment of this word was a vivid way of suggesting to his readers that the truth of capital was to be grasped from a perspective alien to that of bourgeois understanding, which knows capital exclusively through its own categories. One of the claims of this essay is that Marx appealed to the language of magic and theology in general, and fetishism in particular, as a way of evoking the materialist imaginary proper to a communist mode of apprehending capitalist reality. At the most, Marx's mature discourse about fetishism expresses a dialectical and materialist critique of both religion and political economy—one which identifies political economy as an atheological "religion of everyday life"[31] and which revalues both in terms of their effective relation to exploitive divisions of social labor. That is, the discourse about fetishism redescribes both religion and political economy from the perspective of class struggle.

Marx's use of "fetishism" has a deliberately strange effect of erudition and vulgarity: when he speaks about capitalist fetishism, he is being theoretically serious and polemically satirical at the same time. In accepting "fetishism" as a historically scientific term, Marx was simply conforming to the learned opinion of his time; throughout his writing, Marx spoke of the fetish worship of "primitive" peoples as historical fact, often employing the term as a synecdoche for primitive religion in general (with Christianity taken as its modern counterpart). But Marx also recognized—in a way Feuerbach did not—that fetishism was a crucial category for the materialist critique of religion and, indeed, of philosophical idealism. As with all his key words, Marx's usage of "fetishism" enacts a dialogic subversion of the way his predecessors and contemporaries theorized social reality. Marx took advantage of the radically historical, materialist problematic implicit in the Enlightenment discourse about fetishism to travesty the idealist and, at best, abstractly materialist social philosophies of his time by means of their own deepest preconceptions.

Although Marx's materialism and his social theory went far beyond those of Enlightenment thought, his synopsis of the historical progress of religious consciousness from primordial fetish worship to an ironic

30. Karl Marx, *Das Kapital: Kritik der politische Okonomie, vol. 1: Der Produktionsprozess des Kapitals* (Frankfurt am Main: Ullstein, 1969), 50.
31. Karl Marx, *Capital: A Critique of Political Economy*, vol. 3, trans. David Fernbach (New York: Random House, 1981), 969.

deism that was the next best thing to atheism ("from the African's fetish to Voltaire's supreme being")[32] bears an eighteenth-century pedigree. This theoretical narrative of the world history of religion was established in European intellectual culture by the end of the eighteenth century, although the very word "fetishism" was coined only in 1757 by Charles de Brosses. Historians of religion around the turn of the century, especially Germans such as Christoph Meiners and Philipp Christian Reinhard, but also French writers such as J. A. Dulaure, discussed fetishism extensively as the earliest stage of religion.[33] Although the notion was controversial in circles where theological faith confronted the new history of religion (scholars argued whether fetishism was historically prior to polytheism and monotheism or was merely the most debased form of degenerate religion), popular and learned writers alike generally accepted that the worship of terrestrial, material objects (as de Brosses had defined his neologism) was the most primitive moment of religion.[34] Invented by a French philosophe and popularized in German texts, "fetishism" is referred to by English writers as early as 1801.[35] The use of the idea by English humanists already appears in 1809 when Coleridge condemned vulgar empiricism by likening it to primitive fetish worship: "From the fetisch of the imbruted African to the soul-debasing errors of the proud fact-hunting materialist we may trace the various ceremonials of the same idolatry."[36]

In the 1840s, the founder of sociology, Auguste Comte, published a theory of fetishism so elaborate and so important to his theory of posi-

32. Karl Marx, *Grundrisse: Foundations of the Critique of Political Economy*, trans. Martin Nicolaus (New York: Random House, 1973), 891.

33. Christoph Meiners, *Allgemeine kritische Geschichte der Religionen* (Hannover, 1806–7); Philipp Christian Reinhard, *Abriss einer Geschichte der Entstehung und Aubbildung der religiösen Ideen* (Jena, 1794); Jacques Antoine Dulaure, *The Gods of Generation: A History of Phallic Cults among Ancients and Moderns* (1805; New York: Panurge Press, 1933); Charles François Dupuis, *The Origin of All Religious Worship* (1794; New Orleans, 1872).

34. It is taken for granted by most nineteenth-century writers on religion, from Saint-Simonian advocates of the New Christianity (see the 1829 lecture of Saint-Emand Bazard, *Développement religieux de l'homme: Fétichisme, polythéisme, monothéism Juif et Chrétien*, in *Oeuvres de Saint-Simon et d'Enfantin*, vol. 41 [Aalen: Otto Zeller, 1964], 121–48) to atheistic anarchists such as Michael Bakunin (in *God and the State*, written 1870–72 [New York: Dover, 1970], 511).

35. A review of a German critical history of religion refers to fetishism as "the worship of tools." W. Taylor, review of D. Heynig, *Sämmthchen Religions arten*, in *Monthly Magazine, or British Register* 11 (1801): 646.

36. Samuel Taylor Coleridge, *The Friend, I*, in *The Collected Works of Samuel Taylor Coleridge*, 4:1 (Princeton: Princeton University Press, 1969), 518. Matthew Arnold's later criticism of "the Nonconformist fetish" (in *Culture and Anarchy* [1869; Cambridge: Cambridge University Press, 1971], 168–70) was more Kantian in its identification of fetishes with "mechanical" rules and maxims.

tivism that subsequent writers in the emerging social sciences were forced to react against his conception of fetishism if they were to approach the problem it named at all.[37] The principle alternative theories subsequently elaborated—around the time the first volume of *Capital* appeared—were E. B. Tylor's "animism," which offered an idealist psychological explanation of fetishistic beliefs, and J. F. McLennan's "totemism," an institutional theory that subordinated fetishism to ancestor worship and kinship organization.[38] In the last decades of the century, there was both an upsurge in "ethnographic" descriptions of primitive fetishism (a result of the colonialist scramble of those years)[39] and increasing distrust of the notion among social scientists,[40] although historians of religion still tended to treat the notion as unproblematic.[41]

37. Auguste Comte, "First Theological Phase: Fetichism," in *The Positive Philosophy of Auguste Comte*, trans. Harriet Martineau (1840; New York: Eckler, n.d.), 545–61; and "Positive Theory of the Age of Fetichism, or General Account of the Spontaneous Regime of Humanity," in *System of Positive Polity, or Treatise on Sociology, Instituting the Religion of Humanity*, trans. J. H. Bridges et al., vol. 3 (Paris: Carilian-Goeury and Dalmont, 1853), 65–130. For a contemporary English exposition of the Comtian view, see G. H. Lewes, "Ages of Fetishism and Polytheism," in *Comte's Philosophy of Science* (1853; London: Bell, 1897), 273–87.

38. E. B. Tylor, "The Religion of Savages," *Fortnightly Review* 6 (1866): 84; J. F. McLennan, "The Worship of Plants and Animals, Part I: Totems and Totemism," *Fortnightly Review*, n.s., 34 (1869): 422–24. John Stuart Mill was already conceiving fetishism as animist superstition in an essay, "Utility of Religion," written in the 1850s, in *Collected Works of John Stuart Mill*, vol. 10 (Toronto: University of Toronto Press, 1963), 418. See also his notion of fetishism in essays of the 1860s, "Theism," in *Collected Works*, 10:442–43; and "Sir William Hamilton's Theory of Causation," in *Collected Works*, 9:300. For Herbert Spencer, see "The Origin of Animal Worship," *Fortnightly Review* (1870), reprinted in *Essays Scientific, Political, and Speculative* (New York: Appleton, 1904), 308–30, and "Idol-Worship and Fetich-Worship," *Popular Science Monthly* 8 (1875): 158–64. For the German social-scientific idea of fetishism, see Adolf Bastian, "Die Fetische," in *Der Mensch in der Geschichte*, vol. 2 (Leipzig: Wigand, 1860), 11–23; and Fritz Schultz, *Fetishism: A Contribution to the Anthropology of Religion*, trans. J. Fitzgerald (1871; New York: Humboldt, 1885).

39. A. B. Ellis, *The Land of Fetish* (London: Chapman and Hall, 1883); E. J. Glave, "Fetishism in Congo Land," *Century Magazine* 41 (April 1891): 825–36; Mary H. Kingsley, "The Fetish View of the Human Soul," *Folk-Lore* 8 (June 1897): 138–51; Rev. Robert Nassau, "The Philosophy of Fetishism," *Journal of the Royal African Society* 17 (1903–4): 257–70; and *Fetishism in West Africa* (London: Duckworth, 1905); Rev. Robert H. Milligan, "The Dark Side of the Dark Continent: The Mental and Moral Degradation of Fetishism," *Missionary Review of the World* 40 (December 1917): 890–903. More serious were Dr. Nina-Rodrigues, *L'animisme fétichiste des nègres de Bahia* (Bahia, Brazil: Resi, 1900); and in an extension of the term that stuck, Frank H. Cushing, *Zuni Fetishes* (1883; Las Vegas: KC Publications, 1974).

40. See the debate between Max Müller and Andrew Lang: F. Max Müller, "Is Fetishism a Primitive Form of Religion?" in *Lectures on the Origin and Growth of Religion* (London: Longmans, Green, 1882), 54–131; Andrew Lang, "Fetishism and the Infinite," in *Custom and Myth* (London: Longmans, Green, 1893), 212–42; and "Mr. Max Müller and Fetishism," *Mind* 16 (October 1879): 453–69.

41. Goblet d'Alviella, "Origines de l'idolâtrie," in *Revue de l'histoire des religions*, ed. Jean Réville, vol. 12 (Paris: Leroux, 1885), 1–25; P. D. Chantepie de la Saussaye,

Meanwhile, the rise of the discourse about sexual fetishism developed by sexologists in the 1880s only intensified the association of the idea (already stressed by such writers as Hegel and Benjamin Constant in the 1820s) with the arbitrary and the idiosyncratically individual, and hence with psychological rather than sociological processes. Added to its association with the scandalous founder of sociology, Comte, this new usage encouraged the fathers of respectable sociology, Emile Durkheim and Max Weber, to avoid the term. In anthropology, while less "scientific" writers such as James Frazer and Wilhelm Wundt continued to use the term, we find it decisively rejected by Marcel Mauss in 1906.[42]

Marx's own appropriation of the theoretical discourse about fetishism began in the 1840s in the context of a repressive, antiliberal German political regime and the philosophical infighting over the legacy of Hegel. It is to this intellectual moment that a study of Marx's theory of fetishism must first turn.

Religious Fetishism and Civil Society:
The Critique of Hegel

In a newspaper article of July 1842 the twenty-four-year-old Marx, claiming the authority of philosophy, defined fetishism as "the *religion of sensuous desire*" ("die Religion der sinnlichen Begierde").[43] Although the remark is made in passing in order to expose the scholarship

---

Manual of the Science of Religion, trans. Beatrice S. Colyer-Fergusson (London: Longmans, Green, 1891); C. P. Tiele, *Elements of the Science of Religion*, vol. 1 (New York: Scribner's, 1897); Frank Byron Jevons, *An Introduction to the History of Religion*, 3d ed. (London: Methuen, 1896).

42. Wilhelm Wundt has much to say about fetishism in *Elements of Folk Psychology*, trans. Edward Leroy Schaub (1912; New York: Macmillan, 1916), esp. 220–29, and it is in denouncing Wundt that Mauss rejects the term completely. See Marcel Mauss, "L'art et le myth d'après M. Wundt," in *Oeuvres*, vol. 2, ed. Victor Karady (Paris: Minuit, 1968), 216–17, and 244–45, where he writes: "The notion of the fetish ought, we think, to disappear definitively from science and be replaced by that of *mana*. . . . Moreover, when one writes the history of the science of religions and of ethnography, one will be astonished at the unmerited and fortuitous role that a notion of the type of that of the fetish has played in theoretical and descriptive works. It corresponds to nothing but an immense misunderstanding between two civilizations, the African and the European." For this period, also see the attempt to sort things out by A. C. Haddon, *Magic and Fetishism* (London: Constable, 1906). Remarkably late is the long discussion of fetishism by William Graham Sumner and Albert Galloway Keller, in *The Science of Society*, vol. 2 (New Haven: Yale University Press, 1927), 979–1058.

43. Karl Marx, "The Leading Article in No. 179 of the *Kölnische Zeitung*," in Karl Marx and Frederick Engels, *Collected Works*, vol. 1 (New York: International, 1975), 189.

of the editor of a rival journal as mere "penny-magazine erudition," he was not just writing off the top of his head. Earlier that year, Marx had studied the notion of religious fetishism in depth, making extensive excerpts from the book in which the term was coined, Charles de Brosses's *Du culte des dieux fétiches* (1760), and from two more recent works, Karl August Böttiger's *Ideen zur Kunst-Mythologie* (1826) and Benjamin Constant's *De la religion* (1824).[44] In one apocryphal incident excerpted by Marx from the book by de Brosses in which the word "fetishism" was coined, we are offered the image of an apotropaic pot-latch improvised by "savages" to ward off the barbaric agents of 'primitive accumulation':

> The *savages of Cuba* considered gold to be the fetish of the Spaniards. So they celebrated it with a feast, danced and sang around it, and threw it into the sea, in order to be rid of it.[45]

This was not the first time that Marx had found some insight in an anecdote in which social conflict was expressed through the contradictory value orders of money and religion. The year before, Marx had concluded his doctoral dissertation with a reflection on the relationship of imagination to social reality, in which the theistic beliefs of ancient cultures and the monetarized relations of secular societies are understood through each other:

> Take for instance the ontological proof.[46] This only means:
> "that which I conceive for myself in a real way (*realiter*), is a real concept for me,"
> something that works on me. In this sense, *all gods*, the pagan as well as the Christian ones, have possessed a real existence. Did not the ancient

44. For his excerpts see Karl Marx, "Exzerpte zur Geschichte der Kunst und der Religion," in *Marx-Engels Gesamtausgabe*, 2:1 (Berlin: Dietz, 1976), 320–34, 342–67. Marx used the German translation of de Brosses by Pistorius, *Ueber den Dienst der Fetischengötter* (Berlin, 1785). Marx also made excerpts at this time from Christoph Meiners's *Allgemeine kritische Geschichte der Religionen* but did not focus on Meiners's discussions of fetishism; he does make a number of notes on Meiners's discussion of priapism, but for late eighteenth- and early nineteenth-century historians of ancient religion including Robert Payne Knight, J. A. Dulaure, and Meiners, phallicism and fetishism were distinct phenomena.

45. Marx, "Exzerpte," 322.

46. In this passage, Marx is presenting the Hegelian criticism of Kant's discussion titled "The Impossibility of an Ontological Proof of the Existence of God," in *Critique of Pure Reason*, trans. Norman Kemp Smith (New York: St. Martin's Press, 1965), 500–507. As is so often the case when reading Marx, it is important to notice that here he is representing in discursive form a critique (Hegel's critique of Kant) that is not his own, which he intends the reader to regard as itself an object for critical analysis.

Moloch reign? Was not the Delphic Apollo a real power in the life of the Greeks? Kant's critique means nothing in this respect. If somebody imagines that he has a hundred talers, if this concept is not for him an arbitrary, subjective one, if he believes in it, then these hundred imagined talers have for him the same value as a hundred real ones. For instance, he will incur debts on the strength of his imagination, his imagination will *work in the same way as all humanity has incurred debts on its gods.* The contrary is true. Kant's example might have enforced the ontological proof. Real talers have the same existence that the imagined gods have. Has a real taler any existence except in the imagination, if only in the general or rather common imagination of man? Bring paper money into a country where this use of paper is unknown, and everyone will laugh at your subjective imagination. Come with your gods into another country where other gods are worshipped, and you will be shown to suffer from fantasies and abstractions. And justly so. He who would have brought a Wendic god to the ancient Greeks would have found the proof of this god's non-existence. Indeed, for the Greeks he did not exist. *That which a particular country is for particular alien gods, the country of reason is for God in general, a region in which he ceases to exist.*[47]

Such problematizations of religion through economics and economics through religion run throughout Marx's writing. This was not merely a rhetorical conceit, a superficial analogy embellishing Marx's arguments and unrelated to the real problems he sought to address. Religion was as serious a problem for Marx as economics; together they delineated a thematics in whose terms he strove to articulate the social theory and critical method proper to a materialism that was neither mechanistic nor deterministic but emerged from the vital tension in his dual commitment to social scientific objectivity, on the one hand, and, on the other, to a moral responsiveness toward those untheorized historical forces grounded in lived experience and personal suffering (a tension that locates the material limit and historical ground of theory itself).

Marx's first definition of fetishism as "the religion of sensuous desire" came in an article attacking the editor Karl Heinrich Hermes, an anti-Semitic Catholic who was urging severer censorship of religious criticism. Because religious belief is the basis of civic morality, and hence of the state, Hermes argued, the national heritage of theological ideas that lead people to such faith requires special public protection: "Religion is

47. "Difference between the Democritean and Epicurean Philosophy of Nature," in Marx and Engels, *Collected Works*, 1:103–4.

the basis of the state and the most necessary condition for every association."[48] That it is, he reasoned, is demonstrated by the fact that even "in
its crudest form as childish fetishism, it nevertheless to some extent
raises man above his sensuous desires."[49] Marx knew that Hermes' view
did not accord with that of the authorities of his day, since he had
recently investigated the notion of fetishism while writing an essay on
religious art.[50] "Fetishism is so far from raising man *above* his sensuous
desires," as Hermes claimed, wrote Marx, "that, on the contrary, it is 'the
religion of sensuous desire.' Fantasy arising from desire [*Die Phantasie
der Begierde*] deceives the fetish-worshipper that an 'inanimate object'
will give up its natural character in order to comply with his desires
[*seiner Gelüste*]."[51]

This notion of the fetish worshiper's desire-driven delusion regarding
natural objects, his blindness to the unprovidential randomness of physical events, was an element in de Brosses's original theorization of
fétichisme as the pure condition of un-enlightenment. To be enlightened, as Voltaire and Kant both stressed, is precisely to disabuse

48. Quoted in Marx, "The Leading Article," 188. Hermes' point echoes Hegel: "In a
general sense, religion and the foundation of the State are one and the same; they are
in their real essence identical." *Lectures on the Philosophy of Religion*, trans. Rev. E.
B. Speirs and J. Burdon Sanderson, vol. 1 (New York: Humanities Press, 1974), 247.
Marx, on the other hand, by 1842 was already moving beyond even a left Hegelian
critique of the relation of religion and the state, holding "that religion should be
criticized in the framework of criticism of political conditions rather than that political conditions should be criticized in the framework of religion." Letter to Arnold
Ruge, 30 November 1842, Marx and Engels, *Collected Works*, 1:395. In his polemic
against "the Cologne Hermes," Marx reminds his readers that the Hermes of Greek
mythology was the servant of the gods; Marx likens his opposing stance to that of
Prometheus, who, wishing to empower humanity, "hates all the gods." Making the
politics of his critique of religion explicit later in his article on Hermes, Marx explains
that in contemporary Germany serving "the gods" means serving the state: "For
where, under Protestantism, there is no supreme head of the church, the rule of
religion is nothing but the religion of rule, the cult of the government's will." Marx,
"The Leading Article," 199.
49. Marx, "The Leading Article," 189.
50. This was originally to be part of a collaborative book with Bruno Bauer attacking Hegel's theory of religion, but Marx subsequently broke with Bauer. In a letter to
Arnold Ruge, 20 March 1842, Marx mentions that his "article 'On Christian Art,'
which has now been transformed into 'On Religion and Art, with Special Reference to
Christian Art,' must be entirely redone." *Collected Works*, 385. A month later Marx
wrote to Ruge that "the article on religious art . . . has steadily grown into almost book
dimensions, and I have been drawn into all kinds of investigations which will still
take a rather long time" (387). In March, however, with the dismissal of Bauer from his
lectureship, Marx had abandoned his own hopes of an academic career and accepted
the position as editor of the *Rheinische Zeitung*, and the book on art and religion was
never finished. Nevertheless, much of Marx's thought on this subject can be found
scattered in his writings of the 1840s.
51. Marx, "The Leading Article," 189.

oneself of the idea that the real world has been designed to promote one's own—or humanity's—happiness. Moreover, it is not merely "desire" but "*sensuous* desire" that Marx's definition (taken directly from Hegel)[52] specifies. The term "sensuous" played a surprisingly prominent role in Marx's early anti-Hegelianism (and anti–left Hegelianism): it is most directly Feuerbach's conception of sensuousness that Marx will rethink.

There was, surprisingly, a great deal at stake for post-Enlightenment philosophy in this formulation of fetishism as the nontranscendental religion of sensuous desire. The term "fetishism" was adopted by *philosophes* such as Baron d'Holbach, Claude Helvétius, and their followers[53] because its discourse displaced the problem of religion from a theological to a materialist problematic congenial to the emerging human sciences and to anticlerical activism alike. It did so by discovering the origin of religious belief in primitive causal reasoning: a mode of thought deriving not from "reason" but from "desire and credulity."[54] Failing to distinguish the intentionless natural world known to scientific reason and motivated by practical material concerns, the savage (so it was argued) superstitiously assumed the existence of a unified causal field for personal actions and physical events, thereby positing reality as subject to animate powers whose purposes could be divined and influ-

52. See the section of Hegel's *Lectures on the Philosophy of Religion* concerning "natural, immediate religion," whose most primitive expression, in accordance with a colonialist imaginary about which neither Hegel nor Marx became significantly self-critical, was African religion. Hegel writes: "In this primal natural religion, consciousness is still natural consciousness, the consciousness of sensuous desire" ("In dieser ersten, natürlichen Religion ist das Bewußtsein noch natürliches und sinnlich begehrendes Bewußtseins"—more literally, "In this first, natural religion, consciousness is still a natural and sensuously desiring consciousness") (264). Within this primordial form of religion, according to Hegel, fetishism emerges as the negation of the moment of "magic" through the first capricious expressions of human subjectivity itself.

53. See Baron d'Holbach's entry "Serpent-Fétiche" in volume 15 (1765) of the *Encyclopédie*, and his other articles mentioning the fetishes of African religion ("Maramba", "Mumbo Jumbo", and "Ovissa"), collected in *Essays on the "Encyclopédie" of Diderot and D'Alembert*, ed. John Lough (London: Oxford University Press, 1968), 159–75; and Claude Helvétius's fetish-worship anecdote in his controversial (and much read) work of 1758, *De l'esprit*, in *Oeuvres d'Helvétius*, vol. 1 (Paris: Briand, 1794), 300–301. The familiarity of the figure of the African fetish worshiper in eighteenth- and nineteenth-century European cultural discourse (as opposed to the way it was *theorized* by intellectuals) was a result of the booming transatlantic slave trade of the time. The ideological function of attributing the slave state of the African to his inherent mental slavishness (bowing down in obeisance before mere blocks of wood) rather than to the plantation commodity-production system of European businessmen, is obvious enough to the twentieth-century reader.

54. Charles de Brosses, "Mémoire sur l'oracle de Dodone," in *Mémoires de littérature de l'Académie royale des inscriptions et belles-lettres* 35 (1770): 89.

enced. Specifically, humanity's belief in gods and supernatural powers (that is, humanity's unenlightenment) was theorized in terms of pre-scientific peoples' substitution of imaginary personifications for the unknown physical causes of future events over which people had no control and which they regarded with fear and anxiety.[55] De Brosses's own book was written to attack the universalist *"figurisme"* of Christian theologians and secular Neoplatonists at the Académie royale des inscriptions et belles-lettres, whose hermeneutic interpreted ancient myths and cult beliefs as allegories of New Testament events or philosophical ideas. Rejecting the adequacy of Euhemerist explanations as well, de Brosses identified a savage "manner of thinking" (*façon de penser*), a "metaphor natural to man,"[56] which located divine power in terrestrial, material entities themselves, and which was purely contingent and particularistic. *Fétichisme* was the term de Brosses used for the cults and superstitions formed from this "natural propensity" toward the nonallegorical personification of material powers (which is what de Brosses means when he defines fetishism as a "direct" cult of terrestrial things "sans figure").

Fetishism was a radically novel category: it offered an atheological explanation of the origin of religion, one that accounted equally well for theistic beliefs and nontheistic superstitions; it identified religious superstition with false causal reasoning about physical nature, making people's relation to material objects rather than to God the key question for historians of religion and mythology; and it reclassified the entire field of ancient and contemporary religious phenomena by identifying primitive fetishism throughout the historical world, from ancient Egypt (their notorious "animal gods") to archaic Greece (the oracle grove at Dodona) to contemporary black Africa (especially the serpent cult at Ouidah) to America (*manitous* and such) to the Holy Bible itself (the Urim and Thummim, among many others). In short, the discourse about fetishism displaced the great object of Enlightenment criticism—religion—into a causative problematic suited to its own secular cosmology, whose "reality principle" was the absolute split between the mechanistic-material realm of physical nature (the blind determinism of whose events excluded any principle of teleological causality, that is, Providence) and the end-oriented human realm of purposes and desires (whose free intentionality distinguished its events as moral action, prop-

55. The original Enlightenment formulation of this argument was David Hume, *The Natural History of Religion*, published in 1757 and more or less transcribed by de Brosses into the last section of his work on fetishism.

56. Charles de Brosses, *Du culte des dieux fétiches, ou Parallèle de l'ancienne religion de l'Egypte avec la religion actuelle de Nigritie* (Geneva, 1760), 215–16.

erly determined by rational ideals rather than by the material contingency of merely natural being). Fetishism was the definitive mistake of the pre-enlightened mind: it superstitiously attributed intentional purpose and desire to material entities of the natural world, while allowing social action to be determined by the (clerically interpreted) wills of contingently personified things, which were, in truth, merely the externalized material sites fixing people's own capricious libidinal imaginings ("fancy" in the language of that day).

Yet the very distinction that constituted Enlightenment rationality was responsible for a contradiction in the way it conceived its unenlightened Other: fetishism was defined as the worship of "inanimate" things even though its paradigmatic historical exemplifications were cults of animate beings, such as snakes. The special fascination that Egyptian zoolatry and African fetishism exerted on eighteenth-century intellectuals derived not just from the moral scandal of humans kneeling in abject worship before animals lower down on the "great chain of being" but from the inconceivable mystery (within Enlightenment categories) of any direct sensuous perception of animateness in material beings. This constitutive contradiction in Enlightenment thought was overcome in Kant's third critique. The first half of his *Critique of Judgment* develops a novel theory of aesthetic judgment as perception of "purposiveness" in objects.[57] This quasi-animistic subjectivity proper to aesthetic experience is identified as a legitimate faculty of the human mind (as opposed to an aberrant mode of superstitious delusion) in order to come to cognitive terms with the scandalous fact of the organism, the purposeful natural being (theorized in the second part of Kant's treatise, the critique of teleological judgment). For Kant aesthetic judgment *is* the "primitive" mentality become self-critical (and, thus, no longer superstitious) after having learned to distinguish between the purposive intentionality of its own practical subjectivity and the teleological systems of the objective world exemplified in biological organisms.

The phrase "sensuous desire" in post-Kantian German philosophy was thus theoretically fraught. Not only is "desire" the term for the purpose-forming subjectivity that characterizes the ethical world of humanity, but "sensuous" indicates that immediate experience of lived reality which is the primordial mode of experience (the object of aesthetic feeling) out of which we subsequently distinguish the two epistemic orders: physical nature (the object of empirical understanding) and mor-

57. Comte's theory of the ineluctable, heuristically valuable mode of "fetishistic" pseudocausal thought closely resembles Kant's treatment of the purposive feelings proper to aesthetic experience, both in its conception and in its role within their general philosophies.

al action (the object of transcendental reason). "Sensuous desire" is thus the direct "aesthetic" expression-apprehension of purposes and intentions within the subjectively objective world of immediate experience.[58] Finally, "religion" was understood to refer above all to worship (or "service," *Dienst*) as the submission-abolition of the individual's arbitrary free will (*Willkür*) to some greater universal (God in Kant's ethical transcendentalism, the state in Hegel's institutional idealism). The "religion of sensuous desire" is thus the perverse submission of intellect and moral will to a sort of libidinal aesthetics; it is, by definition, the crudest form of spirituality because the sensuous object can never—as a *thing* in itself, untransubstantiated into the signifier or allegory of a concept or ideal—attain to any categorical universality, the only proper object of devotion or allegiance. And this is precisely the treatment of "fetishism" that Marx found in Hegel, who defined fetishism as that threshold moment of Spirit which, paradoxically, produced a distinctive world culture (that of African societies) without representing any *universal* principle (hence Africans were a people outside History). The reason why was precisely the one Marx pointed out to Hermes: the fetishist's "consciousness is still natural consciousness, the consciousness of sensuous desire."[59]

Not only did Marx appreciate the subversively materialist implications of this point of unthinkability in the Hegelian system, but he increasingly came to connect the paradoxical status of this nonuniversal cultural object, the fetish, with the homologously contradictory particularity of "civil society" as discussed in Hegel's *Philosophy of Right*. A close reader of Adam Smith, Hegel identified "civil society" as the social region of the self-interested economic activities of individuals, distinguishing it from the family and the state. Like fetishist cultures, civil society achieved its unity not by finding a principle of universality but

58. The method for examining this world of sensuous desire is phenomenological description rather than logical analysis. For a succinct explication of the phenomenological dialectics of the "subjectively objective world" of sensuous, embodied experience, see Vivian Sobchack, "The Active Eye: A Phenomenology of Cinematic Vision," *Quarterly Review of Film and Video* 12, no. 3 (1990): 21–36.

59. In Hegel's view, the fetish never attains the form of religion proper since "religion is the relation of Spirit to Spirit, the knowledge by Spirit of Spirit in its truth [i.e., as the universal], and not in its immediacy or naturalness." *Lectures on the Philosophy of Religion*, 1:263. It occupies a similarly liminal position in relation to art: "The immediate reverence for natural objects—nature worship and fetish worship—is . . . not yet art." *Aesthetics: Lectures on Fine Art*, trans. T. M. Knox, vol. 1 (Oxford: Clarendon Press, 1975), 315–16. For Hegel, the fetishist operates at the brink of the actualization of Absolute Spirit, never transcending the particularity of the immediate sensuous world to enter the actuality of Ideas.

by endlessly weaving itself into a "system of needs"—a libidinal economy—in which people's ability to produce the object of someone else's desire becomes the means for satisfying their own desires. The *general form* realizing—or reifying—this social network of desires and their objects as a market system is money; but, Hegel argues, its *universal principle* is actualized only outside itself, in the state and the civil servants who regulate the economic system for the good of the whole. Civil society is thus viewed as the collective space of particular desires and their objective forms of gratification, but there is one sort of desire that civil society can never satisfy, the desire for the infinite, for some universal actuality to which individuals, in their singular particularity, can never attain. Man (and civil society is conceived by Hegel as a realm of male individuals) can achieve this desire only outside civil society— imperfectly in the family, where man transcends himself in his ontological union with his wife and the real objectification of this transcendent unity in their child, and absolutely in religious worship and state citizenship, when a man's limited, particular will is abolished and subsumed by the universal will of God and nation. In this logic, Marx saw Hegel as simply the most sophisticated ideologue of "the cult of the government's will."

Given Hegel's argument, the modern political order of a free-market civil society supplemented and subsumed by an authoritarian national state could be criticized only by refuting his identification of the state bureaucracy as the universal class of (though not *in*) civil society and of state citizenship as the actualization of individuals' universal identities. The problem, then, for the materialist critique of politics was to locate a universal class and principle of identity *within* the realm of human particularity, the realm that theology conceived as belonging to cults of terrestrial objects and political economics conceived as belonging to the economic activities of civil society. It is from this theoretical problematic that the peculiar twinning of the primitive fetishist and the industrial proletarian found throughout Marx's writing arises. And it is from their perspective (as evoked in Marx's writing) that the bourgeois capitalist is perceived as himself a fetishist, one whose fetish, capital, is believed by its deluded cultists to embody *(super)natural causal powers of value formation*, but which is recognized by the savage, expropriated through "primitive accumulation," and by the worker, exploited through the capitalist accumulation process proper, as having no real power outside its *social power to command* the labor activity of real individuals.

During 1843 and the first half of 1844, Marx's thought seems to advance by means of a critical analogy between religious fetishism and civil society: Christianity (as a religion of the abstract, heavenly universal) is the modern supersession of fetishism (the religion of sensuous, earthly desires), just as the state (in Hegelian philosophy) is the universal secular institution superseding civil society (the realm of particular desires and of individuals). Marx's materialist critique sought to debunk the claim of universalist social institutions (the Christian church and the state) to a superior ontological status by affirming the untranscendable reality of that existential mode of particular sensuous desires and concrete, embodied individuals proper to fetish worship and civil society. For Marx, then, fetishism and political economy are closer to the true world than monotheism and statism. They can thus be used to criticize the fantastic pretensions of monotheism and statism to some sort of transcendent reality; but they, in turn, become the objects of an even more fundamental critique (whose key terms are historical materialism and revolutionary communism) through which Marx sought to articulate the theory of a humane atheist morality and a radical democratic socialism.

This double critique of religion and politics received its most powerful expression in "A Contribution to the Critique of Hegel's 'Philosophy of Right'" (1844). Marx makes it clear that he sees the relation between the political critique of Hegelian constitutionalism and the religious critique of transcendental theology as more than a mere analogy. "The critique of religion is the prerequisite of every critique," he claims, since it returns our understanding from the unearthly realm of religious ideals to the immanent world of man's lived experience. "The critique of heaven is transformed into the critique of the earth."[60] More than just a homologous complement to the political critique of the state as the "inverted" universalized reflection of the particularistic economic world of civil society, the critique of religion locates the real ground of radical democratic political values: the human suffering and frustrated desires experienced by oppressed people within the concrete world of everyday life.

> Religion is the general theory of this world, its encyclopedic compendium, its logic in popular form. . . . The wretchedness of religion is at once an expression of and protest against real wretchedness. Religion is the sigh of the oppressed creature, the heart of a heartless world, and the soul of soulless conditions. . . . The critique of religion ends in the doctrine that man is the supreme being for man; thus it ends with the categorical imperative to overthrow all conditions in which man is a debased, enslaved, neglected, contemptible being.[61]

60. In Karl Marx, Critique of Hegel's "Philosophy of Right," trans. Annette Jolin and Joseph O'Malley (Cambridge: Cambridge University Press, 1977), 131–32.
61. Ibid., 137.

The truth of religion is found in its potently fantastic theorization of the pain and degradation of oppressed people as a form of spiritual resistance to conditions that, in radically threatening people's very humanity, reveal the specific values that constitute our identity as humans.[62] Human experience of material poverty and social oppression is here viewed as the source of a spiritually powerful moral authority that is the concrete subjective ground of a radically democratic emancipatory politics. The materialist subject of this radically human ground is twice located by Marx: in the maximally alien perspective of the primitive fetishist, a cultural other for whom material conditions are themselves spiritual values, who judges civil society from outside all civilization; and in the maximally degraded viewpoint of the proletarian, bourgeois society's internal other, forced to the physical margin of subsistence, whose value judgments express the most fundamental needs of human life.

Having (in 1844) identified the modern bearer of radically emancipatory passion as the proletariat, Marx now saw the aim of philosophy's critique of religion as the recovery of the discourse of the proletariat from its displaced, or "inverted," theological expression. During the period of The German Ideology (1845–1846), this project was elided in the historical-materialist, social-scientific polemic against ideology, false consciousness, and "critical criticism" (today called postmodernist criticism). But after he had absorbed the lessons of the political events of 1848–1850, Marx returned to the discourse about fetishism in 1857 in order to articulate not so much the dis-illusioned class consciousness of the proletariat (its members' self-conception as workers within the categories of civil society) as a communist imaginary that sees the fantastically inhuman anamorphosis of liberal political economy's vision of human life as civil society. Marx evoked the "savage" subject of religious fetishism as a (potentially theoretical) viewpoint outside capitalism capable of recognizing proletarians in their objective social identity as the economic class owning no marketable private property other than their own embodied being and "its" capacity for concrete productive activity, and therefore as the one identity within civil society in which true human being (that is, sensuous, embodied, living being) appears.

Economic Fetishism: Marx on Capital

Much that is valuable about Marx's thought has been obscured by the failure to appreciate the full novelty—and irony—in Marx's appropria-

62. This view has received its most profound theological expression in Latin American liberation theology. See Gustavo Gutiérrez, The Power of the Poor in History, trans. Robert R. Barr (Maryknoll, N.Y.: Orbis Books, 1984).

tion of the term "materialism". Rediscovering the centrality of the notion of the sensuous in Marx's materialism reinforces his own claims that his approach was neither mechanistic (what he calls "French materialism" in *The Holy Family*) nor economistic, neither monocausally deterministic nor dogmatically normative. It was rather a *critical social materialism* that emerged out of his critiques of Feuerbach's humanist anthropology and Hegel's institutional Idealism: notions of natural species-being and the self-acting Concept could be criticized as idealist abstractions once Marx affirmed the primacy of sensuous desire, productive action, and embodied historicity for human being. The clearest statement of Marx's materialist-phenomenological conception of the human subject as a sensuous, active, objective, desiring being is found in the section "Critique of Hegel's Dialectic and General Philosophy" in the last of the "Economic and Philosophic Manuscripts":

> To say that man is a *corporeal*, living, real, sensuous, objective being with natural powers means that he has *real, sensuous objects* as the objects of his being and of his vital expression, or that he can only *express* his life in real, sensuous objects. To *be* objective, natural and sensuous, and to have object, nature and sense outside oneself, or to be oneself object, nature, and sense for a third person is one and the same thing. . . . To be *sensuous*, i.e. to be real, is to be an object of sense, a *sensuous* object, and thus to have sensuous objects outside oneself, objects of one's sense perception. To be sensuous is to *suffer* (to be subjected to the actions of another). Man as an objective, sensuous being is therefore a *suffering* being, and because he feels his suffering, he is a *passionate* being. Passion is man's essential power vigorously striving to attain its object.[63]

Marx conceived human being as an essentially active, material being, one whose objects are *sensuous* objects and whose bodily life and personal self are "produced" in a single process: labor as praxis. Unless forced apart in the class divisions of exploitive societies, "self-activity and the production of material life"[64] form a single "communist" social process. After the critiques of Hegel and Feuerbach, the discourse about fetishism marks the question of the material articulation between the embodied individual of "sensuous desire" and historically specific social divisions of labor.

63. In Karl Marx, *Early Writings*, trans. Rodney Livingstone and Gregor Benton (New York: Vintage, 1975), 390. This passage was brought to my attention in the appendix "The Hegelian System" in Meister's *Political Identity*, 351–57.

64. Karl Marx and Frederick Engels, *The German Ideology*, 3d rev. ed. (Moscow: Progress, 1976), 96.

Marx arrived at his mature use of the discourse about fetishism—along with his mature conception of dialectical materialism—only in the 1850s, after revising his thinking about the ontic and causal status of universal representational forms. As Rancière has said, the farcical but effective masquerade of "democratic" political representations during the events of 1848–1850 fundamentally altered Marx's problematic,[65] forcing him to think beyond the problematic of "ideology" in order to appreciate the way particular representations of the universal (of the social whole) were real, causally important, nontranscendental components of the social-historical world. It was only during the writing of *Capital* in the decade from 1857 to 1867 that Marx worked out a materialist theory of the dialectical, chiasmic structure of social fetishism. As the opening chapter of *Capital* demonstrates, the method that studies social fetishism must be simultaneously phenomenological and historical, treating historically emerging universal forms as the material "power objects" of organized social systems.

In his notebooks of the late 1850s, Marx begins to speak of economic fetishism[66] in criticizing the *naturalistic* materialism underlying David Ricardo's notion of circulating capital and the vulgar economists' idea "that 'material' and half a dozen similar irrelevancies are elements of value."[67] In both these passages Marx is insisting on the *physical immateriality of value*. At first glance, it might seem paradoxical for Marx, a materialist, to be criticizing political economy's theory of value for being too materialistic. But this is the crucial starting point for Marx's mature theory of capitalist fetishism: the materiality of "value" is not physical but social. For Marx, value is a social substance that appears in a series of material forms (labor-selling people, commodified things, money). Although not physically real, the value quantity of products and money can be physically measured. This abstract, aggregate measure is average, socially necessary labor-time.[68]

65. Rancière, "How to Use *Lire le Capital*," 380–81.

66. Long before, Marx had applied the idea of fetishism to economic relations. In the fall of 1842 (three months after his article against Hermes), Marx concluded an article on trials of peasant "thefts" of firewood by citing the anecdote about the Cuban fetish worshipers. What had been a mere rhetorical gesture in that article was elaborated into a more serious theorization of the fetishism of the modern economic order when, toward the end of 1843, he began his serious studies of political economics. (It is not surprising that Marx approached political economy, the theory of civil society articulated in terms of its own categories, as the secular theology of a modern fetishism.) See the third of the "Economic and Philosophic Manuscripts" (written between April and August 1844) in *Early Writings*, 341–42.

67. Karl Marx, *Contribution to the Critique of Political Economy*, ed. Maurice Dobb, trans. S. W. Ryazanskaya (1859; New York: International, 1970), 48. For the criticism of Ricardo, see Marx, *Grundrisse*, 687.

68. A definite quantity of socially necessary labor-time has gone into the making of each type of product; thus each product "contains" a determinate quantity of labor-

Part of the difficulty of *Capital*'s opening chapter is that Marx's argument demonstrating that exchange value is determined by labor-time is presented within the highly abstract conditions posited for the first volume of *Capital*, where he studies capitalist production apart from circulation and capital investment and, therefore, apart from real prices. For this reason, considered apart from the rest of Marx's four-volume argument, it is not especially convincing. The real virtue of this chapter, it seems to me, is to give a phenomenological model of the sort of dialectical-materialist process that, for Marx, produces capitalism, in particular, and historically arising social formations, in general. Marx presents the emergence of a universal form that is itself a material object: money-capital. When a given type of useful thing comes to function as a general-equivalent exchange object in trade activities, it comes to be recognized as embodying a new quality: that of a general form, the very medium of exchange (money). This historically emerging general form expresses, in its being as a material *object*, the exchange *relation* that produced it: it *is* this relation realized as a sensuous object. Money's reversibility (its ability to be the thing exchanged away or the thing exchanged for) allows the differentiation of the act of exchange into two separate acts: buying a thing with money and selling a thing for money. This initiates a real process of deferral-distanciation through differentiation (as opposed to a textual *différance*) in which the spatial and temporal separation of the moments of exchange generate the logistical (financial) instruments enabling a modern economy. This process—the monetarization of social life—culminates in the rise of central banks and the emergence of money as credit-money, an object that seems to embody its own temporal existence in its capacity to bear interest.[69] The magical moment of fetish formation in this process is the transition of

---

value. At the end of a given production cycle, the totality of products thus represents a definite quantity of labor hours. This aggregate value-quantity is reflected in the total money supply at the end of the cycle, so that each dollar also represents a determinate amount of labor-value. Exploitation can be measured by the difference between the labor-value of the money wage paid to a given labor group and the total labor-value of their product. The distribution of surplus value to different sectors of capital can be measured by the difference between the labor-value of a given sector's aggregate product and the labor-value of the money price actually realized in the sale of that product. This is a simplified exposition of the discussion "Class and Exploitation," in Meister, *Political Identity*, 277–312.

69. It is with the development of a banking system that it becomes obvious that the substance of money is time or, more precisely, the temporalization of social power. In his aptly titled *Secrets of the Temple* (New York: Simon and Schuster, 1987), 59–65, William Greider lucidly explains how banks *create* money simply by contracting new credit-debt relations—in effect lending the same money several times in a miraculous multiplication that is possible because deposits are withdrawn, loans are paid off, and interest comes due over varying periods of time.

the general form into a *universal* form, its modal shift from existence and possibility to necessity—the mysterious transubstantiation of common social practices into custom or law sanctioned by the community as a whole. In short, *Capital*'s first chapter illustrates a process of the historical production of universal forms. Arising as the real representation of material social relations, these exist as material objects; they are fetishes insofar as they have become necessary functional parts that are privileged command-control points of a working system of social reproduction. This process is not only material but dialectical: these causally effective representational forms are "universals" that incorporate (i.e., that become the practical substance—the unity—of) the particular social processes that produce them and which they thereby alter.

Because he views capitalist production as a mode in which social value is fetishistically materialized, it is crucial for Marx to make it clear that the physical materiality of things has nothing to do with their value. A quantity of social labor-time is not composed of physical matter (nor is it equivalent to the physical energy expended by the worker); it is nonetheless true, he argues, that "in bourgeois production, wealth as a fetish must be crystallized in a particular substance."[70] Marx presents capital as a three-stage process accomplishing this "crystallization" (i.e., fetishization): "valorization," value creation by labor in commodity production (the subject of *Capital*, volume 1); "realization" of this value in money form during market circulation (the topic of the second volume); and "accumulation" of realized value through capital investments that set in motion further cycles of valorization, realization, and accumulation (studied in *Capital*, volume 3). The drive to extract ever more surplus labor in order to accumulate more exchange value in the fetishized form of invested capital becomes an end in itself. This is the fundamental fetishistic inversion of bourgeois production: monetarized productive capital, which had been merely the means to obtain wealth (the power to gratify concrete human desires whose origins and "logic" are external to its system), becomes identified as wealth itself. The object that had been an accidental means to achieving some desired end becomes a fixed necessity, the very embodiment of desire, and the effective, exclusive power for gratifying it. The human truth of capital is that, as a means that has become an end, it is a socially constructed, culturally real power-object: it is the instrumentalized power of command over concrete humans in the form of control over their labor activity through investment decisions. Capital is a form of rule, of social government. It is this political truth that the chiasmic personification-reification structure of capitalist fetishism conceals.

70. Marx, *Contribution to the Critique of Political Economy*, 155.

In Marx's mature theory, the capitalist social economy is understood as a repeating process of fetishization (that is, of cycles of labor valorization, monetary realization, and capital accumulation). The very legal and financial categories that establish capital's social reality bring about the fetishized consciousness appropriate to it through what Marx describes as a three-level chiasmus between people and things. The most superficial level is that of personified things and reified people; this is expressed in economists' identification of the "factors of production," which they view as the real sources of value. Marx refers to this whole structure as "the Trinity Formula": land, labor, and capital (the things that appear to have the personlike power to produce value); landlord, wageworker, capitalist (the reified identities that personify the factors composing capitalist production); and, lastly, rent, wages, and profits (the forms of money-capital that mediate among them). This level of fetishized objects and individuals is really an expression of the more fundamental level of fetishized relations: here Marx's labor-value critique of the circuits of exchange reveals this level of fetishism as one of reified social relations and personified material relations. People are reified in their relations insofar as their negotiations and other interactions must be expressed through the objectivity of the commodity-price system (that is, in the markets for labor, consumer goods, and capital). Moreover, as already discussed, the material relations between physical things become the social forms for capital's system of reproduction. This level of fetishized relations, in turn, expresses the chiasmic fetishization at the level of systems: the discourse of political economy confuses the scientific knowledge of the technical division of labor (whose logic is that of physical causality) with the politics of the social division of labor (whose logic is that of group entitlements). The identification of the former system with society as a whole is expressed in the Saint-Simonian slogan that socialism will replace "the government of people with the administration of things." That Marx did not stop at this technocratic social vision is demonstrated by his emphasis on class struggle. Even in a "classless" society, class analysis would still function as a critical standard for political arguments in regard to all policy options and administrative decisions whose material impact would not be uniform across the whole of society.

"Capital" is the substantive name for the unity of a socially (if unconsciously) organized material system of growth and reproduction whose effective components and visible forms are things, people, and money. The substance of capital itself is "value," that conserved quantity of social labor-time which seems to move through the metamorphic phases of the capitalist economy from one form to another (from laboring people to the things they produce, from these products to the money that purchases them, from this money to the new labor and materials it buys, etc.). Commodities and capital goods, wageworkers and capitalists, money and credit, are forms or parts of a whole temporal-material system. They (we) are members of the body of Capital, whose value-essence transcends and yet incarnates itself in these material beings like the divine salvational power of Christ in the faithful members and sacramental objects of His church. Indeed, just as the mystery of the Catholic church as the body of Christ is concentrated and expressed in the sacrament of the Eucharist, so the whole mystery of capitalist society appears at its most visible and, at the same time, at its most mysterious in the form of interest-bearing money-capital (money that "breeds" money in the form of interest). "It is in *interest-bearing capital* . . . that capital finds its most objectified form, its pure fetish form. . . . Capital—as an entity—appears here as an independent source of value; as something that creates value in the same way as land [produces] rent, and labor wages. . . . The transubstantiation, the fetishism, is complete."[71] (Capital's fetish forms, it should be stressed, are not subjective illusions: I am hardly hallucinating when I see my money increase in my savings account or when my investment in some aspect of a production cycle returns to me with a surplus.)

Marx argues that the very completion of its fetishistic system brings about the moment of capital's political truth, the moment of historical crisis when "private enterprise" is revealed as social government (and, therefore, as democratically accountable), and the political-economic reality of capitalist society suddenly appears in public culture *as fetishistic* (that is, as an alien and perversely unnatural reality). Marx located this moment not in the extreme development of the commercialization of social appearances, where readers of Baudrillard might look for it, but in the full development of financial fetishism. The credit-debt system is the fullest institutional expression of a society's relation to itself over time: it is the realization of that social metaphysics which Marx believed to be the true transcendent "other world" existing *within* the immanent material world inhabited by human individuals. Marx refused the positivist temptation of a Comtian social physics by understanding political economy as a mode of social temporality and by conceiving social arrangements as a realm of historical intersubjective humanity absolutely distinct from the natural, physical world. (That is, for Marx, the truth of "metaphysics," the suprasensuous or invisible realm

71. Karl Marx, *Theories of Surplus Value*, part 3, trans. Jack Cohen and S. W. Ryazanskaya (Moscow: Progess, 1971), 494, 498.

beyond the sensuous, visible world, is human society—our true "transcendence" is not transcendental but is immanent in the world: time is materialism's transcendent principle.)

In chapters 24 to 27 of *Capital*, volume 3, Marx discusses the evolution of interest-bearing capital (capital's "pure fetish form") into the general (global) credit system. In the consolidation of a unified credit system, capital both fulfills itself for itself and *dis-credits* itself in the eyes of society. Such a moment came early in the eighteenth century with the collapse in France of John Law's system and the bursting of similar Dutch and English speculative bubbles. Marx saw the crucial importance of the credit system during the events of 1848.[72] They are the historical basis for his remark in *Capital* that

> the credit system has a dual character immanent in it: on the one hand it develops the motive of capitalist production, enrichment by the exploitation of others' labour, into the purest and most colossal system of gambling and swindling, and restricts ever more the already small number of the exploiters of social wealth; on the other hand however it constitutes the form of transition towards the new mode of production.[73]

The social truth of capital—that it is a means of materially temporalizing those social obligations (fulfilled in the performance of types of socially valued labor) by which a population seeks to control and determine its collective future—is increasingly visible the more that capital becomes concentrated in big investment funds subject to the global credit-debt system. The micropolitical fact that our *real* social government consists of the private, undemocratic decisions made by corporations and banks becomes visible in the macropolitics of social security funds and international debt.[74] The *global* crisis of capitalism, which Marx believed was the only way a postcapitalist *world history* would come about, reveals—through the very completion of its fetish form—the proximity

72. See the opening chapter of *The Class Struggles in France, 1848–1850*, in Karl Marx, *Surveys from Exile*, ed. David Fernbach (New York: Random House, 1974), 49, where Marx writes: "The revolt of the proletariat is the abolition of bourgeois credit, for it signifies the abolition of bourgeois production and its social order. Public and private credit are the thermometers by which the intensity of a revolution can be measured. *They fall, the more the passion and potency of the revolution rises.*"

73. Marx, *Capital*, 3:572.

74. See Alain Lipietz, *The Enchanted World: Inflation, Credit, and the World Crisis*, trans. Ian Patterson (London: Verso, 1985).

of the apparently uncoercive structure of capitalist accumulation to the violent state terror of what Marx called "primitive accumulation," a perception of the dialectical unity of the voluntary and the violent that makes visible the class struggle that is the hidden political heart of capitalist economics and ideology.

The Point Is to (Ex)Change It: Reading *Capital*, Rhetorically

Thomas Keenan

> We suffer not only from the living, but also from the dead. *Le mort saisit le vif.*
>
> . . . Perseus used a magic cap as protection from monsters. We draw the magic cap down over eyes and ears, so that we can deny the existence of the monsters.
>
> —Karl Marx, Preface to the First Edition of Capital

> In motivation, if not in its claims, Marxism is a poetic thought that lacks the patience to pursue its own conclusions to their end.
>
> —Paul de Man, "The Dead-End of Formalist Criticism" in Blindness and Insight

General Principles, Immediate Questions

"The philosophers have only *interpreted* the world differently; the point is, to *change* it."[1] The eleventh and final thesis on Feuerbach, uninterpreted and unchanged,[2] stands in for a sometimes quiet, sometimes vociferous, hope that regularly circulates through intellectual en-

---

1. "Die Philosophen haben die Welt nur verschieden *interpretiert*; es kommt darauf an, sie zu *verändern*." Karl Marx, "Thesen über Feuerbach," in Karl Marx and Frederick Engels, *Werke*, vol. 3 (Berlin: Dietz, 1958), 7; Karl Marx and Frederick Engels, *Selected Works in One Volume* (New York: International, 1971), 30.
2. Recall that Engels changed things considerably: in his version, the crucial phrase reads "es kommt *aber* darauf an." Marx and Engels, *Werke*, 3:535; Marx, "Con-

counters with ethicopolitical questions. It is a call for responsibility, and its urgency is even more charged when what is encountered is a text by Marx. A reading of *Capital* carries with it, after all, a double promise of relief: not only the promise of the potential for theoretical or meta-rhetorical "progress beyond [the] local difficulties of interpretation,"[3] which too often obstruct or stall the reading of literary texts, but also the even more desirable promise of some intervention in what is called economic or political reality, the last instance or brute facts of capitalism, which call out not just for interpretation and its inevitable difficulties but for change.

It is by no means naive or "untheoretical" to put one's faith in this promise. Indeed, it is the exemplary promise of philosophy or theory itself, the attraction of a reflected conceptual apparatus purified of the local and merely immediate particularities of a text or a situation—not because those peculiar difficulties have been ignored but because they have been bracketed and accounted for at a more fundamental level. One does not have to be a Leninist to subscribe to the dictum that without revolutionary theory there is no revolutionary practice. Philosophy has always thought responsibility as just this articulation of understanding and action, interpretation and change, where each "and" stands in for the "thus" that signifies a foundation. In that final thesis, perhaps, Marx was only recalling the philosophers to their responsibility, which they have often lacked the patience—if not the desire—to pursue to an end: interpret, so as to change. This at least was Heidegger's reading, although he seems to have thought he was criticizing Marx, when he quoted the eleventh thesis to a television interviewer and commented that "changing the world presupposes changing the *representation of the world* [*Weltvorstellung*], and a representation of the world can be obtained only when one has sufficiently *interpreted* the world."[4] If for Marx there was all too much interpretation without change, surely for philosophy there would be no changing without interpreting. The groundedness of, and hence the responsibility for, both the change and the very imperative to change itself would depend on the secure installation of that

---

cerning Feuerbach," in *Early Writings*, trans. Rodney Livingstone and Gregor Benton (New York: Vintage, 1975), 423.

3. Paul de Man, *Allegories of Reading* (New Haven: Yale University Press, 1979), ix, hereafter abbreviated *AR*.

4. "Martin Heidegger im Gespräch," in *Martin Heidegger im Gespräch*, ed. Richard Wisser (Freiburg: Karl Alber, 1970), 69; "Martin Heidegger: An Interview," trans. Vincent Guagliardo and Robert Pambrun, *Listening* 6 (Winter 1971): 35, emphases in original.

Vorstellung. The final thesis, then, serves not only as what Heidegger called an "unspoken demand for a philosophy" (35), for that in philosophy which aims to make a difference (*verändern*) responsibly (a change governed by a prior interpretation), but also as the exemplary demand *of* philosophy.

But can the possibility of this articulation be taken for granted? What interpretation of philosophy, and of politics, is presupposed when theory and its interpretations are required to found or ground the interventions that seek to change? These are the questions most radically posed by the eleventh thesis and by the reading of *Capital*. Paul de Man once figured what he called, ironically, the "highly respectable moral imperative" of a reconciliation between cognition and action by reference to Marx, and "the wishful hope of having it both ways, of being, to paraphrase Marx in *The German Ideology*, a formalist critic in the morning and a communal moralist in the afternoon" (*AR*, 6). Neither this hope nor the investment in moral conscience could properly be attributed to Marx, though. The moral imperative is moral to the precise extent that it considers the passage already secured by an extrapolitical authority. But if interpretation and change *must* be articulated, then the force of the imperative is to admit that this possibility is by no means guaranteed. Indeed, to say simply that "es kommt darauf an" ("what matters") is to make the demand without regard to its possibility. To do so implies that even if the confidence in the passage and the respectability of the demand are forgone, even if the moral foundations give way, the imperative is in no way undone or avoidable. In shorthand, its survival simply signals its transformation from a philosophical or moral imperative to a political one. And in that sense, *Capital* is a political text.

That *Capital* makes the question of reading—the passage, however ungrounded or difficult, between interpretation and change—unavoidably a political one seems to have been the particular effort of the text's prefaces. We can start with Marx's explicit reflections on the problem of reading *Capital*, a text whose "accessibility to the working class," as he wrote in the preface to the French edition, was for him the "consideration which outweighs all others."[5] To encourage its reading by such a

5. Karl Marx, *Capital: A Critique of Political Economy*, vol. 1, trans. Ben Fowkes (New York: Vintage, 1977), 104. This English translation is hereafter abbreviated *C*. The translation (revised by Marx) is found in Karl Marx, *Le Capital*, vol. 1, trans. Joseph Roy (1872–75; Paris: Progrès, 1982), 11, hereafter abbreviated *LC*. The German text appears in Karl Marx, "Vorwort zur ersten Auflage," *Das Kapital: Kritik der politischen Ökonomie*, in Karl Marx and Friedrich Engels, *Werke*, vol. 23 (Berlin: Dietz, 1984 [based on the Hamburg 1890 edition]), 31, hereafter abbreviated *DK*. It has sometimes been necessary to alter Fowkes's English translation in order to bring out certain aspects of Marx's German and French texts more clearly.

public, the French publisher had proposed releasing the book as a serial, so as not to overwhelm its readers. Marx welcomed the temporizing gesture, yet remained wary; making *Capital* more accessible, he wrote, is

> the good side of your medal, but here is the reverse: the method of analysis which I have employed . . . makes the reading of the first chapters rather arduous, and it is to be feared that the French public, always impatient to conclude, eager to know the relation between general principles and the immediate questions which have aroused its passions [*avide de connaître le rapport des principes généraux avec les questions immédiates qui le passionnent*], may be disheartened because it will not have been able, right away, to move on [*parce qu'il n'aura pu pas tout d'abord passer outre*]. That is a disadvantage against which I can do nothing, except to forewarn and forearm those readers who care for truth. (*C*, 104; *LC*, 11)

Like the many *Aesops* that open with the fable of the cock that finds a pearl but does not know what to do with it, *Capital* begins with a warning about failing to move from knowing directly on to doing, and about the temporal structure of the desired articulation. In reading, time will tell . . . but time to read is always also time to stop reading. Guided by this warning—against the eagerness of a reading that wants to skip over the interpretation to get to the change, that wants to know how to relate general principles to immediate questions—Marx advises that articulation takes patience. Impatience frustrates reading and leads to change without interpretation, passionately immediate—and thus unprincipled—answers. But the demand for patience can generate a discouraged or rejecting reader and thus no reading—and no change—at all. Arduous reading always threatens to become impossible; driven by the zeal to relate, the reading public may find itself in a bind, unable, *tout d'abord*, to get out of the difficulty of that very relation and thus unable to go on reading. If reading, from the start, promises the possibility of this inability—not just the inability to make the articulation between general principle and immediate question but, more radically, the inability to move beyond that inability, since what is in question is reading's possibility in the first place—then reading *Capital* can be no more, and no less, than an effort and a chance . . . the chance of the preface's well-known next sentence. "There is no royal road for science, and only those who do not fear the fatiguing climb of its steep paths have a chance of reaching its luminous summits."

There is no road for reading, no path or method; simply the effort and the fatigue of the difficult chance. As chance, reading and its difficulty defy calculation in advance, refuse prediction. If *Capital*'s French public "will have been unable to move on," worries the preface, the text itself is equally powerless before this inability. "Against this I can do nothing," Marx writes, nothing except write the preface itself in which the inability is thematized. Faced with the prospect of a text that is discouraging at best and disabling at worst, which rigorously threatens its "own" impossibility, the preface suggests nothing other than itself as the possible circumscription of the threats it faces. "Against this I can do nothing, except to forewarn and forearm those readers who care for truth." Readers are thus prearmed with nothing, nothing other than this warning, nothing other than the negative knowledge that their impatience for a conclusion and eagerness to connect general with immediate may lead to the disabling of the reading itself. Armed with this would-be prophylactic knowledge about the inabilities of knowledge, the reading public is freed to take its chances. The chance is the chance of difficulty, the chance that something (unexpected) might happen, that something (new) might be learned. Reading, in this sense, if it happens at all, happens only in the encounter with difficulty and without guarantees.[6]

Marx never underestimated this difficulty: "Every beginning is difficult [*Aller Anfang ist schwer*], holds in all science. The understanding of the first chapter, especially the section that contains the analysis of commodities, will therefore make for the greatest difficulty [*die meiste Schwierigkeit*]" (*C*, 89; *DK*, 11), begins the third paragraph of the first German preface. It continues, after a justification hinging on the "power of abstraction" (to which we will return), by not quite excusing itself from its own indictment: "With the exception of the section on the value form, therefore, this book cannot stand accused as being difficult to understand [*Schwerverständlichkeit*]. I assume naturally a reader who wants to learn something new and thus to think for him- or herself" (*C*, 90; *DK*, 12). It would only be in the exposure to this difficulty, in the exhaustion of available knowledge and the ways of learning more, that something new might happen. And if the understanding subject has named the site in which difficulty has always been overcome, this thinking called reading (something new) might mark the troubling as well of that very self for which we (want to) think. One can learn this lesson only if one reads—if one can. As Marx says of *Capital* a paragraph further, *de te fabula narratur!*

---

6. On "difficulty" in reading *Capital*, see Louis Althusser, "Preface to *Capital*, Volume One," in *Lenin and Philosophy and Other Essays*, trans. Ben Brewster (New York: Monthly Review Press, 1971), 71–106, especially his discussion of what it will require for "petit-bourgeois 'intellectuals'" to be able to read *Capital*: not a "mere education" but a "rupture" (101).

Monster, Carrier: Only in Use

All beginnings are difficult. The first two sentences of *Capital* read as follows: "The wealth of those societies in which the capitalist mode of production prevails appears as [*erscheint als, s'annonce comme*] a 'monstrous collection of commodities [*ungeheuere Warensammlung*],' the single commodity as its elemental form. Our investigation therefore begins with the analysis of the commodity" (*C*, 49; *LC*, 43; *DK*, 125). Cutting off the quotation quickly, we can begin rather telegraphically. The matter at issue is the appearance or self-announcement of something *as* something else, the rhetorical structure of simile or metaphor (*als, comme*): semblance, shine, simulation or dissimulation. In those societies where the capitalist mode of production prevails, something (economic) shows itself by hiding itself, by announcing itself as something else or in another form.

Here, what shape or form does capitalist wealth take on in its self-presentation or self-dissimulation? Wealth appears as . . . a monster: something immense,[7] colossal, yes, but also a thing compounded of elements from different forms, wild but not natural and certainly not domesticated, simply thrown together into a heap, grown beyond the control of its creators. The *Ungeheuer* is a *riesenhaftes, häßliches Fabeltier* ("a gigantic hideous fable animal," says the *Wahrig Deutsches Wörterbuch*);[8] etymologically, it is something lacking the security of a settlement or the common comfort of a home. Something(s) assembled or collected, but in such a way that the parts do not add up to a whole— nothing but parts, unnatural and uncommon, *démesuré*. Aberrant, deviant, the monstrous is the form of appearance of wealth, the way it signifies itself, as something(s) else.[9] The figure of this monstrosity, living and dead (the *Wahrig* links *ungeheuer* to *unheimlich*, unhomely monstrosity to ghostly recurrence), haunts this chapter, appearing, as here, when least expected and out of all proportion.

This "monstrous collection" is also a quotation, a self-presentation from elsewhere ("Karl Marx, *Zur Kritik der Politischen Ökonomie*, Berlin 1859, S. 3," says the footnote), and if we follow the lead we find not just the two quoted words but virtually the same sentence, again: "The wealth of bourgeois society, at first sight, presents itself as an

7. The prevailing English translation of *ungeheuere* as "immense" turns the opening sentence into a virtual transposition of Wordsworth's Intimations Ode: "Thou, whose exterior semblance doth belie thy Soul's immensity."

8. Gerhard Wahrig, *Deutsches Wörterbuch* (Munich: Mosiak, 1987), 1330.

9. See Jacques Derrida on the "monstrosity of monstrasity, monstrosity of monstration." "La main de Heidegger (*Geschlecht* II)," in *Psyché* (Paris: Galilée, 1987), 422.

ungeheuere *Warensammlung*."[10] The immediate question is why? Why the gesture of quoting oneself, from an earlier and surpassed draft, for two words, with the apparatus of quotation marks, footnote, etc.? Without answering, it is at least worth remarking that the quotation itself functions as a monster or a ghost, an uncanny visitor accumulated from another text. And it depends on a structural condition of words—they can be reproduced, mindlessly and mechanically reproduced—which acts as if they were nothing but commodities: to be accumulated, moved and removed to and from contexts, delayed and relayed between texts only to be grafted or inserted into some other text, transferred like (als) property or the mechanical limb (a forearm, let's say; after all, forewarned is forearmed) on a monster.

Of what is the monster composed? Marx names the unit or elemental form of this unruly collection the commodity (*Ware*). *Capital*'s investigation, its under-taking (*Untersuchen*, probing beneath the dissimulative appearance of the form), "begins with" the disarticulation of the monster and "the analysis of the commodity," the dissolution of wealth's appearance into *Elementarformen* and then their reductive decomposition. It is this "method of analysis" to which Marx had attributed all the interpretive difficulty in the preface, and the first chapter relentlessly pursues its destructuring mission—both as method and as theme. The commodity as such *is* analyzed, and not merely by Marx.

The initial terms of a reading can now be gathered together as an immediate question. What links the structure by which one thing appears as another, by which something is substituted for something else or transferred to somewhere else, with (1) the advent of monstrosity or haunting and (2) the movement of analysis or reduction?

Without answering, *Capital* begins the analytic decomposition of the commodity. First of all, prior to all other determinations, at its barest and simplest, a commodity is "an external object, a thing" (*C*, 125; *DK*, 49). The commodity is a way of doing things with things, an interpretation of some thing, but to begin, nothing less or more than a thing. This kind of thing is a thing for human beings, for their use or consumption, physical or imaginary, immediate or derived. Simply, the thing is useful (*nützlich*), which is to say, it satisfies or appeases (*befriedigt*) human needs, needy humans, through its properties (*Eigenschaften*). Marx proposes, though, that things—when they are useful—are not simple, not just one thing: "Every useful thing, such as iron, paper, etc., is to be considered under a doubled point of view" (*C*, 125; *DK*, 49). The analy-

10. Karl Marx, *Zur Kritik der politischen Ökonomie* (Frankfurt-am-Main: Europäische Verlagsanstalt, 1972), 7; *A Contribution to the Critique of Political Economy*, ed. Maurice Dobb, trans. S. W. Ryazanskaya (New York: International, 1970), 27.

sis of *Capital* consists in this double viewpoint, in the interpretation as duplicity of a difference that inhabits every useful thing. The manner of this autodivision or -duplication of the thing is both the target and the mode of the analysis. It aims to decompose the *als*-structure (in different vocabularies: appearance, simile, simulation) that gives rise to both quotations and monsters—a certain mutation, othering, in the thing that allows it to be analyzed from (at least) two viewpoints. "Quality and quantity" (*C*, 125; *DK*, 49) make up the two aspects of the analytic point: (1) what a thing is, its properties or elements, understood as a matter of what can be done with it, what its uses are or could be, and (2) how much of it there is, what it is when it's measured. Accounting for the articulation of quality and quantity, or the conversion of the one into the other, which is to say for how quality can be determined reliably enough to allow for comparing and measuring different ones, is the task of Marx's analysis. In this sense at least, we can say that Marx poses the "transformation problem," or that Marxism is a theory of change. But we cannot say that either transformation or change is anything reliable.

Exactly what quality and property mean is not immediately evident, but taking their meaning for granted (interpreting them within a metaphysics of substance and presence) has been the rule in most readings of *Capital*. Marx begins not with the thing's essence but with its use: to the extent that a thing can be used, it can be seen (first viewpoint) as a "use value," *Gebrauchswert* (*C*, 126; *DK*, 50), something that can be inscribed in a differential system of valuation, distinguished or specified, based on the use to which it is put.[11] The term *Gebrauchswert* is not an easy word to read in *Capital*, and its difficulty troubles not only the text's interpreters but the text itself.[12] Not that its definition is complicated; indeed, Marx is matter of fact about the value of use. "The use-value is actualized or realizes itself [*verwirklicht sich*] only in use or consumption" (*C*, 126; *DK*, 50).[13] Marx does not say: Every thing, because it is itself and itself

11. Of course, Marx insists, some *thing* is used, or rather, some "body." Although a thing can be used and hence be a use value, its status as a *value* does not make it nothing or leave it "suspended in mid-air." On the contrary, "limited by the properties of the commodity-body [*Warenkörper*], [use value] does not exist without it." How this limitation works, though, remains unclear throughout the chapter; in any case, this body will return, and I will return to it.

12. Althusser quotes a note by Marx from 1883: "For me use-value plays a far more important role than it has in economics hitherto." *Lire "Le Capital,"* vol. 1 (Paris: Maspero, 1968), 96; *Reading "Capital,"* trans. Ben Brewster (London: Verso, 1979), 79. In my argument, which pursues some hints in the text about this unprecedented category, the encounter with its troubling difficulty requires going against much of the grain not only of Marx interpretation but of *Capital* itself.

13. The *Contribution to the Critique* is more blunt: "a use-value has value only in use. . . . One and the same use-value can be used in various ways" (27). The same? Or does the iteration alter?

alone, is different from every other thing. A use value is and only is the use of a thing when and as it is used (*nur im Gebrauch*), which is to say, a thing has as many use values as it has uses, all of them different and even, in principle, irreducibly so. This formulation implies not an infinity of uses—one cannot do everything with any;hing—but simply an unpredictability, a structural openness to new contexts. Instead of limiting or determining the thing to an essence or a set of fixed properties, the category radically de-limits or opens up the thing for different uses. As soon as the proper (value) of the thing is said to be its use(s), making it entirely dependent on the particularities of its context(s), whatever self-identity it might pretend to have across those different uses is ruptured, emptied out into its possible iterations. "Such a thing is a whole of many properties, and can thus be useful in different ways." The sentence could just as easily be reversed: because it can be used differently, it has many properties, but nothing proper. History, says Marx, is the history of these "different ways [*Seiten*] and thus the manifold ways of using the thing" (*C*, 125; *DK*, 49–50). This potential for radical differentiation or diversity of things as use values not only distinguishes them one from another but fragments any particular thing "itself" into a multiplicity of uses. So it is tautological when Marx states a few paragraphs later that "as use-values, commodities are above all different qualities" (*C*, 128; *DK*, 52), but the unstated corollary must be: different even from "themselves." Being used differently splits the thing from itself, mani-folds it onto or out of itself, since use is all there is, "really." This reusability principle puts the wholeness of the thing or the propriety of its properties into some question, or at least limits its "unity" to the accumulated traces it leaves in its manifold contexts of use.[14] The thing's thingliness is not in doubt—it is certainly not nothing—but the fact of its realization in use exposes it to the possibility of all sorts of trouble. If its "usefulness does not hang in mid-air [*schwebt nicht in der Luft*]," but is rather

---

14. See Jacques Derrida, "Signature Event Context," in *Margins of Philosophy*, trans. Alan Bass (Chicago: University of Chicago Press, 1982): "This is the possibility on which I want to insist: the possibility of extraction and citational grafting which belongs to the structure of every mark, spoken or written. . . . Every sign, linguistic or nonlinguistic . . . as a small or large unit, can be *cited*, put between quotation marks; thereby it can break with every given context, and engender infinitely new contexts in an absolutely nonsaturable fashion. This does not suppose that the mark is valid outside a context, but on the contrary, only that there are contexts without any center or absolute anchoring. . . . What would a mark be that could not be cited? Or one whose origins would not get lost along the way?" (320). On use, the proper, and the question of value (Marx with Nietzsche and Saussure), see also Derrida, "White Mythology: Metaphor in the Text of Philosophy," in *Margins*, 214–19; as well as Jean-Joseph Goux, *Economie et symbolique* (Paris: Seuil, 1973), esp. 53–148.

"limited [*bedingt*] by the properties of the commodity-body [*Waren-körper*]" (*C*, 126; *DK*, 50), then this used body is always threatened with the possibilities of dismemberment, of being torn limb from limb and scattered like Orpheus, or of grafting, of being combined and recombined in some monstrous accumulation of body parts.[15]

But using them is not even the most interesting or pressing thing to do with things. *Capital* must confront an economic fact, the fact of economy as such: use values, different as they are, are exchanged as well as used or consumed. Use values "constitute [*bilden*] the material [*stofflichen*] content of wealth" (*C*, 126; *DK*, 50), but no matter how material it is, how is something that comes into being only in use converted to something that can be not used but accumulated and exchanged? Immediately following the difficult sentence defining use values as realized only in use, Marx pauses—and unleashes the only term that poses more reading difficulties than use value: "In the form of society to be considered by us, [use values] also constitute the material carriers of—exchange-value [*bilden sie zugleich die stofflichen Träger des—Tauschwerts*]" (*C*, 126; *DK*, 50). It seems that use values, as material, carry—support or transport—the possibility of being deported or transferred elsewhere. The *stofflich* character of the thing as use value seems paradoxically tied to the possibility its materiality may be evacuated in exchange, in the act that appropriates it not for use or consumption but for disappropriation, not to realize it but to transfer it elsewhere. It holds, carries, its "own" vacancy; it holds nothing but a place, the site of a possible relocation. As *soutien matériel* (*LC*, 44) of exchange value, the thing's use value has all the materiality of a marker, of the empty "body," as its "properties" are erased to allow it to bear an inscription. How this effacement happens and what a "carrier" looks like are the questions that will obsess the remainder of the first chapter.

15. See Gayatri Chakravorty Spivak, "Speculations on Reading Marx: After Reading Derrida," in *Post-structuralism and the Question of History*, ed. Derek Attridge et al. (Cambridge: Cambridge University Press, 1987), 30–62, especially 40 and n. 13; and "Scattered Speculations on the Question of Value," in *In Other Worlds* (New York: Routledge, 1988), 154–75. "In my reading . . . it is use-value that puts the entire textual chain of Value into question and thus allows us a glimpse of the possibility that even textualization . . . may be no more than a way of holding randomness at bay." "Scattered Speculations," 162. In "Some Concept Metaphors of Political Economy in Derrida's Texts," *Leftwright/Intervention* 20 (1986): 88–97, Spivak argues elegantly that "use-value is not a transcendental principle because it changes on each occasion or heterogeneous case. . . . it is non-transcendental, material, and therefore incommensurable for the logic of binary exchange" (93). The illogic of use voids use value of phenomenality, quality, and particularity (except in the odd sense of contextual particularity).

Possibility of Exchange, Power of Abstraction

Exchange value "first of all appears as . . . the relation [*Verhältnis*]" and, of necessity, a quantitative one, the "proportion" (*C*, 126; *DK*, 50), in which use values exchange for one another. But exchange can take place only on the basis of something common to the things (use values) being exchanged, something shared that allows them to be compared, measured, the proportion or relation to be calculated. The general principle of exchange, as Marx writes it, holds that "in two different things, there exists . . . something common [*ein Gemeinsames*]. . . . The two things must therefore be like [*gleich*] a third, which in itself is neither one nor the other" (*C*, 127; *DK*, 51). When things are exchanged as commodities,[16] they are related to each other not as use values but as exchange values, in terms of something else. This shared third term, the axis of similarity, enables a comparison, makes the different uses or things commensurable, relatable as quantities of the same thing rather than different uses or qualities.

Needless to say, the exchange value of a thing could never belong to it as a property, even as a use, since exchange *is* depropriation; so an "immanent exchange-value is a *contradictio in adjecto*" (*C*, 126; *DK*, 51). But more rigorously, is not exchange value as such a contradiction in terms? Can the difference in use be regulated or controlled in any way that would allow exchange—the relation or proportion "in which use-values of one kind [*Art*] exchange with [*gegen*] use-values of another kind [*anderer Art*]" (*C*, 126; *DK*, 50)—to take place without sacrificing the determining characteristic of use value, namely, its radical contextuality or heterogeneity? *Capital* here meets its structuring question, the question of how exchange, as such, is possible? How can a system put radically different things (uses) into relation with one another when they have nothing in common, since they are defined, acquire a certain identity or value, "only" in being used or consumed? How can things that do not even have the stability to define themselves as things outside of their use, that differ as much within themselves as between themselves, be submitted to the rule of a common system of measurement? How can these uses be exchanged? How is exchange possible?

---

16. Recall that a commodity, as opposed to a mere thing, is a thing "produced for others" and then "transferred" (at least so Engels understood it, in his inserted parenthesis [*C*, 131]). But *commodity* is probably more accurately a historical (or political) term and not a transcendental one, not simply because of the problems of intention inherent in the "produced for" construction but more crucially since (1) exchange is *always* a possibility and thus cannot simply be avoided like an accident and (2) the multiplicity and contingency of use already implies a divergence indistinguishable from exchange at the putative origin.

The radicality of *Capital*'s analysis becomes evident with its answers. First, exchange is a matter of *substitution*, of one thing's standing in for another, on the basis of something similar or equal. If exchange is to occur, this substitution is a necessity: things "must . . . , as exchange-values, be substitutable or replaceable for each other [*ersetzbar*]" (*C*, 127; *DK*, 51). Thus, the thing must be put into relation even with itself (its uses), since it can be exchanged for many different things, which therefore have to be mutually substitutable; by virtue of the mediation implied by substitution, the various exchange values of a thing "express something alike or equal [*ein Gleiches*]."[17] If a thing can be exchanged for many different other things, then its exchange value must be only a "form of expression [*Erscheinungsform*]" (*C*, 127; *DK*, 51) of something else, something like the thing itself. The substitutability of exchange values, organized around an axis of similarity, which "must" occur in exchange, is thus shown to depend on a previous and just as necessary operation, effected on the level of the *useful* thing, called "reduction." No substitution without reduction, without the reduction of the "manifold ways of using the thing." For the relation or equation (*Gleichnung*) to happen, the things exchanged or substituted "must therefore be like or equal to [*gleich*] a third, which in and for itself is neither the one nor the other. Each of them, insofar as it is exchange-value, must thus be reducible to this third [*muß also auf dies Dritte reduzierbar sein*]" (*C*, 127; *DK*, 51). Where the thing was, the third must be.

The reduction—which, echoing the first sentence, we might as well call the analysis, the decomposition or destructuration of the thing into its most elementary components (if there are any)—ought to reveal, as if by distillation or purification, the common core that exchangeable things share, the likeness on the basis of which they can be put into relation, measured proportionally.[18] What can only be called a double

17. Throughout this essay, my translation of all the words in *gleich* hesitates among similar, (a)like, and equal. As soon as comparison has been entered into, the slippage to equation is hard to resist: that is the aberrancy and the economy of the trope. If things were the same, there would be no need to compare or exchange them, but in order to be related, they must have something of the same available for the crossing . . . thus, *Gleichheit*, alike, as the mediation of identity and difference.

18. The text is free with analogies and examples here, for example: "A simple geometrical example will illustrate this. In order to determine and compare the areas of all rectilinear figures we split them up into triangles. Then the triangle itself is reduced. . . . In the same way [*Ebenso*] exchange values must be reduced" (*C*, 127; *DK*, 51). "In the same way," it says—and thus the whole question of exchangeability or substitutability posed in the example of the triangles is posed by it as well. "In the same way" already presumes of course that the analogy, any analogy, can be drawn between economics and geometry, that the two can be reduced to something common to both, exchanged by being reduced to something *eben*. But this is precisely what is at

rhetorical gesture "must" take place here: the substitution of something for something else, based on resemblance and thus structured like simile or metaphor, can occur only on the condition that a prior reduction has occurred within the things exchanged, by which one "part" of the thing has been made to stand in for the "whole." We know this structure as synecdoche, and *Capital* suggests that its part-for-whole substitution is presupposed within any thing as the condition of its exchange with something other. What is this whole? Use value? That strictly contextual, singular, pragmatic difference that defines value only in use? Can use provide the basic core of commensurability?

As use values, things are completely different from each other and from themselves, different with every use or context (rendering even the term "themselves" problematic). Marx repeatedly insists on the *necessity* of the reduction, but as for its condition of possibility, things are a little more difficult. A hint earlier in the chapter might have seemed to suggest that the thingly properties of the thing could provide the third term: the thing's status as a use *value* is not simply ideal or spiritual, as we read, and does not make it nothing or leave it hanging in the air but is, rather, dependent on "the properties of the commodity-body [*Warenkörper*]" (*C*, 126; *DK*, 50). Do these properties of the commodity as a body make exchange possible, provide the irreducible ground or the basic part on which economy is built? Simply, no. "This something common cannot be a geometrical, physical, chemical or other natural property of commodities. Their bodily properties come into consideration only to the extent that they make them useful, as use-values" (*C*, 127; *DK*, 51), and have no role in exchange. Things are bodies only in use, not a priori or as some kind of essential base. Where exchanging is the task, the commodity body functions as heterogeneously as "its" manifold uses. There is no property common to things, no use, not even being a thing (not even, as Marx will show, the labor required to bring them into the economic field). Because use values are at least as different from one another as things are, the common term could not be a property of the thing as a body. The question of the possibility of exchange takes another step backward: if what is common cannot be a natural property, or a use, then how is it produced or where does it come from? *Capital* repeats: How is exchange possible?

Marx answers—in the spirit of the necessity on which he has become accustomed to insisting—with a single word, *abstraction*. He calls it "obvious" and says that it simply happens, regardless of its possibility.

---

stake in the analysis, and in the example language already plays with the terms beside the "argument," taking everything for granted.

"It is obvious [augenscheinlich] that abstraction from their use-value is precisely what characterizes the exchange relation of commodities" (C, 127; DK, 51–52). Samuel Moore and Edward Aveling translate Abstraktion as "total abstraction"[19]—abusive but correct, since the operation must be totalizing if it is to be at all. The radical heterogeneity of use values must be reduced, and that reduction or overcoming is to be accomplished only by an equally radical ("total") abstraction that massively and systematically effaces the differentiation of every use value, every thing. The difference of every use (property, thing) "must" be dissolved by the force of abstraction. And every exchange relation is characterized by (performs) this abstraction. In the face of difference, abstraction is required even if it is not necessarily possible (augenscheinlich).[20]

Abstraction is the erasure of difference in the service of likeness or equality (Gleichheit): "As old Barbon says, 'there is no difference or distinction in things of equal value.'" Abstraction converts the thing from use value to exchange value, transforms it "within" into something exchangeable. "As exchange-values, [things] can be only different quantities, and thus contain not an atom [kein Atom] of use-value" (C, 128; DK, 52). The abstraction is as radical as the differences were irreducible. If it happens, the exchange of commodities must "first" erase use values to the subatomic level, allowing the emergence of the desired third term, but what could survive the utter eradication of the difference— difference in use, difference in quality—that defines use values as such? What is left over if the things that are (to be) exchanged on the basis of it (something alike, gleich, or common) "contain not an atom of use-value"? The thing, obviously, has been emptied out, and what it was is gone: "If we abstract from its use-value, we abstract also from the bodily constituents and forms that make it into a use-value. It is no longer table or house or yarn or even a useful thing. All of its sensible attributes [sinnlich Beschaffenheiten] are extinguished [ausgelöscht]" (C, 128; DK, 52). The subatomic is use-less, thing-less, and sense-less. Nothing—at least, no thing—is left, it seems. And certainly not the fact that things are products of labor. Marx simply dismisses the idea that the leftover might be some attribute of its having been worked on. "Nor is it any longer the product of joining or masonry or spinning or any determined productive labor," because, first, labor is just as particular and singular as use value and, second, it is precisely that differentiation which is made to disap-

19. Karl Marx, Capital, vol. 1, ed. Frederick Engels, trans. Samuel Moore and Edward Aveling (1887; New York: International, 1967), 37.
20. Which accounts, in a certain sense, for the proliferation of the word must over these pages: in the face of impossibility, necessity imposes itself.

pear by the abstraction. "The differentiated concrete forms of labor vanish [verschwinden], they differ from each other no longer, but are all reduced to the same [gleiche] human labor, abstract human labor" (C, 128; DK, 52). Which is only to say that under the pressure of the abstraction necessitated by exchange, people and their labor become commodities too.[21] (And this humanity will return.)

What is required of this abstraction? If it is to make exchange possible, what does it need to accomplish, and how does it do it? To answer these questions, we need to look more carefully at its structure and attempt to distinguish it from the terms it has come to replace: similitude and reduction. One hint that may help has been lying around since Capital's first sentence. Pursuing Marx's footnote to the Kritik, the sentence following the phrase quoted from that earlier text reads: "Every commodity, however, has a two-fold aspect: use-value and exchange-value." The footnote there refers the reader to Aristotle's Politics, and quotes: "Of everything which we possess there are two uses: . . . one is the proper, and the other the improper or secondary use of it. For example, a shoe is used for wear and is used for exchange."[22] In the same way, a word has its proper meaning(s) and its figurative or derived senses, relations in which it crosses over with other meanings. The figurative ones, it is said, consist in exchanging what is proper to one word with another word, in substituting, borrowing, trading, carrying, transporting, even stealing properties. But these exchanges depend on the presence of an axis of substitution, a common term across which the crossing is articulated. Different tropes are defined by the different axes of comparison according to which their substitutions are organized.

Marx had first seemed to propose that economic exchange was simply a matter of metaphor, of exchange based on resemblance or similitude (Gleichheit). But in order to produce this similarity in the absence of any stable or reliable set of properties common (similar) to all things, the

---

21. Otherwise, the whole question would be begged and the critical power of the analysis forgone. The common generality of human labor, as of use value, is what the analysis refuses to take for granted. When the French translation risks "Il ne reste donc plus que le caractère commun de ces travaux" (LC, 46), it cedes to the temptation otherwise resisted: if this commonality or generality could be found, and given things or labors seen as particular species of them, then exchange would not be a problem. But it is precisely the status of this "common" term that is in question, that is at stake in the analysis. Thus Marx, later in Capital, can raise the "possibility of crises" stemming from the asymmetry in "the antithetical phases of the metamorphosis of the commodity," namely, "the personification of things and the reification of persons" (C 209; DK, 128).

22. Marx, Contribution to the Critique, 27n.

analysis was obliged to backtrack and propose that a certain "reduction" occurred within the diversity that marks things as use values, so as to bring them down to some one thing. This reduction was structured like a synecdoche, a part-for-whole substitution. Yet no common part could be determined either, and the analysis stepped further back to reveal the operation of what it called "abstraction."[23]

What is the structure of abstraction? Paul de Man has argued that, at least for Condillac, abstractions are "formed by ceasing to think of the properties by which things are distinguished in order to think only of those qualities in which they agree"; it is a structure that, according to de Man, is "precisely that of metaphor in its classical definition (i.e., substitution based on resemblance)."[24] The rhetorician Pierre Fontanier, though, in Les figures du discours, thought abstraction was a synecdoche, a substitution based not on resemblance but on "comprehension."[25] "Taking the abstract for the concrete" is a synecdochal exchange in that it "designates an object by the name of another object together with which it forms a set, a whole . . . such that the existence or the idea of one finds itself comprised in the existence or idea of the other."[26]

Evidently, neither of these definitions will do, since abstraction has arrived on the scene in order to accomplish what resisted the efforts of, precisely, metaphor and synecdoche. For exchange to take place, some axis of commonality or channel of communication between different things and within different uses must be invented or opened or breached. Something like abstraction is supposed to do it.

23. See Hayden White's extended reading of Marx's "tropological analysis" of value (from metaphor to metonymy to synecdoche to irony) in "Marx: The Philosophical Defense of History in the Metonymical Mode," in Metahistory: The Historical Imagination in Nineteenth-Century Europe (Baltimore: Johns Hopkins University Press, 1973), 281–330, especially "The Basic Model of Analysis," on Capital, 287–302. Although White concludes that "the labor theory of value serves as the base line from which all erroneous conceptions [provided by the tropological reductions] of value can be transcended," because he thinks that for Marx things are "isolated individualities, particulars which appear to bear no essential relationship to one another," the reading of the figurative structure of the exchanges involved is powerful nevertheless (296, 293).

24. Paul de Man, "The Epistemology of Metaphor," Critical Inquiry 5 (Autumn 1978): 13–30, hereafter abbreviated EM. De Man is quoting the section in Condillac's Essai sur l'origine des connaissances humaines (1746) called "Des abstractions." See Condillac's Essai in Jacques Derrida, L'archéologie du frivole (Paris: Galilée, 1973), 174. As Derrida points out, Marx had a certain interest in Condillac in Capital, on "the confusion between use-value and exchange-value" (70–71).

25. Pierre Fontanier, "Synecdoque d'abstraction," in Les figures du discours, ed. Gérard Genette (1821–1830; Paris: Flammarion, 1977), 93–95.

26. Ibid., 87.

Ghosts of an Analysis, or Humanity

So we can return to our guiding question: How is exchange possible? It is obvious that it is characterized by abstraction. Does the abstraction occur on the basis of something besides the thing or its uses and its makers? What is responsible for exchange? Marx's explanation is curious in its temporality, inasmuch as it "finally" seems to presuppose that what must happen (reduction) has already happened (abstraction) in order to let it happen (likeness or equality). After the fact of the exchange, we can "see" what will obviously have had to happen. The answer goes as follows.

If everything sensible is extinguished, and labor has vanished, "let us look at the residue of the labor-products." The impossible abstraction occurs, does its duty, only to the extent that it leaves a remainder, a *Residuum* or a *résidu* (*C*, 128; *LC*, 46; *DK*, 52). Marx undertakes to give a name to this leftover of total abstraction. What remains after the radical reduction of difference, after the vanishing of all "atoms" of use value or productive labor? Its name is ghost, *gespenstige Gegenständlichkeit*, spectral, haunting, surviving objectivity. "There is nothing of them left over but this very same [*dieselbe*] ghostly objectivity, a mere jelly [*Gallert*] of undifferentiated human labor." This phantom makes possible the relation between (or within) things or uses, grants the common axis of similarity hitherto unavailable, precisely because it is a ghost and no longer a thing or a labor. Once abstracted, as Marx's French text puts it, "each one of them completely resembles the other. They all have the same phantomatic reality [*une même réalité fantomatique*]. Metamorphosed into identical *sublimés*, samples of the same indistinct labor" (*LC*, 46). In the rigor of the abstraction, only ghosts survive. The point is to exchange them.

The timing of these ghosts is spectacular. They return just in time to make possible the operation that produces them, that leaves them as its congealed residue. Because they resemble one another, as all ghosts do, having no phenomenal or sensible features by which to distinguish "themselves," the operation of which they are the remnant can finally occur. Thanks to their resemblance, the conditions of exchange are met—the very exchange that leaves them, atomless, behind. Without ghosts, no exchange, since neither resemblance (similitude) nor comprehension (synecdoche) could be taken for granted, given the volatility of use value—which is why Marx turned to abstraction. No common term could be found that belonged properly to the commodity as a thing or as a use-value—which is why Marx turned to ghosts. Abstraction leaves the ghosts as its remainder. But the abstraction *is* the exchange ("it is obvious that abstraction from their use-value is precisely what characterizes the exchange relation of commodities"). Something happens in order to let exchange happen, but it seems to happen *in* the exchange itself. . . .

The detour through the rhetoric of tropes now turns out to have been essential. Is this kind of substitution structured like a typical trope, like metaphor or synecdoche, a symmetrical crossing of properties? Or does the spectral remnant suggest that a certain asymmetry is built into the so-called exchange, since the prior existence of properties or an axis of commonality by which they are to be related is what is most questionable here? The balanced and closed chiasmus of the trope seems to open out of itself temporally and spatially in the abstraction: the ghost is the ineffaceable excess, the oddly material if nonsensible "jelly" of a remnant that resists incorporation, and the condition of possibility for the operation that must already have happened in order to leave it behind. The maneuver succeeds (as it does all the time) only to the extent that the commodity as ghost is a figure for the most rigorous of reductions, the radical elimination of all traces of use value, with one exception: the residue of the abstraction itself. That enables the thing to survive, as a ghost, and not just disappear, and this residue serves as the "common something" on which exchange can be based because it marks, however negatively, *all* commodities with the trace of resemblance. What remains difficult to decide is where the ghosts come (back) from. Were they there already, or did they come into being in the exchange? The operation works to the extent that this is the difference that cannot be told. What can be told, now, in the realm of ghosts, is this: "All these things now tell us is that in their production . . . human labor is piled up" (C, 128; DK, 52).

A specter is haunting this analysis, the specter of humanity. If exchange is possible, is it thanks to humanity, or more precisely, to the human labor embedded in commodities as the source of their value? Certainly this view has been attributed to *Capital*, especially in the encounter with sentences like this one, a paragraph after the ghost: "A use-value or a good has value only because abstract human labor is objectified or materialized in it" (C, 129; DK, 53). But before endorsing or condemning some labor theory of value, we need to ask about the status not so much of labor as of the abstraction, the abstraction that is humanity.

Much later in the first chapter Marx returns to the question of the possible impossibility of exchange, long after it should have been laid to rest by the ghosts or the jelly. In accounting for the development of money, Marx has been led back to Aristotle, the first analyst of value, who in the *Nicomachean Ethics* had argued that exchange, in principle, has no basis. How is exchange possible?[27] What common term could there be between different objects? If, in Aristotle's example, a house is to be exchanged for (is worth as much as) five beds, then the one and the other must be "made qualitatively alike [*gleichgesetzt*]," but since they are phenomenally or "sensibly different things," the two "could not be relatable to each other as commensurable magnitudes without such an essential likeness [*Wesengleichheit*]." And that's impossible. Aristotle concludes, quotes Marx, that

> "there can be no exchange without likeness [*Gleichheit*], and no like-ness without commensurability. . . . It is, however, in truth, impossible [*unmöglich*] for such heterogeneous things to be commensurable," i.e. qualitatively alike. This making-alike [*Gleichsetzung*] can only be something foreign to the true nature of the things, and thus only a "makeshift for practical purposes [*Notbehelf für das praktische Be-dürfnis*]." (*C*, 151; *DK*, 73–74)[28]

In a certain sense, Marx agrees. The analysis has shown that exchange has no secure transcendental foundation, no condition of possibility in the strong sense, but only what is called the power of abstraction and its residue the ghosts. Yet it—abstraction, exchange—happens, even if it is foreign (*etwas Fremdes*), especially to the "true nature" and the "sensi-ble" particularity of things. If there is a difficulty it is with use; nature and phenomenality barely get into the act, and certainly not as ontologi-cal impediments. Aristotle had argued that exchange was purely prag-matic, that all things were likened or measured simply by the fact that they were in demand. Demand's signifier is money, which is "why money is called *nomisma* (customary currency), because it does not exist by nature but by custom (*nomos*)" (*NE*, 5.5.11, 285). But the fact of conventionality does not explain the convention. Why was Aristotle unable to determine *das Gleiche*—he says, quotes Marx, that it "cannot, in truth, exist"—and forced to abandon the investigation of value with-out naming it but only marking its practical place? Marx supplies the missing name: "And it is—human labor" (*C*, 151; *DK*, 74).

27. On the question of the possibility of exchange in *Capital*, see Michel Henry's extraordinary chapter "The Transcendental Genesis of the Economy," in *Marx*, vol. 2: *Une philosophie de l'économie* (Paris: Gallimard, 1976), 138–207; *Marx: A Philoso-phy of Human Reality*, trans. Kathleen McLaughlin (Bloomington: Indiana University Press, 1983), 190–223.

28. See Aristotle, *Nicomachean Ethics*, trans. H. Rackham, Loeb Classical Library, vol. 19 (Cambridge: Harvard University Press, 1975), book 5, chap. 5, 283–289, hereaf-ter abbreviated *NE*; the quoted passage is at 5.5.14, 287.

Aristotle, though, was "unable to read [*herauslesen*]" this—strictly speaking, unable: "The secret of value-expression, the likeness and equivalence of all [kinds of] labor, because and insofar as they are human labor in general, could not be deciphered [*entziffert*] until the concept of human similarity or equality [*Gleichheit*] had already acquired the permanence of a popular prejudice [*Volksvorurteil*]" (*C*, 152; *DK*, 74). This argument would seem to explain things simply: until all believe they are the same as everyone else, no one, even Aristotle, would or could think to consider them comparable. When humanist enlightenment has arrived, a human(-labor) theory of value becomes possible to read. But Marx does not say so. The next sentence ruins the humanist assumptions at their deepest level: "But [the popular prejudice of the concept of common humanity] is *first possible only in a society where the commodity form is the general form* of the labor-product" (*C*, 152; *DK*, 74—emphasis added).

Try to summarize this extraordinary move: exchange is possible because abstraction reveals the common humanity surviving in the things exchanged. Aristotle thought it was strictly impossible and only conventional because the concept of a common humanity was not available to him. But that humanity itself arrives only with the domination of the commodity form. Which it makes possible.

Or rather, it remains impossible, and it happens all the time: *Notbehelf für das praktische Bedürfnis*, emergency placeholder, or more precisely, prejudice. Before there can be the judgment or the justice that balances and exchanges, there is the prejudice (*Vorurteil*) that renders the parties or things commensurable. Before the law of exchange, prejudice. So, if there is humanity, it is as a popular prejudice, and if exchange occurs, in spite of its impossibility, it is thanks to the popular prejudice of *menschlichen Gleichheit*—itself an effect of the abstracting, eviscerating, spectralizing exchange of commodities. Which means that another name for *gespenstig* would be *menschlich*, and vice versa. Here, all humans are ghosts. Humanity as such, empty and abstract, alike and equal (*gleich*), is indistinguishable from the commodity.

As Louis Althusser wrote, Marxism is not a humanism but a "theoretical anti-humanism."[29] Marxism is the critical analysis of capitalism precisely insofar as capitalism is a humanism. Humanity, the abstraction, is the ghostly residue that names the pragmatic necessity of

29. Louis Althusser, "Marxisme et humanisme," in *Pour Marx* (Paris: Maspero, 1967), 236; "Marxism and Humanism," in *For Marx*, trans. Ben Brewster (London: Verso, 1979), 229.

likeness in exchange. To be alike is to be abstract, which is to say, to be a ghost—to be human, or a commodity.[30]

Marx says as much and spells out its political stakes many pages later as the second part of *Capital* comes to a close.

> The sphere of . . . commodity exchange . . . is in fact a true Eden of innate human rights [*Menschenrechte*]. Here alone rule Freedom, Equality [*Gleichheit*], Property, and Bentham. Freedom! Because buyer and seller of a commodity, e.g. labor-power, are determined only by their own free will. They contract as free persons, who are equal before the law. . . . Equality! Because they relate to each other only as commodity-owners, and they exchange equivalent for equivalent. (*C*, 280; *DK*, 189–90)

Thus, Gayatri Spivak has argued, "there is no *philosophical* injustice in capitalism."[31] The commodity structure is the ideal of justice as fairness, as balance, symmetry, reciprocity, between humans as well as things. "Human rights" means that, before the law of exchange, humans meet, like things, as equal (*gleich*), free, responsible . . . as abstract.

At least epistemologically. When abstractions meet, though, knowledge is not the only force involved. When capitalist meets worker—for example, on the question of the length of the working day—the symmetry of balance provides no guarantees, and the exchange is opened onto political struggle: "There is here therefore an antinomy, of right and against right, both equally bearing the seal of the law of commodity-exchange [*beide gleichmäßig durch das Gesetz des Warenaustausches besieglt*]. Between equal rights, force [*Gewalt*] decides." (*C*, 344; *DK*, 249)[32]

Look-alikes, or *Augenschein*

To recapitulate. *Capital* performs the analytic decomposition, the analysis or abstraction, of the system of commodity exchange into its

30. Marx is thus speaking strictly when he writes in a footnote: "In a certain sense, man is like the commodity. As he neither enters into the world in possession of a mirror, nor as a Fichtean philosopher who can say 'Ich bin Ich,' a man first sees or recognizes [*bespiegelt*] himself in another man. The man Peter only relates to himself as a man through his relation to the man Paul as his likeness [*als seinesgleichen*]" (*C*, 144 n. 19; *DK*, 67 n. 18).

31. Spivak, "Some Concept Metaphors," 96; and compare Spivak, "Speculations," 50.

32. Spivak quotes the final sentence here in "Some Concept Metaphors," 94. See also Henry, *Marx*, 194.

basic unit and of that unit into the duplicity of use value ("quality") and exchange value ("quantity"). As use value, the thing differs irreducibly from everything else, including other uses of the "same" thing. But the thing carries, bears the burden of, exchange value, which is to say it transports the possibility of being transported, converted into or traded for something else. Yet nothing immanent in the thing as thing makes such exchange possible: there is no *Ding-an-sich* in exchange, neither use nor nature. Some mediation "must" intervene, some redefinition or metamorphosis within the things which provides the axis of resemblance or comparison (*Vergleich*) around which they may exchange. This preparatory operation within, this *perestroika* or *Gleichsschaltung* at the interior of the thing, is called abstraction. It "characterizes" the exchange. In abstraction—the operation that readies the things for exchange, that makes them exchangeable, and that exchanges them—not an atom of use value remains. Nor is anything left of the labor that has produced them, no thing but a strange "residue." There is nothing left over but ghosts (*gespenstige Gegenständlichkeit*), as practical possibility— or should we say, as necessity.

This haunting can only be thought as the difficult (simultaneous and impossible) movement of remembering and forgetting, inscribing and erasing, the singular or the different. On the one hand, difference is the reason for economy; were things not different, there would be no possible interest in exchange: "Were each of the things not qualitatively different use-values and hence not the products of qualitatively different useful labors, they would be utterly incapable of encountering each other [*gegenübertreten*] as commodities" (*C*, 132; *DK*, 56). Exchanging something for itself would be tautology, not economy. "Heterogeneous [*vershiedenartigen*] use-values" (*C*, 132; *DK*, 56) are the condition of the system—no substitution of identicals, only of different things in differing uses.

But this difference, the raison d'être of the system, is also its target. "La différence de leurs valeurs d'usage est éliminée, de même disparaît" (*LC*, 52): "Just as in the [exchange] values coat and linen there is abstraction from the difference of their use-values, so in the labors represented in these values, from the difference of their useful forms" (*C*, 135; *DK*, 59). Only when this abstraction occurs, an abstraction from use value as from human labor, can things come into relation as (exchange) values (*C*, 136; *DK*, 60). The only "labor theory of value"[33] here reads as follows: "It is in this property of being similar or abstract [*gleich*

33. As Althusser points out in *Reading "Capital,"* Marx wrote quite directly in the "Critique of the Gotha Programme": "Labor is not the source of all wealth" (171). "In *Capital*," writes Althusser, "Marx breaks with the idealism of labor . . . 'as the essence of man'" (172).

. . . *oder abstrakt*] human labor that [labor] forms commodity's value" (*C*, 137; *DK*, 61) and *only* insofar as it is abstract(ed) and no longer particular labor but its ghostly residue. But the emphasis is on "human" rather than "labor," which is to say, alike because abstract. This is the definition of humanity—abstract, similar, spectral.

This *Doppelcharakter* of the commodity requires the ghosting of an abstraction—different and alike, used and exchanged. Insofar as they are exchanged, commodities have no materiality. "In direct opposition to the coarsely sensible objectivity of the commodity body, not an atom of natural material [*Naturstoff*] enters into their objectivity as values." It is indeed ghostly. "You may twist and turn [*drehen und wenden, tourner et retourner*] a single commodity as you wish; it remains ungraspable as a value-thing" (*C*, 138; *LC*, 55; *DK*, 62).

That (commodity) exchange is not natural but social is a commonplace, but the self-evidence of the politicizing cliché obscures its force. The analytic decomposition of the thing of value suggests that exchange is not simply possible, that the entry of different things-uses into exchange relations has no transcendental guarantee or basis at all. Exchange is at best pragmatic and thus aberrant, seeking out differences in order to eliminate them, recalling them to oblivion. A coat is not a house, and they have nothing in common, just as Achilles is not a lion. Their substitution occurs only when the uses or things disappear and return as ghosts, different but alike to the extent that they are all *unfassbar* . . . or more precisely, words.

Although it receives its sharpest thematization only in the final section on fetishism, the analytic necessity of this linguistic turn is what is at stake throughout the third section of the first chapter. Carefully measuring the implications of the theory of the doubled character and the ghosting abstraction, Marx suggests that the ghost means, paradoxically, that commodity exchange is not something visible, not sensory, not something to see or feel. It has nothing sensible or phenomenal (*sinnlich*) about it, nothing "real" as philosophy or political economy has interpreted reality (within oppositions such as matter/spirit, essence/appearance, real/ideal, etc.).[34] Exchange is a matter of signification, expression, substitution, and hence something that must be read. The like-ness of the ghosts is invisible, untouchable, ungraspable by human hands. So when two things, such as value, "look alike," the emphasis falls on the like rather than the look. It is obvious but worth

---

34. See Althusser's amusing and pointed discussion of the encounter with the sign that says "cross the frontier and go on in the direction of society and you will find the real," in "Marxism and Humanism," 244.

emphasizing: the economy is a system of differences or relations, relations that precede the things they relate to the extent that they are values. And when things are exchanged they are exchanged not as things but as values, values within a system that traffics only in abstractions, idealizations, prejudices, and their ciphers or markers. Ghost: *Geist* and *Gespenst* at once.

Value[35] is always value in a relation, in an exchange. "The simplest value-relation is evidently that of a commodity to a single heterogeneous commodity: . . . x *Ware A = y Ware B*" (*C*, 139; *DK*, 62–63). The relation makes the value happen, since neither commodity brings its value with it, independent of the other. One thing uses the other as the medium of its expression as value; "the value of the linen can therefore be expressed only relatively, i.e., in another commodity" (*C*, 140; *DK*, 63). The relation is structured as something like a dialectical staging of self-recognition through contradiction and mediation (expression) in an other (recall the example of Peter and Paul). (Exchange) value emerges only relatively, without (and as a result of the evisceration of) anything intrinsic, absolute, especially sensible or phenomenal. "In the value-relation of one commodity to another its value-character emerges or steps forth [*hervortritt*] through its own relation to the other commodity" (*C*, 141– 42; *DK*, 65). Commodities relate not as things but as values, ghostly or jellied abstractions: "It is only as value that [the linen] is related to the coat as equal in value [*Gleichwertiges*] or exchangeable with it." Nothing sensible happens here, but simply the transformation by substitution of values. Thus Marx can write that "weaving, insofar as it weaves value [which is no sensible activity], has nothing to distinguish it from tailoring" (*C*, 141; *DK*, 64).

What "allows" exchange to happen is neither the labors nor the uses nor the things themselves but their abstracts, abstractions, operating as tokens (practical necessities) in a relation. Being alike is being abstract. And in relation, one thing counts as the "qualitative equal [*Gleiches*]" of the other, "as a thing of the same nature, *because it is a value*" (*C*, 142; *DK*, 66, emphasis added). Relation is abstraction, and the "expression" or equation of one unit in the other, accomplished in the event of the abstraction, is unavoidably a matter of signification or figuration—to be read: "The coat, the body of the coat-commodity, is sheer use-value. A coat as such no more expresses value than does the first piece of linen we came across. This proves only that, within its value-relation to the linen, the coat signifies more [*mehr bedeutet, signifie plus*] than it does

35. Recall that early in the chapter Marx stops writing "exchange value" and substitutes simply "value."

outside it, just as some men signify more when inside a gold-braided uniform than they do otherwise."[36] Marx presents the event of the relation, the signifying encounter, as a drama of mutual recognition, a little fable of things looking at—and like—each other and thus saying "I = I" thanks to the entrance of the other. But the recognition cannot, by definition, be an (aesthetic, sensory) experience; the only "experience" of exchange is the extinguishing of all that is phenomenal. You can twist and turn the ghosts, but you'll see or feel or hear or touch nothing of their value.

> And in the value-relation with the linen, the coat counts therefore only under this aspect, as embodied value, as value-body [Wertkörper]. Despite its buttoned-up appearance, the linen recognizes in it [the coat] a beautiful kindred value-soul. C'est le côté platonique de l'affaire. Nevertheless, the coat cannot represent value toward the linen unless value, for the latter, simultaneously assumes the form of a coat. . . . As use-value, the linen is a sensibly different thing from the coat; as [exchange] value, it is "coat-like or -identical [Rochgleiches]," and therefore looks like a coat [sieht daher aus wie ein Rock]. (C, 143; LC, 58; DK, 66)

This appearance, this look, cannot be seen; if it were capable of being perceived phenomenally, if it could be seen, it wouldn't be a value. Value is a signification and must be read, a purely verbal "like." This is what Marx calls the "language of commodities," der Warensprache, the discourse of likeness without likeness, engaged in by commodities as soon as they enter into the abstracting-ghosting relation of exchange.

> We see then, that everything our analysis of the value of commodities previously told us is repeated by the linen itself, as soon as it enters [tritt] into association with another commodity, the coat. Only it reveals its thoughts in a language with which it alone is familiar, the language of commodities. . . . In order to say that its sublime value-objectivity differs from its stiff and starchy body, it says that value looks like a coat, and therefore that insofar as it [the linen] itself is a value-thing, it and the coat are like as one egg and another. (C, 143–44; DK, 66)

Or should we say, like as two ghosts?

As for the linen, it is a figure, and a figure of figure at that: "Its

36. Note that the example, the figure of the coat as commodity, has begun to slip into something more literal here.

existence as value appears in its likeness [*Gleichheit*] with the coat, just as the sheep-nature of the Christian [appears] in his likeness with the Lamb of God" (*C*, 143; *DK*, 66). Thus the commodity is like something that is like something else *only as a figure*, as something that can be looked at only on paper.

It now becomes obvious why the original sentence that introduced the problem of abstraction in all its force had recourse to the strange little word "obvious," *augenscheinlich* (*C*, 127; *DK*, 52). To the eye, it demands to be read. The look of and at the commodity is finally, if it is ever finally anything, a purely *material* vision, but material in the sense that language is material, not phenomenal or sensible. It appears, it looks like, but merely as an inscription. It appears to the eye (*Augenschein*) of a reader, but abstractly (*unfassbar*). If it turns and returns, the movement is that of the trope and the ghost, but only insofar as they are written down. That is why Walter Benjamin could speak of the commodity as "material that is dead in a double sense . . . anorganic matter, matter that has been eliminated from the circulation process" or, quoting Baudelaire, "oublié sur la carte":[37] doubled, both ghost and inscription.

The ghosts are there to be read, again and again.

Doing without Knowing

Having decomposed the commodity to present it as doubled, abstracted, ghosted, aberrant, *Capital* quickly reintegrates it, if rather ironically. The mechanism of the recomposition is itself rhetorical, a fabulous movement of personification superimposed on the metaphorical abstraction. Luce Irigaray has described the process precisely: "Commodities among themselves are thus not equal, nor alike, nor different. They only become so when they are compared by and for man. And the prosopopeia of the relation of commodities among themselves is a projection through which producers-exchangers make them replay be-

37. Walter Benjamin, "The Paris of the Second Empire in Baudelaire: The *Flâneur*," in *Charles Baudelaire*, trans. Harry Zohn (London: Verso, 1983), 55–56 n. 41. Paul de Man calls attention to Jauss's discussion of this phrase in his Introduction to Hans Robert Jauss, *Toward an Aesthetic of Reception*, trans. Timothy Bahti (Minneapolis: University of Minnesota Press, 1982), xxiii, referring to Jauss, 178–79. De Man comments, "The commodity is anorganic because it exists as a mere piece of paper, as an inscription or a notation on a certificate." And see de Man's reading of *Augenschein* in Kant, in "Phenomenality and Materiality in Kant," in *Hermeneutics: Questions and Prospects*, ed. Gary Shapiro and Alan Sica (Amherst: University of Massachusetts Press, 1984), 121–44.

fore their eyes the operations of specula(riza)tion."[38] To a certain extent the possibility of prosopopeia had already begun in the text's fourth paragraph, when commodities were embodied (Warenkörper). The ghosts of the analysis, which "allow" the passage to a specular system of likeness or equality (called, abstractly, "humanity") now return with a vengeance. With the entrance into the analysis of Warensprache, Capital takes its figure (body, ghost, humanity) literally, deploys it narratively, and soon commodities are walking, standing, choosing, carrying, dressing (indeed, the coat, however threadbare, wraps itself around the very commodity of which it is the privileged example [C, 143; DK, 66]) . . . and talking commodity talk. "The linen [as a value form] no longer stands in social relation with only one other kind of commodity, but with the commodity-world [Warenwelt]. As commodity it is a citizen [Bürger] of this world" (C, 155; DK, 77).

The system of commodity exchange within which these reanimated if somewhat spectrally abstract figures enter into relations with each other is itself spectacularly powerful. Having been artificially dissolved, the formalized rigor of the exchange relation (so the story goes) can be all the more thoroughly reconstructed. Like the geometry of forms with which Marx regularly compares it, its equations or likenesses are symmetrical, mirrorlike, and totalizing. Equipped with the resources of dialectical negativity (the commodity's mediation of itself in the other as its other), the system maps out the time and space of the exchange and binds its terms tightly together. The exchange of commodities is a "system of formalization and notation rigorous enough to be patterned on the model of mathematical language," or more precisely, "its model is that of analytic geometry," as Paul de Man says of Heinrich von Kleist's marionette theater.[39]

Growing through a series of stages (the different "forms of value"— simple, expanded, general [recapitulated at C, 158; DK, 80]), the isolated substitution of one thing for another is multiplied into the general system of economy ("it is an embryonic form which must undergo a series of metamorphoses before it can ripen into the price-form" [C, 154; DK, 76]). The system begins as a simple equation, and the symmetry of the substitution allows others to be added to it infinitely, in a movement of

38. Luce Irigaray, "Le marché des femmes," in Ce sexe qui n'en est pas un (Paris: Minuit, 1977), 173; "Women on the Market," in This Sex Which Is Not One, trans. Catherine Porter with Carolyn Burke (Ithaca: Cornell University Press, 1985), 177. See also her discussions of the ghost, abstraction, and the question of analogism, between the exchange of commodities and of women, but also within Capital itself. "Le marché des femmes," 170–71; "Women on the Market," 174–75.

39. Paul de Man, "Aesthetic Formalization: Kleist's Über das Marionettentheater," in The Rhetoric of Romanticism (New York: Columbia University Press, 1984), 265.

specularization ("every other commodity-body becomes a mirror of the linen-value" [*C*, 155; *DK*, 77]) and infinite incorporation (one thing's "isolated value-expression is transformed into the indefinitely expandable series [*stets verlängerbare Reihe*] of its different simple value-expressions" [*C*, 154; *DK*, 76]). Although the series is entirely ad hoc, "a motley mosaic of disparate and heterogeneous value-expressions" (*C*, 156; *DK*, 78), any equation within this endless chain of substitutions or transformations can be reversed—since all "commodities, when taken in certain proportions, must be equal [*gleich*] in value" (*C*, 136; *DK*, 60)—and the chain "remains constantly extendable" by any new *Wertgleichung* (*C*, 156; *DK*, 78). Being a commodity, an exchangeable thing, means being inscribed in this transformational system of crossings and reversals, illimitable in principle. The commodity is this perpetual motion machine, at least until its enumerative stutter is temporarily halted with the emergence of a general value form, a commodity set apart from the rest as "immediate[ly] exchangeable with all other commodities" (*C*, 161; *DK*, 82), a kind of zero excluded from the system in order to guarantee its totality and closure. "This form, for the first time, actually relates commodities to each other as values or lets them appear to each other as exchange values" (*C*, 158; *DK*, 80); it is "immediate universal exchangeability" (*C*, 162; *DK*, 84).

With the emergence of universal exchangeability arrives the moment for which *Capital* is justly best known, the final section, "The Fetishism of Commodities and the Secret Thereof." The *Geheimnis*, though, of the section is what it says. Those who claim to understand it usually argue that *Capital*'s so-called theory of fetishism is (1) an explanation of how human beings, through buying and selling (exchange), come to relate themselves to commodities and not to each other and (2) a reminder, thus, that every commodity is the product of a human social relation, one of "our" creations and not something to be endowed with the independent existence we tend to grant it. It is a warning to recognize our "own" offspring as such and to refuse their domination over us—because we made them. This is perhaps the central commonplace of the talk that goes on under the name Marxism. As Lukács pointed out, "The essence of commodity structure has often been pointed out." That it has did not stop him from repeating it: "Its basis is that a relation between people takes on the character of a thing and thus acquires a 'phantom objectivity,' an autonomy that seems so strictly rational and all-embracing as to conceal every trace of its fundamental nature: the relation between people."[40]

40. Georg Lukács, *History and Class Consciousness*, trans. Rodney Livingstone (Cambridge: MIT Press, 1971), 83.

This interpretation is not without its basis in *Capital*, and there is even reason to see the analysis of the commodity structure as a critique with practical implications, thanks to Marx's indulgence in an analogy to religion with a decidedly negative tone.

> The commodity-form . . . is nothing but the determined social relation between humans themselves which assumes here, for them, the phantasmagoric form of a relation between things. In order, therefore, to find an analogy we must take a flight into the misty realm of religion. Here the products of the human head appear as endowed with a life of their own, entering into relations both with each other and with humans. This I call fetishism. (*C*, 165; *DK*, 86–87)

Perhaps *Capital* is saying, forewarned is forearmed—not simply against the errors classically described as fetishism[41] (confusing one's creations with one's creator, fixatedly mistaking the substitute for what it replaces) but against the double danger of the commodity form: abstraction *and* reanimation. Here, warning would be preparation for action: whether the danger is the aberrant totalizations and exchanges of tropes or commodities, the reader and consumer might acknowledge their existence, understand their mechanism, and by that cognitive advance stand some chance of circumscribing or regulating their impact. So the question would be: does it suffice to become aware of the rhetorical or commodified nature of our exchanges in order to control their tendency to error, or at least in order to avoid the delusions of the fantasy apparently criticized as "fetishism"?

If Marx is any example, the answer would have to be no. Needless to say, the reading sketched here suggests that the *phantasmagorische Form* of fetishism is an exact description of the story we have just been reading. So, does *Capital* conclude by denouncing the very errors it practices? Does it practice the very errors it denounces? Or does it protect itself from error and denunciation by a self-critical turn at the end? Perhaps it does none of these, and the practice of fetishism is a little more complicated than the standard definition suggests. We would do well to heed Marx's admonition to the French reader and slow down, suspend our eagerness to connect immediate questions with general conclusions, and pursue the fatiguing reading just a bit further.

41. See the series of articles by William Pietz, "The Problem of the Fetish," *Res* 9 (Spring 1985): 5–17, *Res* 13 (Spring 1987): 23–45, and *Res* 16 (Autumn 1988): 105–23, as well as "The Historical Semantics of Fetishism," ms.

The section begins:

A commodity appears at first sight a self-evident [*selbstverständliches*], trivial thing. Its analysis brings out that it is a very strange [*vertracktes*] thing, abounding in metaphysical subtleties and theological niceties. Insofar as it is a use-value, there is nothing mysterious about it, whether we consider it from the point of view that by its properties it satisfies human needs, or that it first takes on these properties as the product of human labor. It is absolutely clear that, by his activity, man changes the forms of the materials of nature in such a way as to make them useful to him. The form of wood, for instance, is altered [*verändert*] if a table is made out of it. Nevertheless, the table remains wood, an ordinary sensible thing. But as soon as it emerges [*auftritt*, steps forth] as a commodity, it changes into a sensible supersensible thing [*ein sinnlich übersinnliches Ding*]. (*C*, 163; *DK*, 85)

The opening paragraph of the section conspicuously echoes the first paragraph of the chapter, rehearsing the progress it has performed. It returns us to the question of exactly how something can step forth as a commodity, how use value is transformed into exchange value in the process of exchange. We have reached the analytic determination that a certain abstraction must (have) take(n) place in order for exchange to occur, and that, in fact, abstraction is the name of what goes on in exchange. But the ghosts of the abstraction have proved to be less an answer than a practical necessity, replacing the missing measure with the prejudice of "humanity."

The turn to fetishism finally grants us the rhetorical room to theorize this place-holding prejudice. There is nothing at once particular and common that an abstraction could substitute for, no common trait: if use values (or productive labors) have nothing in common, by definition (being *only* ways of use or working themselves), and thus their radical (subatomic) erasure is required, then doesn't the so-called common or third term have to be substituted for nothing? The *Gespenst* that Marx calls abstraction is a substitution for nothing, which, in constituting the nothing as a something that could be substituted for, institutes an originary simulation of exchange between something (common, abstract) and nothing. But the institution is structured like a substitution. It looks like the positing of an improper name (a common noun)—say, "exchange value" or just "value" or "abstract human labor" or, more precisely, "human"—for something that has no name at all of its own. Could this positing be in any way distinguished from the act of exchange itself?

If abstraction is structured like the imposition of an improper name on something that has none of its own, then another turn to rhetoric will be helpful. The situation is that described by the rhetoricians as catachresis: "If for lacke of naturall and proper terme or word we take another, neither naturall nor proper, and do untruly applie it to the thing which we would seem to express," said George Puttenham, then we have used the figure he called "abuse, or catachresis."[42] It exposes the symmetrical and totalized field of the trope to something that troubles its closure. Catachreses, as Paul de Man comments,

> are capable of inventing the most fantastic entities by virtue of the positional power inherent in language. They can dismember the texture of reality and reassemble it in the most capricious of ways. Something monstrous lurks in the most innocent of catachreses: . . . the word can be said to produce of and by itself the entity it signifies, [one that] has no equivalence in nature. When one speaks of the legs of the table or the face of the mountain . . . one begins to perceive a world of potential ghosts and monsters. (EM, 21)

The first chapter of *Capital* is this world of monsters and ghosts, from the first sentence's hideous assemblage to the abstraction's spectral remnant to this final section's misty fetishes. Ghosts and monsters are the (figurative) names of the commodity. And the story of these figures, the one narrated by this chapter and allegorized under the name "fetish" here, runs the full tropological spectrum, from simile or metaphor to synecdoche to prosopopeia and now to catachresis. The question is whether we're still within a continuous spectrum, or if we ever really were. Is catachresis a matter of substitution, of exchange, or does it rupture the closure of the tropological system?

Can you *exchange* something for nothing? That you can get something for nothing should be clear by now, and if it isn't, the privileged example of the fetish ought to make it so. Think of a table.[43] The vertical things that keep the flat top off the ground have no name of their own, no natural or proper signifier. But by catachresis we impose the borrowed or stolen term "legs" (or even "feet") and invent a name where before there was nothing. Which is the story of fetishism; we can pick up quoting *Capital* right where we left off.

42. George Puttenham, *The Arte of English Poesie* (1589; Kent, Ohio: Kent State University Press, 1970), 190–91.

43. Deborah Esch, " 'Think of a Kitchen Table': Hume, Woolf, and the Translation of Example," in *Literature as Philosophy, Philosophy as Literature*, ed. Donald G. Marshall (Iowa City: University of Iowa Press, 1987), 262–76.

The form of wood, for instance, is altered if a table is made out of it. Nevertheless, the table remains wood, an ordinary sensible thing. But as soon as it emerges [*auftritt*] as a commodity, it changes into a sensible supersensible thing [*ein sinnlich übersinnliches Ding*]. It not only stands with its feet on the ground, but, in relation to all other commodities, it stands on its head, and evolves [*entwickelt*] out of its wooden head whims [*Grillen*] more wonderful even than when of its own accord [*aus freien Stücken*] it began to dance. [The footnote adds: One may recall that China and the tables began to dance when the rest of the world appeared to be standing still [after 1848]—*pour encourager les autres.*] (*C*, 163–64; *DK*, 85)

Whether this state of affairs is good or bad is difficult to say at this level of rhetorical complexity. After all, this turning table is not just one example among others but is, quite simply, the example of the commodity, the common commodity, the effective universal equivalent for all the rest. As the figure for the commodity—for the useful thing become exchangeable, for the doubled structure—the table can be substituted or exchanged for any other commodity in Marx's demonstration, "in the same way" that commodities can be exchanged for other commodities. Exemplary commonplace, commodity of commodities, in more ways than one. The commodity as such (e.g., the table) is already structured like a figure, since use values cannot be directly exchanged, having nothing in common around or across which the substitution could be organized, but must instead be mediated or figured by being transformed into so-called exchange values. The medium is the ghost, here.

The structure of this violent figure is that of catachresis, a placeholder, the opening of the tropological spectrum beyond the symmetry of an exchange the possibility of which can no longer be taken for granted. Dissolved or volatilized by the reductive force of abstraction-in-exchange, use values become exchangeable only as ghosts. Or (abstract) humanity. But these specters are traded with a vigor and an urgency approaching that of living bodies themselves. The force of abstraction (*Abstraktionskraft*) both de- and reanimates commodities; we could say it "ghosts" them, giving them whatever life (*überleben*) or animation (suspended) they have, without presuming that they had any prior to the abstraction. The same *coup de force* institutes and destitutes them at once—thus violating the propriety of any "same" or "at once"—which means that "monster" would be as good a name as "ghost" for the structure Marx analyzes under the name *Ware*.

Perhaps the difficulty of the exemplary table can be measured. The table is a figure of the commodity, which is itself structured as a figure. Besides being the example of the commodity, the table is also an exemplary figure, a catachresis. And the catachresis itself provides the example for the structure of the commodity. Thus, as they say, it could be no accident, and nothing less than a certain textual necessity, that the table steps forth (not to mention standing on feet and head, and rising off the ground altogether) as the ghostly residue of the monstrous collection of commodities the chapter has analyzed. This table, "more wonderful even than when of its own accord [aus freien Stücken] it began to dance," stands here not only on its feet and head but for the commodity as such: ghost of a monster, monster of a ghost. Freely.

What is called exchange or substitution has always already begun with an act that can only be unthinkably different from it, an act of institution—the wild, random, uncontrolled, and utterly arbitrary positing of a status, a relation or a name to be related (Gespenst, Menschheit). That act can only be described as the simulation in advance, the pre-simulation or the simulacrum (the radically nontranscendental condition of possibility, nontranscendental because, strictly speaking, it is the condition of the impossibility of any exchange worthy of the name) of exchange. Abstraction would thus itself name neither the institution of exchange nor the substitution that is exchange, neither catachresis nor metaphor.

So when the question of commodity fetishism turns into the question of what is to be done, it should come as no surprise that it is figured as a problem of reading and writing: "Value, therefore, does not have its description branded on its forehead; rather, it transforms every product of labor into a social hieroglyphic. Later on, men try to decipher the hieroglyphic" (C, 167; DK, 88). All the emphasis here is on the effort, the difficult labor of decipherment. Try as we may, though, the interpretation does not help much. Learning what we have learned from reading Capital, Marx says, "in no way banishes the semblance [Schein] of objectivity," which mists the commodity and which locks in fetishistic pursuit (the hermeneutic gesture itself). The ghosts may be linguistic, but that does not make them any easier to read. Indeed, precisely to the extent that they are placeholders, markers, catachreses, they become more linguistic and more trouble to read. "Matter that is dead in a double sense"—that is language (at least) twice: abstracted, inscribed.

Faced with this conundrum, augenscheinlich, the interpreters (exchangers) succeed only in redeploying the double bind that structures commodity exchange. No matter how forewarned we are, thanks to the forearmaments of the knowledge of the secret of commodity exchange and its resulting fetishism, as long as exchange (language) goes on we are powerless to overcome its difficulties. And knowing only makes it more scary. "Je sais bien, mais quand même."[44] As Marx says, this is the path of madness: "If I state that coats or boots stand in a relation to linen because the former is the universal embodiment of abstract human labor, the craziness [Verrücktheit] of the expression hits you in the eye. But when the producers of coats and boots bring these commodities into relation with linen . . . the relation . . . appears to them in this crazy [verrückten] form" (C, 169; DK, 90).[45] "Humanity" is this madness, its subject and its object. It is not simply the ignorance of not knowing what to do; it is rather the terror of still having to do, without knowing. And we have no magic caps, only ghosts and monsters.

44. See Octave Mannoni, "Je sais bien, mais quand même . . . ," in Clefs pour l'imaginaire (Paris: Seuil, 1969), 9–33.
45. Spivak, in "Some Concept Metaphors," cites a passage from the Grundrisse to the same effect: "madness . . . as a moment of economy" (93).

Marxian Value Theory and the Problem of the Subject: The Role of Commodity Fetishism

Jack Amariglio and Antonio Callari

An unnecessary gulf has come to exist between two important areas of theoretical work in contemporary Marxism, with the theory of value (the economics, if you will) on one side and the nature and role of subjectivity in historical materialism (an antieconomism) on the other. Those concerned with the problem of subjectivity have argued that Marxism needs to reject its "theory of value." The situation (an apparent schism) has not been helped by traditional academic disciplinary separations, which, to the extent that they have influenced Marxists, have made the economists among them less than totally sensitive to the insights and theoretical propositions of students of subjectivity.[1] At the

The first versions of this essay were presented (and subsequently published as Discussion Paper 1 in its discussion paper series) at the Association for Economic and Social Analysis, First Annual Conference on Marxian Social Theory, held at the University of Massachusetts, Amherst, in April 1983 and at the History of Economics Society annual meeting in Pittsburgh, May 1984. Since then, it has been presented to, read by, and discussed by various audiences. An earlier version of this essay appeared in *Rethinking Marxism* 2 (Fall 1989). Among the many people who commented on the essay in its multiple disguises, we wish to thank especially Dean Saitta, John Davis, Bruce Roberts, Fred Curtis, and members of the Association for Economic and Social Analysis for their helpful comments.

1. Three books that treat at some length the "problem of the subject" in relation to contemporary Marxian social thought are Lucien Sève, *Man in Marxist Theory and the Psychology of Personality*, trans. John McGreal (Hassocks, Sussex: Harvester Press, 1978); Paul Smith, *Discerning the Subject* (Minneapolis: University of Minnesota Press, 1988); and Anthony Giddens, *The Constitution of Society* (Berkeley: University of California Press, 1984). For a kindred reading of value theory that treats "subjectivity" as an inherent part of its investigation, see Gayatri Chakravorty Spivak, "Scattered Speculations on the Question of Value," in *In Other Worlds* (New York: Routledge, 1988), 154–75.

same time, disciplinary isolation has tended to leave precisely those academics most immersed in recent theories of subjectivity insensitive to the relevance of debates about the problem of value in Marxian economics.

The disciplinary separations, in fact, are so severe that radical thinkers in both realms are mostly ignorant of and unreceptive to the normal discursive work and theoretical breakthroughs in each other's fields. As a result, Marxist (and non-Marxist) economists perusing texts (which they rarely do) written by poststructuralist and postmodern cultural critics often complain about both the complete impenetrability of these texts and, in the end, the uselessness for economic theory of deconstructive readings and, especially, of the "decentering" of the subject by now taken for granted in much of this literature. Likewise, it may come as a surprise to those few cultural critics who admirably attempt to cross disciplines and to link literary strategies to "political economy" to learn that for the overwhelming majority of professional Western economists concepts such as "late capitalism," "consumer society," and "postindustrial society," sometimes mentioned with studied casualness, have no particular standing or following, even in radical circles. Nor, for that matter, would most economists evince the slightest recognition of such terms as the "political economy of signs," the "exchange of signifiers," and "libidinal economy" as extensions in any way of their own disciplinary language. On their side, students of subjectivity would be equally baffled, we think, by the near hegemony of the notion of rational behavior as the preeminent statement of subjectivity underlying most approaches (including radical ones) to economic activity. Many of our colleagues in the economics discipline, Marxists included (in our view, to their great detriment), show no understanding of, interest in, or tolerance for notions of "decentered" subjects and the like as a substitute for the premise that unfragmented, rational choice is the obvious basis for all economic behavior. In fact, the hostility to such alternative conceptions of subjectivity is so severe at present that many erstwhile radicals have now concluded that economics as a discipline or set of conceptual tools must be essentially identified with the idea of rational choice undertaken by maximizing agents. Thus, whereas many poststructuralist critics, even those influenced by Marxism, have been uninterested in or oblivious to the contours of contemporary economic theory and have concluded that Marxist economics has no insights into the question of subjectivity, many radical economists ironically have refused Marxism's long-standing insistence on the critical importance of scrutinizing the historical production of economic subjectivities (including rational choice) in theorizing value relations.

To be sure, Marxism has had a theory of the subject, the theory of commodity fetishism. To the extent that it attempts to join the analysis of commodity production and circulation with a discussion of "ideology," commodity fetishism does discuss the peculiar subjectivity typical of capitalist social formations.[2] The most typical renditions of commodity fetishism, however—and this is the crux of the matter—have presented that particular subjectivity as the effect of an underlying economic reality, rather than as one (overdetermined and overdetermining) element in the constitution of that very reality. These renditions of commodity fetishism thus have not so much treated subjectivity as an object for analysis in its own right as they have functionally subsumed it within an economistic understanding of "the commodity."[3]

No matter how many levels of subjectivity traditional accounts of commodity fetishism put forward to "mediate" the economy, these ac-

2. See Duncan Kennedy, "The Role of Law in Economic Thought: Essays on the Fetishism of Commodities," *American University Law Review* 34 (Summer 1985): 939–1001, for a brief but incisive description of what we refer to as the "traditional" reading of commodity fetishism. Kennedy's meditations on Marx's discussion have some similarity, in key parts, to our view. This similarity is especially true of Kennedy's insight (993) that far from nailing down an economistic view of "superstructural" elements, Marx's discussion completely integrates the necessary effects of particular legal concepts in the constitution of commodity relations. Kennedy, however, criticizes Marx's understanding (borrowed, as he points out, mostly from the classical political economists) of legal concepts, particularly Marx's views on contract and property. Kennedy's rendition of commodity fetishism differs most from ours in his retention of the notion that people misperceive—they possess a "false consciousness" of—the role of "nature" in economic outcomes.

3. There are many renditions of commodity fetishism; in our view, most of them, despite their differences, are based on some type of economism. In this vast literature, readers can consult early classics, such as Nicolai Bukharin, *Historical Materialism* (1921; Ann Arbor: University of Michigan Press, 1969), 237–39, and his *Economic Theory of the Leisure Class* (1919; New York: Monthly Review Press, 1972), 48–50, or more recent (but perhaps no less classic) texts such as Paul Sweezy, *The Theory of Capitalist Development* (New York: Monthly Review Press, 1970), 34–40; M. C. Howard and J. E. King, *The Political Economy of Marx* (London: Longman, 1985), 39–42; Bertell Ollman, *Alienation* (Cambridge: Cambridge University Press, 1975), 198–204; Maurice Godelier, "Fetishism, Religion, and Marx's General Theories concerning Ideology," in *Perspectives in Marxist Anthropology*, trans. Robert Brain (Cambridge: Cambridge University Press, 1977), 169–85, John Weeks, *Capital and Exploitation* (London: Edward Arnold, 1981), 41–47, for succinct presentations of the issues at stake. One classic and early defense of determinism which attempts to handle the relation between an economy and the "psychology" of society is Georgi Plekhanov, *The Development of the Monist View of History* (1894; New York: International, 1972). His account is noteworthy because he denies that for Marxism the economy is "the prime social cause," while he holds on to the view that "the psychology of society adapts itself to its economy" (168). This defense is made possible by substituting for a strict determinism the notion that psychology can and must eventually be appropriate to (but not an effect solely of) the economic relations. But the motor force of historical change, in the last analysis, rests with "the development of productive forces" (169). See also Maurice Cornforth, *Historical Materialism* (New York: International, 1954).

counts remain embedded in, or at least infected by, an economic determinism.[4] They seem to provide a solution to the problem of locating subjectivity within the terrain of "material relations." But this solution has meant asserting the primacy of the economy "in the last instance," rendering particular forms of subjective consciousness (and action) as inevitable effects, even in those subtler versions in which these forms are said to have "feedback" effects on the economy.[5] This "solution," then, ultimately negates the problem of subjectivity. To the extent that fetishism is treated as a mere effect, the implicit message to economists and others interested in explicating the economic "base" of commodity relations is that there is no need for them to consider too deeply the role of such fetishism in *producing* the conditions of existence of that base.

By contrast to the economic determinist who ultimately negates the problem of subjectivity, some critics have fully embraced it, allowing an "autonomy" of cultural and ideological realms from economic activities and institutions. But this strategy, we think, is no less problematic since some of the "autonomists," freed from the straitjacket of economic determinism, turn around and embrace some alternative determinism— privileging culture, ideology, power, and so on—in positing the determinations that constitute modern subjects and subjectivities.[6] These

4. In some versions, commodity fetishism permeates all spheres of social action and self-consciousness, so that one can say, as does Ernest Mandel in *The Formation of the Economic Thought of Karl Marx*, trans. Brian Pearce (New York: Monthly Review Press, 1971), that "Marx reduced human alienation in society based on commodity production essentially to the reification of human and social relations caused by commodity relations" (184).

5. At times, it is difficult to evaluate the extent to which some Marxists fall back on economism to describe commodity fetishism. For example, in *Marx's Method* (Hassocks, Sussex: Harvester Press, 1983), Derek Sayer quotes Marx from the *Theories of Surplus-Value* to the effect that Thomas Hodgskin, the Ricardian socialist, believed that when "the effects of a certain social form of labour are ascribed to objects," this ascription is a "pure subjective illusion which conceals the deceit and the interests of the exploiting classes" (33). Marx's summary comment was that Hodgskin "does not see that the way of looking at things arises out of the relationship [between objects] itself; the latter is not an expression of the former, but vice versa." Sayer goes on to say that for Marx, commodity fetishism "arises specifically from the value-form—a form Marx is careful to describe as a 'prosaically real, and by no means imaginary, mystification'" (33). We have no disagreement with Marx's quotation or Sayer's interpretation, provided that we all understand the terms "imaginary," "subjective illusion," and so forth in the same way. If the point is that fetishism is a "material" force or a description of a consciousness that is necessary for commodity trade, then this reading avoids precisely the economism we criticize. If Sayer is treating fetishism solely as an effect of the "real relations" established by the value form, however, and if this treatment does not see the constitutive role of fetishism in creating those relations, then Sayer's rendition falls within the purview of our criticisms.

6. It may thus happen, in the rise of such other determinisms, that Marxism itself is portrayed as the grandest of illusions: commodity fetishism and all that it implies

critics contribute to the schismatic situation by "leaving" the concerns of value theory to the economists.

Our point, of course, is that the gulf that exists within Marxian discourse is unnecessary and unproductive. The remainder of this essay introduces an alternative rendition of commodity fetishism in order to argue for a necessary conjunction, within Marxian thought, of a value theory and a theory of the subject under conditions of commodity production and trade. Our primary concern is to show that Marx, in considering the peculiar consciousness he summarized as commodity fetishism, provided the means to break substantially with any economistic derivation of subjectivity from supposedly objective social relations in the accounts of commodity exchange. We believe that Marx employed the concept of commodity fetishism to introduce questions about the "social constitution of the individual" with the aim of urging his readers to locate the manifold forces that give rise to the particular form of subjectivity involved in the "exchange of equivalents" under conditions of generalized commodity trade. Premised on a nondeterminist approach, our rendition of commodity fetishism depicts the social constitution of the individual as a "precondition" for commodity trade as much as an effect of this trade.

A word of warning is in order. We are concerned that noneconomist readers may mistake our interest in using Marx's concept of commodity fetishism to explain the particular forms of subjectivity produced within capitalist society, especially that of economic "individuality," as a sign of our own presuppositions, shared with our disciplinary colleagues, regarding the existence of unified Cartesian cogitos as the basis of economic and social behavior. This would be a mistake indeed. The point of our reading of the section on commodity fetishism is that Marx is not presupposing—he does not treat as "always already" existing—any particular form of subjectivity as the universal, eternal, and uniform basis for economic activity. To the contrary, Marx's discussion (and our own) is directed to showing, on the one hand, the overdetermined historical constitution of any and all forms of subjectivity, individuality included, and, on the other, one particular form of subjectivity (and its "self-consciousness") which is constructed in and is necessary to the market relations that are part and parcel of a capitalist economy. Although such demonstrations may be old hat for postmodern students of subjectivity who have no problem deconstructing individual subjectivity and show-

---

about the determination of subjectivity under commodity capitalism may itself be an obfuscation and reification, perhaps the inevitable mystification resulting from a "productivist" mentality. See Jean Baudrillard, *The Mirror of Production*, trans. Mark Poster (St. Louis: Telos Press, 1975), for one such position.

ing the totalizing pretensions and destructive effects of Cartesian cogitos, it is important for us to stress that in crucial ways these deconstructive strategies are anticipated by Marx's discussion of commodity fetishism and the social constitution of individuality. Our argument, then, contrasts sharply with those of poststructuralist critics who have viewed Marx as complicit with rather than in opposition to totalizing visions of subjectivity.

Post-Marxism and Analytical Marxism

To help our readers better situate our theoretical project, we briefly compare it with two other highly contested approaches, that of the "post-Marxism" of Ernesto Laclau and Chantal Mouffe, on the one hand, and that of Analytical Marxism, on the other. Taking Laclau and Mouffe's post-Marxism first, we note our general agreement (holding aside minor differences) with their rejection of economism and their preference for notions of overdetermination and "articulation" in presenting the constitution of subjects, subject positions, and much else. With these notions, Laclau and Mouffe seek to avoid the "fixity" assigned by economistic Marxism to the nature, positions, and "interests" subjects are presumed to have or occupy as a function of the ultimate effects of the economy. However, and this is our point of contention, Laclau and Mouffe consider their alternative presentation to be at odds with *all* strands of Marxism, including those that, as they acknowledge, have gone farthest to overcome economism (they single out Gramsci). In their view, Marxism must be superseded or rejected in toto since all versions can be shown to founder on an essentialist conception of the economy.

As an instance of such essentialism, Laclau and Mouffe argue that the debates between economistic and antieconomistic versions of Marxism have been "necessarily reduced to the secondary problem of the weight that should be attached to the superstructures in the determination of historical processes."[7] According to them, this reduction thus misses the "primary problem" since even "the most 'superstructuralist' of conceptions retained a naturalist vision of the economy—even when it attempted to limit the area of its effects."[8] Calling this naturalist vision "the last redoubt of orthodox essentialism," Laclau and Mouffe declare it to be their intention to "demonstrate that the space of the economy is

7. Ernesto Laclau and Chantal Mouffe, *Hegemony and Socialist Strategy* (London: Verso, 1985), 76.
8. Ibid., 76.

itself structured as a political space, and that in it, as in any other 'level' of society, those practices [they] characterized as hegemonic are fully operative."[9]

While we are in full agreement with Laclau and Mouffe's intention, we entirely disagree with their view that an antiessentialist depiction of the economy eludes Marxism per se. We believe that Marx's discussion of commodity fetishism allows not only for an investigation of how the economy interacts with elements "external to itself" but, more pertinently, for a nondeterminist depiction of how the economy itself cannot be constituted and understood except by reference to these "non-economic" elements. Understood in this way, commodity fetishism requires a rejection of naturalist portrayals of the economy. Commodity fetishism is Marx's device to show just how economic relations influence subjectivity, ideology, discourse, politics, and so on and, most important, how economic relations are themselves the "articulated" and overdetermined outcomes of the combined effects of these "superstructural" and other processes. Marx's theory of value and his treatment of subjectivity—conjoined in the notion of commodity fetishism—permit us to raise just the types of questions regarding the overdetermined constitution of the economy, politics, and subjectivity which Laclau and Mouffe believe cannot be discussed within Marxism.

Turning now to Analytical Marxism, we defend the role of "value theory" within Marxian thought in opposition to the Analytical Marxists' ultraeconomism.[10] Reminiscent of the criticism in the early 1960s by the famous Cambridge economist Joan Robinson,[11] Analytical Marxists view the theory of value as nothing more (and no more useful) than Hegelian metaphysics. For these analysts, market behavior is determined by subjects' preferences and initial endowments (much as bourgeois economics would have it), though they argue that the set of questions they ask and their focus on exploitation qualify their work as

9. Ibid., 76–77.

10. For an introduction to Analytical Marxism, see John Roemer, ed., *Analytical Marxism* (Cambridge: Cambridge University Press, 1986); his *Free to Lose* (Cambridge: Harvard University Press, 1988); and Jon Elster, *Making Sense of Marx* (Cambridge: Cambridge University Press, 1985). For criticisms of this school, readers should look at Jack Amariglio, Antonio Callari, and Stephen Cullenberg, "Analytical Marxism: A Critical Overview," *Review of Social Economy* 47 (Winter 1989): 415–32; David Ruccio, "The Merchant of Venice, or Marxism in the Mathematical Mode," *Rethinking Marxism* 1 (Winter 1988): 36–68; Michael Lebowitz, "Is 'Analytical Marxism' Marxism?" *Science and Society* 52 (Summer 1988): 191–214; Andrew Levine, Elliott Sober, and Erik Olin Wright, "Marxism and Methodological Individualism," *New Left Review* 162 (March–April 1987): 67–84.

11. Joan Robinson, *Economic Philosophy* (Garden City, N.Y.: Doubleday, 1964), especially 35–42.

Marxist. Be that as it may, our project in this essay is structurally differ-ent from that of the Analytical Marxists because we do not at all intend to take "subjects" as given; rather, we intend to find a way of theorizing about exchange, values, and prices which compels a set of critical ques-tions regarding just how subjects come to be constituted.

In opposition to the traditional readings of commodity fetishism and to the rejection of Marxism, we insist that it is possible to retain a commitment to Marxian value theory and yet avoid the relegation of subjectivity to a mere "superstructure," determined in the last instance by the economic base. In opposition to the Analytical Marxists, we insist on retaining a value theory that can allow a concerted and rigorous analysis of the intersection of the economic with the noneconomic— something that their economic positivism does not allow. In proposing a new, nondeterminist reading of commodity fetishism, we are cognizant of the thesis that the value concepts in *Capital* are necessarily structured into an economic determinist discourse.[12] But, although Marx's dis-course on value theory has been read along determinist lines, such a reading is not inevitable. To defend this contention, we briefly discuss the strategy and effects of economic determinism on Marxian thought and develop, even more briefly, the alternative discursive strategy made possible by the concept of overdetermination.[13]

The Concept of Value and the Overdetermination of Social Practice

The construction of value relations presumes and exemplifies a gener-al conception of the relationship between economic processes (e.g., commodity circulation) and forms of social agency and subjectivity (e.g., individuality). The confrontation between economic determinism and the critique of economic determinism is partly about the nature of this relationship.[14] Whereas economic determinism reduces forms of social

12. See, for example, Anthony Cutler et al., *Marx's "Capital" and Capitalism To-day*, vol. 1 (London: Routledge and Kegan Paul, 1977).

13. The concept of overdetermination was borrowed from Sigmund Freud, *The Interpretation of Dreams* (1900), in *Standard Edition*, vols. 4 and 5, and introduced into Marxism by Louis Althusser, *For Marx*, trans. Ben Brewster (London: Verso, 1979), and has been further developed by Stephen Resnick and Richard Wolff in *Knowledge and Class* (Chicago: University of Chicago Press, 1987).

14. While critical of the thesis in Cutler et al., *Marx's "Capital,"* we are much in debt to Barry Hindess and Paul Q. Hirst's *Mode of Production and Social Formation* (London: Macmillan, 1977) for the critique of empiricist and rationalist epis-

agency to effects of the economy, the critique questions just this reduction; whereas economic determinism conceives of the political and cultural processes necessary to the social constitution of forms of agency as themselves secured by the economy, the critique assigns to these processes a degree of autonomy with respect to the economy.

Economic Determinism

Economic determinism, as an essentialist discourse, is based on a translation: the translation of a discursive privilege that Marx gave to the concept of labor and to the concept of an economic process into an ontological claim about the universality—the historical eternality and all-pervasiveness—of labor and economy. This translation is evident in the economic-determinist reading of the concept of value, which has two parts. First, a "law of value" (the distribution of the labor of society) is immanent in the very definition of "society"; that is, a society is defined as an organization that must solve the problem of allocating labor in such a way as to secure the existence and reproduction of that society. Second, the determination of the value of commodities is but a practical expression of the operation of this universal law of value; commodities are stamped with the mark of a solution to the problem of allocating social labor. Each commodity "represents" a part of the system of allocation of labor time through its value. It is in order to preserve the privileged, ontological status of this law—the idea that labor is chosen simply because it reflects the "real," forever-existing, and necessary basis for a society to meet its material needs[15]—that economic determinism proceeds to reduce cultural and political moments of social practice to effects of the economy, an economy itself conceived as a structural expression of the law of value. Hence, in economic determi-

---

temologies. See also Dominique Lecourt, *Marxism and Epistemology* (London: New Left Books, 1975). We are also indebted to Louis Althusser et al., *Reading "Capital,"* trans. Ben Brewster (London: Verso, 1979), for conceiving of the project of criticizing essentialism. See also Jack Amariglio, "Marxism against Economic Science: Althusser's Legacy," *Research in Political Economy* 10 (1987): 159–94. Stephen Resnick and Richard Wolff have carried out this critique of essentialism the farthest, without abandoning the basic Marxian categories of class and value, in *Knowledge and Class.* We agree with Resnick and Wolff's treatment of the concept of overdetermination within the context of this critique of essentialism.

15. See, for example, Ernest Mandel, *Marxist Economic Theory*, vol. 1, trans. Brian Pearce (New York: Monthly Review Press, 1970), chap. 2.

nism, this law of value functions as an essence, first for the economy and then for culture and polity.

To grasp how the essentialism of economic determinism is related to the "ontological claim" that the law of value is more than just a historically constituted theoretical "choice," it may be useful to dwell for a moment on the treatment of what Marx called "abstract labor" in his elaboration of the theory of value. Quite a few Marxists have pointed out that Marx did not regard abstract labor—the idea that not concrete labor but labor in general is embodied in the exchange value of a commodity— as a mere choice (in opposition, for example, to a different choice, the "utility" of the classical political economists). Rather, as Norman Fischer sees, Marx's discursive choice is due to his "discovery" of the "real" existence of abstract labor within the capitalist labor process.[16] Thus, some Marxists (Fischer cites, for example, an article by Geoffrey Kay) claim that "abstract labor, a generality, can be actual."[17] Usually, such readings proceed to show either that regularized commodity exchange can take place only if exchanged goods possess some quantity of a "real" element common to all, such as abstract labor, or that since the tendency to "homogenize" labor increases in capitalism, then the "abstraction" of labor makes utter sense and does, indeed, exist as a "reality" of capitalism. Note, then, that the ontological position—that abstract labor really exists—is consequently granted a discursive privilege. Note as well that Marx's discourse here, the theoretical discussion of value, is likewise considered privileged since it alone rests on empirically extant conditions. The real basis for the law of value is thus shown, and the theory of value is simply an expression of its existence.

The essentialist structure of economic determinism is evident also in the way it constructs the concept of consciousness as "false consciousness." Economic determinism in Marxist discourse identifies the consciousness of the agents of commodity circulation as an objectification of human relations—commodity fetishism or reification. With characteristic reductionism, economic determinism locates the *origin* (essence) of this objectification in the supposedly universal relations described by the law of value. It explains this objectification as the necessary product of the disjuncture between the economic processes of

16. Norman Fischer, "The Ontology of Abstract Labor," *Review of Radical Political Economics* 14 (Summer 1982): 27–35.

17. Ibid., 28. For other such readings, see Anwar Shaikh, "Neo-Ricardian Economics: A Wealth of Algebra, a Poverty of Theory," *Review of Radical Political Economics* 14 (Summer 1982): 67–83; and Roberto Finelli, "Some Thoughts on the Modern in the Works of Smith, Hegel, and Marx," *Rethinking Marxism* 2 (Summer 1989): 111–31.

production and circulation in the system of private producers. Since producers do not come into contact with each other except through the process of circulation, the law of value can assert itself only by reference to commodities as objects of circulation and not of production, that is, by reference to "things" and through a consciousness of reification.

Moreover, economic determinism, consistently reductionist, uses Marx's concept of commodity fetishism to argue that the self-identification of economic agents as private individuals derives from a structurally produced inability of these agents to recognize their true social nature, which consists of their essential constitution by the social function of commodity circulation as a distribution of labor time. The misrecognition, which some authors contend is entirely appropriate to the circumstances in which commodity producers find themselves,[18] is that they fail to see that the circulation of goods takes place according to the particular mechanism (every society must have one) through which their socially productive activity is organized in order to meet socially constructed needs. Consequently, economic determinism has labeled Marx's concept of fetishism a theory of false consciousness.

The Effects of Economic Determinism on Marxian Discourse

Now, we reject economic determinism—the derivation of the consciousness of objectification from a pregiven economic structure and the labeling of this consciousness as *false*[19]—mostly because it has a destructive practical effect. The determinist construction of individuals

18. E.g., E. K. Hunt, "Marx's Concept of Human Nature and the Labor Theory of Value," *Review of Radical Political Economics* 14 (Summer 1982): 7–25; Marco Lippi, *Value and Naturalism in Marx*, trans. Hilary Steedman (London: New Left Books, 1979).

19. The concept of "false consciousness" is discussed by Georg Lukács in *History and Class Consciousness*, trans. Rodney Livingstone (Cambridge: MIT Press, 1971). Lukács argues that "the dialectical method does not permit us simply to proclaim the 'falseness' of this consciousness and to persist in an inflexible confrontation of true and false. On the contrary, it requires us to investigate this 'false consciousness' concretely" (50). While we agree with Lukács on the need for a concrete investigation of forms of consciousness, we disagree with his use of the term "false consciousness." Indeed, it is likely that Lukács himself found it rather uncomfortable, as can be seen in his qualification that the term does not allow us to dispense with a concrete investigation of this consciousness.

as agents possessing a false consciousness has led to a relative absence in Marxist discourse of a concrete analysis of the concept of individuality.[20] For if, as economic determinism has it, the process of historical social transformation rests on the playing out of contradictions immanent in the economy, then in principle it is not necessary, *either* for tracing out the historical social transformations of the past *or* for mapping out a potential political transformation, to produce concrete analyses of individuality, of the social processes that constitute it, and of the effects it has on social practices. The results of this neglect have been a tendency to view political events as inevitable consequences of transformations in an economic structure and a consequent dismissal of forms of struggle that are not typically economic. Economism displaced onto the terrain of political practice can result in what, in our view, is a mistaken denigration of the questions of agency or subjectivity and of the relation of forms of agency to the overdetermination of class (and nonclass) struggles.

In opposition to this economistic tendency, we believe that forms of social agency, such as individuality or race, gender, and nationality self-ascription, affect the constitution of the agency of class. These forms of social agency must be analyzed in terms of their own historically specific determinations and effects. The critique of economic determinism is a call for Marxist discourse to adopt a theoretical strategy that does not hinder analyses of the cultural and political as well as economic constitution of such forms of social agency as individuality—a theoretical strategy that would challenge the discursively produced determinist instinct to dismiss the concept of the individual as a figment of bourgeois imagination.

---

20. In this article, we treat the notion of the "individual"—and we do so only in abstract terms—because this form of agency has rarely been a primary object of analysis in Marxist discourse, though, for one exception, different as it is from our views, see D. F. B. Tucker, *Marxism and Individualism* (New York: St. Martin's Press, 1980). It is not our intention to preclude a more complex analysis of this or other forms of social agency in a capitalist social formation. (The individual is not the only form of social agency within a capitalist social formation.) In fact, our concern is with the possible effects of this form of agency on class processes and on the class form of agency, which we regard as the main concerns distinguishing Marxist from non-Marxist discourse. Further, we believe that the individual as a form of agency is not without its contradictions. The concept of overdetermination suggests that the individual is a form of agency whose constitution is always produced/reproduced within the context of historically specific conjunctures, that is, as a changing ensemble of qualities that influences and is effected partly by the historical transformation of capitalist social relations.

The Alternative Conceptual Structure
of Overdetermination

Although Anthony Cutler and his colleagues have suggested in Marx's *"Capital" and Capitalism Today* that the critique of economic determinism requires a rejection of "the value categories in *Capital*," we do not think that such a repudiation is necessary in order to introduce into Marxist discourse the constitutive role of politics and culture as well as the economy in the determination of forms of social agency.[21] It is, in fact, possible to theorize this role of politics and culture into the very construction of the concept of value.

In order to exemplify the effects of noneconomic processes in the constitution of value, let us briefly anticipate our reading of that concept. Recall first that Marx defined the value of a commodity as a magnitude not simply of labor time but of labor time deemed *socially necessary* to the production of that commodity. Marx's construction of value, then, introduces an element of social estimation. It is through exactly this element that Marx allowed for the complexly combined effectivities of all social processes (noneconomic as well as economic) in the constitution of his value categories.

The constitution of the products of labor as commodities and the determination of value require more than the mathematical averaging (of the various magnitudes of labor time expended by the different pro-

21. The argument in *Marx's "Capital" and Capitalism Today* is that Marx presents the concept of value in an essentialist way. But even if such a reading of how Marx developed the concept of value were beyond dispute, it would not follow that the concept itself has the power to structure the whole discourse of *Capital* as an essentialist discourse and that, therefore, the concept of value has to be abandoned. Such an argument, by assigning such omnipotence to a single concept, would itself be an essentialist argument. Allin Cottrell, "Value Theory and the Critique of Essentialism," *Economy and Society* 10, no. 2 (1981): 235–42, has criticized Cutler et al. for their wholesale rejection of the categories in *Capital*. A similar argument can be found in Antonio Callari, "History, Epistemology, and the Labor Theory of Value," *Research in Political Economy* 9 (1986), 69–93, which contains a critical commentary on the tension between economic determinism, as exemplified in Isaac Illich Rubin, *A History of Economic Thought*, afterword by C. Colliot-Thélène (London: Ink Links, 1979), and the critique of economic determinism, as exemplified in Cutler et al. Although we agree with the gist of Cottrell's argument, we disagree with his separation of Marx's value problem into quantitative and qualitative strands and with his judgment that "the critique of essentialism hits home" on the question of a quantitative relationship in commodity relations. The quantitative relation of equality is theoretically introduced in the analysis of commodity relations because of the nature of individuals as specifically historical social agents and *not* because it is a property of an objective act of exchange. To present commodity relations as quantitative does not necessarily imply an essentialist rendition of the value categories.

ducers in the production of each unit of the commodity) required in economistic treatments of the concept of value. They require just that confluence of cultural, political, and economic processes which effects the constitution of social agents as individuals, agents who recognize each other as equals, who objectify human activity, and who act as rational (economic) beings. It is the presence of such individuals that creates the possibility for, and gives meaning to, any calculation of mathematical averages to begin with.

The notion of "combined effectivities of all social processes" is summarized in the concept of overdetermination. We use *overdetermination* to refer specifically to the nature of the *relationship among* cultural, political, and economic processes that are discursively designated as participants in the constitution of practices and forms of agency in a social formation. Specifically, *overdetermination* refers to the conception of a relation of *mutual intereffectivity* among these processes. Thus, the concept of overdetermination is different from, say, the concept of a multiple determination, according to which forms of social agency would be affected by a variety of processes that exist separate and distinct from each other.

Overdetermination permits the rejection of the ontology that supports economic determinism. It is not our concern, however, to replace one ontological position (the empirical preeminence of the economy or the law of value) with another one (the "real" preeminence of relations of overdetermination) on the grounds that the former is a simple and the latter is a complex ontological assertion—or, indeed, on any other grounds. We make no ontological claim for the ensuing analysis *because* we seek no epistemological guarantee for Marx's discourse or for our reading of it.

Marx's Discourse in History: Confronting the Economism of Classical Political Economy

Borrowing loosely from contemporary theories of semiotics—the linguistic and cultural analysis of "signs"—we view the structure of Marx's value concepts as a structure of signs, a chain of signifiers whose order and meaning is not reducible to an expression of given signifieds (the economy, quantities of labor time, etc.). Instead, these signifiers—here, Marx's value concepts—are discursively constructed in a particular historical conjuncture and with a particular set of politicotheoretical (discursive) priorities.[22] All discourses (not only Marx's but also Adam Smith's or David Ricardo's or the neoclassical economists') can be read as comprising different orders in which signifiers are articulated into discourse to produce different meanings; that is, different discourses are different constitutions of signs rather than different interpretations of an empirically given object of analysis.

In order to make sense of the set of meanings produced in a particular discourse, we must take into account the relations of confrontation between this particular discourse and other discourses. These relations of confrontation are themselves the partial result of the operation of different politicotheoretical priorities in discourse. Thus, for example, the meanings that Marx ascribed to his key concepts (e.g., value, economy, ideology) do not have fixed, empirical referents. These meanings are construed as they are because Marx, facing the meanings produced by classical political economy, confronted this school of thought—its politicotheoretical priorities—by setting out to produce a *different* set of meanings exhibiting a *different* set of priorities.

The task of reading value and commodity fetishism as nondeterminist concepts is greatly facilitated by placing them in the context of a theoretical confrontation between Marx and the classical political economists.[23] In our view, the roots of economic determinism are to be found in classical political economy, not in Marx. Marx developed his own value concept not to enshrine the economic determinism of the classicals, or to replace their economism with an economism of his own, but to dispose of economism and to create the discursive conditions necessary to carry out a nondeterminist theoretical construction of the capitalist social formation.

The economism of classical political economy is expressed in the concept of "the economy" as a self-regulating market structure.[24] The

22. See Rosalind Coward and John Ellis, *Language and Materialism* (London: Routledge and Kegan Paul, 1977).

23. It is interesting that Cutler et al. in *Marx's "Capital"* have not paid much attention to the relationship between Marx and the classical political economists. They argue that the problem of a theory of value begins with Marx and not with the classicals and, thus, they concentrate their attention on the internal structure of Marx's discourse. By so doing, they disregard Marx's commentaries in which he criticized the classicals' economism. Had they approached Marx's discourse historically and intertextually, Cutler et al. would have faced a more difficult task in attempting to read that discourse as an economistic one.

24. In *Primitive, Archaic, and Modern Economies*, ed. George Dalton (Boston: Beacon Press, 1971), Karl Polanyi argues that the concept of "the economy" was a specific historical construction. In *The Great Transformation* (Boston: Beacon Press, 1957), he presents an extended discussion of the historical conditions under which this concept of an economy as a "self-regulating market system" emerged.

conception of the economic process as a self-regulating structure allows and urges the classicals to present "society" as an expression of the economy. As a self-regulating process, the economy is autonomous and, thus, can be conceived as a "subject" that expresses itself in culture and politics. The classicals produced this subject by making the economic process itself the expression of the economic rationality of given individuals and by reducing cultural and political behaviors as well to expressions of this given economic rationality (which then functions as an essence in classical discourse).[25] In short, classical political economy conflated economy and society.

Marx criticized this conflation by producing a concept of value which is not the result of a *given* economic rationality or an expression of a universal law of value or a sign whose fixed signified is "the economy" but a discursive sign of the effects of the complex relations of overdetermination among economic and noneconomic processes in a capitalist social formation (nowhere can this procedure be seen better than in his sporadic discussions in the *Grundrisse*,[26] where, in opposition to classical political economists, he adumbrates the legal, political, cultural, and psychological presuppositions for the appearance of value, money, and capital). Thus, the concept of value, far from being an economistic concept, questions the economism of classical political economy. It is an attempt to displace the presumably economic categories from the comfortable ground on which they had rested since Smith onto a critical discursive terrain that questioned the ontology/universality the classicals had assigned to the bourgeois concept of rationality.

Marx attempted to criticize this ontological/universal concept of rationality by exposing it as a historically specific concept, a concept produced and sustained by a historically specific confluence of economic and noneconomic processes. Marx theorized the historical specificity of this concept of a supposedly eternal rationality with the concept of commodity fetishism, which functions, then, to create a new (different) discursive space in which it becomes possible to carry out a nondeterminist, nonbourgeois construction of the capitalist social formation.

---

25. Adam Smith's discussion of property rights in *Lectures in Jurisprudence* (ed. R. L. Meek, D. D. Raphael, and P. G. Stein [Indianapolis: Liberty Press, 1978]) makes it clear that he viewed the source of these rights in the acts of labor with which human beings appropriate nature. Antonio Callari, "The Classicals' Analysis of Capitalism" (Ph.D. diss. University of Massachusetts, Amherst, 1981), discusses how, in the analytical structure of the classical political economists, "the economy" appears as an expression of the concept of rationality with which bourgeois discourse constructs itself.

26. Karl Marx, *Grundrisse: Foundations of the Critique of Political Economy*, trans. Martin Nicolaus (New York: Random House, 1973), 136–264.

The concept of commodity fetishism plays a crucial role in a non-determinist reading of Marx's discourse. Economic determinists have viewed it as an expression of the ability of the economy to structure the consciousness of the social agents of commodity circulation and, thus, to shape cultural and political relations into a mirror image of economic relations. The nondeterminist view, in contrast, treats this concept as a sign—a strategically located sign—that the relations between economic and noneconomic processes are neither unproblematic nor unidirectional. The very location of the concept of fetishism in the chapter on value argues for our view that value relations do not exist independently of a consciousness of objectification—an objectification that is a determining trait of the social constitution of individuals. The key to the concept of value lies not in any universal law of value, but in the historical conjunctures that reproduce that objectification of human relations which is the content of bourgeois consciousness and which Marx began to theorize with the concept of commodity fetishism. Far from being proof of the closure of Marx's discourse at the level of the economy, the concept of commodity fetishism is Marx's way of overturning the discursive privilege of the economy.

The Practice of Exchange and Commodity Fetishism

The language of fetishism that enters Marx's chapter on value is striking, of course, for conjuring up both the mystificatory nature of commodity relations and the necessary "sight" that one must possess to pierce the vapors, to comprehend and unravel the mysteries. Marx's language suggests that the problem of a commodity's value cannot be solved by a simple appeal to the necessary and fixed subjectivity of the commodity's owner/trader; neither the form of subjectivity nor the relation of value to the exchanging subject can be transparently "read." The distinctly analogical language in parts of the section on commodity fetishism—its explicit reference to religious mysteries and an accompanying interpretive hermeneutics—invites an openness on the question of the subject's essential nature. In contrast, to read Marx's exchanging subject as essentially fixed would mean that there is no continuing "mystery" in the ongoing reproduction of capitalist market relations. The "appropriate" literary figures in this event would be strictly representational and most likely realist or naturalist. But Marx uses the language of fetishism to imply that the mystery of commodity exchange continues to be reproduced, even while he shows that at least some deconstruction of this mystery is possible. In our view, Marx's choice of the figure of fetishism to convey the mystery of commodity exchange suggests his own commitment to depicting the creative, innovative, and even fantastic process that creates the reality/myth of the "individual," the form of subjectivity that is continually shaped by and, in turn, shapes market relations. Even Marx's slight departure from a descriptive "scientific" language here precisely invites readers to enter into the continuing mystery, never fully resolvable, regarding the lack of ultimate closure (the absence of the "last instance" determinant) of the individual and of the commodity relations this form of subjectivity makes possible. When he then discusses the apparent disjuncture between agents' simultaneous perceptions of equal and unequal exchange rates, Marx shows that this conundrum—this seemingly formal "objective" economic problem of exchange rates—necessarily depends upon the historically produced, "open," but mystified subject for its tentative resolution.

The mystery of commodity exchange to which commodity fetishism refers, then, is a question primarily for and about the subject. Yet, as part of the mystery, this question emerges in Marx's text and in capitalist society as a problem of rates of market exchange. Exchange, a particular form of trade, has come to be synonymous with "equal exchange." There is nothing in trade per se, however, that requires this qualification of equality, and indeed, specific social conditions are required for this equality of exchange to be operative in trade.[27] For us, the concept of the "individual" summarizes just these conditions. Bourgeois economic theory, in either its classical or its neoclassical variant, has derived equal exchange from its assumption of the individual with a set of given attributes. If trade is understood as taking place between agents naturally constituted as individuals, then this trade appears, and is immediately explained, as an exchange of equivalents. In Marxist discourse, however, the agents of trade in a capitalist social formation are constituted as individuals only historically. Hence, that trade should be an exchange of equivalents cannot be simply assumed but must be theoretically produced.[28]

The first chapter of *Capital* analyzes the conditions under which trade takes place as an exchange of equivalents. Marx conceived the circulation of commodities as a process that continually tends toward equal

27. See Polanyi, *The Great Transformation*, 56–57.

28. Here we are not posing the concept of equal exchange in opposition to the concept of unequal exchange. Both concepts stand together: to say that an exchange is unequal would presume that standards for equality had been established. What we are opposing are two different concepts of trade—one in which standards for (in)equality are present and another in which no such standards are operative.

exchange. In our reading, however, this equality of exchange is posed not as an affirmation but as a theoretical problem. Marx conceived the trading of commodities as a trade of "labor times."[29] The theoretical problem we see emerges from the absence of any guarantee that these acts of trade involve equal magnitudes of labor time. In fact, these are trades of *unequal* magnitudes of *actual* labor time.[30] But this inequality notwithstanding, for commodity circulation to take place, trade must be conceived by the agents of circulation—by individuals—as an exchange of equivalents. There is thus a contradiction: the same process of circulation is at once both an *unequal* exchange of quantities of actual labor time and an exchange of *equivalents*. The theoretical problem that *Capital* presents is the resolution of this (theoretically posed) contradiction.

The social constitution of the agents of commodity circulation as individuals is but a resolution of this contradiction in favor of the equality of exchange. Marx uses the concept of commodity fetishism to theorize both this contradiction and its resolution in favor of equality. Commodity fetishism, then, summarizes the qualities of individuals that transform the unequal exchange of actual labor time into an exchange of equivalents.

Unequal Exchange

In commodity-producing societies, the social allocation or distribution of labor time is conceptualized as taking place through relations of

29. To begin the conceptualization of value relations in terms of this category of labor time is not to assign to this category an ontological privilege. In our view, Marx began his construction of the capitalist social formation with this category of labor in order to locate his discourse in opposition to the discourse of the classicals, that is, in order to problematize the classical conception of value and of labor. Marx's point of entry is not labor per se, or production per se, or value per se, but class relations (Marx, *Grundrisse*, 100–108). But of course, a discourse is not erected in a vacuum. Rather, the specificity of a discourse is constructed only in opposition to other discourses. Marx began his elaboration of the class relations of a capitalist social formation by attacking the classical conception of class relations at its strongest point, at the point where the concept of labor was used to construct a concept of value—the classical concept of value—which had as its effect the externalization of capitalist class relations.

30. Here, we are not referring to the transformation problem and to the corresponding deviations of prices of production from the exchange values of *Capital*, vol. 1. The trading of unequal quantities of actual labor time occurs in a "volume-one world" and is as much a part of the definition of exchange value as of the definition of prices of production. A nondeterminist conception of the transformation problem itself is found in Richard Wolff, Bruce Roberts, and Antonio Callari, "Marx's (not Ricardo's) Transformation Problem: A Radical Reconceptualization," *History of Political Economy* 14, no. 4 (1982): 564–82.

supply and demand. When the society's labor has been distributed in such proportions that, for each commodity, quantities supplied and demanded are equal, a (notional) state of equilibrium exists. Equilibrium is achieved through price changes, which act as "signals" that lead to the proper distribution of labor time. Marx conceived the (notional) state of equilibrium as a state in which the price of each commodity is equivalent to its exchange value. He determined this exchange value as a quantity of *socially necessary* labor time (SNLT)—necessary, that is, for the production of one unit of the commodity in question. This quantity of SNLT is a numerical average. For example, if the social demand for commodity X were satisfied by 100 units of the commodity, and if 1000 hours of the society's labor were necessary to produce these 100 units, then the SNLT, and the exchange value, of commodity X would be 10 hours.

Now, given this formula, it follows that the exchange of any two commodities by their respective producers could be conceptualized as an equal exchange of actual labor time only if two very strict conditions were satisfied: first, that there be an actual state of equilibrium in each market; second, that for the production of each commodity there prevail one, and only one, technique of production. As for the first condition, by definition, the absence of equilibrium implies a divergence of price from value and, thus, an exchange of unequal quantities of actual labor time. In the case of the second condition, a diversity of techniques in the production of each of the various commodities would guarantee an unequal exchange of actual labor time *even if* there were an actual state of market equilibrium. The SNLT attached to each unit of the commodity is an average and not the quantity of actual labor time required to produce the unit of the commodity being exchanged. To return to the numerical example given in the text, let us assume that the SNLT per unit of commodity X is 10 hours. But since these 10 hours are an average, it is possible for any one unit of this commodity to have required more or less than this average number of hours for its production (some producers, who work with a technique that results in above-average productivity, may require only 8 hours of labor time per unit; other producers, who work with less than average efficiency, may require not 10 but 12 hours of labor time).

To continue with our example, let us assume two commodities, X and Y, both with a SNLT of 10 hours—so that, at equilibrium, one unit of X would be exchanged with one unit of Y. It can be shown that unless the two producers exchanging X and Y had produced their respective commodities with the same relative degree of efficiency (relative, that is, to the average efficiency in their respective branches of production), the exchange of one unit of X for one unit of Y would involve an exchange of unequal quantities of actual labor time. The producer working with the relatively higher (lower) degree of efficiency would trade a lower (higher) for a higher (lower) quantity of actual labor time. One of the parties to this exchange would be a net gainer and the other would be a net loser of actual labor time.

Neither of these two conditions is theorized by Marx as a normal state of affairs in a capitalist social formation, however. In general, then, exchange involves a trading of unequal quantities of actual labor time.[31]

Equal Exchange: Individuals and Commodity Fetishism

The trading of unequal quantities of actual labor time is a theoretical problem because the agents of trade are constituted as "individuals" whose self-identity is in conflict with an unequal exchange. Those agents are defined as individuals who are "rational economic beings" both in their consciousness and in their behavior, who conceive of the network of social relations within which they are inscribed as a network of (political and economic) equality (at least potentially), and who treat the things they bring to market, and the things they receive in exchange, as possessions. That is, they identify themselves, and behave, as private proprietors. Inequality in exchange would violate this ensemble of qualities that defines individuals.[32]

31. As Engels explained in his Introduction to Karl Marx, *The Poverty of Philosophy* (New York: International, 1963), the exchange of unequal quantities of actual labor time is *necessary* if the price system is to function as a mechanism for the distribution of social labor time in a capitalist social formation. According to Engels, any required redistribution of labor time could be effected only by a deviation of market price from SNLT. Thus, social reproduction, since in general it requires a redistribution of labor time, can be effected only through an exchange of unequal quantities of actual labor time. An additional reason can be given for this inequality in exchange. When we allow for competition and technical progress, social reproduction entails a lack of intraindustry uniformity of techniques. As we have seen, this lack of uniformity results in unequal exchanges of actual labor time.

32. Marx spoke of the sphere of exchange, within which individuals operate, as "a very Eden of the innate rights of man, the exclusive realm of Freedom, Equality, Property and Bentham." *Capital: A Critique of Political Economy*, vol. 1, trans. Ben Fowkes (New York: Vintage, 1977), 280. Freedom, Equality, Property and Bentham are, of course, allusions to the qualities of private proprietorship, equality, and economic rationality. Marx's reference to Eden has to be understood as a critical reference to the bourgeois conception of the individual as a being with innate attributes. The biblical metaphor is exemplary of Marx's critique of the bourgeois eternalization of exchange relations (175 and n. 35).

There is, then, a contradiction in the requirement that trade be both an equal exchange and an exchange of unequal magnitudes of actual labor time. For Marx, the need to resolve this contradiction arises out of a theoretical strategy bent on affirming the historical specificity of the capitalist social formation as one in which trade (the prevalent form of distribution) is constructed as an exchange of equivalents.

It was in order to resolve this contradiction that Marx developed the concept of commodity fetishism. A resolution that affirms the existence of individuals must theorize the possibilities for a transformation of trade (of unequal quantities of actual labor time) into exchange (of equivalents). Such a transformation is possible only on the condition that the object of exchange not be, and not be conceived as, actual labor time. Equality of exchange can be theorized only by reference to a property of the objects of trade other than actual labor time. It is possible to define this property in a variety of ways, each of which signifies particular, hence, different forms of consciousness and agency.

With the concept of commodity fetishism, Marx theorized that particular consciousness which "objectifies" human activity and thus defines the property of the objects of trade as a property of "things." The neo-classical concept of utility is one such theoretical expression of this consciousness (perhaps among several), one that defines this property as the ability of things to provide satisfaction to individuals. In this neo-classical theoretical construct, a property is chosen to serve as a standard for the measurement of equality in exchange. This property is contained within the relationship of one human being, or of a group of human beings (e.g., a household), to nature and thus preserves the individuality of these human beings.

Marx, for his own discursive purposes, chose a property not inherent in "things" themselves. To theorize a standard of equality, he devised the concept of *socially necessary* labor time, which is not contained within the concept of the relationship of a human being to nature. Through this concept, Marx could simultaneously theorize the historical specificity of individuality as a form of social agency and the social code through which market practices shape the activities of the many individual private producers.

Significantly, Marx's own reference to things in the exposition of the concept of commodity fetishism does not refer to empirical givens. Rather, things stand as signs with somewhat shifting meanings. Most often, however, under conditions of commodity exchange, things signify both the particular type of consciousness that objectifies human activity into things and the set of social processes that overdetermine this particular type of consciousness.

The Social Constitution of Individuals

Exchange (of equivalents) is made theoretically necessary by the presence of individuals. Thus, the concept of commodity fetishism is used by Marx *not to derive* the consciousness and behavior of individuality as an effect of the structure of commodity production and circulation but only *to summarize* the qualities of individuality that construct trade as "exchange." Commodity exchange, then, is an *effect* of the social constitution of individuals and cannot be used—as it is in economic determinism—to derive the consciousness of individuality functionally (such a derivation could only proceed on the assumption that trade must, by its nature, be constituted as an equal exchange—an assumption that, if made, would only *naturalize* commodity production and distribution). Commodity fetishism, therefore, allows Marxist discourse to conceptualize the political and cultural, as well as economic, constitution of individuality as a form of social agency.

There are (at least) three qualities that define the self-identity and behavior of individuals: economic rationality, equality, and private proprietorship.[33] In the following pages, we first briefly outline the content of each of these qualities as they are overdetermined by economic, political, and cultural processes;[34] then, we discuss how these qualities are condensed into the practice of exchange.

Economic Rationality

The attribute of economic rationality implies that individuals treat the objects they possess and trade as quantities that can be calculated. Rational economic agents are so constituted that, first, they conceptualize use values as *objects*, separate and distinct from themselves, which po-

33. For a related discussion of these qualities and their importance to value theory, see David Harvey, *The Limits to Capital* (Oxford: Basil Blackwell, 1984), 17–24.

34. Our discussion, although it identifies and discusses the effects of noneconomic processes in the overdetermination of the qualities of individuality, is structured in terms of the effects of the economic process of exchange more than those of noneconomic processes. This focus on the effects of an economic process, however, is *not* a way to reintroduce—through the back door, so to speak—an economic determinism. The reason for our focus on the economic process of exchange is our professional training as economists and, no doubt, an effect of the tradition of economic determinism within Marxism. This deficiency notwithstanding, we believe that we have laid out our argument in a way that assigns to noneconomic processes as much effectivity as to economic processes. Clearly, the effects of economic processes are not *sufficient* to constitute individuals.

tentially have the ability to satisfy perceived needs; second, they *quantify*, assign numbers to, these objects; third, they construct a set of procedures by which the *calculation* of these objects is conducted; and fourth, they undertake action based on the results of these calculations (actions that are perceived as "rational" because they take advantage of opportunities recognizable only through these calculations).

Rational economic agents are therefore not only defined by a particular consciousness (objectification, quantification, and calculation) but also actively produce exchange as a site in which this consciousness is concretized. Rational economic beings *actually* treat the social products that satisfy their desires as entities that reside outside of themselves. They *actually* assign "objectively" measurable values to these objects. They *actually* calculate these values according to a given set of rules.[35]

Economic rationality presupposes the constitution of agents as "selves" distanced and differentiated from "others." Objectification, and indeed the very notion of "object," presupposes a consciousness of difference. Individuals are agents that perceive differences not only among one another but also between themselves and the products they produce, possess, or consume. Without this differentiation, there would be no objectification; and without objectification, neither quantification nor calculation would be possible. Thus, without this culturally constituted differentiation, trade could not be conceived as "exchange," either equal or unequal.

The constitution of agents as "selves" differentiated from "others" is the result of both economic and noneconomic processes. Thus, we may use Freudian theory as one guide to understand this constitution as (partly) effected during childhood and in the family—a cultural and political, as well as an economic, site. The consciousness of objectification in a capitalist social formation, however, is also partly produced by the participation of agents in the process of exchange. Individuals may come to market with an ability to objectify. Participation in the market, however, "teaches" individuals that objectification must take a *particu-*

---

35. Our view here shares something with that of Michel De Vroey, "Value, Production, and Exchange," in Ian Steedman et al., *The Value Controversy* (London: Verso, 1981), when he states that "if commodity exchange is to be possible, a theoretical space of measurement must exist, so that the heterogeneous products of private labour can be transformed into equivalent categories" (178). Thus, value "constitutes a space of commensurability without which no relation of equivalence could be established. Prior to any measurement, an abstraction must be constructed" (178). He concludes that since value "refers to a measurement whose validity is limited to the point of exchange," then it is "an instantaneous measurement"; thus, "the idea of an ever-existing value, an 'embedded' value, makes no sense" (178).

lar form: the treatment of the objects of trade as quantifiable and as subject to calculation.[36]

Equality

Individuals are agents who identify themselves through, and shape their behavior in accordance with, the principle of equality (or inequality). This equality has cultural and political, as well as economic, aspects. "Equality" is as dependent on an operation of objectification as is "economic rationality." In other words, objectification (and, with it, quantification and calculation) is constituted not only through and in economic rationality but also through and in relations of equality. Thus, equality, through objectification, has economic and noneconomic determinations, as does economic rationality.

In the sphere of exchange, the consciousness and behavior of equality take the form of each agent's identifying other agents involved in trade as essentially equal (or unequal) to him/herself and treating the objects of trade as, likewise, standing in relation to one another as equal (or unequal). In the market, the operative social status of agents is that of owners/traders of objects. In exchange, each individual looks at another in terms of the qualities that the other's objects possess. Since the perception that individuals have of each other is narrowly focused on the things they each possess, the possibility of equating commodities allows individuals to construct themselves as equal (or unequal), at least in exchange.

But the construction of relations of equality is not purely economic. In a capitalist social formation, the concept of equality is based on a quan-

36. In the remainder of this essay, we use the terms "teach" and "learn" to describe the construction of the particular subjective knowledge that we call the consciousness of individuals, at least as it pertains to exchange. By placing them in quotation marks, we signal a problem with these terms. The concepts of teaching and learning are problematic for us because they imply cognition, recognition, realization, discovery, etc., by an already constituted subject of an empirical "given" outside of that subject. This is not a conception of consciousness we support. What we wish to convey with the terms "teach" and "learn" is the notion that the subjective knowledge of individuals in exchange is partly and actively constructed in the process of exchange itself. We reject the idea that individuals, wholly formed, come to comprehend what is objectively "there." Rather, the subjectivity of individuals and the process of exchange are articulated in a relation of overdetermination. It is interesting to note that we could not find (perhaps another of our deficiencies) in the English language a word, or a short phrase, that avoided the empiricist epistemological connotations that teach and learn have.

tification of human relations that depends on cultural and political, not just economic, forms of objectification. Agents come to view each other as equal (or unequal) insofar as they themselves "represent" a quantitative accumulation of universally shared properties—rights or qualities— as well as use values. In order for agents to construct their social relations as relations of equality (or inequality), they must "see" themselves and others as differentiable entities that embody amounts of common qualities. Different accumulations of these qualities constitute inequality of social status. Now, "different" means "unequal" and "same" means "equal" only when the standards are quantitative. Thus, to have the social status of "equals," agents must themselves be objectified, and that objectification must permit the divisibility of these agents into quantities of attributes. The constitution of these agents as quantities of attributes has a partial economic determination in the activity of exchanging objectified and quantified articles of trade. But it is not difficult to point to political processes (the quantification of political effectivities in the "one person, one vote" rule) and to cultural processes (the quantification and, thus, differentiation of intelligence with the concept of an "intelligence quotient") that also partly constitute agents in relations of equality (or inequality).[37]

In the history of Marxism, the bourgeois concept of equality is formulated and taken apart most brilliantly in Lukács's essay, "Reification and the Consciousness of the Working Class."[38] Lukács claims that the determination of relations of equality stems from commodity fetishism. To discuss the connections between economic and noneconomic expressions of equality, Lukács works with a concept of commodity fetishism that is linked to the concept of a false consciousness. Thus, for reasons that we have given already, Lukács's exposition of the concept of equality is for the most part reductionist. For him, all bourgeois consciousness, including the idea of equality, is implicated in the analysis of capitalist economic relations.

By contrast, we argue that equality is not exclusively constituted (through objectification, quantification, and calculation) in the economic process. Equality, as a form of consciousness and a directive for behavior, is not merely a mystification of the "real" relations of production and distribution. On the contrary, equality is a relation—a historically specific relation, to be sure—whose effectivity is partly to constitute the agents of trade as individuals in both economic and noneconomic spheres.

37. See, for example, Stephen J. Gould, *The Mismeasure of Man* (New York: Norton, 1981).
38. Lukács, *History and Class Consciousness*, 83–222.

The equation of individuals to one another is the result of treating agents *themselves* as things and is not just the result of measuring agents in terms of the commodities they own. This treatment of individuals as possessors of measurable qualities or rights is partly a *displacement* of the equality of things from the economic to the political and cultural realms. Thus, we agree with Lukács that the concept of equality, as it is "learned" in exchange, does have an effect of reifying social relations elsewhere. But we disagree with Lukács's implication that the ideology of economic and political equality is the effect of an underlying economic "reality." Agents become individuals by learning to construct themselves as equals in the economic process; but conversely, the cultural and political construction of equality is partially constituted prior to and outside of exchange.

Private Proprietorship

The third, and last, quality of individuality is agents' self-identification as proprietors of commodities. Agents must view the products of their labor and the fruits of trade as theirs to dispose of however they see fit—as long as this disposal does not prevent other agents from acting similarly.

Proprietorship is partially determined by political and cultural processes. The self-identification of agents as proprietors is possible only if these agents are recognized by others as proprietors. In bourgeois society this recognition of proprietorship is codified in private property laws, but it also depends on the ideological conception and defense of these laws, and particularly on the objectification through which agents are defined as selves differentiated from others. Agents are viewed as individuals who have a "natural right" to some portion of the products of social labor, a right usually attributed to "their" contribution to that social labor.

What is at stake here is the particular identity of agents as proprietors. Proprietorship is not exclusively defined by the objects that are owned (as property). Rather, proprietorship is at least partly constituted by the network of social relations within which labor functions as that which designates a right (ideologically recognized as legitimate and politically defined) to the objects that are owned. Individuals, then, enter into trade with an already established legal and cultural status as private proprietors. In addition, the identity of agents as proprietors is, of course, not solely an economic identity. For example, proprietorship can extend to the possession of political rights or of cultural or supposedly natural attributes (such as an "intelligence quotient").

The Condensation of Economic Rationality, Equality, and
Private Proprietorship in the Social Practice of Individuals

The qualities of economic rationality, equality, and private proprietorship are overdetermined by economic, political, and cultural processes. They are also condensed in those social practices of individuals that constitute market relations. Economic rationality, equality, and private proprietorship entail one another in their particular respective definitions.

For rational economic agents, objectification is connected to the quantification of the objects of trade. This quantification, however, is inseparable from the self-identity of agents as equals. Exchange is a process within which agents learn to quantify objects partly in order to ascertain their own location in a social network partly constituted as relations of equality. The quantification of objects of trade and the trading of equal quantities of these objects—according to whatever standards of equality are used—concretize the relations of equality among these agents. Economic rationality and equality mutually condition each other and are condensed in any act of exchange.

Economic rationality and equality mutually condition each other in at least one other way. In the market, agents learn not only to calculate but also to deploy a particular form of calculation. Individuals may come to market already having learned rules of calculation (in, for example, educational institutions). In order for an ongoing system of commodity circulation to exist, however, individuals must learn, in the market, to join *abstract* rules of calculation with particular *concrete* conditions of trade. The ongoing participation of individuals in the market requires that all individuals use the same set of rules of calculation.

A further condition of generalized commodity trade would be that each individual use this set of rules of calculation consistently. This condition is required if the agents of this social formation have learned, through cultural processes, to objectify their very needs and to express their individuality as a given set of needs. If these agents quantify their needs, the satisfaction of these needs—through the consumption of use values—proceeds by calculable degrees. If the rules used by an individual to calculate the value of a use value to be acquired in exchange are not used consistently, then the continued ability of this individual to meet his/her needs in the market will be threatened. In the absence of a set of rules that an individual can follow with regularity, the provision of the means to satisfy needs through exchange would, at best, be a coincidence. There would be no way to predict that any given act of exchange would lead to the satisfaction of a given set of needs. Individuals can, of course, change the rules they use to calculate their needs and to calculate the degree to which a set of use values would satisfy these needs. Such a change, however, may very well entail, or be brought about by, a transformation of "personality."

There is nothing in trade per se that prohibits different agents from using different systems of calculation for either the same or for different commodities. The mere act of quantification is not sufficient to establish exchange as a mutually perceived trade of equivalents. In a general system of exchange, however, agents must come to *equate* amounts of different objects in the same ratio (e.g., four apples = two oranges). Thus, there must be an "agreed upon" system of calculation that is followed by all agents.[39] The concept of equal exchange is an outgrowth of the operation of this common system of calculation. The moment of equality is understood by all agents concerned as the moment of equilibrium, when their mutual calculations are in agreement.[40]

The quality of proprietorship also has relations of mutual intereffectivity with both economic rationality and equality. In order to recognize others—and hence themselves—as proprietors, agents must be able to treat these others as subject to the same laws, rights, and calculations as they are. Private proprietorship is equally conferred on those who are able to show themselves as capable of being equated in law to all others—slaves cannot be proprietors—and who are able to demonstrate that their property is not possessed through a transgression of the "rights" of others. The legal and legitimate accumulation of commodities is protected by a guarantee of equal rights to all.

Proprietors are partly defined by their prerogative to alienate their possessions in trade. This prerogative, though, depends on a particular form of objectification of the products of social labor. To be exchangeable, these products must be construed ideologically as quantifiable in addition to being the private property of agents. Proprietors may recognize one another's rights to consume or alienate their possessions. If these rights are not to be violated, however, any alienation of com-

39. Money is the medium through which this "agreement" is enforced by the state.

40. Of course, *inequality* in exchange is not only possible but constitutes the actual norm in a capitalist social formation. Marx's *Capital* exemplifies the view that market relations are always relations of disequilibrium. As Marx attempted to capture with the concept of commodity fetishism, however, the principle of equality in exchange is ideologically projected onto all social spheres and is "internalized" by individuals as the underlying rule. This principle of equality is also theoretically necessary to the conceptualization of a state of equilibrium as brought about by forces of competition (in the Marxian and the classical or neoclassical conceptions of competition). Interindustry movements by commodity producers are determined on the basis of a calculation by some producers that, were they to remain in a particular industry, they would lose by having to sell their commodities at less than "their" values (i.e., the principles of equality would be violated).

modities must proceed according to the logic of equality. Since private proprietorship is measured to some extent by the quantities of commodities each agent possesses, the system of exchange must preserve not only the right to consume or alienate commodities but also the basis of that proprietorship, the quantities accumulated by individual agents. But this basis is crucially dependent upon relations of equality. Inequality in exchange would lead to an increase or diminution of the quantities of wealth possessed by each of the agents of commodity circulation.

The Problem of Exchange

From our perspective, the structure of Marx's argument in *Capital* is such that, far from taking the exchange of commodities as a given, it presents this exchange as a problem—a problem we have reproduced here as the contradiction between equal and unequal exchange. The theoretical resolution of this problem lies in Marx's reference to a particular form of subjectivity and consciousness, a subjectivity and consciousness of objectification, which is characteristic of "individuals" as specifically historical agents of a capitalist social formation. Our discussion of the category of value in the context of this theoretical problem makes it clear, we believe, that the structure of Marx's argument can be insightfully read as nondeterministic. In fact, our location of Marx's discourse in opposition to the discourse of the classical political economists suggests a way of construing Marxism as a pointedly antideterminist discourse. In place of economic determinism, the concept of overdetermination can be used to structure Marx's categories as depictions of a complex, historical interaction among economic, political, and cultural processes.

In our presentation, the act of exchange is not simply the site of an *economic* process but also one of the key locations within capitalism where a symbolic order is partially constituted and learned. Thus, the consciousness of individuality does not *reflect* objective economic conditions. If individuality as a form of social agency were secured by the economy, then we would only need to read the objective economic conditions and deduce from them a consciousness and behavior whose determinations would necessarily derive from a knowledge of those conditions. If this were the case, *either* agents would themselves have to "know" the concrete economic conditions objectively and turn that knowledge into their own subjectivity, *or* we, the theorists, would have to presume that the consciousness of these agents would have to mirror unconsciously—and, perhaps, in an inverted, "false" form—the concrete processes in which these agents would be inscribed. Presentations of the consciousness of individuality as a false consciousness usually employ one or both of these presumptions.

The treatment of exchange as an overdetermined site in which a symbolic order is partly constituted differentiates our reading from those that presume already-formed agents whose false consciousness prevents them from recognizing the reality of an economic process that is external, but necessary, to their essential constitution. The fact that individuals treat trade as an exchange of equivalents does not warrant the conclusion that these agents have a false consciousness. No discursive privilege should be assigned to the ability, or willingness, of these agents to "see," or "not see," exchange as a trading of equal, or unequal, labor time.

Marx argued that "value transforms every product of labour into a social hieroglyphic."[41] But in our view, this statement and his ensuing discussion can be read to suggest that the construction of commodity exchange in terms of labor values (a form of "decipherment," as Marx puts it) is itself a particular consciousness produced within the capitalist social formation. If the agents of exchange do *not* read commodity relations in terms of the exchange of labor time, this must be explained in terms of the sociopolitical generation of a particular form of subjectivity and consciousness—individuality—and not in terms of an inability of these agents to perceive an underlying reality *correctly*.

In a capitalist social formation, given the existence of individuals, trade is constructed as an equal exchange. There are, however, different bases for conceiving or enacting that equality. Marx constructed a conceptual basis for equal exchange with the concept of socially necessary labor time. Neoclassical theorists conceive equal exchange on the basis of utility. Of course, the establishment of equality on the one or the other basis—assuming that agents behave exactly in the ways depicted by Marx or the neoclassicals—does have different economic, political, and cultural effects.

What Marx was getting at with the concept of commodity fetishism was exactly a recognition of these different effects, not a reduction of bourgeois ideology to an expression of a given economic structure. It is this reduction, to which our argument stands opposed, that continues to deprive Marxism to this day both of a theory of subjectivity founded on the premise of the "relative autonomy" of forms of consciousness and action, and of a theory of value in which social agency is a necessary and constituent aspect of the depiction of the economic practices of market capitalism.

41. Marx, *Capital*, 1:167.

Maleficium: State Fetishism

Michael Taussig

> We spent our time fleeing from the objective into the subjective and
> from the subjective into objectivity. This game of hide-and-seek will
> end only when we have the courage to go to the limits of ourselves
> in both directions at once. At the present time, we must bring to
> light the subject, the guilty one, that monstrous and wretched bug
> which we are likely to become at any moment. Genet holds the
> mirror up to us: we must look at it and see ourselves.
>
> —Jean-Paul Sartre, *Saint Genet*

The State as Fetish

Fetishism elucidates a certain quality of ghostliness in objects
in the modern world and an uncertain quality of fluctuation between
thinghood and spirit ("fleeing from the objective into the subjective and
from the subjective into the objectivity"—as Sartre puts it in his work on
Genet). But unlike Walter Benjamin and Theodor Adorno, the celebrated
theorists of commodity fetishism, I wish to focus attention on what I call
State fetishism.[1] For the pundits this can be seen as an element in the
necessary task of bringing German theory into closer connection with a
stream of French radicalism that surfaces with Bataille and Genet. But it
is also very much a personal quest concerning the mystical foundations
of State authority.

---

1. My own introduction to the cultural study of the modern State and grasp of this
as a problem worth thinking about comes from Philip Corrigan and Derek Sayer, eds.,
The Great Arch: English State Formation as Cultural Revolution (Oxford: Basil Blackwell, 1985), by way of the insights and encouragement of Professor Bernard Cohn of
the University of Chicago.

It is to the peculiar sacred and erotic attraction, even thralldom, combined with disgust, which the State holds for its subjects, that I wish to draw attention in drawing the figure of State fetishism. And here we would do well to recall that for Nietzsche, good and evil, intertwined in the double helix of attraction and repulsion, are so many aesthetic-moralistic renderings of the social structure of might. In the considerable, indeed massive, might of the modern State we encounter the most fabulous machination for such rendering. "I know nothing sublime," wrote the young Edmund Burke in his inquiry into our ideas of the beautiful, "which is not some modification of power."[2] But how is it possible to emote an abstraction, and what do I mean by State fetishism?

By State fetishism I mean a certain aura of might as figured by the Leviathan or, in a quite different mode, by Hegel's intricately argued vision of the State as not merely the embodiment of reason, of the Idea, but also as an impressively organic unity, something much greater than the sum of its parts.[3] We are dealing with an obvious, yet neglected topic, clumsily if precisely put as the cultural constitution of the modern State—with a big S—the fetish quality of whose holism can be nicely brought to our self-awareness by pointing not only to the habitual way we so casually entify "the State" as a being unto itself, animated with a will and mind of its own, but also by pointing to the not infrequent signs of exasperation provoked by the aura of the big S—as with Shlomo Avineri, for instance, writing in the introduction to his book *Hegel's Theory of the Modern State*:

> Once one writes "State" rather than "state," Leviathan and Behemoth are already casting their enormous and oppressive shadows.[4]

While the celebrated anthropologist A. R. Radcliffe-Brown (in his student days nicknamed "Anarchy" Brown), in the preface to the classic *African Political Systems* (first published in 1940), also puts his finger on the palpable unreality of State fetishism when he denounces it as *fictional*.[5] Yet he writes as if mere words, very much including his own,

2. Edmund Burke, *A Philosophical Inquiry into the Origin of Our Idea of the Sublime and Beautiful*, ed. and with an Introduction by Adam Phillips (New York: Oxford University Press, 1990), 59.

3. Thomas Hobbes, *Leviathan, or The Matter, Forme, and Power of a Commonwealth Ecclesiasticall and Civil* (New York: Macmillan, 1962), 132.

4. Shlomo Avineri, *Hegel's Theory of the Modern State* (Cambridge: Cambridge University Press, 1972), ix.

5. A. R. Radcliffe-Brown, Preface to *African Political Systems*, ed. Meyer Fortes and E. E. Evans-Pritchard (1940; New York: Oxford University Press, 1970), xxiii.

were weapons that could whisk away even the spell of their own mischief.

> In writings on political institutions there is a good deal of discussion about the nature and origin of the State, which is usually represented as being an entity over and above the human individuals who make up a society, having as one of its attributes something called 'sovereignty,' and sometimes spoken of as having a will (law being often defined as the will of the State) or as issuing commands. *The State in this sense does not exist in the phenomenal world; it is a fiction of the philosophers.*[6]

"What does exist," Radcliffe-Brown goes on to declaim, "is an organization, i.e. a collection of individual human beings connected to a complex set of relations." He insists that "there is no such thing as the power of the State; there are only, in reality, powers of individuals—kings, prime ministers, magistrates, policemen, party bosses and voters." Please note here the repeated emphasis on Being—on "what does exist," and powers contained therein. It's all so plausible at first and so desirable too, this seduction by real reality, real policemen, real kings, and real voters. And don't think I'm pulling your leg here. Jean Genet might pull at the policeman's penis in search of the really real. But we who might learn some lessons about Stately reality from Anarchy-Brown and the genealogy of Anthropology figured by his stately presence should pause and think about why he is so hostile to what he describes as the fiction of the State—the big S. For what the notion of State fetishism directs us to is the existence and reality of the *political power* of this *fiction*, its powerful insubstantiality.

The State as Mask

Some thirty years after Radcliffe-Brown's dismissive *pronunciamento* on the unreality of the big S, Philip Abrams in a truly path-breaking analysis referred to this fiction in a way at once more clear and more complicating:

> The state is not the reality which stands behind the mask of political practice. It is itself the mask which prevents our seeing political practice as it is [and] it starts its life as an implicit construct; it is then reified—as the *res publica*, the public reification, no less—and acquires

6. Ibid., emphasis added.

an overt symbolic identity progressively divorced from practice as an illusory account of practice.[7]

And he calls on sociologists to attend to the senses in which the state does not exist. Like Avineri he sees the big S as misrepresentation— Radcliffe-Brown's "fiction"—yet credits it, as does Avineri, with mighty force, not merely in the maw of Leviathan but more to the point in workaday "democracies" such as Great Britain's, where "armies and prisons, the Special patrol and the deportation orders as well as the whole process of fiscal extraction" critically depend on State fetishism.[8] For, he argues, it is the association of these repressive instruments "with the idea of the state and the invocation of that idea that silences protest, excuses force and convinces the rest of us that the fate of the victims is just and necessary."[9]

Now the question has to be raised as to what can be done to this misrepresentation by means of which reification acquires alarming fetish power? Abrams's striking figure of mask and reality—of the State not as the reality behind the mask of political reality but as the mask that prevents our seeing political reality—is a dazzling and disturbing representation. For it not only implicates the State in the cultural construction of reality but delineates that reality as inherently deceptive, real and unreal at one and the same time—in short, a thoroughly nervous Nervous System.

Therefore how strikingly fitting, how (unintentionally) magical, is Abrams's response to the power of the reality effect of the mask. "My suggestion," he writes,

> is that we should recognize that cogency of the *idea* of the state as an ideological power and treat that as a compelling object of analysis. But the very reasons that require us to do that also require us not to *believe* in the idea of the state, not to concede, even as an abstract formal-object, the existence of the state.[10]

And as an inspired Dada-like shock-tactic exercise in how to pull this off, he recommends that we should, as an experiment, try substituting the word *God* for the word *state*—which is exactly what I intend to do

7. Philip Abrams, "Notes on the Difficulty of Studying the State," *Journal of Historical Sociolcgy* 1, no. 1 (1988): 58.
    8. Ibid., 77.
    9. Ibid., 79.
    10. Ibid., 79.

since State fetishism begs just such an excursus, provided one is up to dealing with the profound ambiguity that, according to one track of influential Western analysis, the sacred is said to contain.

The Impure Sacred

What I want to consider is the everlastingly curious notion, bound to raise hackles, that not only God but evil is part of the notion of sacredness—that bad is not just bad but holy to boot. Emile Durkheim in 1912 labeled this holy evil the "impure sacred" and scantly illustrated it in but seven pages of his major work on primitive religion by references to the fresh human corpse, to the forces conjured by the sorcerer, and to the blood issuing from the genital organs of women—all of which, he insisted from his ethnographic evidence from central Australia as much as from W. Robertson Smith's *Religion of the Semites*, inspired men with fear, into which horror generally entered, yet could, through a simple modification of external circumstance, become holy and propitious powers endowing life. While according to this formulation there is the most radical antagonism between the pure and the impure sacred, there is, nevertheless, close kinship between them, as exhibited in the fact that the respect accorded the pure sacred is not without a measure of horror and the fear accorded the impure sacred is not without reverence. Hence not just Genet the homosexual in a homophobic society, not just Genet the thief in a State built on the right to property, but *Saint* Genet.

Reason and Violence

> Before you use military force, you should use the force of reason.
> —Governor Mario Cuomo, speaking during the violent New York
> State dispute over gambling on the Mohawk reservation

Where this confluence of the pure with the impure sacred is most relevant to the modern State is at the point where the crucial issue of "legitimacy" of the institution abuts what Max Weber regarded as a crucial part of the definition of the State—namely, its monopoly on the legitimate use of violence within a given territory. The other part of that definition, of course, as with Hegel's, is the State's embodiment of Reason, as in the bureaucratic forms.

What needs emphasis here is how this conjuncture of violence and reason is so obvious, and yet is at the same time denied, and therefore how important it is for acute understanding of the cultural practice of Statecraft to appreciate the very obtuseness of this obviousness, as when we scratch our heads about the concept of "war crimes"—it being legal for the U.S. State to bomb the Iraqi enemy incessantly but a crime for the Iraqi State to beat up the pilots dropping the bombs. Such legal niceties testify to the self-contradictory and ever more absolutely necessary attempts to rationalize violence. That is why there is something frightening, I think, merely in saying that this conjunction of reason and violence exists, not only because it makes violence scary, as if imbued with the greatest legitimating force there can be, reason itself, and not only because it makes reason scary by indicating how it's snuggled deep into the armpit of terror, but also because we so desperately need to cling to reason—as instituted—as the bulwark against the terrifying anomie and chaos pressing in on all sides. There has to be a reason, and we have to use reason. Yet another part of us welcomes the fact that reason—as instituted—has violence at its disposal, because we feel that that very anomie and chaos will respond to naught else. And consider how we slip in and out of recognition and disavowal. Consider this as Stately cultural practice. Nothing could be more obvious than that the State, with its big S rearing, uses the sweet talk of reason and reasonable rules as its velvet glove around the fist of steel. This is folklore. This is an instinctual way of reacting to the big S. But on the other hand this conjunction of reason and violence rapidly becomes confusing when we slow down a little and try to figure it out: So much reason versus so many units of violence? The mere threat of violence hovering way in the background of Kafka's cave? Different types of people affected in different places, and different times getting a different mix? And so forth. Weber himself registers this latent yet vital presence of violence when he notes in his famous essay "Politics as a Vocation," delivered at Munich University in 1918, that even with the legitimacy of domination based on rationally created rules (which he portrays as "the domination exercised by the modern 'servant of the state' and by all bearers of power who in this respect resemble him"), "it is to be understood that, in reality, obedience is determined by highly robust motives of fear and hope."[11]

In noting Weber's inclusion of if not emphasis on violence as what defines the modern State, we cannot forget how decidedly flat, how instrumental, his notion of violence generally seems to be; how decidedly reified it is, as if violence were a substance, so many ergs of

11. Max Weber, "Politics as a Vocation," in *From Max Weber: Essays in Sociology,* Trans. Hans Gerth and C. Wright Mills (London: Routledge and Kegan Paul, 1948), 79.

spermatic effluvial power that the father exerts in the private fastness of the family, with permission of the State, and that the State exerts over civil society and, at times, over other States. What are missing here, and I mean this to be a decisive critique, are the intrinsically mysterious, mystifying, convoluting, plain scary, mythical, and arcane cultural properties and power of violence to the point where violence is very much an end in itself—a sign, as Benjamin put it, of the existence of the gods.[12]

So, what I wish to suggest with considerable urgency is that what is politically important in my notion of State fetishism is not only that this necessary institutional interpenetration of reason by violence diminishes the claims of reason, casting it into ideology, mask, and effect of power, but also that *it is precisely the coming together of reason and violence in the State that creates, in a secular and modern world, the bigness of the big S*—not merely its apparent unity and the fictions of will and mind thus inspired, but the quasi-sacred quality of that very inspiration, a quality we quite willingly impute to the ancient States of China, Egypt, and Peru, for example, or to European absolutism, but not to the rational-legal State that now stands as ground to our being as citizens of the world.

1886, A Surreal Moment, the Reemergence of the Sacred: Torture Should Give Way to Totemism

I hope that Messrs. Black [publishers of the *Encyclopaedia Britannica*] understand that Totemism is a subject of growing importance, daily mentioned in magazines and papers, but of which there is no good account anywhere—precisely one of those cases where we have an opportunity of being ahead of every one and getting some reputation. There is no article in the volume for which I am more solicitous. I have taken much personal pains with it, guiding [James George] Frazer carefully in his treatment; and he has put about seven months hard work on it to make it the standard article on the subject. We must make room for it, whatever else goes. "Torture," though a nice paper, is not at all necessary, for people can learn about torture elsewhere, and the subject is one of decaying and not of rising interest.

> —W. Robertson Smith, author of *The Religion of the
> Semites,* in a letter of 1886 to the publisher of
> the *Encyclopaedia Britannica,* of which he was editor

12. I am indebted to Adam Ashforth for bringing this observation of Benjamin's to my attention.

The State as Sacred: Rejuxtaposing the Colonial Gaze

Elsewhere—always elsewhere. Decay. But a nice paper. Such is the fate of torture, especially in the face of the rising star of totemism. So much for the decline of the sacred. That is why the restoration of the sacred as an object worthy of study by Georges Bataille's College of Sociology group in the late 1930s, and precisely its attempt to examine the place of the sacred in the modern State, strikes me as being an eminently timely task—a task that I myself see as involving a somewhat larger project, yet to be worked out—namely, that of rejuxtaposing the terms of the colonial inquiry, recycling and thus transforming the anthropology developed in Europe and North America through the study of colonized peoples back into and onto the societies in which it was instituted, where the terms and practices imposed upon and appropriated from the colonies, such as *fetish*, *sorcery* (the *maleficium*), and *taboo*, are redeemed and come alive with new intensity.[13] As will become obvious from even this short attempt, such a rejuxtaposition is hardly a simple practice, certainly more than just reversing the light from the dark zones of empire. Let us begin with the fetish.

The Fetish: Genealogy of Making

Bill Pietz has presented us with a genealogy of the *fetish* that grounds this eminently strange word in the praxis of *making*, rooted in strategic social relationships of trade, religion, slaving, and modern science.[14] To this end, he discusses certain social practices in the commerce of ancient Rome (separating natural products from *factitious*, artificially cultivated, ones), in early Roman Christianity (with God making man in

13. In his Foreword to an exhaustive collection of essays and talks prepared by the group around Bataille, Roger Caillois, and Michel Leiris (to name the best known), Denis Hollier indicates the college's vexed dependence on Durkheim and his school, especially in relation to the place of the "primitive" and "the sacred" in modern West European society. Denis Hollier, ed., *The College of Sociology, 1937–39* (Minneapolis: University of Minnesota Press, 1988). While many of the key concepts of Durkheim, almost by default, would be theirs too, there were also profound differences, beginning with the question that formed the basis of their project—namely, the place of the sacred in modernity. Another outstanding difference is the college's notion of the sacred as not only a force for Durkheimian social solidarity but also the opposite, the sacred as an excess, as "the outburst," as Caillois (*College of Sociology*, 152) put it in 1938, "of violations of the rules of life," which is, of course, thoroughly consistent with Bataille's fascination with taboo and transgression—a "post-Durkheimian" rewriting of the liberal problematic of reason and violence.

14. William Pietz, "The Problem of the Fetish," part 1, *Res* 9 (Spring 1985): 5–17.

his image, but man denied, therefore, similar sorts of making), the "bad making" of the *maleficium* of the magic of the Middle Ages, the notion of the fetish or *fetisso* in the Portuguese pidgin trading language of the West African slave routes, and finally, the positivist rendering of fetishism as the sheen or mystical counterpart to their virtual worship of objectness. Quite a story.

To develop and bring to our comprehension a genealogy like this strikes me as curiously analogous to the fetish itself, in that such genealogizing assumes that the meaning of the word bears traces of epochal histories of trading with the edges of the known universe and that, although it is these traces that endow the word—as Raymond Williams in his *Keywords* might have said—with an active social history pushing into and activated by the present, these trace meanings are nevertheless largely or completely lost to present consciousness.[15] What is left, active and powerful, is the word itself—enigmatically incomplete. Just the signifier, we could say, bereft of its erased significations gathered and dissipated through the mists of trade, religion, witchcraft, slavery, and what has come to be called science—and this is precisely the formal mechanism of fetishism (as we see it used by Marx and by Freud), whereby the signifier depends upon yet erases its signification.

What Pietz does with his genealogizing is to restore the traces and erasures and weave a spell around what is, socially speaking, at stake in *making*. This amounts to a European history of consciousness making itself through making objects, and this involves a compulsion to fuse and separate and fuse once again the maker with the making with the thing made, wrestling poignantly and urgently with what we might call Vico's insight, which is also Marx's: God made nature, but man makes history and thus can come to understand history by understanding this making. In short, the fetish takes us into the realm of praxis, and to genealogize the fetish the way Pietz does is in effect to problematize praxis—the subject making itself through making the object—and by the same token to take us into the realm of "agency"—the vexing problem of individual versus social determination. Now, in the genealogy of fetishism as I write it, this vexing issue can be translated into a confrontation of sorcery with sociology, the sorcery that informed the fetish word in the era of Iberian expansion into Africa and the colonization of the New World, namely, the sorcery of the *maleficium*, on the one hand, and *sociology*, as with Comte's successor Emile Durkheim, the sociologist's

15. Raymond Williams, *Keywords: A Vocabulary of Culture and Society* (New York: Oxford University Press, 1976).

sociologist, on the other. It is to sociology as a form of inquiry enlivened by fetish powers that I now turn, and later, with Genet, to the revelatory epistemology of the *maleficium*.

Sociology

> It was Durkheim and not the savage who made society into a god.
> —E. E. Evans-Pritchard in *Nuer Religion*

How strange and multitudinous a notion "society" becomes when we thingify it, as if this very act makes it slip away from us. "Social facts are things," Durkheim grimly reiterated time and again in *The Rules of Sociological Method* (first published in 1895), as if desperate to nail down this elusive thinghood. Things of God or things made? we might ask in turn, with a twinge of anxiety, perhaps, pondering the place of things-made in the abyss created in the curt language of Colombian sorcery between God and the sorcerer. And in keeping with that discourse should we not allow the terminology to express its sacral bent more fully and instead of saying social facts are *things* say that social facts are *reification*, thus entering not only into the sacrosanct language of Latin but into the holy darkness created by the Lukácsian *thing* (as in "Reification and the Consciousness of the Proletariat")? Thus Steven Lukes in his study of Durkheim aptly pinpoints the crucial flip-flop from *res* to *deus*, the instability at the heart of the fetishization of "society"—from thing to god.

> Hence, above all, [Durkheim's] talk of "*la société*" as a "reality" distinct from the "individual," which led him to reify, even deify "society," to treat it as a *deus ex machina*, to attribute to it "powers and qualities as mysterious and baffling as any assigned to the gods by the religions of this world."[16]

The dismay expressed by exponents of Anglo common sense at what is seen as mysticism in Durkheim's sociology is as ubiquitous as it is self-defeating. Hence the valiant attempts (as with Radcliffe-Brown and Evans-Pritchard, for example) to extract social facticity clean of its mystical penumbra. Take this heroic attempt to sever the Durkheimian

16. Steven Lukes, *Emile Durkheim: His Life and Work* (Harmondsworth, Eng.: Penguin Books, 1973), 34–35.

twins, the social *fact* from the social *conscience collective* in the Introduction to the English translation of the *Rules:*

> Durkheim's method, most suggestive in itself, yet involves, it so hap-
> pens, the use of the hypothesis of a collective consciousness; it results
> in a deplorable effort to interpret social phenomena in terms of this
> alleged consciousness [and thus] Durkheim is not singular among men
> of science in being more valuable in respect of the by-products of his
> theory than in his main contention.[17]

And that erratic genius, Georges Sorel, himself no slouch when it came
to both using and theorizing the powers of mystery in modern society (as
in his *Reflections on Violence,* 1915), claimed that Durkheim said it was
unnecessary to introduce the notion of a social mind but reasoned as if
he were introducing it.[18]

In that formidably important book *The Structure of Social Action*
(1937), Talcott Parsons represents this flip-flop from thing to god not as
the inevitable outcome of the very concept of "society" but as a movement embedded in a more familiarly acceptable form, that of narrative—
an adventure of ideas in which first there was the Durkheim of the *Rules*
and *The Division of Labor* (the positivist empiricist who understood
social facts to be things, external and constraining *faits sociaux*), and
then, years later, emerged a new Durkheim, the idealist, beginning with
his desire to identify the crucial quality of social facticity as legal and
normative rules resulting, finally, in his emphasis on the weave of moral
obligations as the constitutive basis of "society."[19]

We will have need to recall this adventure of ideas from *res* to *deus*
through the various types of rules—of fact, of law, of norm, and of
morality—when we come to a certain sexual quality of the law and of
breaking the law, the beauty and libidinality of transgression, the place
of the sacred in the profanity of modern life, particularly French versions of that life, from Georges Bataille's College of (non-Parsonian) Sociology of the late 1930s, to the postwar period with Jean Genet. Suffice
it to say that this noble attempt to invent for the Founding Father of
Sociology a narrative of the concept "society," first thing, then God, is

17. George Catlin, "Introduction to the Translation," in Emile Durkheim, *The Rules
of Sociological Method,* trans. Sarah A. Solovay and John H. Mueller (New York: Free
Press, 1964), xiv.
18. Lukes, *Durkheim,* 12.
19. Talcott Parsons, *The Structure of Social Action: A Study in Social Theory with
Special Reference to a Group of Recent European Writers* (New York: Free Press,
1937).

the consequence of the inability to appreciate that the concept may be *both things simultaneously* and, in any event, the fetish character of the "social fact" as sheer thing and as moral thing is here strikingly conveyed. Which brings us to totems, their sacred power, and the rule of old men.

Intoxication

The fetish is extensively theorized—not as fetish but as totem[20]—in what is in many ways Durkheim's greatest work, *The Elementary Forms of Religious Life* (1912), the work that Parsons sees as occupying the crucial point in the adventure of ideas where the thing becomes a god.[21] There is poignancy in Parsons's representation of this travail of ideas from thing to God for it is an inexorable journey and the stakes are high: the base of knowledge itself. Parsons writes:

> This tendency [to emphasize the idea and value factor in the constitution of society] culminated in his sociological epistemology where he identified the social factor with the a priori source of the [Kantian] categories, thus finally breaking the bond which had held it as a part of empirical reality. But having done this it was impossible for him to get back to empirical reality.[22]

20. As far as I can determine, Durkheim uses the term *fetish* but once in *The Elementary Forms of Religious Life*, trans. Joseph Ward Swain (New York: Free Press, 1965), 144, and does so in order to disassociate the totem from it. But this dissociation is implausible and probably reflects his need to distance himself from the theory of animism and fetishism put forward by the British anthropologist E. B. Tylor. Durkheim's sociological analysis of "totemism" (guided by extant ethnography), in particular his tying sacred designs to a specific and bounded social grouping (hence "society"), is now considered quite wrong in important ways, ways that reflect profoundly on the present-day politics of land claims by Aboriginal people against the Australian State. For important revisions of the sociology of Australian "totemism," see W. E. H. Stanner, "Religion, Totemism, and Symbolism," in *White Men Got No Dreaming* (Canberra: Australian National University Press, 1979), 106–43, and also his "Reflections on Durkheim and Aboriginal Religion," in *Social Organization: Essays Presented to Raymond Firth*, ed. Maurice Freedman (Chicago: Aldine, 1967), 217–40. For a debunking of the social philosophical basis of the anthropology of totemism, see Claude Lévi-Strauss, *Totemism*, trans. Rodney Needham (Boston: Beacon Press, 1963).

21. Parsons, *Structure of Social Action*, 469, footnotes that Durkheim failed to admit that there was any such transformation.

22. Ibid., 469.

It must be chilling to lock yourself out of empirical reality. But when confronted by the fact that it was this very "sociological epistemology" that allowed for the brilliance of the *Année sociologique* school, I wonder if it was such a terrible fate. My argument, of course, is that this brilliance was not the result of a step-by-step development from social fact as thing to social fact as moral web and the fetishization of Society (as *deus*), but instead, it was the result of a specific epistemic tension within the very notion of the Social as both thing and godly at one and the same time. In other words, far from being an unfortunate side effect, it was Durkheim's very fetishization of "society" that provided the intellectual power of his sociology. Reification-and-fetishism—*res* and *deus*—was a powerful mode of reckoning in modern society, nowhere more so than when applied to "society" itself, and Durkheim was correct in problematizing—to the degree of fanaticism—the invisible presence, the intangibility, the literally unspeakable but begging to be spoken nature of "society." That is why I think it is so halfhearted, so mindlessly self-congratulatory to incessantly make the criticism that he (to follow Lukes): "reified" the distinctions between society and the individual "into the abstractions of 'society' and the 'individual.' Indeed as Morris Ginsberg justly observed, 'in general "la société" had an intoxicating effect on his mind, hindering further analysis.' "[23]

But as against these strictures of Messrs. Ginsberg and Lukes, isn't it this very intoxication that, far from hindering, facilitates further analysis? Instead of trying to cleave what is taken to be sober from intoxicated thought, why not seize upon the intoxication itself and wonder why—as so named—it is so necessary and powerful a force in this influential sociology centrally located in the positivist tradition? As Walter Benjamin, following the surrealists, might have elaborated in his analysis of modern society as animated by new mythic powers located in the tactility of the commodity image, the task is neither to resist nor to admonish the fetish quality of modern culture but rather to acknowledge, even submit to, its fetish powers and attempt to channel them in revolutionary directions. Get with it! Get in touch with the fetish! This exhortation points the way to an aptly critical, aptly synergistic, sociology of modernity.[24]

---

23. Lukes, *Durkheim*, 21.
24. Walter Benjamin, "Surrealism: The Last Snapshot of the European Intelligentsia," in *Reflections*, trans. Edmund Jephcott (New York: Harcourt Brace Jovanovich, 1978), 177–92. Of course I have taken great liberties here with Benjamin's suggestion.

In Touch with the Fetish: Inscription and Erasure

A picture keeps swimming in and out of focus in *The Elementary Forms*. It comes from Baldwin Spencer and F. J. Gillen's two pioneering ethnographies (1899, 1904) of people native to central and north-central Australia, and it concerns the character of sacred objects called *churinga*, the way in which they are touched and rubbed, the way in which they are emblematized with abstract designs and—according to Durkheim—stand in some ineffably complex way, involving the erasure of their meaning as signs, for the abstraction that is our old, otherwise unrepresentable friend "society" itself. It turns out that it is from the peculiar way in which these objects embody and erase that embodiment of society that their sacred power derives.

To read Durkheim is to feel the force of these mysterious objects, standing at the center of group cults and at one time thought by many anthropologists to represent, as "totemism," a universal stage in the history of religion, serving, among other functions, to hold a group together. Concentrating great power, which "radiates to a distance and communicates itself to all the surroundings," having marvelous properties to heal sickness and ensure the reproduction of animal and plant life, the powers of these sacred objects can be communicated to officiants and their assistants by being "rubbed over the members and stomachs of the faithful after being covered with grease."[25] Throughout the *Elementary Forms* (as Rodney Needham and Roger Keesing have pointed out) Durkheim reifies whatever it is that is meant by sanctity, representing it as a spreading force such as might be conveyed by electricity or by fluids, unprepared contact with which can be shocking and even fatal.[26]

It is, strangely enough, the designs on the churinga that seem to Durkheim necessary to this force: "Now in themselves, the churinga are objects of wood and are distinguished from profane things of the same sort by only one particularity: this is that the totemic mark is drawn or engraved upon them. *So it is the mark and this alone which gives them their sacred character.*"[27] Absolutely crucial to this argument is that the mark, which bestows sanctity, is in itself not only sanctifying but *is more*

25. Durkheim, *Elementary Forms*, 142–43.
26. Roger Keesing, "Rethinking Mana," *Journal of Anthropological Research* 40 (1984): 137–56. Also Rodney Needham, "Skulls and Causality," *Man*, n.s., 11 (1977): 71–78. I thank Nick Thomas for these references. This image of magical force as miasma is also crucial to Freud's analysis of imitation and contagion in *Totem and Taboo*.
27. Durkheim, *Elementary Forms*, 144, emphasis added. It is obvious from Spencer and Gillen that the designs and the churingas are far from being all that goes into invoking sacred power. These elements are inserted into performative routines in which singing the dreamtime and dance are essential. Durkheim himself cites many passages indicating as much. Nevertheless, it is to the designs on the objects that he attributes central importance.

This empty space is where I would like to have presented Spencer and Gillen's drawing of the frog totem because it seems to me next to impossible to get the points about representation across without this amazing image. But my friend Professor Annette Hamilton, of Macquarie University, Sydney, tells me that to reproduce the illustration would be considered sacrilege by many Aboriginal people—which vindicates the power not only of the design but of the prohibitions against its being seen.

sacred than what it represents—the totem, animal species, whatever. Let us take this step by step.

Durkheim stresses that the sacred nature of the object comes not from imputations of an inner soul or from the object's being an image of an ancestor's body, but "from some other source, and whence could it come, if not from the totemic stamp which it bears? It is to this image, therefore, that the demonstrations of the rite are really addressed; it is this which sanctifies the object upon which it is carved."[28]

The designs represent definite and specific things, what he calls *totems*, such as trees, frogs, kangaroos. But the designs themselves are stupendously abstract, dots and circles—which fact Durkheim's seizes upon with the curiously mimetic argument that this abstraction indicates the diffuse and abstract character of "society" (which, in his reading, the design stands for).[29] In the picture of a design of the frog totem (dreaming) I would have liked to have presented from Spencer and Gillen's 1899 monograph, the three large concentric circles—according

28. Ibid., 145.
29. He employs this argument vigorously with regard to what he identifies as sacred force in the principles *mana* in Oceania, and *wakan* in North America, and so forth.

to their "level" of interpretation—represent celebrated eucalyptus trees along the Hugh River at Imanda, which, Spencer and Gillen say, is the center of the particular group of the frog totem to which the owner of the totem belonged.[30]

The straight lines on one side of the churinga represent the trees' large roots, and the little curved lines at one end stand for the smaller roots. Note that frogs are said to come out of the roots of these trees. Smaller concentric circles represent smaller roots of trees, and, in what to me is a radical shift in representational logic, the dotted lines alongside the edge of the churinga are tracks of frogs hopping in the sand of the riverbed. We would probably want to call this an abstract—a superabstract—representation, but it also has a decidedly mimetic concreteness, as registered by those frog tracks. This type of abstraction thus turns out to be curiously complex, somewhat like the fetish itself—spiritually material, materialistically spiritual.

Now the peculiar conflation and destabilization of (what we generally take to be) abstraction and figuration are intimately bound to the most decisive operation Durkheim carries out in order to derive the very notion of "society" and its sacred quality. I want you to hold these things together—the image of the old men hugging their totems; the terrific physicality of those mysterious objects; the central importance Durkheim gives to the design over and beyond what the design represents; the curious abstractness of the design—and I want you to realize that everything turns on his proposal that the representation is more important than the represented, that the totemic design itself is not only sacred and powerful but more so than the totemic species or entity it represents, and more so than the clan it also represents, because it *in some way* represents the great and complex abstraction "society." The question then fairly becomes: what is this way—the way, we might say, of the fetish itself?

What seems crucial in this predominance of the signifier over the signified is a certain materialization: materialization by inscription. The elementary forms are not, to Durkheim's way of thinking, to be saddled with the ur-presence of voice, nor with the handwringing of Lévi-Strauss's appraisal of *civilization* (as in White Man's Civilization) as a writing lesson.[31] To the contrary, writing is the elementary form, lying at

---

30. Baldwin Spencer and F. J. Gillen, *The Native Tribes of Central Australia* (1899; New York: Dover, 1968), 145–47.

31. Claude Lévi-Strauss, "A Writing Lesson," in *Tristes Tropiques: An Anthropological Study of Primitive Societies in Brazil*, trans. John Russell (New York: Atheneum, 1968), 286–97.

the very beginnings of thought itself, in its aboriginality. For Durkheim it is the visual and tactile image that is crucial, not the spoken sign.[32] Furthermore, the representation of the totem by means of a design is, he feels, in response to the basic need to create an image, *no matter what the image is itself!* Put otherwise, the image here is an image of the need for images. In Durkheim's words, the Australian's urge to represent the totem "is in order not to have a portrait of it before his eyes which would constantly renew the sensation of it; it is merely because he feels the need of representing the idea which he forms of it by means of material and external signs, *no matter what these signs may be.*"[33] Given that these signs confer aesthetic value as well as being "above all, a written language," it follows, he says—in one breathtaking swoop—that the origins of design and writing are one and the same and that man "commenced designing, not so much to fix upon wood or stone beautiful forms which charm the senses, as to translate his thought into matter."[34]

The Fetish Is Where Thought and Object Interpenetrate in the Significance of Collective Sentiment

It is, of course, in this very reciprocation of thought in worked matter and of worked matter in thought that much of the puzzle of fetishism lies. This is where I began, following Pietz's genealogy of the fetish from ancient Roman trading through modern slaving as a genealogy of praxis, of the maker making him/herself. And this reciprocation of thought in worked matter and of such matter in thought is crucial to Durkheim's most basic propositions concerning the nature of thought and its relation to "society." Elsewhere in *Elementary Forms* the Father of Sociology states that "in general a collective sentiment can become conscious of itself only by being fixed upon some material object; but by virtue of this very fact, *it participates in the nature of this object, and reciprocally, the object participates in its nature.*" He also states that "the emblem is not merely a convenient process for clarifying the sentiment society has of itself; it also serves to create this sentiment; it is one of its constituent elements."[35]

Thus does matter itself—the object—displace the social character of the social construction of signs.

---

32. Durkheim, *Elementary Forms,* 266.
33. Ibid., 149, emphasis added.
34. Ibid.
35. Ibid., 269, emphasis added.

Sociology as the Art of Magical Correspondences

This reciprocation of collective thought in matter and of matter in collective thought, such that worked-upon matter itself acquires an animated and hence a fetish character, is crucial for what Talcott Parsons calls Durkheim's "sociological epistemology," whereby Durkheim sociologizes Kant's schematism with often wonderful results (as is also the case, for instance, in the gemlike essay of his colleague Robert Hertz, "On the Predominance of the Right Hand").[36] What I think is exceedingly remarkable here is not just the boldness of Durkheim's sociological argument that Kant's a priori categories of space, time, cause, and so forth stem from and express socially established classification, as in settlement pattern and kinship, but that the epistemic basis of the science of sociology he was forging completely depends on an unacknowledged yet profoundly magical notion of natural correspondences.[37]

He asks whether the (Kantian) categories, because they directly translate social organization, can be applied to the rest of nature only as metaphors, as "artificial symbols" with "no connection with reality." And he answers with a decisive No! The connections are real and not artificial because society is part of nature; that is why "ideas elaborated on the model of social things can aid us in thinking of another department of nature."

It is at least true that if these ideas play the role of symbols when they are turned aside from their original signification, *they are at least well-founded symbols*. If a sort of artificiality enters into them from the mere fact that they are constructed concepts, it is an artificiality which follows nature very closely and which is constantly approaching it still more closely.[38]

In other words, it is the *social* origin of the ideas of time, space, class,

36. Parsons, *Structure of Social Action*, 268.
37. See also Durkheim and Marcel Mauss, *Primitive Classification* (1903), trans. Rodney Needham (Chicago: University of Chicago Press, 1963).
38. Durkheim, *Elementary Forms*, 31, emphasis added.

cause, or personality that leads to the theorem "that they are not without foundation in the nature of things."[39]

Where does this leave us with regard to (Durkheimian) Sociology—the modern science of man? What seemed like the most rigorous case that could ever be put for a science of society as an autonomous sphere, now suddenly collapses in on itself, imploding into nature with which it becomes subtly congruous.

This I take to be the law of the fetish itself. The most rigorously sociological sociology in the history of Western Man turns out to be bound, tooth and claw, to fetishism, from which it is itself inseparable and of which it becomes exemplary.

The Peeling Off of the Signifier and the Power Thereof

Durkheim provides spellbinding evocations of what I can only call imageric seduction, first of the natives, then—through them—of us. "It is the emblem that is sacred," he reiterates, and in noting that it can be painted on the body and on the rock face of caves, he attempts to invoke the attitude of the beholders toward the image drawn in human blood on the sand for the *intichiuma* ("life-endowing") ritual of the emu totem: "When the design has been made the faithful remain seated on the ground before it, in attitude of the purest devotion. If we give the word a sense corresponding to the mentality of the primitive, we may say that they adore it."[40] What we are inching toward here is a critical dismantling of the sign in which the image lifts off from what it is meant to represent. In this peeling off of the signifier from its signified, *the representation acquires not just the power of the represented but power over it as well.*

The representations of the totem are therefore more actively powerful than the totem itself.[41]

What is fascinating here is that what we might call (with some perplexity) the *image itself* should be granted such a power—not the signified, the sacred object, the totemic species, animal, vegetable, and so

39. Ibid., 32.
40. Ibid., 148. See Spencer and Gillen's version, *Native Tribes of Central Australia*, 181.
41. Durkheim, *Elementary Forms*, 156.

forth, but the signifier in itself prized apart from its signification so as to create a quite different architecture of the sign, an architecture in which the signified is erased. Thus can Durkheim make his final claim that what is "represented" by sacred objects is "society" itself, that "totemism is the religion, not of such and such animals or men or images, but of an anonymous and impersonal force, found in each of these beings but not to be confounded with any of them."[42]

Which force for Jean Baudrillard in the form of the image would be the anonymous and impersonal one of the latest form of the commodity, the force of the capitalist market functioning at its silkiest postmodern best. Which force for Marx in the form of commodity fetishism would exist and be effective *precisely on account of erasure*—of the erasure locked into the commodity in its exchange-value phase, ensuring its dislocation, its being prized apart from the social and particularist context of its production. Which force for Durkheim is "society."[43]

This process of inscription and erasure finds an uncannily mimetic representation in Spencer and Gillen's description of the churinga of the Arunta people of the central desert, and like all mimesis, it inheres in the biological organism, in this case the aged male body, the hands and the stomach, into which the design disappears. While most churinga have patterns incised with the tooth of an opossum, they write, many are "scarcely decipherable, owing to the constant rubbing to which they have been subjected at the hands of generation after generation of natives." For "whenever the churinga are examined by the old men they are, especially the wooden ones, very carefully rubbed over with the hands" and pressed against the stomach.[44]

Maleficium; Bad-Making

In Pietz's genealogy of the fetish, the *maleficium*, or the sorcerer's "bad-making," enjoys a substantial place in the layering of histories that stratify the fetish word. This seems particularly the case for the contribution of the *maleficio* in the Iberian peninsula at the time of Portuguese

---

42. Ibid., 217.
43. Many are the ironies created by such a comparison. Chief of these is that for Marx the primitive world is one in which the social character of the (economic) object is transparent to all involved—quite opposite to the situation he describes for the capitalist economy of nineteenth-century Western Europe. But in Durkheim's argument this is not the case; in primitive society the social character of the (sacred) object is erased.

slave trading along the west coast of Africa and later on during the time of the Spanish expansion into the New World. Hence, as an instance of what I propose as the rejuxtapositioning of the terms of anthropology, I would now like not so much to *study* the sorcerer's tool of the *maleficium* as to *deploy* it as a tactic for drawing out some of the fetish power of the modern State. My deployment is unabashedly plagiaristic and comes in the name of Genet, Saint Genet, who, because of the maleficent role in which Society cast him, and which he so manifestly made the most of, was able, to the extent that love be not blind, to illuminate the fetish force of its Stately prowess. My use of Genet as *maleficium* is not to ensorcell anyone, least of all readers or the State, but rather to do what I have seen the *maleficio* so good at doing over my years spent with healers in southwest Colombia, which is to stir the pot of discussion and scratch heads over the perennial problems of understanding evil and misfortune in relation to social process. The *maleficio*, in other words, brings out the sacred sheen of the secular, and this ability is especially germane to an inquiry into State fetishism in that, as I have said, following Durkheim's view of the sacred, the pure and the impure sacred are violently at odds and passionately interlocked at one and the same time. It is to this ability to draw out the sacred quality of State power, and to out-fetishize its fetish quality, that the *maleficium*—as I use it—speaks eons.

Taboo: Transgression and Fantasy

Predictably, given his emphasis on the representation over the represented, Durkheim states that, "contrarily to all that could be foreseen," the prohibitions referring to the *representation* of the totem are "more numerous, stricter, and more severely enforced than those pertaining to the totem itself." He emphasizes that uninitiated men and all women are prohibited access to the representations. Indeed, the very first thing Spencer and Gillen have to say in their chapter on the churinga is that they are sacred objects "which, on penalty of death or very severe punishment, such as blinding by means of a fire-stick, are never allowed to be seen by women or uninitiated men."[45]

We are then in a situation in which "society," inscribed and erased in thereby sacred objects, can, in this peculiarly objectified and highly concentrated form, be seen and touched only by one presumably rather

44. Durkheim, *Elementary Forms*, 144, 288.
45. Spencer and Gillen, *Native Tribes of Central Australia*, 129.

small group of persons within "society." This situation raises two somewhat unsettling questions. First, whether the sacred force of these objects arises only in conjunction with such seeing, touching, and absorption into the old (or, at least, initiated) male body. Second, whether it is
the object's sacred force that impels such powerful taboos as vividly
expressed in the punishment of blinding with fire or, to the apparent
contrary, *is it the societal prohibition itself*—the taboo—that is decisive
to the sanctification of the object?

This second question tends to undermine a lot of things. It opens us
into another type of world where not the solidity of substance but the
diaphanous veil of negation bears the world on its back, and it makes us
pose further questions: Is the sanctity of the whole that is "society"
always, throughout history, in the hands of a few select men? What
happens to this sacred power, expression of the whole, with the decline
of the power of religion and the emergence of the modern secular State
(the question posed by Bataille's "College of Sociology")? Finally, if it is
restriction to a small group, together with the prohibition, that is decisive in sanctification, might it turn out not that it is the sacred knowledge of myth and ritual *of the initiated* that constitutes the power of the
sacred but that instead such power derives from the *fantasies of the
people prohibited* concerning the nature of that sacred knowledge?

Secrets of State

The real official secret, however, is the secret of the non-existence
of the state.
—Philip Abrams, "Notes on the Difficulty of Studying the State"

Not the anthropology of Australian aborigines but the memoir of a
sheep farmer born in 1874 in Tierra del Fuego provides me with the
secret of the secret, which is to say the real, official secret. The son of
British missionaries, E. Lucas Bridges grew up speaking the language of
the Ona Selk'nam people, with whom he played as a child. Toward the
end of a long life spent in the land of the Fuegians he wrote down the
curious history of his now-legendary family, in which he paid a good
deal of attention to the Indians, especially some Onas, into whose lodge
he had been initiated. Only men were initiated and only initiated men
were allowed close to or into the lodge. No woman was allowed close,
under penalty of death. But long ago, so the story went, things were
different. For then the lodge belonged exclusively to the women. There
they practiced and passed on to the younger women the secrets of magic

and sorcery of which the men were ignorant. Frightened, the men banded together and massacred the adult women. They married the young ones and, so as to prevent them from reconstituting the link between the feminine and magical power, made their own secret society wherein they supped on supernatural nourishment brought them by a handful of monstrous and short-tempered women-hating spirits such as the two fierce sisters, the red one from clay, the white one from cumulus clouds, and the horned man who came out of the lichen-covered rock. When Bridges was taken into the lodge he was told that he would make a good impersonation of *Short*, a spirit who came from the gray rocks and wore a piece of parchmentlike skin over the face and head. Gray down from birds was applied to the body, and there was a good deal of variation in that the arm and the opposite leg could be painted in white or in red, with spots or stripes of the other color superimposed. Periodically in the company of the men *Short* would emerge from the lodge, a large wigwam set a quarter of a mile or so from the village, and dart unpredictably around the village, causing the women to flee and hide their heads. On other occasions the women and uninitiated men would be summoned to appear in front of the lodge, where, to the accompaniment of an unearthly noise, the cruel sister from the clouds, dressed in heaped-up furs covered in white chalk, would slowly make her way from a clump of trees to the lodge's entrance. When the horned man appeared with his mask of red-rimmed eyes, the women fled home, threw themselves face down on the ground in groups, and covered their heads with skins.

The initiation of a man demanded ordeals and solitary journeys in which he would be shadowed by a spirit-monster, and the culminating moment arrived in the lodge when he had to fight one of them. Bridges was present when a terrified novice was forced to engage in combat with *Short*, whose anger and disgust at the novice had grown almost to a frenzy. Unbeknownst to the novice, the outcome was set in advance such that the novice would always win; in this case, when the novice finally threw his spirit opponent to the ground and the identity of his attacker was revealed to be a fellow human in disguise, he attacked him with such fury, writes Bridges, "that he had to be dragged off, to the accompaniment of roars of laughter, in which *Short* joined heartily." Now the novice had become an inner member of the lodge.

As this laughter finally, after many adventures of transmission through the colonial lifeline, reaches through me to you, we can appreciate a certain plenitude in the hollowness, the catharsis following the vicious struggle by the firelight leading to the eventual revelation of the monster's true nature, previously concealed by its appearance of parchment, paint, and bird-down. But the catharsis is far from fulfilling. The revelation makes the novice rage. The duped becomes the duper. The basis of this primitive "State" is male theater organized for a female audience, and the State exists as a hollow core, a meticulously shielded emptiness and magnificent deceit in whose making all members of the society, so it would seem, conspire. When Bridges suggested to the men that the women might only be acting so as to please them, the men's reaction left him in no doubt as to "their firm conviction of the women's blind credulity." To Bridges it seemed impossible that the women could be deceived, yet he noted that the male initiates, who lived constantly with their mothers for twelve years or so and would surely have heard any expression of disbelief, were undoubtedly terrified when they came face to face with *Short* for the first time. He leaves us with this reminder. "One thing is certain: that if any woman had been indiscreet enough to mention her doubts, even to another woman, and word of it had reached the ears of the men, the renegade would have been killed—and most likely others with her. Maybe the women suspected; if they did they kept it to themselves."[46]

Might it turn out, then, that not the basic truths, not the Being or the ideologies of the center, but the fantasies of the marginated concerning the secret of the center are what is most politically important to the State idea and hence State fetishism? Here the secret takes on the burden of protecting not merely the deceit practiced by the initiated men but a great epistemology, one that drives philosophers, scientists, social scientists, and policemen: the epistemology of appearance is thought to shroud a concealed truth—but not the truth that there is none. Insofar as you can trust a thief, it is here where Jean Genet's thief's journal can be our guide, juxtaposing to the majesty of the State the homoerotic emblem-fetishes of the criminal, Saint Genet.

Saint Genet and the Supreme Organ

The State is above all, supremely, the organ of moral discipline.
—Durkheim, *Professional Ethics and Civic Morals* (1904)

It is one of Genet's triumphs to have brought the fetish character of the modern State into a clear and sensual focus, and this could be accomplished only by someone deft in the management of the ancient art of the *maleficium*, the fetish power intrinsic to the impure sacred. By means of

46. E. Lucas Bridges, *Uttermost Part of the Earth* (London: Hodder and Stoughton, 1951), 424–25.

his remorselessly holy yet secular blend of crime and homosexuality Genet does for the State what Sartre would have him do for us: he holds out the mirror in which we might see the holiness of its monstrous self. Is it necessary, here, to recall Durkheim's notion, drawn from his theorizing from turn-of-the-century monographs about primitive societies, of the kinship between the pure and the impure sacreds? And Nietzsche: "It might even be possible that what constitutes the value of these good and revered things is precisely that they are insidiously related, tied to and involved with these wicked, seemingly opposite things—maybe even one with them in essence."[47]

In Genet's case, to be deft in the management of the *maleficium* means above all to be deft with the logos. I think of him not only as the transgressor of the taboo but as the one who ably registers a vision born from its diabolical logic of mystical attraction and repulsion. This is the vision of persons who, in being prohibited access to the sacred, ensure its sanctity, which, far from being a thing in itself, is what we might call a self-fulfilling fantasy of power projected into an imagined center—like that of the old men rubbing their fetishes into their bodies, their adoration of these objects, as revealed to us, but not to the tribe, by the anthropologists of long ago. But this adroit anthropology stumbles on its own taboos when it comes to gaining access to, let alone revealing, the seminal centers of fetish-riddled power in its own society, where male knowledge, sanctity, and age coalesce. There is no anthropology of the ruling class that rules over us, just as there is no sociology of it either. And the time is long past for that project to have been initiated. There are institutional reasons for its not having happened. Failing that revelation, we fall back on our fantasies about the center, fantasies that in some curiously backhanded and utterly effortless manner constitute that center. It is here where the great guides, the Dantes of our era, the super-marginal such as Genet, come forth to lead us underground. For they are, thanks to their structural malposition, blessed with vision.

A Dominating Order

He loves criminals. Yet it seems to me that he loves crime even more. And this is the point. For when I say love I mean a love so strictly spiritual that it has to be carnal. For to love the abstraction "crime" there is naught else to do but make love with the infamous, the practitioners of

47. Friedrich Nietzsche, *Beyond Good and Evil,* trans. Walter Kaufmann (New York: Vintage, 1966), 10.

crime, which is where another strange catch arises. As Durkheim himself made much of, there can be no spirit of crime without its other, no crime without law.[48] And so we find the thief that is Saint Genet hopelessly in love with the abstraction that is the State, and carnally involved with its policemen as well as with the spirit of crime as incarnated in criminals.

Here he is, this handsome thief, caught by the Spanish coast guard on the lookout for smugglers. It is a cold night by the ocean stretching to Morocco. Who seduces whom, the criminal or the cop? It does not matter. The policeman needs the criminal and the criminal. . . . "In submitting to the whims of the coastguard I was obeying a dominating order which it was impossible not to serve, namely, the Police. For the moment I was no longer a hungry, ragged vagabond whom the dogs and children chased away, nor was I the bold thief flouting the cops, but rather the favorite mistress who, beneath a starry sky soothes the conqueror. When I realized that it was up to me whether or not the smugglers landed safely, I felt responsible not only for them but for all outlaws."[49]

In That Skin

Genet, the thief, says that for him the police form a sacred power that acts directly on his soul. Please note, first and foremost, that when he speaks of the sanctity of the police he is speaking of them as an institution, that "dominating order," not of individual policemen. And here's the rub. It's not a question of the particular as an instantiation or symbol of the general order. These terms are of some secondary relevance, to be sure, but there's something else, more metonymic, more carnal, tactile, and sensuously material that is central here—and this is the issue of the fetish, of the State with its big S rearing, of the Dominating Order as that which oscillates, like Durkheim's "society," between res and Deus, be-

48. Durkheim, Rules, 70: "Thus, since there cannot be a society in which the individuals do not differ more or less from the collective type, it is also inevitable that, among these divergences, there are some with a criminal character. What confers this character upon them is not the intrinsic quality of a given act but that definition which the collective conscience lends them. If the collective conscience is stronger, if it has enough authority practically to suppress these divergences, it will also be more sensitive, more exacting; and, reacting against the slightest deviations with the energy it otherwise displays only against more considerable infractions, it will attribute to them the same gravity as formerly to crimes. In other words, it will designate them as criminal.
"Crime is, then, necessary; it is bound up with the fundamental conditions of all social life, and by that very fact it is useful, because these conditions of which it is a part are themselves indispensable to the normal evolution of morality and law."
49. Jean Genet, The Thief's Journal (Harmondsworth, Eng.: Penguin, 1967), 141.

tween thing and God, with a carnal and ritualized relation to objects, as with the totems. Here the policeman and his gear are precisely that—a totem—with whom the saint that is the thief establishes just such a carnal and ritualized relationship. Hence Bernardini, the secret police-man whom the thief met in Marseilles, "was to me the visible, though perhaps brief manifestation on earth of a demoniacal organization as sickening as funeral rites, as funeral ornaments, yet as awe-inspiring as royal glory. Knowing that there, in that skin and flesh, was a particle of what I would never have hoped could be mine, I looked at him with a shudder. His dark hair was flat and glossy, as Rudolf Valentino's used to be, with a straight white part on the left side. He was strong. His face looked rugged, somewhat granite-like, and I wanted his soul to be cruel and brutal."[50] Or again, as instantiation of this, the most crucial, the ultimate State fetish-move and one which we all make and succumb to: "Little by little I came to understand his beauty. I even think that I created it, deciding that it would be precisely that face and body, on the basis of the idea of the police which they were to signify."[51]

The Invisible Presence of the Object in Which the Quality of Males Is Violently Concentrated

Again, the fetish that is the other side of the reification that is the big S: Bernardini "was not aware that, beside him, at the bar, crushed by his huskiness and assurance, I was excited chiefly by the invisible presence of his inspector's badge. The metal object had for me the power of a cigarette lighter in the fingers of a workman, or the buckle of an army belt, of a switchblade, of a calliper, objects in which the quality of males is violently concentrated. Had I been alone with him in a dark corner, I might have been bold enough to graze the cloth, to slip my hand under the lapel where cops usually wear the badge, and I would have then trembled just as if I had been opening his fly."[52]

Bernardini's virility was centered on that badge just as much as in his penis. Had his penis "been roused at the touch of my fingers," continues the thief, deftly picking his pocket as well as ours, grasping at the finest nerves connecting the State with sex, reification with its fetish-creation, then that penis "would have drawn from the badge such force that it might have swelled up and taken monstrous proportions."[53]

50. Ibid., 157.
51. Ibid.
52. Ibid., 159.
53. Ibid.

The Body of the Nation

This circulation of forceful swellings between the State and its fetish objectifications knows other circuits and byways as well. These are formed by the vital organs of the big S, its cities, its ports and railway stations of entry, its language, and its borders. In reality and in fantasy this thief's journal is a record of contested journeying through the erotic zones of the Nation-State, a sexual picaresque into the abstractions Nation and State, very much including the reification of the nation's language itself.

The Language Mass

Reflecting on his vocation as a thief and his return to France to practice it once again, the thief writes—and he is as much concerned with writing as with language—"I think that I had to hollow out, to drill through, a mass of language in which my mind would be at ease. Perhaps I wanted to accuse myself in my own language."[54] For him, crime is synonymous with treason, and it is very much as a traitor to his country that he understands his activity as attaining the status of art. But only with language, the language of the nation, can this art be practiced. This language binds the thief not only to his victim but to the thief's own victimization at the hands of the Law and the laws of Language. The reifications are as endless as they are full-bodied. "To be a thief in my own country and to justify my being a thief who used the language of the robbed—who are myself, because of the importance of language—was to give to being a thief the chance to be unique. I was becoming a foreigner."[55]

Ports

The city blurs into the male body burning with desire, and it is the city as port, entry to the nation, that establishes this incarnation. "'What do you feel like doing?'

"'With you, everything.'

"'We'll see.'

"He didn't budge. No movement bore him toward me though my whole being wanted to be swallowed up within him, though I wanted to

54. Ibid., 94.
55. Ibid., 95.

give my body the suppleness of osier so as to twine around him, though I wanted to warp, to bend over him. The city was exasperating. The smell of the port and its excitement inflamed me."[56]

This entry to the nation is immovable. "No movement bore him toward me." Yet in its very stolidity its animate quality emerges, swallowing one up into its fixed, great, and beautiful self. This figuration of the port city as man's body is no simple substitution. The port is not a symbol of the entrance to a body. Nor is the body a symbol of the nation. The thief's journal strains to establish the connection, but it will always succeed for it is predestined in desire, the desire accompanying fetishization, whereby the body is the idea of the Nation-State here by the port where the ships of many nations lie at anchor. But how can a body be an idea? You see, this thief is hell-bent on naturalization. He desperately wants to be in-*corporated*—em-*bodied*—and he has to work at it. It is his body that has to move and be supple so it can twine around, warp, and bend over the other. Hard labor. The city is exasperating. You smell the sweat, the inflammatory smell of the port. His semiosis is sensuous—or, rather, from his vantage point of forbidden desire he can visualize the sets of mimetic correspondences that link the body to the Nation's ports.

Borders

Why is this thief so fascinated by borders? With his innumerable border crossings, is he not caught up in his own restless form of State-craft, circumnavigating the body of the nation? "After many stays in jail the thief left France. He first went to Italy. The reasons he went there are obscure. Perhaps it was the proximity of the border. Rome. Naples. Brindisi. Albania. I stole a valise on the 'Rodi' which set me ashore in Santi Quaranta. The port authorities in Corfu refused to let me stay. Before I could leave again, they made me spend the night on the boat I had hired to bring me. Afterwards it was Serbia. Afterwards Austria. Czechoslovakia. Poland, where I tried to circulate false zlotys. Everywhere it was the same: robbery, prison, and from every one of these countries, expulsion. I crossed borders at night, and went through hopeless autumns when the lads were all heavy and weary, and through springtimes when suddenly, at nightfall, they would emerge from God knows what retreat where they had been priming themselves to swarm in alleys, on the docks."[57]

56. Ibid., 101–2.
57. Ibid., 75.

Death and the Country

Like the Nation-State, the fetish has a deep investment in death—the death of the consciousness of the signifying function. Death endows both the fetish and the Nation-State with life, a spectral life, to be sure. The fetish absorbs into itself that which it represents, leaving no traces of the represented. A clean job. In Karl Marx's formulation of the fetishism of commodities it is clear that the powerful phantasmagoric character of the commodity as fetish depends on the fact that the socioeconomic relations of production and distribution are erased from awareness, imploded into the made-object to become its phantom life force. In the thief's view of the Nation-State, the policeman's badge displaces his organ, which has, in turn, displaced and erased Durkheim's ("the State is the supreme organ of moral discipline"). In like fashion the State solemnly worships the tomb of the unknown soldier and (many) young men are (at least sometimes, crucial times), as Benedict Anderson reminds us, not only prepared to go to war and kill their nation's enemies, but ready to die themselves.[58] With this erasure we are absorbed into the object's plenitude of emptiness.

Less into a Country than to the Interior of an Image

But far from anesthetizing awareness, this involution of reference intensifies sensuousness, breaks sense into the senses, and annuls the distance between subject and object, subject and the State. The subject enters into the object as image, into the State as tomb of the unknown soldier and, with this sensuous entry, breaks radically with mere contemplation of the object. As the thief writes, "The crossing of borders and the excitement it arouses in me were to enable me to apprehend directly the essence of the nation I was entering. I would penetrate less into a country than to the interior of an image."[59]

The State as Fetish

So, we are back into the strange world of (Durkheim's) totems where the territory was bound to the group by means of the sacred objects—by means of the images (so the argument runs) on those objects. In that

58. Benedict Anderson, *Imagined Communities* (London: Verso, 1983), 16.
59. Genet, *Thief's Journal*, 39.

world, so the first anthropologists reported back to what was to become our patrimony, only the initiated men were allowed to see those images which, on account of their adoration, they erased over time and by loving, caressing into themselves. But the thief, who needs to be carefully distinguished from the anthropologist, with whom in some ways he overlaps, and from the men at the center, sees it differently. He likewise caresses the images of the State, the policeman's hidden badge, but instead of his body being penetrated by the sacred image, he says he penetrates it. His time is modern and godless, and he is bound hand and foot to the impure sacred of the margin, not the sacred center of power. He does not see the tabooed objects but imagines himself to be one. "A picture is worth a thousand words," it is said. Then what of a tabooed object? Imagine if it could talk? Imagine this thing called Genet as a taboo object, epitome of the impure sacred, writing the sacred designs on himself as a churinga of the modern Western underworld, where he gathers and concentrates into himself all the fantasies of those at the center. Now he is one of Walter Benjamin's treasured devices, that infamous "dialectical image" striking like lightning on the anvil of mimetic correspondence—Genet the petrified object being jolted awake to give voice to the modern dreamtime compacted within, opening up to the little hunchback of history that through cunning, will win every time so long as it enlists the sacred, wizened though it be. For Durkheim something called "society" spoke through—or, rather, was written into—sacred objects. That's what made them sacred, so long as society itself was blocked, silenced, and the discourse bounced back into the object's design and substance. That's what made them fetishes. But as a bad fetish object, as a *maleficium* of what we might call Durkheim's "own society" and Nation-State, which is in many respects "ours" too, Genet, like the little hunchback, does something terribly instructive to this displaced speech and balmy concept of "society." First of all he speaks back, as fetish. He defetishizes. Then he displaces the term *society*, replacing it with the State and its sexuality, and thereby writes with clarity and beauty the endless story of its seductive bodily prowess and the sensuous trafficking between rationality and violence as writ into the Law itself. He reenchants. That is how he gained sainthood.

SCOPIC FIXATIONS

The Art of Fetishism:
Notes on Dutch Still Life

Hal Foster

I want to begin with the fetish as a form of protection. After all, an art historian who writes about fetishism (or a modernist who publishes on seventeenth-century Dutch still life) needs some sort of defense, and mine is this. I am fascinated by modernist works that involve an encounter between different cultures or, more precisely, different economies of the object. These works emerge in an interstice between, say, the ritual order of tribal artifacts and the exhibitional status of modern art, as in primitivism; between the mundane realm of commodities and the hermetic realm of autonomous art, as in the readymade; between the sexual register of part objects and the social field of *objets trouvés*, as in the surrealist object. Such practices are posed in these interstices ambivalently—as if to make us ambivalent, as if to turn the psychic conflict and social contradiction that underlie them into a critical provocation. No given model can grasp modernist art as such a symbolic figuration of conflict and contradiction—except, perhaps, one based on an expanded concept of fetishism.

Many modernisms point to conflict and contradiction only to point away from them, just as Freudian fetishism affirms castration only to disavow it. In both cases, however, there *is* a recognition of contradiction, not just a denial of it, and this recognition is active, not merely passive. The problem is that these two intuitions—that certain modern-

Thanks to David Freedberg for an incisive reading of this essay and to audiences at Cornell, Princeton, Michigan, Rochester, and the University of California, Santa Barbara, for helpful comments.

isms involve contradictions between cultures or economies of the object, and that each responds to its given contradictions fetishistically—are difficult to reconcile. No one concept of fetishism—anthropological, Marxian, or Freudian—suffices to explain the process, and an amalgamation of all three may simply issue in the empty formula that all art is fetishistic. This is why I turn here, in a fetishistic displacement of my own, to an art form that seems to negotiate conflict and contradiction more transparently—in a way that also appears to permit an expanded understanding of fetishism precisely as the discourse of this negotiation. . . .[1]

"Oysters, lemon pulp, heavy goblets full of dark wine, long clay pipes, gleaming chestnuts, pottery, tarnished metal cups, three grape seeds—what can be the justification of such an assemblage if not to lubricate man's gaze amid his domain, to facilitate his daily business among objects whose riddle is dissolved and which are no longer anything but easy surfaces?"[2] So Roland Barthes writes of seventeenth-century Dutch still life, and I believe he is right: this is a primary goal of such painting. It is rarely achieved, however, for the gaze of the viewer and the riddle of objects are not so easily treated. In this art the gaze (which is assumed to be masculine) is more often fixed, as in the Freudian scenario of the sexual fetishist who turns to a surrogate object, and the riddle of things is simply posed again and again, as in the Marxian metaphor of commercial fetishism whereby such products appear as "hieroglyphs" in "the riddle" of our own social labor. To argue thus is to advance both a general thesis and a methodological approach: that, far from a golden mean, Dutch still life expresses an anxiety about the gaze and a confu-

1. I grope toward such an understanding in (Dis)agreeable Objects (New York: New Museum of Contemporary Art, 1986) and The Future of an Illusion, or The Contemporary Artist as Cargo Cultist (Boston: Institute of Contemporary Art, 1986). Since then I have benefited enormously from three essays by William Pietz, "The Problem of the Fetish," pt. 1, Res 9 (Spring 1985): 5–17, pt. 2, Res 13 (Spring 1987): 23–45, and pt. 3a, Res 16 (Autumn 1988): 105–23. His Jamesonian formula—"the fetish is situated in the space of cultural revolution"—may stand for this expanded concept of fetishism.

Occasioned by the exhibition A Prosperous Past: The Sumptuous Still Life in the Netherlands, 1600–1700 (catalogue text by Sam Segal [The Hague: SDU, 1988]), my essay is also inspired by four important texts (which I sometimes, usually tacitly, argue with here): Norman Bryson, "Chardin and the Text of Still Life," Critical Inquiry 15 (Winter 1989): 227–52; Svetlana Alpers, The Art of Describing: Dutch Art in the Seventeenth Century (Chicago: University of Chicago Press, 1983), and Rembrandt's Enterprise: The Studio and the Market (Chicago: University of Chicago Press, 1988); and Simon Schama, The Embarrassment of Riches: An Interpretation of Dutch Culture in the Golden Age (Berkeley: University of California Press, 1988).

2. Roland Barthes, "The World as Object," in Calligram: Essays in New Art History from France, ed. Norman Bryson (Cambridge: Cambridge University Press, 1988), 108.

sion about the value of objects; and that the best way to explore this structure of feeling is through the discourse of fetishism.

At first glance it is problematic to relate the discourse of fetishism to Dutch still life: the discourse hardly appears coherent, and given its modern provenance, it seems anachronistic to apply it to a distant practice.[3] And yet seventeenth-century Holland is a crucial site for its articulation. To a great extent the term was developed by Dutch traders in order to posit a perverse conception of value among the Africans of the Gold and Slave coasts—a discourse of exploitation that has underwritten its prejudicial use ever since as the sign of the most primitive—whether the subject be religious systems (Brosses), historical stages (Hegel), social orders (Comte), or representational forms.[4] Moreover, on a general level, the composite figure of the fetishist as drawn by Marx and Freud—the capitalist patriarch—is first fully formed at this time and place; and on a local level, Dutch still life manifests too many of the attributes commonly associated with fetishism not to be considered in its terms. The three primary models of fetishism—anthropological, Marxian and Freudian—all define the fetish as an object endowed with a special force or independent life (Marx writes explicitly of "transference," Freud of "overvaluation"). Too many viewers have remarked upon the strange energy that emanates from the objects of Dutch still life for us not to admit a connection, and this observation is especially true of the "pronk" paintings that concern me here, lavish displays of fine objects and extravagant food (in Dutch *pronken* means "to show off).[5]

If only a superficial sheen or shine, this visual intensity cannot be explained away as an effect of a disguised symbolism or a residue of a religious gaze; a fetishistic projection on the part of artist and viewer alike is involved.[6] Often in Dutch still life the inert appears animate, the familiar becomes estranged, and the insignificant seems humanly, even

3. For Jean Pouillon, fetishism is not discursively coherent. See his "Fétiches sans fétichisme," *Nouvelle revue de psychanalyse* 2 (Autumn 1970): 135–47. For Pietz, on the other hand, it is tropologically consistent, involving questions of materiality, historicality, and value, and processes of displacement, overvaluation, bodily subjection, and psychic fixation. See Pietz, "Problem of the Fetish," pts. 1, 2, and 3a.

4. Marx and Freud inherit this evolutionist scheme, which they transvalue only partially (e.g., we too are fetishists . . .).

5. See Segal, *A Prosperous Past*, 15.

6. Panofsky suggested a mutuality of naturalist observation and religious symbolism in Early Netherlandish painting. In *Dutch Still-Life Painting*, trans. Christina Hedstrom and Gerald Taylor (London: Faber and Faber, 1956), Ingvar Bergstrom elaborated this insight into a general interpretation of Dutch still life: "Certain artists were attempting to separate the customary symbols from the religious scene and to give them an independent existence as a symbolical still life" (14). My account is obviously not very concerned with the "symbolical."

preternaturally, significant, in a way that transvalues the ancient term for still life, *rhyparography*, the depiction of insignificant things. In one way or another, all these effects are attributes of fetishism not only in the anthropological sense but also in the Marxian and Freudian senses. Marx maintained that in commodity exchange people and things trade semblances: social relations take on the character of object relations, and commodities assume the active agency of people. An inkling of this inversion of subject-object relations is evident in many Dutch still lifes, as if the objects were endowed with life to the degree that the viewer is sapped of it. Similarly, Freud argued that in experiences of the uncanny, which he specifically related to castration anxiety and its fetishistic defense, animate and inanimate states are confused, things are subsumed by representations, once-homey images return as *unheimlich*, and a whiff or whisper of death hangs over the scene. Again, many of these qualities are present in Dutch still life. Indeed, the insistence of such terms as still life, *still leven*, and *nature morte* on the mortal state of the motif suggests an anxiety that it might be otherwise, that an uncanny animation, a fetishistic projection, is active here. It hardly suffices, I know, to read such attributes in(to) such painting, but that is not really my purpose. Rather, I want to propose that the very dynamics of fetishism, at least as described in its three primary models, structure this art. I begin with the anthropological account and then proceed to the Marxian and Freudian conceptions.

The term *fetish* was first used in relation to the amulets of witches, that is, to marginal others within the culture, persecuted peasant women; then it was adopted by fifteenth-century Portuguese traders to refer to the cult objects of West Africans, that is, to alien others outside the culture, subjected tribespeople.[7] These are the loci of the common anthropological meaning of the fetish as a thing possessed of a (super)natural quality or force—and of the typical imperial excuse that beings possessed of such belief need not be accorded the rights of Christian (or rational) subjects. Less known is the elaboration of the term by seventeenth-century Dutch merchants who had ousted the Portuguese from the Gold and Slave coasts by 1642, or roughly the high moment of the Dutch still-life tradition. In this case African fetishes were directly related to Catholic sacramental objects. In 1602 Pieter de Marees, who introduced the pidgin term to northern Europe, associated *Fetissos* with saints; and in 1704 Willem Bosman, former chief merchant of the Dutch

7. For contemporary etymologies of the term, see Pietz, "Problem of the Fetish," 1:5, and 2:24–25; and Jean Baudrillard, "Fetishism and Ideology," in *For a Critique of the Political Economy of the Sign*, trans. Charles Levin (St. Louis: Telos Press, 1981), 91.

West Indies Company, wrote: "If it was possible to convert the Negroes to the Christian Religion, the Roman-Catholicks would succeed better than we should, because they already agree in several particulars, especially in their ridiculous Ceremonies."[8] This, of course, is a Protestant claim: to deny that any material object has a special capacity of spiritual mediation. Yet in this religious point is hidden an economic agenda: to denounce as primitive and infantile the refusal to assess value rationally, to trade objects in a system of equivalence, in short, to submit to capitalist exchange. (Note that in this proto-Enlightenment discourse the great figure of modernist fixation—the savage-child-madman—is already announced.) As an irrational relation to objects, fetishism was not just an abomination in the eyes of the Lord; it was also a damned nuisance to market activity.[9] To a great extent, then, Dutch object relations in the seventeenth century were articulated in relation to "fetishism," Catholic and African, in such a way as to privilege not only Protestant individualism but also commodity exchange; and still life can be seen as one important site where this new contradictory complex of subject-object relations was mediated and expressed.

An ironic displacement occurs here, however, which can also be read in the art. As religious fetishism was suppressed, a commercial fetishism, a fetishism of the commodity, was released; the Dutch denounced one overvaluation of objects, only to produce another of their own. For Marx commodity fetishism is analogous to religious projection. I want to argue one step further, that commodity fetishism partly replaced religious fetishism, or at least compensated for its partial loss. This displacement-overvaluation is symbolically enacted in pronk still lifes. Even today, positioned reverently before these gold chalices, fine porcelain pieces, and exquisite glasses like so many worshipers before the Golden Calf, we might believe, as perhaps did the Dutch, that these things have a *mana* or power of their own—a *mana*, moreover, that redounds to the *mana* or value of painting. For baroque artists, still-life practitioners in particular, the nobility of painting, its art value if you like, was hardly secure. Thus it was important to display that the art of painting could go beyond other crafts, that the value of the work could subsume other values. In this agenda painting was to become the ultimate golden calf, as it is for us today, as it had begun to be for the seventeenth-century Dutch.[10]

8. Willem Bosman, *A New and Accurate Description of the Coast of Guinea* (1704; London: Cass, 1967), 154. Both Marees and Bosman are quoted in Pietz, "Problem of the Fetish," 2:39; see also Pietz, 3a, passim.
9. See Pietz, "Problem of the Fetish," 2:41, and 3a:116.
10. It was somewhere in-between for Goethe, who, in a remark on a pronk still life,

My point here is not simply that the Dutch, in default of fetishistic religious icons, fetishized objects of exchange, especially (in) paintings. It is rather more that they employed fetishism as a category with which to negotiate the different economies of the object that they encountered in the course of market expansion.[11] Pronk still lifes in particular seem like tabulations or mappings of the most diverse objects from the most disparate classes and cultures. A given painting by Jan Davidsz de Heem or Willem Kalf may include not only metalware from Nurnberg and glass from Venice but also porcelain from China, tobacco from America, shells from the Far East, rugs from the Near East, exotic spices from the Indian archipelago, and on and on—so many synecdoches, if not of the Dutch empire, then at least of the Dutch market. Often these synecdoches threaten to burst open the circumscribed space of traditional still life, the limited scene of its domestic setting, to outside, other worlds.[12] Yet this is a necessary risk, for it appears that the objects of disparate classes and cultures are depicted precisely so that they may be mastered in representation, so that the domestic space and capitalist subjectivity of the seventeenth-century Dutch may be secured from its outside and others by a synecdochic incorporation of these very things. It is this fetishism—fetishism as a negotiation of divergent representations and dangerous realities—that pronk still life embodies.

Such negotiations must also be made within cultures, and Dutch still life operates in this arena too. For instance, there is a tension, especially as the focus of the tradition passes from meal themes to pronk motifs,

---

attests to the ennobling this genre had achieved by his time: "Gold and silver vases by Kalff [sic]—they highlight the masterly skill of this man in this branch of art. One must see this painting in order to understand in what respect art is superior to nature and what the spirit of man lends to these objects when he observes them with a creative eye. For me there is no question: If I would have to choose between the golden vases or the painting, I would choose the painting." Quoted in Segal, *Prosperous Past*, 185. Ironically, what Goethe thus praised was a copy.

11. Pietz: "This novel situation began with the formation of inhabited intercultural spaces along the West African coast (especially that stretch known as the Mina coast) whose function was to translate and transvalue objects between radically different social systems. Specifically . . . these spaces, which endured for several centuries, were triangulated among Christian feudal, African lineage, and merchant capitalist social systems. It was within this situation that there emerged a new problematic concerning the capacity of material objects to embody—simultaneously and sequentially—religious, commercial, aesthetic, and sexual values. My argument, then, is that the fetish could originate only in conjunction with the emergent articulation of the commodity form that defined itself within and against the social values and religious ideologies of two radically different kinds of non-capitalist society, as they encountered each other in an ongoing cross-cultural situation." "Problem of the Fetish," 1:6–7.

12. Bryson, "Chardin," 248, speaks of this effect of the market in terms of leveling rather than rupturing.

among objects of direct use, objects produced for exchange, and objects of display or prestation. In early still lifes, use objects predominate, and they are often depicted matter-of-factly; as Marx says, there is nothing mysterious about such things. In later still lifes, objects of exchange or display predominate, and they are often represented in a mystificatory way—at once phantasmagorical and palpable, as Marx notes of commodities. The difference in these types cannot be ascribed only to different artistic subjects, styles, milieus; it also concerns different social aspects of the economy differently apprehended. This apparent transition from paintings primarily of use objects to paintings primarily of exchange or display objects may well reflect the increased presence of the market as a mediator of Dutch social life in the seventeenth century—and the increased pressure on pictorial representation to come to terms with this market, to articulate its different objects, registers, effects. Of course, commodity production was hardly total as yet, but it was general enough to effect regimes of vision and modes of representation.[13] And the effects can be seen in certain still lifes. Often it is as if natural things such as flowers and shells, or useful objects such as knives and glasses, are coated with a special shellac before our very eyes, as if the painter were compelled to endow them with a pictorial value to match the commercial value they had already acquired on the market. Fetishism thus is almost a mandate: In order to reassure patrons, objects must be represented as if value were inherent in them (as the intensive pictorial elaboration of flowers and shells in particular suggests). Marx derided this mercantilist endowment of natural substances with social properties: "Hitherto, no chemist has been able to discover exchange value in a pearl or in a diamond."[14] And yet this was part of the task of the pronk painter. No wonder, then, that the objects in these still lifes often attest as much to the speculative investments of the patron as to the physical marks of the painter. The transformation, however, is never complete: old referents, contexts, and object relations remain. As a result, the objects appear caught between worlds—not alive, not dead, not useful, not useless, as if lost between the tangibility of the common thing and the visibility of the distanced commodity. And the pictorial effect is often one of deathly suspension or, as remarked before, of eerie animation, with the objects at once chilled and charged by the speculative gaze fixed upon them.

13. Significantly, Marx makes an analogy between the fetishistic projection of value in the commodity and the illusory projection of vision as an objective fact rather than a subjective experience. See *Capital: A Critique of Political Economy*, vol. I, trans. Ben Fowkes (New York: Vintage, 1977), 165.
14. Ibid., p. 177.

This pall is occasionally cast over meal pieces too, and the effect is to invert the structure of feeling implicit in the genre since its beginnings. Extant Greek still lifes mostly depict food, as do many Roman examples; still life was designated a *xenion*, a present made to a guest.[15] In its purported origins, then, still life was less about a display than it was about an offering: it represented a gift exchange. Such gift exchange is only very residual in a commodity system (indeed, Marcel Mauss implicitly opposed the two orders),[16] and the structure of feeling, the welcome if you like, of the still-life genre is adversely affected. Certainly in pronk pieces the concern with social position, with excess and ostentation, or, even less generous, the emphasis on moral probity, on "remonstrance against excess and ostentation,"[17] overwhelms the sense of offering or gift vestigial in still life. The offering is somehow denied before the fact; the gift has a social, moral or economic tag attached; the presentation intimidates more than it welcomes. Even when pronk paintings represent food, which implicitly is ours by carnal right, it seems somehow spoiled, tabooed, inedible. Again the chill of the commodity is felt, and in heretofore removed spaces. For just as the new market invades the intimate space of the still life, so too it erodes the old Aristotelian distinction between the economy of the household and the accumulation of value through commerce; and directly or indirectly, many still lifes comment on this penetration.[18]

The becoming-commodity of things produces other paradoxes as well. On the one hand, as the market becomes more intensive, objects are referred to the order of money; they become, in principle or potential at least, more equivalent. On the other hand, as the market becomes more extensive, objects become more diverse. Is it too much to suggest that pronk still life negotiates this illusory paradox too? From the moderate styles of the 1620s and 1630s to the coloristic modes thereafter, the representational grid of the typical still life becomes not only more pictorially consistent but also more referentially porous to objects of all sorts. Such paintings often appear as sites that can accommodate almost

15. See Charles Sterling, *Still Life Painting: From Antiquity to the Twentieth Century*, 2d rev. ed. (New York: Harper and Row, 1981), 28; also see Bryson, "Chardin," 238.

16. "The pattern of symmetrical and reciprocal rights [in gift exchange] is not difficult to understand if we realize that it is first and foremost a pattern of spiritual bonds between things which are to some extent parts of persons, and persons and groups that behave in some measure as if they were things." Marcel Mauss, *The Gift: Forms and Functions of Exchange in Ancient Societies*, trans. Ian Cunnison (New York: Norton, 1967), 11.

17. Segal, *A Prosperous Past*, 169.

18. Alpers discusses the effects of this erosion on Rembrandt in *Rembrandt's Enterprise*, 96.

any kind of represented thing—natural or culinary, homemade or elaborate, mundane or exotic. Is there a logic to this tabulation of difference within sameness, or is the effect not one of heterotopia? Certainly there seems little taxonomic logic either to the typical pronk still life or to its more artisanal cousin, the cabinet of curiosities (actual or depicted). The principle of order here cannot be found in the nature of the objects alone, and the transcendental guarantee of God no longer appears automatically. Rather, the primary plane of consistency is the shared status of the things as more or less precious or rare commodities—even when they appear most natural (e.g., flowers or shells). It is this common condition that allows for the difference within sameness in the still lifes. Diverse objects can be brought together in these paintings because they are *already* brought together not so much in the domestic space as in the marketplace. They already exist to be exchanged, collected, consumed. In effect, it is this abstractive economic field that the paintings map. Since they are implicated in it, however, they cannot frame it, and one result is that they frequently appear in this mapping alongside other commodity collectibles. In this way, the ultimate principle of order of these paintings may well be the imperial market; it is a first support and a final referent of this art. And this claim may in turn support another assertion: that the fall of the metaphoric or symbolic order of things in religious art coincides with the rise of a metonymic or synecdochic tabulation of objects in capitalist art.[19]

Of course, art does not simply submit to economic logic; apart from myriad other things, it can also expose or mediate contradictions within an economy. Painting for the open market was common in mid-seventeenth-century Holland, and there was a high division of artistic labor. Whether or not one subscribes to the old saw that scarcity of land encouraged speculation in pictures, it does appear that the Dutch were generally at ease with the status of art as commodity and investment.[20] Certainly, the value of paintings was subject to the fluctuations of the market and the whims of speculation. Yet there was a tension or negotiation here as well. I noted a negotiation within pronk still lifes between objects of use and exchange value; there is a related negotiation around the paintings between value fixed according to labor time (in the old guild manner) and value determined by the marketplace. This negotiation of values was very important for the mid-seventeenth-century Dutch (witness the tulip mania), and once again, pronk still life was a

19. To me this distinction is more important than that between the descriptive and the emblematic in Dutch art. See Alpers, *The Art of Describing*, 166–67, 229–33.
20. See Alpers, *Rembrandt's Enterprise*, 94.

symbolically significant site of such negotiation. Indirectly, in its making, still life allowed the Dutch to think the pros and cons of different
kinds of value creation. So, too, in its styles and subjects, still life enabled the Dutch to reflect on the related ethical-economic tension between control and consumption. As Simon Schama argues in *The Embarrassment of Riches*, this issue was hardly black and white morally or
economically: better expenditure, it was felt, than avarice; better circulation than accumulation.[21] Like the Reaganomic subject of our own era of
fundamentalism and greed, the seventeenth-century Dutch subject was
positioned schizophrenically: moral restraint and economic expenditure were both encouraged. Pronk still life was asked to represent these
imperatives simultaneously—thus its negotiation between order and
disorder, godliness and greed, a negotiation that helps to explain
emotively conflicted tableaux such as a spilled chalice immaculately
composed or a spoiled pie exquisitely glazed. The viewer may revel in
this consumption but see it controlled, not only through the caution of
destructive excess or implicit *Vanitas* but also by skilled craft. The productive labor of the artist and the measured value of the work helped to
assuage anxiety about affluence, expenditure, speculation—and so, in
some sense, abetted these activities. In any case, in pictorial art as in
economic society there existed an interplay between spending and sav-
ing, luxury and frugality, an attraction toward the sovereignty of possession and a renunciation of this possessive sovereignty, and still life was
called upon to work through this general contradiction between "acquis-
itiveness and asceticism"—in effect, to caution the subject about the two
extremes but to allow him to have it both ways.[22] Indeed, still life treated
these extremes not only in its subjects, compositions, and craft but also
in its stylistic development, which oscillated between "acquisitive" and
"ascetic" poles.

Such a great cultural contradiction can hardly be resolved in art, but it
can be intuited, even invoked there. And by way of a conclusion I want

21. Schama reads Dutch still life perhaps too directly in these terms: the monochromatic breakfast pieces are said to express humanist balance, the coloristic pronks
ostentatious display. But the emphasis of the pronk mode is clear. In fact, it suggests
another economic value represented in such still lifes: sumptuary value—still life as a
site of prestige garnered through expenditure. Again, one of the meanings of *pronken*
is to "show off." Segal translates its pictorial derivative as "sumptuous still life," and
Schama notes that Dutch culture had "a rich tradition of ceremonial waste." *Embarrassment of Riches*, 310.
22. Schama, *Embarrassment of Riches*, 338. Schama suggests that Dutch culture
dealt with this ambivalence adequately: "This moral pulling and pushing may have
made for inconsistency, but it did not much confuse the artisan, the merchant or the
banker in their daily affairs. The peculiar coexistence of apparently opposite value
systems was what they expected of their culture" (371).

to suggest that Dutch still life treats such anxieties but cannot finally assuage them. In part it fails to do so because it produces an anxiety of its own, and in order to understand this effect we must turn to the third primary model of fetishism, that of Freud. For Freud, of course, the fetish is a substitute for the (maternal) penis thought to be castrated; it screens out this supposed castration and so wards off its implied threat—that the same fate may befall the subject (here, as elsewhere, the little boy is privileged). The ambivalence of this subject, torn between knowledge and belief, is never resolved.[23] Thus fetishism is not simply an act of disavowal: it is a compromise formation that effectively allows the subject to have it both ways: to see the woman (the mother) as both whole and castrated. As such, the fetish is not only a "protection" against castration but also a "memorial" to it—a point of some importance if we are to locate a critical moment in the fetishistic structure of art. My purpose here is not to relate the ambivalence of seventeenth-century Dutch society regarding material culture directly to this ambivalence of the fetishist. Rather, I want to suggest that Dutch still life is, like the Freudian fetish, a structure of ambivalence, which, on the one hand, points to social contradictions beyond its reach and, on the other hand, tends to a psychic splitting of the subject (as Freud argued regarding the most extreme fetishists) even though it seems disposed to his mastery. At first glance, this assertion is at odds with the influential argument of Svetlana Alpers regarding Dutch art generally: that its descriptive (Keplerian) basis privileges the priority of the seen world, not, as in the narrative (Albertian) mode of Italian art, that of the viewer addressed. But surely the techniques of immediacy intended, as Alpers argues, to "deanthropomorphize vision" in this art constitute a supreme fiction (as, for that matter, do the strategies of absorption intended, according to Michael Fried, to detheatricalize beholding in eighteenth-century French painting).[24] That is, Dutch conventions of visual immediacy

23. In the case of the little girl, it is Freud who is too precipitous: "A little girl behaves differently. She makes her decision and her judgement in a flash. She has seen it and knows that she is without it and wants to have it." "Some Psychical Consequences of the Anatomical Distinction between the Sexes," (1925), *Standard Edition*, 19:252. Essentially he sentences her to a chain of metonymic substitutes (penis, child . . .). His account of fetishism is also very problematic for gay men and lesbians. He argues that fetishism is one way to "ward off" homosexuality ("Fetishism", in *Standard Edition*, 21:201), and he suggests that lesbians outstrip fetishists in their disavowal of castration. "Some Psychical Consequences," 253. I do not address these problems here, but I hope it is clear that I want to rethink fetishism and not merely rehabilitate or otherwise valorize it.

24. Alpers, *The Art of Describing*, 36; Michael Fried, *Absorption and Theatricality: Painting and Beholder in the Age of Diderot* (Berkeley: University of California Press, 1980), passim.

(e.g., no fixed viewpoint, an apparent framelessness, a mirror mimesis—all brilliantly detailed by Alpers) may serve to negate the artist as maker, the painting as medium, and most of all, the viewer as presence, but they do so finally to affirm the subject, that is, to protect his voyeuristic interests, specifically his capitalist apprehension of objects as possessions and his scopophilic pleasure in human figures (or fetishistic surrogates) as sexual objects.[25] In short, the Dutch art of describing is also pledged to the mastery of the subject; in its still-life mode at least, however, this mastery is disrupted from within.

In many ways Dutch still life is perfect—perfectly composed, perfectly finished, with no hint of lack or loss. We may look at these shiny canvases in the way an infant of six to eighteen months is said to look at a mirror: with joy that the image reflected there is made whole. Although some objects in the still lifes are distanced, others remain corporeally, even psychically intimate; and although they appear scattered as objects, they are composed as motifs in a way that somehow echoes our bodily image in perfected form.[26] This very perfection thus points to a preexistent loss or castration in the subject—which is precisely why the perfection is demanded, and perhaps why finish is such a fetish in this art.[27] Moreover, this perfection may reflect our gaze in a way that finally threatens it. Possessed of this art, of its material riches and visual splendors, we may also be threatened with dispossession. (At a more obvious level, meal and pronk still lifes are often so abundant as to deny the very possibility of incompletion, and yet right before our eyes, in the guise of a split peach or a cut wedge of cheese, there may lie a displaced image of castration.)[28]

25. I discuss this in an unpublished manuscript, "The Baroque as a Brisure of Art History," as does Louis Marin in "Toward a Theory of Reading in the Visual Arts: Poussin's The Arcadian Shepherds," in The Reader in the Text, ed. Susan R. Suleiman (Princeton: Princeton University Press, 1980), 293–324.

26. My allusion to the mirror phase is only partly tongue in cheek. If the paradigm of Dutch art generally is the mirror (to which Alpers adds the map), its still lifes somehow reflect a subject that is precisely not represented otherwise.

27. In his etymology of fetishism, Baudrillard detects antithetical connotations (which might have interested Freud)—both natural, even supernatural, and artificial, even fraudulent. I see a related doubleness in Dutch still life, particularly in its finish, which was intended to signal both natural perfection and skilled artifice. See Alpers, Rembrandt's Enterprise, 98. This doubleness may be related to the fetishistic structure of classical representation in general, which both affirms and disavows the objectness of the painting and the presence of the viewer.

28. Perhaps one need not be so iconographically literal here; perhaps any detail can serve as a fetishistic punctum that arrests the viewer. It strikes me that the distinction between narration and description detected by Alpers in Renaissance painting may be related to the tension between narrative and spectacle detected by Laura Mulvey in Hollywood cinema ("Visual Pleasure and Narrative Cinema," Screen 16 [Autumn 1975]: 6–18), who associates the first term with the diegetic control of the masculine

Perhaps we can grasp the stakes here if we turn to the mini case history that Freud presented in his 1927 essay on fetishism. Freud tells us of a young man who, born in an English environment but raised in a German one, fetishized a "shine on the nose." Now this *Glanz auf der Nase*, Freud writes, "was in reality a '*glance* at the nose'"; the man had confused the two words, *Glanz* or shine and *glance*. "The nose was thus the fetish, which, incidentally, he endowed at will with the luminous shine which was not perceptible to others."[29] There is much to develop here, but Freud does little with it. Intent on the formula of the fetish as (maternal) phallic substitute, he does not listen to his own analysand. So what actually happens in this scenario? A man fetishizes a shine on the nose of a woman. That is to say, a masculine subject projects onto a female object (or part object) the condition of loss or castration, and he does so with his gaze—perhaps *as* his gaze. The suggestion is that the loss preexists her in him, that she is simply his projected representation of it.[30] In short, the castration is his, and indeed, many losses or separations (from the womb, the breast, the feces . . .) precede the hypothetical sighting of castration—even if they are understood as such only retrospectively through this optic.[31] It is this preexistent loss in the subject that demands fetishistic perfection in the object (a recognition that puts a very different spin on "art appreciation"). Significantly here, although the fetishistic displacement of glance to *Glanz* is linguistic, the fetishistic projection is visual: the glance is projected by the subject onto the object, which returns this gaze as a *Glanz*, "a luminous shine which was not perceptible to others." I have suggested that the capitalist gaze of the Dutch subject endows the object with a special luminous life; here the fetishistic gaze of the Dutch subject can be seen to project a similar "shine." (Could it be that artistic aura in general is produced by this very projection-reflection of the regard of the subject? For Walter Benjamin an object is auratic if it retains the traces of the practiced hand; this "shine"

---

protagonist/viewer in depth and the second term with the fetishized image of the feminine figure held to the surface of the screen. This association may in turn relate the Alpers "art of describing" to my "art of fetishism." Alpers also discusses her distinction in "Describe or Narrate? A Problem in Realistic Representation," *New Literary History* 8 (1976–77): 15–41.

29. Freud, "Fetishism," 200.

30. As Kaja Silverman notes, this is also suggested when Freud terms the sighting of castration "uncanny"—that is, somehow a repetition—a term he also uses to describe the primal scene. Her rereading of Freud on fetishism, which I had not read when I drafted this essay, is more developed than mine but similar in many respects. See *The Acoustic Mirror: The Female Voice in Psychoanalysis and Cinema* (Bloomington: Indiana University Press, 1988), 1–41.

31. At several points (most famously in the Little Hans study) Freud objects to the use of the term *castration* for these other losses or separations.

of the crafted thing is thus very different from that of the commodity fetish. But aura is also effected for Benjamin by an object that somehow returns our gaze, and clearly in this regard the ur-auratic object is the gaze, the body, of the preoedipal mother.)[32]

The question then becomes: Why might this glance-Glanz of the fetishist, this auratic shine, be received as a threat? There are (at least) two reasons, one of which is suggested in the notion that the fetish is also a memorial to castration. As a fetishistic projection, the glance-Glanz might include a reminder of the very loss that haunts the subject. Certainly still life seems so marked: a ghost of a lack hangs over its very abundance. The second reason concerns the psychic association of the threat of castration with the threat of blindness (which, again, is discussed by Freud on the uncanny and by Lacan on the gaze). Perhaps more than any other genre, still life is disposed for our gaze.[33] And yet the very intensity of our gaze causes it to be reflected; pronk pictures in particular seem to return it, so to speak. But this returned gaze is not the maternal one of Benjaminian memory that speaks of a restored psychic unity. The luminous shine of these still lifes is more faultily fetishistic: it recalls our lack even as it distracts us from it. It is as if we are seen as we see—only it is objects that "see" us.[34]

32. Benjamin discusses these aspects of aura in "On Some Motifs in Baudelaire," in *Illuminations*, ed. Hannah Arendt, trans. Harry Zohn (New York: Schocken, 1969), 186–92. For an important discussion of the connection between aura and fetishism, see Miriam Hansen, "Benjamin, Cinema and Experience: 'The Blue Flower in the Land of Technology,'" *New German Critique* 40 (Winter 1987): 179–224.

33. Barthes extends this principle to cover all seventeenth-century Dutch art. Is it coincidental that the great glazes of the still lifes are contemporaries of the great gazes of the group portraits? Barthes writes: "It is the gaze that is the *numen* here, the gaze that disturbs, intimidates, and makes man the ultimate term of the problem." "The World as Object," 119.

34. Norman Bryson sees a similar effect of threat in Albertian perspective: as equal and opposite to our viewing point, the vanishing point doubles our gaze, returns it in alienated form, threatens us with the nullity this point represents. See *Tradition and Desire: From David to Delacroix* (Cambridge: Cambridge University Press, 1984), 63–84; also see, for an initial critique of this "paranoid" model, Bryson, "The Gaze in the Expanded Field," in *Vision and Visuality*, ed. Hal Foster (Seattle: Dia Art Foundation/Bay Press, 1988), 86–108. In the neo-Kantian tradition of art history, Renaissance perspective is typically seen as the reconciliation of subject and object (e.g., Panofsky), as a form devoted to the mastery of the viewer. Contemporary readings influenced by Lacan, however, see it as a point of potential crisis for the subject. In this light, much baroque painting may appear in part as an unconscious response to the castrative charge of Renaissance perspective—as so many attempts to opacify it or to defuse it through excessive elaboration. Dutch still life can also be seen as such a defense; yet it is precisely here that the repressed returns. Although still life seems pledged against traditional perspective—that is, pledged to invert it or to push it forward, as if to expel the viewer from the position of a masterful sight—it overcomes perspectival threat only to reproduce it in another form, in the "look" of the object, which doubles our

Disposed for our gaze, still life threatens to dispossess us of our sight. Our gaze, made intense in still life, even Medusal (as Norman Bryson says), looks back from things, and threatens us. Could it be that the intensity of the gaze, religious in nature, has nowhere to go once freed of its transcendental anchor in God but to return to the subject? Whatever the case, this anxiety, this ambivalence is fundamental to Dutch still life; it is an ambivalence to which the other ambivalences produced by the genre and its objects—as tokens of different classes and exotic lands, as examples of the strange new form of the commodity—must be related.

---

own. Baudrillard writes similarly of trompe-l'oeil: "In trompe-l'oeil the effect of per-spective is somehow thrown forward. . . . Nothing to see: it is things that see you, they do not fly from you, they bear themselves before you like your own hallucinated interiority." "The Trompe-l'oeil," in *Calligram*, 58. Certain Dutch still lifes seem to intuit as much; certainly there are moves that might be construed as defenses against this possibility. For example, the more monochromatic compositions of the 1620s and 1630s, especially of Pieter Claesz and Willem Claesz, not only suggest moral modera-tion or economic equivalence; they also mute the gaze, relieve it of its Medusal intensity, free the subject from his own scopic fascination/fixation/fetishism. So too the more painterly style of van Beyeren; so too the coloristic saturation of the glutted object field of de Heem—this last can serve to disorder or scatter the gaze, to block its reflected return.

The Legs of the Countess

Abigail Solomon-Godeau

> Subjectivity denied to woman: indisputably this provides the finan-
> cial backing for every irreducible constitution [of her] as an object:
> of representation, of discourse, of desire.
>
> —Luce Irigaray, "Any Theory of the 'Subject' Has
> Always Been Appropriated by the 'Masculine'"

Historians of photography tend to divide the staggering number of images that constitute their object of study into two separate but
hardly equal realms: that of the typical and that of the anomalous. The
photographs of the countess de Castiglione fall within both. On the one
hand, the countess was merely one of thousands of well-to-do clients
who passed through the doors of the fashionable Second Empire photographic firm of Mayer & Pierson, official photographers to the emperor
and his court. The majority of photographs made of the countess by
Louis Pierson are neither technically nor formally dissimilar to those of

Reprinted from *October* 39 (Winter 1986): 65–108, by permission of the MIT Press,
Cambridge, Massachusetts, copyright © 1987 by the Massachusetts Institute of Technology and October Magazine, Ltd.

This essay, a short version of which was presented at the College Art Association in
February 1986, is part of a work in progress, a study of femininity, sexuality, and
photography in nineteenth-century France. I acknowledge the assistance and advice
of Jean Sagne, who first told me about the photographs of the countess de Castiglione;
Maria Morris Hambourg, who led me to the Montesquiou text and facilitated my
research in every way; Grant Romer and Lynn Garafola, who generously shared their
research with me; and especially Joanne Serador, who helped me at every stage of the
work.

any other aristocratic and elegant woman who engaged his services.[1] But the frequency with which the countess presented herself to the camera and, in a certain number of startling instances, the *ways* in which she did so are exceptional. What are we to make of the countess's having herself photographed in her chemise? Or exposing her legs? With some justice, one could dispense with these anomalies as the whims of an eccentric, if not deranged, woman. But considered in the context of her culture and milieu, her eccentricity seems remarkable only in degree, and in relation to the fact that she herself was the architect of her own representations. Indeed, much of the significance of these photographs, initially so unclassifiable, resides in their homology with other kinds of photographs, their contiguity with other images, both licensed and illicit. For, as I shall argue, the logic of these images is not only that of a unique expression of the countess's obsessions but that of a talisman of the culture that produced her.

Accordingly, the photographs of the countess require a contextual examination as much as they do a biographical one. However bizarre or idiosyncratic the appearance of these images, the elements of their con-

---

1. Louis Pierson, who began his professional career as a daguerreotypist, joined the firm of Mayer Frères sometime before 1854. The Mayers' commercial success was based on the invention, patent, and sale of various photographic supplies, including fully equipped darkrooms, and the sale of already prepared paints and tints for hand-coloring photographs, a specialty of the firm. Their first commissioned portrait of Napoleon III in 1853, followed by a number of portraits of Eugénie, established their commercial success and social cachet. By 1855 the firm had an address on the boulevard des Capucines and branches in London and Brussels.

In 1862 Ernest Mayer, the remaining brother in the firm, withdrew from the business, leaving Pierson as sole owner, although the original name was retained. In that year the firm could boast a collection of a thousand to fifteen hundred celebrity *cartes-de-visite*. The same year saw the precedent-setting lawsuit (Mayer and Pierson were the plaintiffs) establishing the copyright protection of photography under the law of 19 July 1793.

In 1873 Pierson's daughter married Gaston Braun, whose photographic firm, based in Dornach, specialized in industrial photography. The following year Gaston Braun purchased the entire contents of the Mayer & Pierson studio, which was then consolidated into the firm of Braun & Cie. Pierson continued to administer the affairs of the company until his retirement in 1909. Many of the photographs of the countess de Castiglione have thus been erroneously attributed to Adolph Braun, and the ones taken in her old age to Gaston Braun, because of the studio stamp they bear. I am convinced that all the photographs of the countess that I have seen were taken by Pierson.

The extant plates from the firm of Mayer & Pierson now in the collection of the Musée d'Interlinden, but housed in the Archives du Haut Rhin in Colmar, number ten thousand. See Pierre Tyl, "Mayer et Pierson (2)," in *Prestige de la photographie*, no. 7 (Paris, e. p. a., 1979), 36–63; and the unsigned article, "Pierson's portretten van 'La Castiglione,'" *Foto* (December 1974): 36–39. For the implications of the Mayer & Pierson lawsuit, see Giselle Freund, *Photography and Society* (Boston: David Godine, 1983).

Mayer & Pierson. Countess de Castiglione. c. 1856–1860. © Musée d'Unterlinden Colmar. Reproduction Christian Kempf.

struction are to be located in various representational sites whose common denominator could be termed the semiotics of the feminine. Their
reading thus needs to be both symptomatic and dialectical: symptomatic
in that they are the personal expression of an individual woman's investment in her image—in herself *as* image—dialectical in that this individual act of expression is underwritten by conventions that make her less

an author than a scribe. Such a reading raises the status of the photographs, transforms historical curios into significant testimonials to the power of patriarchy to register its desire within the designated space of the feminine. This reading devolves on the confluence of three fetishisms, a confluence that can also be observed in other social and cultural phenomena of the period: the psychic fetishism of patriarchy, grounded in the specificity of the corporeal body; the commodity fetishism of capitalism, shrouded in what Marx terms the "veil of reification" and grounded in the means of production and the social relations they engender; and the fetishizing properties of the photograph, a commemorative trace of an absent object, the still picture of a frozen look, a screen for the projective play of the spectator's consciousness. That Marx wrote "The Fetishism of Commodities" at the very moment when the countess was photographically documenting her toilettes and bodily parts, and also when the photographic industry was experiencing its own massive commercial expansion, suggests not only the temporal proximity of the three forms of fetishism but the site on which they come together.[2]

That site is, of course, woman, and the confluence of these fetishisms on the body of woman is everywhere to be found in the Second Empire and the Third Republic. But it is above all found within the representations of three types of women: in the image (both textual and iconic) of the prostitute, who unites in her person both seller and commodity; in the dancer or actress, the spectacle within the spectacle, who is perceived as a type of circulating goods; and in the notion of the beautiful, worldly woman, endlessly hypostatized, scrutinized, and dissected. That these three fetishisms converge in and around the representation of the feminine is surely not fortuitous. Luce Irigaray contends that Marx's analysis of commodities as the elementary form of capitalist wealth may be applied to an understanding of women's status in patriarchy. Irigaray's attempt to integrate Marxist and psychoanalytic approaches illuminates one of the problems in much recent literary criticism concerned with the mechanisms and consequences of sexual positioning. Focusing on only the first of the three fetishisms tends to dehistoricize the phenomenon. The structures of fetishism, like the oedipal scenario that is its source, are presented as transhistorical, transcultural, and immutable givens, hermetically distinct from changing material deter-

---

2. The structural homologies between the commodity fetish and the woman in patriarchy is the subject of Luce Irigaray's extraordinary essay "Women on the Market." My own essay is to a great extent indebted to her analysis. See Luce Irigaray, *This Sex Which Is Not One*, trans. Catherine Porter with Carolyn Burke (Ithaca: Cornell University Press, 1985), 170–91.

minations. Granted that nineteenth-century culture manifests a heightened fetishization of the woman's body, it is equally important to acknowledge that the period also witnesses the penetration of the commodity into all spheres of life, experience, and consciousness. Is it not possible to see in the emerging reign of the commodity new forms of the commodification of the feminine?

Examined in this perspective, photography appears to function as a crucial agent in the articulation and dissemination of both forms of commodification. Moreover, insofar as the camera fragments and abstracts its living subject, its mechanisms optically parallel those of reification. In producing and reproducing the image world of capitalism, photography is simultaneously a commodity and an instrument of commodification.[3] Such mid-nineteenth-century cultural developments as an expanded conception of celebrity, with its auxiliary discourses of fashion and publicity, are inseparable from the rise of camera culture. Furthermore, photography plays a critically important role in fostering that condition of modern life which the situationists have dubbed spectacle. Finally, photography brings into being new configurations and articulations of the body, new images of masculinity and (especially) femininity which intersect with older modes of representation to produce their own potent and transfiguring admixtures of modernity. It is within this dense matrix of sexual ideology, economic and social transformation, and inexorable expansion of commodity culture that the historical significance of the countess's photographs may be glimpsed. To the extent that they also raise questions about the nature of feminine self-representation, they are somber reminders that the psychic determinations of patriarchy and the material ones of capitalism are as inescapable for us as they were for the countess.

The Image of Desire

Writing in her journal near the age of sixty, the countess de Castiglione considered her youthful beauty: "The Eternal Father did not realize what He had created the day he brought her into the world; He formed her so superbly that when it was done He lost His head at the contemplation of this marvelous work."[4] The extravagant narcissism of the countess's self-

3. A thorough discussion of this double role of photography may be found in Judith Williamson, *Decoding Advertisement* (London: Marian Boyars, 1985).
4. Quoted in Frédéric Loliée, *Les femmes du second empire* (Paris: Talladier, 1954), 48.

appraisal is somewhat startling, but less so than the objectification to which it attests, evidenced both by the use of the third person singular and by her designation of herself as a work (*maravigliosa opera*).

This hyperbolic praise was echoed by other commentators during the period of the countess's prominence as a Second Empire court celebrity from 1854 until the early 1860s. "There has never been another woman," wrote Gaston Jollivet, "at least not in my lifetime, in whom immortal Venus, as deified by the brushstrokes and chisels of the great masters, was more perfectly incarnate."[5] Even Princess Pauline de Metternich, who thoroughly disliked the countess, admitted, "I have never in my life seen such beauty and I do not expect to see its like again."[6]

Virginia Verasis, née Oldoini, countess de Castiglione, has been the subject of two kinds of posthumous acknowledgment, succeeding those contemporary descriptions of her that appeared in the memoirs and diaries produced during the Second Empire and the Third Republic.[7] In the standard political histories of the period, she figures only as a footnote in the annals of the empire. Briefly the mistress of Napoleon III, she appears to have acted as an agent of Camillo Cavour, to whom she was distantly related, in order to help ensure the emperor's cooperation in King Victor Emmanuel's designs for the unification under his crown of the kingdoms of Piedmont, Lombardy-Venetia, and the two Sicilies. The countess's second discursive afterlife was a function of her fabled beauty and her brief notoriety as the emperor's mistress. In this guise, the countess was the subject of Second Empire republican propaganda (Benjamin Gastineau's *Sottises et scandales du temps présent*), Third Republic potboilers (Frédéric Loliée's *Roman d'une favorite*), modern historical romances (Jacques Chabanne's *Poison sous le crinoline*), and perhaps most interesting, a hysterical panegyric by the self-styled "sovereign of the transitory," the epicure and dandy Comte Robert de Montesquiou (*La divine comtesse*).

One of the pretexts of Montesquiou's curious book is the collection of photographs of the countess, together with many of her personal effects—letters, jewelry, and memorabilia—which he had purchased at auction after her death in 1899. It is this collection of over four hundred photographs that more than anything else suggests the countess's sin-

---

5. Quoted in Alain Decaux, *La Castiglione: Dame de coeur de l'Europe* (Paris: Le Livre Contemporain, 1959), 151.

6. Quoted in Robert de Montesquiou, *La divine comtesse: Etude d'après Mme de Castiglione* (Paris: Goupil, 1913), 26.

7. These include the memoirs of Count Horace de Viel-Castel, Countess Stéphanie Tascher de la Pagerie's *Mon séjour aux Tuileries*, and the memoirs of the count de Maugny.

Mayer & Pierson. Countess de Castiglione. c. 1856–1860. © Musée d'Unterlinden Colmar. Reproduction Christian Kempf.

gularity.[8] For whereas many of the female celebrities of the Second Empire and Third Republic were frequently photographed, their images reproduced, sold commercially, and widely circulated, the countess's photographs, though *taken* by a professional photographer, could with some justice be seen as having been *authored* by her. Far from passively following the directives of the photographer, the countess substantially determined her own presentation to the camera, dictating the pose, costume, props, and accessories and occasionally deciding upon the coloring or retouching of the photographs. Alternatively, we might consider the hundreds of photographs taken of her by Louis Pierson as a working collaboration—one that extended over thirty years.

In whatever proportion we wish to mete out credit for these images, however, what concern me here are the problematic and contradictory aspects of the countess's attempt at photographic self-creation. The apparent imbrication of narcissism and fetishism and the subject's collusion in her own objectification transform these idiosyncratic artifacts into disturbing emblems of the aporia of women and their representations. For what is repetitively played out in the countess's choreography of the self—a choreography she attempts to appropriate for her own ambiguous ends—is the difficulty, if not the impossibility, of the attempt to represent herself. Thus, in venturing to raise the issue of authorship in relation to these photographs, my intention is not to wrest the honors from Pierson and give them to the countess, or even to demonstrate the complexity of the issues pertaining to photographic authorship, but rather to emphasize that the singularity of the countess's photographs intersects with the problem of feminine self-representation.

There is little need to underscore the fact that, historically, women have rarely been the authors of their own representations, either as makers or as models. Prior to the twentieth century there are a few exceptions in literature and in letters, fewer in the visual arts, and virtually none in photography. Indeed, even the most cursory consideration of the photographic representation of women reveals that they are typically constructed in ways scarcely less coded, hardly less "already-written," than they were in other representational systems. Marx's description of the politically and socially disenfranchised—"they do not represent themselves; they must be represented"—is surely as applicable to women as to the proletariat or the colonial subject. But the countess did, in a quite literal sense, produce herself for the camera, and in a manner she alone determined. When a nineteenth-century woman

8. These photographs are now in the collection of the Metropolitan Museum of Art, New York.

provides us with an example of self-representation, we would do well to attend to the terms of its articulation.

In addition to the 434 photographs assembled by the count de Montesquiou, there exist between 250 and 350 negatives of the countess from the photographic firm of Mayer & Pierson, incorporated into the collection of Maison Adolph Braun in 1873, and now in the photographic archives of the city of Colmar.[9] The great majority of the photographs were made between 1856 and 1865, at the height of their subject's fame and beauty. In addition, a few years before her death, the countess commissioned Pierson to make another series of photographs, one set of which is now in the collection of the Gilman Paper Company and another, larger group in Colmar.[10]

These photographs—running the gamut from entirely conventional studio portraits, in either *carte-de-visite* or cabinet format, to theatricalized or narrativized tableaux, to stunning and formally unusual full-figure portraits and odd, crudely hand-colored images[11]—are exceptional for a number of reasons. First, there is the sheer quantity. Surely no woman of the mid-nineteenth century, irrespective of fame or notoriety, was photographed so extensively within so short a time span as was the countess. Moreover, whereas individual women were much photographed (for example, Queen Victoria or the courtesan Cleo de Merode), their images were intended for commercial consumption; by contrast, the bulk of the countess's photographs appear to have been commissioned for herself. We must also bear in mind that in this period the photographic portrait, made principally within a specialized photographic atelier, was by no means cheap, involving as it did the skills of a number of professionals and technicians; it was, in short, anything but a casual and impromptu

9. Many but not all prints in the Montesquiou collection are in the Colmar Archives, which in turn contains prints not represented in the Montesquiou collection. The lack of precision in giving the number of photographs of the countess is due to the fact that there are often several exposures on the same plate, with only slight variations.

10. The photographs in the Gilman Paper Company are attributed to Gaston Braun. Quite possibly there exist other photographs of the countess, but these are the collections I have worked from and are the only ones with which I am familiar.

11. Mayer & Pierson were well known for the quality of their hand-coloring. A number of the countess's biographers claim that she particularly valued the hand-coloring of her photographs by M. Gustave Schad, one of their employees. Many of the colored photographs in the collection of the Metropolitan Museum, however, are crude almost to the point of defacement. Moreover, the paint applied to them looks more like tempera, or occasionally india ink, rather than the tints specifically manufactured for coloring photographs. Since a number of these photographs are annotated in the countess's hand (usually specifying the colors, accessories, and jewelry she wore with the depicted outfit), it seems reasonable to suppose that it was she who painted them.

Mayer & Pierson. Countess de Castiglione. c. 1856–1860. © Musée d'Unterlinden Colmar. Reproduction Christian Kempf.

affair.[12] The countess's photographs, in which she appears, variously, in extravagant court dress, in masquerade, in narrative tableaux enacting such roles as drunken soubrette, Breton peasant, or cloistered nun, were necessarily elaborate productions.

No less remarkable are the photographs she commissioned of herself en déshabillé—in chemise or nightgown—or the closeups of her feet in the sandals she wore for the costume of the queen of Etruria, or the pictures of herself feigning sleep and awakening, terror and rage, or even a photograph where she weeps within the rectangle of an empty picture frame, propped on a table. The genre of still life was also conscripted to the ends of self-portraiture. There are two prints that depict a profusion of her personal effects—photographs of herself shown en abyme, along with shawls, keepsakes, dried flowers, and half buried in their midst, one of her lapdogs, together with his leashes, collars, and dog clothes. That it was the countess, however, who directed the camera is nowhere more evident than in the extraordinary group of photographs in which she removed her shoes and stockings, raised her petticoats and crinoline, and had her naked legs photographed from several viewpoints.

The shocking impropriety of this gesture, even though these photographs were in no sense intended to circulate, becomes even clearer when we note that in those contemporary photographs of dancers, actresses, and demimondaines produced for public consumption, legs are always sheathed in tights. Tights were virtually the prerequisite for the transformation of carnal flesh into the sublimated, sculptural form of aesthetic, albeit eroticized, delectation. For Baudelaire, the work of the tights was analogous to that of cosmetics:

> Anyone can see that the use of rice-powder, so stupidly anathematized by our Arcadian philosophers, is successfully designed to rid the complexion of those blemishes that Nature has outrageously strewn there, and thus to create an abstract unity in color and texture of the skin, a unity, which, like that produced by the legs of the dancer, immediately approximates the human being to the statue, that is, to something superior and divine.[13]

This conception was so prevalent that the naked leg appears only in the context of the nude or in the specifically erotic gesture of removing or putting on stockings. In the latter case, it is, of course, the stocking that

12. See in this regard Jean Sagne, L'atelier du photographe, 1840–1940 (Paris: Presses de la Renaissance, 1984).

13. Charles Baudelaire, "The Painter of Modern Life," in The Painter of Modern Life and Other Essays, ed. and trans. Jonathan Mayne (London: Phaidon, 1964), 33.

constitutes the supplementary sign that codes the woman's body erotically, whether in eighteenth-century pornographic imagery or in the current *Playboy*.

That an aristocratic woman, however notorious, would so display her legs to the official photographer of the court breached one of the several boundaries of what was normatively representable in Second Empire photography. This breach alone establishes these photographs' oddity. But the images are neither coded for the erotic (as are the commercially produced erotic or pornographic images in which the fetishistic display of the leg mandates particular modes of presentation) nor purely clinical and evidentiary, although they resemble the latter genre far more than the former. Rather, the countess's desire was to image parts of her body and to reserve those images for her own gaze—an enterprise that suggests the activities of the fetishist.

Freudian theory, however, insists on the impossibility of female fetishism.[14] The fetish is clinically defined as a substitute object, simultaneously disavowing and commemorating the penis perceived as missing from the maternal body. Accordingly, the significance of the theory lies in its value as a model for simultaneously sustaining two mutually contradictory beliefs. But insofar as it hinges on the threat of castration, the definition effectively forecloses a structural model of female fetishism. Indeed, clinical instances of female fetishism (defined as a libidinal investment in an object indispensable for sexual gratification) appear not to exist. Thus, within the terms of psychoanalytic theory, it is not possible, at least in a clinical sense, to describe the countess's relation to her photographs as fetishistic. Symptomatically, one is on more solid ground in describing the countess's captivation with her photographic image as a classic instance of narcissism or, as it would have been under-

14. That Freud's theory of fetishism is fundamentally predicated on the male subject accounts for at least some of the lacunae and inconsistencies in the theory (for example, the different correlation between vision and significance attributed to boys and girls): see Sarah Kofman, *The Enigma of Woman: Woman in Freud's Writings*, trans. Catherine Porter (Ithaca: Cornell University Press, 1985). Recently, attempts have been made to theorize female fetishism. See, for example, Mary Kelly's artwork and book *Post-Partum Document* (London: Routledge, Kegan Paul, 1983). In this work, Kelly formulates a woman's fetishism in terms of the mother's relation to her (male) child. See also Naomi Schor, "Female Fetishism: The Case of George Sand," in *The Female Body in Western Culture: Contemporary Perspectives*, ed. Susan Rubin Suleiman (Cambridge: Harvard University Press, 1986), 363–72. Theories of the fetish character of the photograph, on the other hand, do not distinguish between male and female spectators and so tend to beg the issue of how women could have a fetishistic relation to them. See Christian Metz, "Photography and Fetish," *October* 34 (Fall 1985): 81–90; and Victor Burgin, "Photography, Phantasy, Function," in *Thinking Photography*, ed. Burgin (London: Macmillan, 1982), 177–216.

stood in her own time, a familiar, if excessive, expression of feminine vanity. But thinking back to her characterization of herself as a "work," it is more suggestive to consider the countess's narcissism within the problematic of feminine subjectivity, for with whose eyes does the countess gaze at images of her face? her legs? her body? Having no culturally privileged organ of narcissistic identification and being positioned outside the symbolic order of patriarchy, defined only as other in relation to the masculine one, the feminine position, it is argued, precludes an achieved subjectivity—subjectivity here understood as a positively, rather than differentially, defined identity. Consequently, the woman, whose self-worth and social value is contingent on her status as object of desire, has so internalized the male gaze as to produce a near total identification with it. In this sense, the commonplace desire to see oneself as one is seen—from outside the confines of subjectivity—is complicated by the concept of sexual difference, because for woman, to see oneself as one is seen is not a supplement to subjectivity but its very condition. But the conditions that inform the subjectivity of women, including the internalization of the male gaze, are hardly the symmetrical complement of those informing the subjectivity of men. In this light, the countess's obsessive self-representations are less an index of narcissism—although they are that too—than a demonstration of a radical alienation that collapses the distinction between subjecthood and objecthood.

Despite the countess's authorship of her own presentation, then, we confront in these photographs a fundamental contradiction. In the very act of authoring her image—a position that implies individuality and a unique subjectivity—the countess can only reproduce herself as a work of elaborately coded femininity, a femininity that, as always, derives from elsewhere. "The life of this woman," wrote Robert de Montesquiou, "was nothing but a lengthy *tableau vivant*, a perpetual *tableau vivant*."[15]

Contemporary descriptions of the countess emphasize the sculptural, marmoreal aspect of her beauty, a quality doubtless heightened by her habitual hauteur. Princess de Metternich, for example, describing the countess's scandalous ball costume as Salammbô, with arms and legs bare and no corset, concludes, "Despite our indignation, I must swear that the sculptural beauty she revealed was so complete that there was nothing indecent about it. One could call her a statue come to life."[16]

15. Montesquiou, *La divine comtesse*, 81.
16. Quoted in Pierre Labrachérie, *Napoléon III et son temps* (Paris: Julliard, 1976), 49.

And Marshal François Canrobert agrees, "Mme de Castiglione was of an incomparable beauty. She resembled at one and the same time a Virgin of Perugino and an antique Venus; but she remained always in a state akin to marble or painting, without animation and without life."[17]

This totemic and reified conception of feminine beauty is a leitmotif in nineteenth-century French culture, changing very little between Balzac and Zola. The highly conventionalized language in the descriptions of feminine beauty may be more specific and detailed in the later period, but their status as already-written texts remains the same.[18] Consequently, the discursive formulas employed in conveying the beauty of a woman are not only quite generalized but usually little related to the specific attributes of the individual on whom they are inscribed. This abstraction accounts for the frequent dissonance between the written accounts and the visual record of famous nineteenth-century courtesans and beauties. For the most part, the faces and bodies of woman such as Cora Pearl, La Paiva, Liane de Pougy, Anna Deslions (the first two were the composite models for Zola's Nana) seem wholly ordinary. Similarly, looking at the plump and rather flaccid legs of the countess, it is difficult to understand what the fuss was about. To be sure, standards of feminine beauty change constantly; Second Empire canons encompassed both the plump and the slender. Moreover, the importance of various body parts waxes and wanes. In her youthful glory, even the countess's elbows were eulogized, compared to ripe peaches. According to Montesquiou and several other biographers, molds were made of her feet and arms.

Of course, the terms according to which the countess was perceived, and those through which she came to perceive herself, were so mediated as to make any reference to her corporeal reality almost beside the point. A historical and feminist examination of her photographs must therefore shift to a consideration of the stereotypical aspect of their construction. In this respect, one of their most striking qualities is their theatricality. In substituting performance for any attempt at presence, the countess may be said to provide a series of representations of the feminine as a form of theater, of masquerade. The impassive face she offers to the camera, the utter formality and iconicity of her self-presentation, refuses the viewer any psychological access, whether real or imagined. We are

17. Quoted ibid., 48.
18. "Beauty (unlike ugliness) cannot really be explained: in each part of the body it stands out, repeats itself, but it does not describe itself. Like a god (and as empty), it can only say: I am what I am. The discourse, then, can do no more than assert the perfection of each detail and refer 'the remainder' to the code underlying all beauty: Art. In other words, beauty cannot assert itself save in the form of a citation." Roland Barthes, S/Z, trans. Richard Miller (New York: Hill and Wang, 1974), 33.

here far from the interest in physiognomy. By her own estimation and that of others, the countess is equivalent to her beauty, and her beauty is itself a form of mask, of disguise. The extravagance of her toilette, even by the bloated and parvenu standards of the Second Empire court, is the incarnation of a femininity that has become wholly theatrical and impersonal, a tribal mask of idealized display. If the photographs of the countess often suggest the stylized exaggerations of a female impersonator, it is because the spectacle of this elaborated femininity is so overweening as to abolish any impulse in the spectator to imagine a character, a personality, a psychology, behind the mask.

In this regard it is important to recall that femininity has been theorized as an operation of masquerade. Initially formulated by the French psychoanalyst Joan Riviere, this concept has been revived by contemporary feminist psychoanalytic theorists (Luce Irigaray) and feminist film theorists (Claire Johnston, Mary Ann Doane) for its relevance to the project of defining the conditions of feminine subjectivity (or its lack).[19] "Masquerade," as Doane writes, "is not as recuperable as transvestism precisely because it constitutes an acknowledgment that it is femininity itself which is constructed as a mask—the decorative layer then conceals a non-identity. . . . The masquerade, in flaunting femininity, holds it at a distance."[20] Doane's formulation departs somewhat from that of Riviere, who had argued that femininity, in a fundamental way, *was* masquerade. Doane inflects the concept differently, enabling her to argue for the destabilizing and defamiliarizing aspects of the feminine as masquerade and thereby imputing to its operations a subversive, or at least disruptive, charge. But taking the case of the countess as a (once) living instance of the mechanisms of feminine masquerade, one perceives less a refusal of patriarchal positioning than a total capitulation to its terms.

Nevertheless, in this psychoanalytic sense of masquerade, the fact that

19. "Masquerade (*la mascarade*): An alienated or false version of femininity arising from the woman's awareness of the man's desire for her to be his other, the masquerade permits woman to experience desire not in her own right but as the man situates her." Irigaray, *This Sex Which Is Not One*, 220. The problem with such formulations lies in their presumption of an at least hypothetically "authentic" femininity. For a different interpretation of the concept, see Mary Ann Doane, "Film and the Masquerade: Theorising the Female Spectator," *Screen* 23 (September–October 1982): 74–87.

20. Doane, "Film and the Masquerade," 81. Doane's consideration of masquerade within the problematics of feminine self-representation draws on the work of the French psychoanalyst Michèle Montrelay, who argues that, since women lack the means to represent lack and can never wholly lose or repress the maternal body, they manifest an excessive proximity to their own bodies that precludes representation. "Woman," writes Montrelay, "is the ruin of representation." See Michèle Montrelay, "Inquiry into Femininity," trans. Parveen Adams *m/f* 1 (1978): 83–101.

many of the photographs of the countess depict her in actual fancy-dress costumes—the queen of Etruria, the lady of Hearts, the hermit of Passy, the Breton peasant, the geisha—is less significant than the more profound sense in which the feminine itself is constituted as an elaborate construction of pose, gesture, dress, or undress. Femininity is not a costume that a woman might remove at will but a role that she lives. Still, there is something about the rituals of masquerade to which the countess was profoundly responsive. This fascination with willful transformation was extended to, imposed upon, her only child, her son, Georges. In a number of photographs the little boy is sometimes dressed as a girl, sometimes as an eighteenth-century cavalier out of Reynolds or Gainsborough, even, in one startling suite of images, as a little-girl version of his mother—hair identically coiffed and ornamented with flowers, neck and shoulders bare. There are also photographs in which he is cast as his mother's page, facing the camera while the countess poses in imperious profile.[21]

The countess's enthusiasm for acting out roles, even to the extent of casting her child as supernumerary in her photographic mise-en-scènes, can perhaps be read as a synecdoche for the role of court beauty, a role fully determined before she ever came to occupy it. In other words, the terms of this part, like the standardized and formulaic descriptions of her beauty, were in every sense given in advance. The babble of the popular press, the gushing of her admirers, the ritualistic tributes to feminine beauty are not only overdetermined but serve, crucially, to mask the nonidentity of the feminine position, its nullity in relation to an acknowledged subjectivity. Many of the anecdotes attached to the countess (that she immured herself behind closed doors and shutters, mirrors veiled, to avoid seeing the fading of her beauty or having it seen, that as she aged she went out only at night) bear witness above all to her textual construction, just as the photographs reveal a persona rather than a person. But the awe, admiration, even panegyrics that La Castiglione inspired in her brief celebrity in the glitter of the Tuileries should not distract us from the material facts that determined her life as a woman. Her relative freedom was a function less of her station and her income than her widowhood, Count Verasis having died at the age of twenty-eight, five years after their marriage. Moreover, the countess, whose face was truly her fortune, came from a noble but not especially solvent

21. Not surprisingly, relations between the countess and her son were deeply troubled from Georges's adolescence on. The countess was perceived, even by her admirers, as a negligent and indifferent mother. This was, in fact, one of the charges made by Count Verasis when, at one point, he contemplated divorce proceedings. Georges died at the age of twenty-four from scarlet fever.

family. The count was wealthy, and she was given in marriage—the terminology is significant—at the age of fifteen. Neither rank nor beauty exempted the countess from her woman's fate as object of exchange.

In her old age, the countess returned to the studio of Louis Pierson. She had known him by then for more than three decades, and for a number of years they had been neighbors. Given the difference in class and circumstance, it is unlikely that they were friends, but there must have existed the kind of peculiar intimacy that aristocratic women would sustain with their servants, physicians, or corsetieres. She had, after all, exposed her legs to him. By the time these photographs were taken in the 1890s, the countess had become stout and possibly toothless. She seems, as well, to have lost much of her hair. Nonetheless, her face appears unlined (it was probably retouched on the negative), her eyebrows were penciled, her eyelids shadowed. She had Pierson photograph her in a number of ensembles: in a ball gown she had worn in her youth; in street costume; in what looks like mourning attire. Again, she had her legs photographed, this time from an odd angle, extended on a chair or hassock. The camera must have been directed down toward her lap from over her shoulder. The dead whiteness of these limbs, along with the shape and blackness of the hassock that supports them, suggest nothing so much as a corpse in a coffin. In one photograph she opened the bodice of her dress, revealing not the lace underwear of an aristocrat, but a poor-looking undershirt, an undergarment that might have been worn by a beggar woman. Her expression here is hard to pin down, hovering as it does between grimace and smile. Her hands are strangely posed; consciously placed or not, they point to her sex.

From this photographic session the countess selected a group of prints and sewed images together with a few stitches. On a slip of paper, in her large, sweeping hand, under the heading "Série des Roses," she listed the places she had worn the ball gown between 1856 and 1895 (Tuileries, Compiègne, etc.). With straight pins, she attached slivers of paper to the surface of several of the photographs, as though to whittle down her girth. But certain of these pieces of paper are applied with seeming randomness, precluding the possibility that in every instance this was a crude attempt to mask the image for rephotographing.

These last photographs are a somber coda to the several hundred images of the countess. For an old woman to restage the postures, costumes, and attitudes of her youth is a staple of the gothic, the grotesque, or the comedic. This too is a text that is already written. Old and fat, forgotten by almost everyone, annotating references to herself in the memoirs of the Second Empire as they appeared in print, the countess looked to the photographer not only to stop time but to undo it. That she

Louis Pierson. Countess de Castiglione. c. 1895–1898. The Gilman Paper Company.

went so far as to tamper with the images suggests the depth of her identification with them. *They* were herself as much as she was herself, perhaps more so. After she had lived her life effectively as a representation, it is not so surprising that identity came to be located in the image perhaps even more than in the flesh.

If we are willing to see the countess's investment in her image as pathological only in degree, then her photographic legacy can be read as a melancholy excursus on the conundrum of feminine self-representation. The lack of any clear boundary between self and image, the collapse of distinctions between interiority and specularity, are familiar, if extreme, manifestations of the cultural construction of femininity. In this sense, it is tempting to see her relation to photography as a bleak parable of femininity attempting its own representation. Mirror of male desire, a role, an image, a value, the fetishized woman attempts to locate herself, to affirm her subjectivity within the rectangular space of another fetish—ironically enough, the "mirror of nature."

The Bazaar of Legs

> The commodity, like the sign, suffers from metaphysical dichotomies. Its value, like its truth, lies in the social element. But the social element is added on to its nature, to its matter, and the social subordinates it as a lesser value, indeed as a nonvalue. Participation in society requires that the body submit itself to a specularization, a speculation, that transforms it into a value-bearing object, a standardized sign, an exchangeable signifier, a "likeness" with reference to an authoritative model. *A commodity—a woman—is divided into two irreconcilable "bodies"*: her "natural" body and her socially valued, exchangeable body, which is a particularly mimetic expression of masculine values.
>
> —Luce Irigaray, "Women on the Market"

The photographs of the countess suggest that she is less the incarnation of a reified femininity than a particularly adept medium of it. In this interpretation, the grotesquerie of the countess's narcissism moves beyond the individual case history to find its constituent terms in the cultural construction of femininity. Accordingly, if the countess can be understood as actively involved in fetishizing parts of her own body—in this instance, her legs—it makes sense to examine this impulse in its historical specificity. Insofar as femininity (the cultural) is never simply a given, as is femaleness (the natural), the countess's staging of herself may be seen as an extreme and immensely stylized recapitulation of fetishistic mechanisms dispersed throughout the culture that produced her.[22]

22. In the nineteenth century, the opposition female-nature/feminine-culture is heavily inflected in terms of class. Femininity or womanliness is the purview of the lady, in contrast to the animal femaleness of working-class or peasant women. "Woman," state the Goncourt brothers, "is an evil, stupid animal unless she is educated and civilized to a high degree. . . . Poetry in a woman is never natural but always the product of education. Only the woman of the world is a woman; the rest are females [*femelles*]." Entry dated 13 October 1855, *Pages from the Goncourt Journal*, ed. and

It is with respect to the specific fetishism of legs and the more generalized fetishism informing the construction of femininity that I want to
consider aspects of the social history of ballet from the romantic period
through the Second Empire. My purpose is twofold. On the one hand,
the development of the ballet permits us to see sexual ideology in the
making: the cult of the ballerina, and the corresponding eclipse of the
danseur noble are indexes of new concepts of masculinity and femininity. On the other hand, the history of ballet provides a particularly
clear case of the imbrication of fetishism and commodification on the
bodies of women. It is important to acknowledge the metastasizing properties of capital as it transforms, insofar as it illustrates, the relationship
between the fetishizing of the feminine and the prostitutionalization of
the women workers who represent that femininity, and the imperatives
of the market, which underpin both developments.

My information on the social history of nineteenth-century ballet is
drawn almost entirely from the works of Ivor Guest, the standard references in the field. But the information I have culled from his book and
essays, and the emphases I have given it, is in every sense partial. In
producing his detailed and indispensable accounts of the French and
English ballet, Guest appears to be oblivious to the sexual politics enacted not only on the level of ideology but also on the material circumstances of the dancers who literally embody that ideology. Feminist
dance historians such as Lynn Garafola, however, have been able to
reread Guest's histories with a clear grasp of the hitherto unacknowledged factors of sexual ideology that operated reciprocally both
inside and outside the institutional boundaries of dance. The importance of both sources for this essay lies in their examinations of a cultural phenomenon from which the countess assimilated the generalized
fetishism of legs, as well as the more dispersed mythology of the feminine.

All considerations of the nineteeth-century ballet stress that it produced the most highly articulated and aestheticized expression of idealized femininity. With the development of pointe in the second decade
of the century, the ballerina became an etherealized vision of sublimity.
Her airy weightlessness, embodied in the darting, floating movement of
her body *en pointe*, is the emblem of a femininity purged of earthly
dross and carnality. Like the fairy spirits, ghosts, and apparitions that

---

trans. Robert Baldick (London: Oxford University Press, 1963), 18. This discursive
opposition is reflected in the Goncourts' literary production as well: on the one hand,
the historical studies of eighteenth-century aristocratic women, and on the other, the
realist novels featuring working-class heroines.

populate the librettos of romantic ballet, the ballerina is a figure of another, more rarefied world. At the same time, this new primacy of the ballerina signals, in Lynn Garafola's description, the historical movement in which "femininity itself becomes the ideology of the ballet, indeed the very definition of the art."[23]

This spiritualized representation of the ballerina as the incarnation of an idealized femininity is, of course, ballet's own representation of itself to itself; this is the language and perception of choreographers, librettists, and dancers, of dance critics, afficianados, belletrists, and those for whom the beauty and pleasure of the ballet lay first and foremost in its expression as an expressive and rigorous art. But whereas the internal development of the ballet in London and Paris from the 1820s through the Second Empire hinged on the new primacy of the ballerina, on a range of technical refinements and elaborations in the dance vocabulary, on the abolition of genres,[24] and on the assimilation of romanticism into dance librettos, music, and narrative, what mattered for the new, enlarged dance public were legs.

Here, for example, is a wholly unexceptional excerpt from an unsigned article of 1843, a moment dance historians consider a benchmark in the artistic and technical evolution of ballet:

> Whenever we hear that a *danseuse* is coming out we white-waistcoat, pantaloon, and double-opera ourselves up to the hilt . . . so that nothing may interrupt our study and contemplation of the "new gal's legs." The stage, particularly the stage of Her Majesty's Theatre, is a kind of gallery of sculpture, a studio in which Phidias might have revelled, and the conceptions of Canova have been enslaved. The legs at the opera are reflections from the best masters—we beg pardon—we mean *mistresses*, yes *mistresses* is precisely what we mean. We have seen gentlemen, even old gentlemen, deeply affected by this glorious display. . . . Oh! the legs of Fanny [Elssler] displayed a vast deal of propriety and frightened sober men from their prescribed complacency. Taglioni's legs encompassed a great deal of attention; Cerrito's leg magnified excite-

23. Lynn Garafola, "The Travesty Dancer in Nineteenth-Century Ballet," *Dance Research Journal* 17–18 (Fall 1985–Spring 1986): 35–40. The ideological structuring of the feminine mystique of ballerinas was further implemented by their division into two categories, an ethereal (Taglione's legendary quality), and an earthly (Elssler's specialty). This binary opposition was codified by Théophile Gautier in his distinction beween ballerinas as "Christians" and "Pagans." See Ivor Guest, *The Romantic Ballet in Paris* (London: Pitman, 1966).

24. The three traditional genres were the *noble* (in which the male dancer was of special importance), *demi-caractère*, and *comique*. See Guest, *The Romantic Ballet in Paris*.

A. A. E. Disdéri. *Les jambes de l'Opéra* (*carte-de-visite*). 1856. International Museum of Photography at George Eastman House.

ment; Duvernay possessed a magic leg, but to dilate is useless—the Opera is a bazaar of legs, and a stall costs ten and sixpence.[25]

That a significant proportion of the audiences that thronged the ballet in London and Paris were there to ogle the dancers' bodies—and particularly their legs—was a fact of ballet life that varied only in the outrageousness of its expression. By the 1830s the pit of the Covent Garden Opera House, popularly known as "Fop's Alley," had become an unruly debauch in which the dandies from White's and Crockford's loudly commented upon the physical merits and deficiencies of the dancers' bodies, regularly interrupting the ballet with catcalls, obscenities, or the equal furor of their approbation. The salaciousness of the aristocratic male spectators was often baldly repeated in the written accounts and commentaries on various performances.

Thus, from the privileged vantage of the omnibus box, one writer described the erotic locus of ballet, "drawing innumerable glasses to a common center, decked in flowers and a confusion of folds of gauze scarcely secreting that particular part of the leg whereon the fastening of the stocking is generally clasped and smiling and making others smile to see her *pirouette* as the star of the *ballet*."[26]

That the legs of the dancers are the focus of the fetishizing gaze of the male spectator is only the reflection of a far more generalized phenomenon that superimposes a map of (erotic) significance on the woman's body. In Western culture, women's legs were covered by robes, skirts, or dresses until after the First World War. Although hemlines historically migrated from the arch of the foot to several inches above the ankle, no expanse of leg was ever normally exposed, and this protocol was as applicable to agricultural laborers as to aristocrats and bourgeoises. Still, that women's legs were not normally seen is a necessary but not sufficient argument for the erotic significance accorded them at least from the eighteenth century on. Certainly, the fact that European women did not routinely wear drawers until well after the mid–nineteenth century is relevant. Above the stocking, the leg was bare; under the skirts and petticoats, the woman's body—her sex—was exposed. Yet the existence of the fetishism of legs as, in Kleinian terms, a part object is such as to trivialize attempts at an empirical understanding. The legs of Betty

---

25. *Illustrated London Life*, 16 April 1843, cited in Ivor Guest, "Dandies and Dancers," *Dance Perspectives* 37 (Spring 1969): 4. The leering quality of this quotation is particularly striking in that Taglioni was popularly perceived as the incarnation of virginal spirituality.

26. Ibid., 12.

Grable or Marlene Dietrich, or the prominence of legs in modern advertising, are evidence of the enduring potency of this particular mapping of the erotic. Within the historical period under discussion here, however, the salient fact is that until the twentieth century it was only the legs of dancers or entertainers that were publicly on display.

We confront here the first of the cultural contradictions of the mystique of the feminine inscribed in the dance. Discursively constructed to represent a purified essence of femininity, enacting the body's transformation into art, the dancers themselves are simultaneously erotic spectacle, bazaar of legs, panoply of potential mistresses.

In this regard, two crucial and interrelated phenomena accompany the ballet's evolution from a courtly art, wholly supported by royal patronage, to a public, increasingly bourgeois spectacle, dependent on sales and subscriptions. First and foremost, there was the prostitutionalization of the dance; second, there was the eclipse, if not banishment, of the male dancer and his replacement by the female travesty dancer. That these developments are the direct outcome of the ballet's new economic exigencies and its consequent reliance on a free-market economy is further substantiated by comparison with conditions of the Royal Ballet in Copenhagen and the Mariinsky Theater in St. Petersburg. Licensed and subsidized by crown and czar, patronized by the court, the ballet in both countries retained its aristocratic status. Consequently, the *danseur noble*, although certainly rivaled by the ballerina, never lost his position. And the female corps de ballet, underpaid and overworked as were their sisters in France and England, were employees of the court and thus legally protected by it. But in both England and France the privatization of the ballet led inexorably to the debasement of the female corps and eventually to the trivialization of the ballet itself.

One of the immediate results of privatization was the need for advance subscriptions and private subsidies, which made the finances of the ballet contingent upon the largess of wealthy men. One of the first acts of John Ebers, appointed director of the Covent Garden Opera Ballet after its bankruptcy in 1820, was to open the passages to the stage to gentlemen and to construct a greenroom where they could mix with dancers. Almost as soon as it was completed, it became a cruising ground for the members of the private clubs, whose patronage was so crucial to the economics of the ballet. Contemporary accounts make very clear the extent of sexual trafficking within the dancers' world, including the presence of procuresses as go-betweens and erstwhile managers. This is not to say that dancers had not sold themselves prior to the adaptation of the ballet to a market economy. Rather, the new arrangements tended to encourage and institutionalize a situation in which wealthy and powerful men could regard the corps de ballet as a sanctioned flesh market.[27]

The sexual commodification of the dancer was further facilitated by the disintegration and eventual disappearance of a guild and clan system that had traditionally provided training, social identity, and protection. Whereas many of the greatest ballerinas of the romantic era were the offspring of theatrical clans, an increasing number of girls entering the profession were products of urban slums.[28]

In Paris the sexual economy of the ballet, which was privatized in the wake of the 1830s revolution, mirrored that of London. In the same way that the greenroom was made into a site of sexual commerce, so was the *foyer de la danse* under the directorship of Dr. Véron. Albéric Sécond's description of this development is worth quoting at length:

Before the Revolution of 1830, when few strangers were admitted backstage and guards and lacqueys in royal livery were stationed to warn off intruders, the Foyer de la Danse served merely as a room for the dancers to gather and limber up before going on to the stage. But all that was changed by Dr. Véron, who transformed the bare working room into a glittering center of social life. This was an adroit move, which made the Opera fashionable overnight. The dancers were then joined by a select band, consisting of the *corps diplomatique*, the more important *abonnés*, and other distinguished men, who found in this an added source of pleasure in the evening's entertainment. Many of these men, young men-about-town who were for the most part members of the Jockey Club, acquired the habit of looking on the *coulisses* of the Opera as their private seraglio. The most fashionable of them watched the performances from the proscenium boxes which abutted on the stage itself and were known as the *loges infernales*. "The Opera," it was

27. "Poverty, naturally, invites sexual exploitation, especially in a profession of flexible morals. . . . In the 1830s, however, the backstage of the Paris Opera became a privileged venue of sexual assignation, officially countenanced and abetted. Eliminating older forms of 'caste' separation, the theater's enterprising management dangled before the select of its paying public a commodity of indisputable rarety and cachet— its female corps of dancers." So writes Garafola, "The Travesty Dancer," 36. To this recipe for exploitation must be added the straitened economic circumstances of most dancers after the loss of royal subsidy. New budgetary restrictions in the wake of privatization diminished pensions (when they were not altogether eliminated) and curtailed other benefits. In 1848, with the Paris Opera confronting enormous deficits, the corps's salaries were reduced. With the exception of the immense pay drawn by the ballet stars, salaries were extremely low, and dancers had to pay out of pocket for extra classes and *classes de perfectionnement*. That so many dancers sold themselves has as much to do with poverty as with the freer sexual mores among professional entertainers.

28. Ibid., 36.

explained, "provides them with their amorous pleasures, just as the Pompadour stud-farm provides them with their equestrian pleasures; they consider it as a storehouse for remounts, no more." The real nature of the coulisses, in the words of an intelligent dancer, was "bourgeois, which is the worst of natures. No one is too virtuous, because that would be stupid, but no one is too sinful, because that becomes fatiguing. The coulisses of the Opera have, above all, an air of boredom. They have the spleen, like a fat English millionaire, and it would be difficult for it to be otherwise. A large proportion of the abonnés have frequented the Opera for years. For them, the coulisses no longer have any mystery, savour, novelty or poetry. The others, the newcomers, do nothing but look on, being not rich enough to touch."[29]

But if the bourgeois spectator could afford only to look, he was given more to look at. In the 1840s the ballet skirt was shortened from midcalf to knee length, although the longer skirt was retained for certain roles. Of much greater significance, however, was the disappearance of the danseur noble and the rise of the travesty dancer as partner to the ballerina.

In large part, this disappearance was a consequence of altered definitions of masculinity engendered by bourgeois culture. An aristocratic, courtly ideal of masculine grace and elegance was incompatible with a new ideology of gender in which concepts of beauty and grace were coming increasingly to be identified exclusively with the feminine. The stately adagios of the danseur noble, the gravity and poise of his partnering, were far less appealing to an increasingly bourgeois audience than the athleticism of the leaps and spins performed by the danseur de demi-caractère. Associated with the ancien regime, the art of the danseur noble was politically suspect as well.[30]

By 1840 these attitudes had solidified to such an extent that even a critic as knowledgeable and sophisticated about dance as Jules Janin professed to find male dancers ridiculous:

You know perhaps that we are hardly a supporter of what are called grands danseurs. The grand danseur appears to us so sad and heavy! He is so unhappy and self-satisfied! He responds to nothing, he represents nothing, he is nothing. Speak to us so of a pretty dancing girl who displays the grace of her features and the elegance of her figure, who

29. Albéric Sécond, Les petits mystères de l'Opéra (Paris, 1844), quoted in Guest, The Romantic Ballet in Paris, 28.
30. Garafola, "The Travesty Dancer," 35–36.

reveals so fleetingly all the treasures of her beauty. Thank God, I understand that perfectly. . . . But a man, a frightful man, as ugly as you and I, a wretched fellow who leaps about without knowing why, a creature specially made to carry a musket and a sword and to wear a uniform. That this fellow should dance as a woman does—impossible! That this bewhiskered individual who is a pillar of the community, an elector, a municipal councillor, a man whose business is to make and unmake laws, should come before us in a tunic of sky-blue satin, his head covered with a hat with a waving plume amorously caressing his cheek, a frightful *danseuse* of the male sex, come to pirouette in the best place while the pretty ballet girls stand respectfully at a distance—this is surely impossible and intolerable.[31]

The rise of the travesty dancer, from the 1820s on, represented more than a technical solution to the problem posed by the shift in the ideology of gender. The thinly veiled prurience in the descriptions of the ballerinas who specialized in travesty roles indicates the extent to which their popularity was inseparable from the spectacle of their bodies. The corseted midriff emphasized bosom and hips, the skintight breeches displayed buttocks, hips, and legs. Thus, everything in the costume of the travesty dancer proclaimed her womanliness even as the choreography positioned her as the lover/partner of the ballerina. Accordingly, a pas de deux between ballerina and travesty dancer produced its own, distinctive eroticism, subtly evoking a lesbian pairing that the libretto disavowed.[32]

During the Second Empire, as the ballet became diminished as art, it became ever more elaborate as spectacle, with great attention paid to lighting, decor, special effects, and an accompanying increase in the corps of dancers. The number of venues for dance, both popular and balletic, increased; for the period 1847 and 1870, Guest lists seventeen theaters, vaudevilles, and *bals* where dance could regularly be viewed. This proliferation produced an expansion in the number of dancers who obtained a living, however precarious, from the dance. The introduction of new popular forms (the cancan, for example, which, although invent-

31. Jules Janin, *Journal des Débats*, 2 March 1840, quoted in Guest, *The Ballet of the Second Empire* (Middletown, Conn.: Wesleyan University Press, 1974), 21.

32. "In the formalized mating game of the travesty *pas de deux*, two women touching and moving in harmony conveyed an eroticism perhaps even more compelling than their individual physical charms. The fantasy of females at play for the male eye is a staple of erotic literature, a kind of travesty performance enacted in the privacy of the imagination. Ballet's travesty *pas de deux* gave public form to this private fantasy, whetting audience desire, while keeping safely within the bounds of decorum." Garafola, "The Travesty Dancer," 39.

ed in 1832, swept through Paris as a craze in the 1860s) produced a new crop of celebrity dancers, such as the notorious Mlle Rigolboche.[33] The proletarian background of the majority of these women, combined with the now fully sexualized associations of the dance, guaranteed that the dancer was perceived a priori as a sexual commodity. Her lower-class origins presumed, her legs exposed, her favors for sale, the equivalence of the dancer with the prostitute had by midcentury become fully acknowledged. The virtuous exceptions, such as the tragic Emma Livry, function dialectically as the necessary virgins in a discourse of whores. In a figure such as Lola Montes (who in the 1840s and 1850s was the subject of a number of scandalous or moralizing books, much space in the popular press, and innumerable lithographs and wood engravings), the mythology of the dancer and that of the courtesan were fully united.

To an already substantial market for lithographs and wood engravings of ballet dancers, the advent of the photographic *carte-de-visite*, by virtue of its relative cheapness, quasi-industrial means of production, and indexical qualities, guaranteed a second life and even greater dissemination. In her book on *carte-de-visite* portrait photography, Elizabeth Ann McCauley stresses the technical determinations governing subject and pose (e.g., exposure time, studio location, etc.), which effectively precluded conveying any real impression of dance choreography or movement.[34] If we understand, however, that the dancer had become, virtually by definition, an icon of the erotic, the massive production of photographs of dancers need not attest to any particular interest in ballet per se. Additionally, the preponderance of travesty dancers in the dance photographs of the Second Empire tends to substantiate the perception that these were, in some sense, fetish objects.

The traffic in (dance) photographs, like the traffic in (dance) women, was charged in this period with another discursive current—namely, an intensified and expanded notion of celebrity, a phenomenon reciprocally fueled and in part constructed precisely by that traffic in images, particularly *carte-de-visite* and stereopticon photographs. McCauley indicates that by 1860, the first, second, third, and ninth arrondissements (the center of the photographic industry) included 207 pho-

33. Ephemeral celebrities at the intersection between popular dance and the demimonde, women such as Rigolboche at the height of her fame, inspired books (e.g., *Rigolbochemanie, Mémoirs de Rigolboche*), caricatures in the popular press, and of course, photographs. See Ivor Guest, "Queens of the Cancan," *Dance and Dancers* (December 1952): 14–16; and Francis Gribble, "The Origin of the Cancan," *Dancing Times* (April 1933): 19–21.

34. Elizabeth Ann McCauley, *A. A. E. Disdéri and the Carte-de-Visite* (New Haven: Yale University Press, 1985).

tographic establishments, of which sixteen employed more than ten workers each. Although the commissioned portrait was the staple service of all such businesses, celebrity *cartes* represented a significant part of the sales of the larger firms.[35] Similarly, celebrity stereos were marketed either individually or in thematic ensembles. McCauley indicates that 37 percent of A. A. E. Disdéri's published *Galerie des contemporains* was devoted to theatrical personalities and entertainers; 53 percent of the celebrity *cartes* advertised in an 1861 issue of the *Journal amusant* were likewise of entertainers. While the top of the photographic pyramid was occupied by esteemed tragediennes such as Rachel, Ristori, or for ballet, Muravieva and Merante, the bottom was made up of the *figurantes*, dance-hall girls, café-concert singers, and the troupes of the popular theaters and *bals*. Somewhere between the two were the *cartes* of the famous courtesans La Paiva, Cora Pearl, Anna Deslions, and so forth.

Accompanying the circulation of these images were books hastily produced by journalists, books with such titles as *Ces dames*, *Les jolies actrices de Paris*, *Les cocottes*, *Rigolbochemanie*. These were themselves supplements to the extensive coverage of entertainers and demimondaines churned out by the illustrated press, publications such as *Le Boulevard* (established 1862), *La Lune* (1866), *Journal Amusant* (1856), *La Vie Parisienne* (1863).

While it is indisputable that the development of the illustrated press and the celebrity gossip/scandal/fashion ephemera it purveyed were among the results of the draconian press laws imposed after Napoleon III's 1851 coup d'état, this new construction of celebrity in the Second Empire had broader ramifications. For insofar as this expanded notion of celebrity is predicated on an economy of the spectacle (an image of Ada Isaacs Mencken in tights is not to be understood in the same terms as one of the duc de Morny with accompanying biography), we are witnessing a shift from an older conception of celebrity defined through power and exemplarity to one of consumable—constantly replenished—evanescence. And insofar as a major part of this spectacular realm is populated by more or less eroticized images of women, the attraction of this new

35. The vogue for assembling celebrity *cartes-de-visite* into bound albums was widespread, indulged in as much by the aristocracy as by the bourgeoisie. What is particularly striking about these albums is the promiscuous mix of images of the powerful, the royal, the fashionable, the notorious, and the ephemeral. For example, an album in the collection of the Museum of Modern Art (Accession no. 42.135), assembled 1865–75, brings together in its pages victims of the Commune, the British Royal Family, generals of the Second Empire, various crowned heads of Europe, artists (Edwin Landseer, Adolph Menzel, Horace Vernet, Ary Scheffer, Gustave Courbet, Camille Corot, Jean Meissonier), actresses (Rachel, Adelaide Ristori), and freaks (General Mite, Tom Thumb's wedding). Such an ensemble is by no means exceptional.

image world is underwritten by fantasies of imaginary possession. Although the image of the woman is not yet conscripted to the marketing of commodities (this would be the accomplishment of the Third Republic), the erotic allure of the commodity and the woman herself as erotic commodity are inexorably moving into a shared orbit. For the bourgeois men at the opera who could not afford to touch, only to look, the diminutive image of the living woman—sexualized, compliant, immobilized— is the token of their power.

The Legs of the Prostitute

> The economy of exchange—of desire—is man's business.
> —Luce Irigaray, "Women on the Market"

The nude, the prostitute, pornography—what kinds of relations on the register of representation obtain among these three avatars of femininity? The first, legacy of classical antiquity, had by the nineteenth century all but excluded the male, whose idealized body had originally provided the conceptual model for its expression. The second, the prostitute, whether in the glamorized incarnation of the *grande courtisane* or the debased and sordid image of the *fille publique*, is one of the most pervasive and allusive motifs of the Second Empire and Third Republic. The third term of this set, pornography, intersects with and upsets the category of the nude, particularly to the extent that it incorporates certain elements of it within its own conventions.[36] And insofar as it is assumed that the women depicted in pornographic and erotic photography are prostitutes, the aristocratic *hôtel*, the bourgeois interior, can be said to have been in some sense penetrated by that which the entire reglementary system was designed to sequester and contain.

In placing these three terms in relation, what I hope to suggest is the failure of a discursive cordon sanitaire—an attempt at segregating the licit from the illicit, which constantly founders, not simply because

---

36. This distinction I am implicitly drawing between erotic and pornographic photographic imagery is neither systematic nor theoretical. I would categorize as erotic a frontal photograph of a female nude, more or less artfully posed. If, however, she were masturbating, or exposing her genitals, I would consider it to be (within the terms of this discussion) pornographic. From the coup d'état of 1851 through the 1860s, censorship of photography was fairly stringent. *Académies* were legal, but could be sold only within the wall of the Ecole des beaux-arts. Soft-core erotica, which was openly sold, was subject to the vagaries of the government censors; one man's art was often another's indecency.

the various boundaries prove permeable but because the mechanisms (psychic, social, economic) that underwrite them are ultimately the same. The evidence of this failure of containment shows itself in various guises in the Second Empire. The anxiety cathected onto the image and body of the prostitute is one symptom. The "crisis of the nude"—so termed by T. J. Clark—is its manifestation in the framework of aesthetic discourse. And finally, the apparently enormous production of pornographic imagery attests to the impulse to master and possess the object of desire while debasing it and neutralizing its power and threat.

Of the three terms I am treating, photographic pornography is the most empirically elusive.[37] Then, as now, it represented an underground aspect of photographic production, and as such it figures not at all in the standard photography histories. Collectors of pornographic photography tend not to publicize their holdings, and their reticence is paralleled by libraries, museums, and other public institutions. Nonetheless, a few generalizations can be made with certainty.

First, almost as soon as there were easily produced daguerreotypes, there were pornographic ones. Until the early 1850s—that is to say, until the industrialization of photography—photographic pornography appears to have been a luxury item. Daguerreotypes are, of course, unique images; calotype technologies were not employed much in France until after 1850, and the collodion process, which also produces unlimited prints, was not invented until 1851. Daguerreotype pornography is often exquisitely hand-colored, the models are carefully posed and lighted, and the trappings are often luxurious. Grant Romer of Eastman House describes pornographic daguerreotypes concealed inside watch covers, opened by hidden springs, or lining the interior covers of snuff boxes or made into jewelry. By the early years of the Second Empire, much daguerreotype pornography was stereoscopic.[38] Possessing a compelling illusion of three-dimensionality and preternatural detail, painstakingly tinted, entirely grainless, the visual effect of the hand-colored daguerreotype stereo is the acme of verisimilitude. Moreover, viewing an image through the stereopticon masks out everything but the image; the illusion of being in the picture is extremely powerful. The fineness of detail is often striking; in a number of daguerreotypes in the Cromer Collection at Eastman House the necklace and earrings of the model are picked out

37. For most of my information on Second Empire pornography, I am indebted to Grant Romer, of Eastman House, who has generously shared his substantial, and unfortunately unpublished, research with me.

38. See Uwe Scheid, *Das erotische Image* (Dortmund: Die bibliophilen Taschenbücher, 1984).

with a needle on the surface of the plate. Viewed through a stereopticon, they glitter and shine.

Romer suggests that the production of these deluxe examples of the pornographer's art crested at the time of the 1855 and 1867 universal exhibitions, when Paris was packed with wealthy foreigners. By the mid-1850s, though, the production of pornography for the discriminating connoisseur was joined by a mass-produced form, with an accompanying decline in quality and craftsmanship.[39]

What did these images depict? Here is an instance of the ways in which photography either draws on existing representational conventions and alters them or invents its own. Of the former, images of coitus, oral sex, lesbians, and masturbation all have graphic-arts precedents—in many cases, immediate ones, such as in the pornographic lithography of the July Monarchy. These, however, undergo modification. On the level of technique, the immobility of the tripod-mounted camera, the relative slowness of exposure, and the resistance of real bodies to positions possible for the graphic artist all tend to enforce a repertory of pose and display in one sense more limited, in another more expansive, than existed previously. For example, pornography had traditionally privileged sexual activity; with photography, the emphasis shifted more and more to the presentation of the woman or of parts of her body, as spectacular display for scopic consumption. With the leg as a locus of erotic interest, poses were invented to provide new arrangements for the delectation of the viewer. Dancers and demimondaines were frequently shown with their legs straddling the backs of chairs. And photography can be credited with the invention of the beaver shot, an image so constructed that its sole purpose is the exposure of the female genitalia.[40] Within this genre neither a surrogate for the male viewer nor a simulation of the woman's pleasure—indeed very little of the woman at all—is necessary for the image to do its work. In fact, one of the suggestive tropes of this kind of presentation is the disappearance of the woman's face, covered by her thrown-back petticoats or shrouded in veils.

But if one representational pole concerns the elimination of every-

39. Some notion of the scale of the photographic pornography industry of the nineteenth century may be obtained from the following: "The *Times* of 20 April 1874 reports a police raid on a London shop in which 130,248 obscene photographs were seized, plus 5,000 stereoscopic slides." Stephen Heath, *The Sexual Fix* (New York: Schocken, 1984), 110.

40. A conspicuous predecessor is Gustave Courbet's notorious painting *L'origine du monde*, recently discussed in Linda Nochlin, "The Origin without an Original," *October* 37 (Summer 1986): 76–86; Neil Hertz, "Medusa's Head: Male Hysteria under Political Pressure," *Representations* 4 (Fall 1983): 27–54; and Denis Hollier, "How to Not Take Pleasure in Talking about Sex," *Enclitic* 8 (Spring–Fall 1984): 84–93.

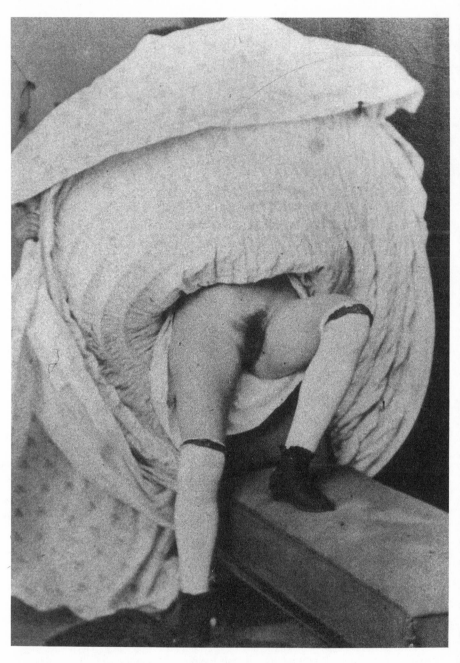

Anonymous. Albumen print. c. 1865. Private collection.

thing but the woman's sex, another privileges the specificity of her gaze. It is these photographs—in which the woman model looks directly into the lens of the camera, thus meeting the gaze of the spectator—that depart so emphatically from traditional modes of pornography. Inasmuch as it is a real woman so deployed, a real woman who receives and returns the look, pornographic photography detaches itself from an image world of fantasy and comes to occupy an ambiguous realm between the real and the imagined.

It was around this problem of the indexical property of the photograph that the debate on the acceptability of the photographic nude unfolded. For members of the prestigious Société Française de la Photographie, who actively debated the issue in the 1850s, the photographic nude, almost by definition, could not accede to the aesthetic. Photographic nudes were therefore formally banned from the society's competitions and exhibitions. This exclusion had two components, one explicitly articulated, the other implicit within the larger framework of the debate. The former hinged on the purported lack of mediation between living model and photographic image; the generalizing, idealizing, and abstracting operations of the artist were voided by the very nature of mechanical reproduction. The absence of these mediations—so the argument went—precluded the metamorphosis from naked to nude. The second, implicit aspect of the debate turned on what could not be said about either category.

Primarily, this aspect devolved on the nature of the conventions that confirm the attributes of the nude as, on the one hand, a sublimation of the erotic and, on the other hand, a fetish. In its sublimatory capacity, the nude functions both formally and discursively as an aesthetic grid on which is figured the representation of a woman's body. A field of pleasurable looking, for the free play of desire and imaginary possession, it must nonetheless distinguish itself from the real world of individualized, corporeal bodies. As fetish, the nude must deny or allay the fear that the real female body always risks producing—hence such conventions as the suppression of the vagina and the elimination of body hair, as well as a prescribed repertory of acceptable poses.

The photographic nude inevitably disrupts these structures of containment and idealization, disrupts, in short, the propriety of the nude. What the painter elided, the photographer showed: not just pubic hair but dirty feet and, perhaps most disturbing, the face of the real woman, often including her direct and charmless gaze. The look of these women is rarely the inviting compliant expression that signals complicity between the desiring subject and the object of desire. In other photographs the look is utterly straightforward, unflinching, devoid of seduction. Occasionally it is challenging. This is, in fact, the look of Manet's *Olym-*

pia, and part of the scandal the painting provoked undoubtedly lay in the widespread recognition, albeit unacknowledged, of the covert and illicit imagery that paralleled the representation.[41]

In this context, T. J. Clark's discussion of *Olympia's* reception in 1865, which in most respects is so inclusive, entirely neglects the ways in which the crisis of the nude, the scandal of *Olympia*, and the intensifying fetishism of women's bodies were integrally related to the proliferation and dissemination of pornographic and erotic photography. Clark's discussion hinges on the notion that the courtesan—the mythologized, expensive, and publicly acknowledged manifestation of commercial sexuality—constituted the horizon of iconographic representability for the Second Empire.[42] To the extent that *Olympia* violated that boundary, to the extent that the model was anxiously recognized as a denizen of the lower ranks of prostitution—"woman of the night from Paul Niquet's" as she is designated in one of Clark's critical citations—the painting wrought havoc on the discursive limits within which prostitution could be imaged. The problem with this formulation is that it ignores the extent to which images of prostitutes (or women imagined to be prostitutes) of all ranks and levels actually circulated. Although the courtesan may have been the only prostitutional representative appropriate for salon walls, an iconographic tradition depicting the less privileged members of the profession had produced its own mythologies, conventions, modes of representation. Moreover, the women who posed for the

41. Gerald Needham's essay "Manet, *Olympia*, and Pornographic Photography" made this claim in 1972. Needham reproduced a number of photographs in support of the argument that Manet had been strongly influenced by what Needham terms "pornographic" photographs (I would consider them to fall within the category of erotic imagery). Needham's essay is reprinted in *Woman as Sex Object: Studies in Erotic Art, 1730–1970*, ed. Thomas B. Hess and Linda Nochlin (New York: Newsweek Books, 1972), 80–89. The essay appears to have had little influence in the field; T. J. Clark, for example, neither cites nor lists it in the bibliography of *The Painting of Modern Life* (New York: Knopf, 1984).

42. "The category *courtisane* was what could be *represented* of prostitution, and for this to take place at all, she had to be extracted from the swarm of mere sexual commodities that could be seen making use of the streets." Clark, *The Painting of Modern Life*, 109. On this point, I disagree with Clark, although I would wish to add that his chapter on *Olympia* is brilliant and illuminating. In arguing for the courtesan as representational limit, Clark needs to collapse all sorts of categories of the sexualized or venal woman under the sign of the courtesan, whom he characterized as floating either above or below fixed class determinations. The grisette of the romantic period and the lorette of the Second Empire (so named by Nestor Roqueplan, director of the Paris Opera), to cite two examples, were associated with bohemia, however, not with the flashy world of courtesans and financiers. Further, in numerous texts, including *Nana*, the courtesan is very explicitly linked to commerce and commodification; her glamour and costliness in no way detached her from her position as goods on the market.

pornographic images (whether the deluxe or mass-market versions), the women who spread their legs, feigned masturbation, engaged in lesbian or heterosexual sex, were surely assumed to be prostitutes—*filles publiques*—not artist's models. In fact, a broad spectrum of sexualized and more or less venal feminine identities—the *grisette, lorette, lionne, biche, cocotte, grande cocotte, grande horizontale*—were initially imagined in the lithographic production of the 1830s and 1840s and later in photographs.[43]

These various lexical distinctions in the vocabulary of gallantry warrant discussion, particularly insofar as their variety and ambiguity have some bearing on the iconographic sphere. To begin with the obvious, such a rich and nuanced lexicon for sexually active or venal woman, like the Eskimo's reputed twenty-seven words for snow, attests to the central importance of defining women by their sexual activity. How that importance was articulated and what kind of significance was attributed to it, could, however, be inflected in different ways. Within the framework of the judicial, legislative, medical, or sociological coordinates of prostitution, the crucial issues were surveillance, control, and confinement. The terms of this *discours prostitutionelle*, laid down in encyclopedic detail by the "Newton of Harlotry," A. J. B. Parent-Duchâtelet, were largely instrumental.[44] If the public prostitute could be identified, registered, and confined to certain areas; her activity limited to certain hours; her person segregated in a licensed brothel; if she could be monitored by the madame, the police, the gynecologist—then prostitution, considered by Parent-Duchâtelet and his heirs a necessary evil (like the sewer system, indispensable for public health), could be managed and contained.[45] The threat to this rationalized system lay in the growing ranks of clandestine, that is to say, nonregistered prostitutes.

But the alarm produced by the increase in clandestine prostitution

43. See in this regard Beatrice Farwell, *The Cult of Images: Baudelaire and the 19th-Century Media Explosion* (Santa Barbara, Calif.: University of Santa Barbara Art Museum, 1977).

44. Alexandre Parent-Duchâtelet's *De la prostitution dans la ville de Paris*, a demographic study of twelve thousand prostitutes who had been registered during the period 1816–31, was published in 1836. Its influence cannot be overemphasized. It provided the model not only for fifty years of French reglementary systems but also for British laws and investigations. See Alain Corbin's seminal work *Les filles de noce: Misère sexuelle et prostitution aux 19ième et 20ième siècles* (Paris: Aubier, 1978). In his chapter on *Olympia*, T. J. Clark provides an excellent account of the legacy of Parent-Duchâtelet.

45. Parent-Duchâtelet was additionally a specialist in sewers, drains, and cesspools. For a discussion of the linkage among prostitution, sewage, purification, and death, see Alain Corbin, "Commercial Sexuality in Nineteenth-Century France," *Representations* 14 (Spring 1986): 209–19.

(reflected in the corresponding decrease in the number of licensed houses in both Paris and London) as well as what were widely perceived as increasingly "public" manifestations of it, masked a more fundamental anxiety. For what is ultimately at stake in the effort to define the prostitute—whether through demographic and sociological analysis, as in the work of Parent-Duchâtelet and the British Blue Books of the 1840s, or in the many works in the popular press on the subject of the demimonde—is the uncertainty of differentiation. How does one distinguish between the honest woman and the prostitute? Or as Alain Corbin asks, "Is it not precisely the goal of this discourse to create a difference and thus finally to marginalize the registered prostitute as a counterideal in order to permit the honest woman to be better defined?"[46] The urgency of the need to define the nature of the prostitute was further heightened because the work of Parent-Duchâtelet and the British researchers had indicated that women frequently moved in and out of prostitution with some fluidity; the loss of employment or other economic factors could propel a woman into prostitution temporarily, but she could leave it just as abruptly.[47] Thus the encrustation of folklore,·legend, and myth that functioned to fix the definition of the prostitute (she was frigid, lazy, improvident, liked sweets, and so forth) was undercut by a body of empirical documentation that put in question the very terms of the discourse itself.

All the more reason, no doubt, that Zola's Nana, the Golden Fly, the Goncourts' Elisa, Huysmans's Marthe, or Balzac's Esther should possess the hard and brilliant clarity of archetypes, whether as representative of the heights of prostitution or of its depths. Not only do they all come to suitably bad ends, but their sexuality is described as deficient or deformed. In this way, the etiology of venal sexuality could be fully explained in terms of heredity, malign influence, or moral corruption. Such explanations, like the archetypal cast of the descriptions of the prostitute, provided reassurance; they are apotropaic devices against uncertainty.

46. This conception was taken to its logical conclusion in the substance of the Contagious Diseases Acts, passed in Great Britain in 1864, 1866, and 1869 and no⁺ repealed until 1886. In the interest of controlling venereal disease in garrison citie: and ports, any woman could be accosted by a special plainclothes policeman and accused of being a "common prostitute." If she could not prove otherwise, she could be subjected to an internal examination and, if found to be carrying a venereal disease, interned for up to nine months in a certified lock hospital. Needless to say, men (who were also known to be carriers of venereal diseases) were exempt from medical or judicial control and examination. See Judith Walkowitz, *Prostitution and Victorian Society: Women, Class, and the State* (Cambridge: Cambridge University Press, 1980).

47. Clark cites Jill Harsin's book *Policing Prostitution in Nineteenth-Century Paris* (Princeton: Princeton University Press, 1985), which he says refutes the idea that prostitution was in many cases occasional and temporary.

This uncertainty is fully built into the language of feminine sexuality and identity. Even as the words proliferate, the slippery, protean reality that the words attempt to govern constantly threatens to overcome them. The word *demimonde*, which from the very outset referred to an especially feminine condition, was invented by Alexandre Dumas *fils* in the 1840s. In the play in which it originally appeared, it referred to those women "become free" (widows, wives separated from their husbands, and foreigners), who, though respectable, were nonetheless "marginal" insofar as their marital status was perceived as ambiguous.[48]

The suggestive vagueness of the term is characteristic of the shifting, unsecured meaning of the sexualized woman drifting between the sturdy fixities of *femme honnête* and *fille publique*. Consequently, gray areas in this topography of the sexualized feminine—the kept woman (of high or low station), the *lorette*, the *grisette*, the occasional prostitute, the dancer, the actress—all confound the social need to define that is an inseparable component of the power to name, regulate, survey, and control. But the real question underlying the specific debates between prostitutional regulationists and abolitionists, or between the celebrators of the demimonde and its Jeremiahs, is perhaps more fundamental than the stated problem of prostitution as such. Rather, the question is the culturally—and temporally—overarching one of femininity, the enigma of woman, the sphinx without a riddle, the mystery without a solution. Who is she? What is she? How can she be known? What does she want?

Predictably, these are the rhetorical questions asked about the countess de Castiglione in the popular press. The tone is bantering, sly, insinuating—the cheap sophistication of the journalist/*boulevardier*. "Paris at this moment possesses a *lion* and a *lionne*," wrote a journalist for *L'indépendance belge* in 1856.[49] The countess is a "mysterious stranger" destined to sow heartbreak and discord in the fashionable salons. Who is she? What does she want? The lion is the aged Prince Orloff, emissary of the czar, present in Paris for the peace negotiations following the conclusion of the Crimean War. The lioness is the countess, not yet a widow, and in no way associated with the demimonde. Nonetheless, the Count Orloff is described as a lion, that is to say, prominent and powerful (the term is still current, both in English and French), and the countess is described as a lioness, that is to say, a sexual predator—a courtesan.[50] That the countess was not protected by

48. See Novelene Sue Ross's excellent discussion in *Manet's Bar at the Folies-Bergères and the Myths of Popular Illustration* (Ann Arbor: University of Michigan Press, 1982).

49. Jules Lecompte, in the "Courrier de Paris," *L'indépendance belge*, quoted in Loliée, *Les femmes du second empire*, 226.

50. The lithographer Eugène Guérard, for example, produced a suite of twelve plates titled *Les lionnes* between 1845 and 1848. "This series of lithographs . . . de-

her marital status, her title, her reception at court, from being publicly labeled a courtesan indicates the extreme instability of the epistemological system that attempted to secure the meanings of feminine virtue and vice. The nefarious power of the woman perceived as sexually active was such as perpetually to subvert the taxonomies constructed to label and contain her. The cultural hysteria produced by the courtesan and the prostitute (Zola's notes for *Nana* or Maxime du Camp's wildly inflated descriptions of the numbers and influence of prostitutes are prime examples) exceeds the conventional categories in which the sexual activity of women is circumscribed, for the anxiety that attaches to the figure of woman is that of a difference that escapes the discourses of containment.

To a certain extent, the nude, erotic and pornographic imagery, and the discourse of prostitution propose various responses to this threat. In the female nude of Western culture, patriarchy produces a representation of its desire; sexual difference, like the structure of fetishism, is both there and not there. Nothing to see and nothing to hide. Pornography emphatically exhibits the physical sign of that difference, even to the extent of making the woman's genitals the subject of the image. But any potential threat is neutralized by the debased situation of the woman thus portrayed and the miniaturization and immobilization inherent in photographic representation. The mastery and possession accorded the spectator's look, a mastery doubled in the structure of the photograph itself, dispels whatever menace or unpleasure the sight of the woman might provoke. Lastly, the discourse of prostitution, in its epistemological rigor and exhaustive typologies, attempts to provide the reassuring edifice of knowledge and power, which, despite its lacunae, is nonetheless a monument to the possibility of total control and domination.

The failure of the cordon sanitaire to which I earlier referred has more far-reaching implications than the disruption of academic painting conventions or the perceived failure to contain and control prostitution. Moreover, to the degree that this latter cultural anxiety confuses effect with cause and imputes to the prostitute those destructive and corrosive powers that are everywhere at work in society, it produces a symbolization of social crisis in which woman becomes the figure of guilt, corruption, and decomposition. The barriers between what is deemed licit or illicit, acceptably seductive or wantonly salacious, aesthetic or prurient, are never solid because they are contingent, never steadfast because they traffic with each other—are indeed dependent upon one another. Hence,

---

picts the activities of the *grandes courtisanes* who, from frequent association with the dandies, or *lions*, derived their appellation *lionnes*. Farwell, *The Cult of Images*, 123.

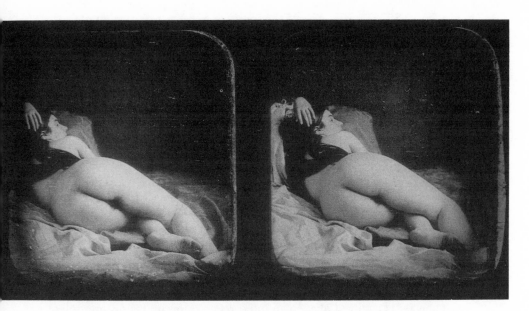

Anonymous. Hand-colored stereoscopic daguerreotype. c. 1855. Private collection.

an entire system, of distinctions, elaborations, signs, and codes—a system that pretends to be founded on differences—is in reality a tendentious elaboration of the same. To the patriarchal norms that govern this wonderland of sexual economics, the court beauty, proletarian dancer, courtesan, and streetwalker are equally subject, if not equally abject.

> In other words, for the commodity, there is no mirror that copies it
> so that it may be at once itself and its "own" reflection.
> —Luce Irigaray, "Women on the Market"

Considering the hundreds of photographs that the countess commissioned of herself, particularly those that feature the use of mirrors, the hollowness of the attempt to claim the countess as author is apparent. Like the conventionalized femininity she was believed to incarnate, the edges of the photographic frame are a Procrustean bed to which body and soul must accommodate themselves. The masks, the disguises, the postures, the poses, the ball gowns, the display of the body—what is the countess but a tabula rasa on whom is reflected a predetermined and delimited range of representations? And of what does her subjectivity consist if not her total absorption of them, her obedience to a scopic regime that inevitably undercuts her pretended authority as orchestrator of the look? It is in this sense that the photographs of the countess de Castiglione are finally so troubling.

In a number of photographs she included within the stagelike space of the studio a similar photograph of herself, doubling her own image *en abyme*. Image within image, it is as though the countess were providing a commentary on her own specularization. In another series of photographs—the best-known ones of her—she frames her eye within the oval space of a black passe-partout frame. In another, she doubles her gaze in a small hand mirror, deflecting it outward toward the spectator in a manner that permits her to be at once subject and object of the gaze. For whom does the countess effect this framing of the look? Knowing that these images of her were only for her, to what purpose this isolation and emphasis of her gaze?

The profound ambiguity of this gesture, the confusion of subject and object positions it occasions, might be said to expose the very reification it enacts. The appeal of such an interpretation lies in its presumption of a critical space, however minimal or problematic, from which the woman can speak herself. But in their entirety the images of the countess do not suggest her occupancy of such a space, or anything but a total embrace and identification with the look of the other. Consequently, the look with which she fixes herself, and the fixing of herself for the reception of the look, cannot be understood as a disappropriation—a theft—of the masculine prerogative. Nor can it be understood as an act of intentional mimicry, an act that potentially subverts the authority it apes. Rather, the countess, a living artifact, has so fully assimilated the desire of others that there is no space, language, or means of presentation for any desire that might be termed her own. In its broadest implications, the photographic legacy of the countess de Castiglione—image and object of desire—confronts us with the question of whose urgency is a function of whatever empowerment women can thus far claim: whose desire?

Reading Racial Fetishism: The Photographs of Robert Mapplethorpe

Kobena Mercer

This essay splits into two parts. The first is based on an essay contributed to *Photography/Politics: Two*, published in Britain in 1986.[1] The second consists of a partial revision of my earlier views, which has led me to reevaluate Robert Mapplethorpe's black male nudes. The splitting is not a repudiation of the Freudian concept of fetishism so much as an inscription of important changes in the cultural and political context of Mapplethorpe's work. If anything, recent developments in black and gay art practices *and* in the cultural politics of Jesse Helms and the New Right renew the relevance of "fetishism" in cultural criticism as they point to the political dimension of the kind of ambivalence that arises at the intersection of the psychic and the social. Insofar as the splitting also circumscribes the position(s) from which I speak, as a black gay writer and critic, the ambivalence I have tried to negotiate and describe in "reading" Mapplethorpe, and then changing my mind, speaks to the lived relations of difference that characterize the complex and incomplete construction of any social identity.

From *Lost Boundaries: Essays in Black Cultural Studies* by Kobena Mercer. Forthcoming from Routledge. By permission of Routledge, Chapman and Hall, Inc.
1. Patricia Holland, Jo Spence, and Simon Watney, eds., *Photography/Politics: Two* (London: Comedia/Methuen, 1986), 61–69. My contribution to the book came about as a result of a conversation with Pat Holland after the "Cultural Identities" conference in March 1986, during which I participated in a panel discussion with Gayatri Spivak, Jacqueline Rose, and Angela McRobbie; see *Undercut* no. 17 (Spring 1988).

Imaging the Black Man's Sex (1986)

I want to talk about Robert Mapplethorpe's pictures of black male nudes as a cultural text that says something about certain ways in which white people "look" at black people and how, in this way of looking, black male sexuality is perceived as something different, excessive, other.[2] Certainly this particular work must be set in the context of Mapplethorpe's photographic oeuvre as a whole. Mapplethorpe made his name in the world of art-photography taking portraits of patrons and protagonists in the post-Warhol New York avant-garde milieu of the 1970s. In turn he has become something of a "star" himself as journalists, critics, curators, and collectors have helped to weave a mystique of transgression around his public persona—creating a portrait of the artist as author of "prints of darkness."

As he extended his repertoire across flowers, bodies, and faces, the conservatism of Mapplethorpe's aesthetic became all too apparent—a reworking of the old modernist tactic of "shock the bourgeoisie" (and make them pay), given a new aura by his characteristic signature, the pursuit of perfection in photographic technique. The vaguely transgressive quality of his subject matter—gay sadomasochistic ritual, lady body builders, black men—is given heightened allure by his self-evident mastery of photographic technology. Once we consider the author not as the origin or guarantee of the meanings produced in the text, however, but as a "projection, in terms more or less psychological, of our way of handling texts,"[3] then what is most interesting about work such as *Black Males* and *The Black Book* is the way the text facilitates the imaginary projection of certain racial and sexual fantasies about the "difference" of the black man's body. Whatever his subjective motivations or creative alibi, Mapplethorpe's ambiguous imagery opens an aperture onto the fetishistic structure of stereotypical representations of black masculinity that circulate across a range of everyday surfaces, from newspapers, cinema, and television to advertising, sport, and pornography.

The first thing one notices about *The Black Book*—so obvious it almost goes without saying—is that all the men are *nude*. Through its

2. References are primarily to Robert Mapplethorpe, *Black Males*, Introduction by Edmund White (Amsterdam: Gallerie Jurka, 1982); Robert Mapplethorpe, *The Black Book*, Introduction by Ntozake Shange (Munich: Schirmer/Mosel, 1986); and Robert Mapplethorpe, *1970–1983*, Introduction by Allan Hollinghurst (London: Institute of Contemporary Arts, 1983).

3. Michel Foucault, "What Is an Author?" in *Language, Counter-Memory, Practice*, trans. Donald F. Bouchard and Sherry Simon (Oxford: Basil Blackwell, 1977), 127.

Robert Mapplethorpe. *Man in Polyester Suit.* 1980. © 1980 (The Estate of Robert Mapplethorpe.)

catalogue of vantage points, shots, and takes, the camera's gaze is directed to a unitary vanishing point that organizes the erotic and aesthetic objectification of individual black male bodies into the idealized form of a homogeneous "type." We look through sequences of personally named Afro-American men (invariably young, healthy, dark complexioned), but we "see" only their sex as the essential sum total of the meanings signified around the attributes of blackness and maleness. It is as if, according to Mapplethorpe's line of sight, Black + Male = Aesthetic/Erotic Object. Regardless of the sexual preference of the spectator, the connotative yield of the text thoroughly saturates the black male body with sexual predicates. Whereas the photographs of gay male S/M couples invokes a subcultural sexuality that consists of "doing" something, black men are confined and defined in their "being" as sexual and nothing but sexual, hence hypersexual. In *Man in Polyester Suit*, apart from his hands, it is the penis and the penis alone that identifies the model in the photograph as a black man.

This ontological reduction is accomplished through the specific visual codes brought to bear on the construction of pictorial space. Sculpted and shaped through the artistic conventions of the nude, the image of the black male body presents the spectator with a source of erotic pleasure in the act of looking itself. As a generic code established across fine-art traditions in the West, the conventional subject of the nude is the (white) female body. Substituting the socially "inferior" black male subject, Mapplethorpe nevertheless draws on some of its generic codes and conventions to frame the objectification of black male bodies into abstract beautiful "things." As all references to a social, historical, cultural, and political context are ruled out of the frame, this visual codification abstracts and essentializes the black male body in the realm of a transcendental aesthetic ideal. In this sense, because the erotic and aesthetic idealization is so totalizing in its effect, the text reveals more about the desires of the hidden and invisible white male subject behind the camera than it does about the anonymous black men whose beautiful bodies we see depicted.

Within the dominant tradition of the female nude, patriarchal power relations are symbolized by the binary relation in which, in crude terms, men assume the active role of the looking subject, while women are passive objects to be looked at. Laura Mulvey's radical contribution to feminist film theory revealed the normative power and privilege of the "male gaze" in dominant systems of representation.[4] The visual con-

4. Laura Mulvey, "Visual Pleasure and Narrative Cinema," *Screen* 16 (Autumn 1975): 6–18.

struction of the female nude can thus be understood not so much as a representation of (hetero)sexual desire but as a form of objectification that articulates masculine hegemony and dominance over the very apparatus of representation itself. Paintings abound with self-serving scenarios of phallocentric fantasy in which male artists paint themselves painting a naked woman, which, like depictions of feminine narcissism, construct a mirror image of what the male subject wants to see. The fetishistic logic of mimetic representation, which makes present for the subject what is absent in the real, can thus be characterized as a masculine fantasy of mastery and control over the "objects" represented and depicted in the visual field, the fantasy of an omnipotent eye/I who sees but who is never seen.

In Mapplethorpe's case, however, the fact that both subject and object of the look are male sets up a tension between the active role of looking and the passive role of being looked at. This frisson of (homo)sexual sameness transfers erotic investment in the fantasy of mastery from gender to racial difference, and the traces of this metaphorical transfer underline the highly charged libidinal investment in the most visible element that signifies racial "difference"—the fetishization of black skin. In his analysis of the male pinup, Richard Dyer suggests that when male subjects assume the passive, "feminized" position of being looked at, the risk or threat to traditional definitions of masculinity is counteracted by the role of certain codes and conventions, such as taut, rigid, or straining bodily posture; character types; and narrativized plots—all of which aim to stabilize the dichotomy of seeing/being seen.[5] Here Mapplethorpe appropriates elements of commonplace racial stereotypes to regulate, organize, prop up, and fix the process of aesthetic/erotic objectification in which the black man's flesh becomes burdened with the task of signifying the transgressive fantasies and desires of the white gay male subject. The glossy, shining, fetishized sheen of black skin thus serves and services the white man's desire to look and to enjoy the fantasy of mastery precisely through the scopic intensity that the pictures solicit.

Homi Bhabha has suggested that "an important feature of colonial discourse is its dependence on the concept of 'fixity' in the ideological construction of otherness."[6] Mass-media stereotypes of black men—as criminals, athletes, entertainers—reinscribe the logic of such colonial fantasy, permitting black male subjects to become publicly visible only

5. Richard Dyer, "Don't Look Now—the Male Pin-up," Screen 16 (Autumn 1982): 61–73.
6. Homi K. Bhabha, "The Other Question: The Stereotype and Colonial Discourse," Screen 24 (Winter 1983): 18.

through a rigid and limited grid of representations that therefore reproduce certain idées fixes, ideological fictions and psychic fixations, about
the "difference" black masculinity is constructed to embody. As an artist, Mapplethorpe engineers a fantasy of "absolute" authority over his
subjects by appropriating the function of the stereotype to stabilize the
erotic objectification of racial otherness and thereby affirm his own identity as the sovereign I/eye empowered with mastery over the abject
"thinghood" of the other—as if the images implied, "I have the power to
turn you, base and worthless creature, into a beautiful work of art." Like
Medusa's look, his camera-eye turns the black body into stone, each
"shot" enslaves the black man's flesh to the representational space of
the white male imaginary, fixed and frozen in space and time, immobilized and made silent in the name of a transcendental aesthetic ideal.
There is another aspect to the objectification inscribed here: as each
black man's proper name is taken from the person and given to the
artwork as its title or caption, the creative labor invested in the intersubjective relation between artist and model is alienated and effaced by the
commodity value of the object produced. And as art objects Mapplethorpe prints fetch exorbitant prices on the international market in art
photography.

The fantasmatic emphasis on mastery is also evident in the isolation
effect, whereby only one black man appears in the field of vision at any
one time. As an imprint of a narcissistic, ego-centered fantasy, this is a
crucial component in the erotic objectification of otherness not only
because it forecloses the representation of a collective or contextualized
black male body but because the solo frame is the precondition for a
voyeuristic fantasy of unmediated and unilateral control over the other,
which is the function it performs in gay and straight pornography. Su-
perimposing two ways of seeing—the nude, which eroticizes the act of
looking, and the stereotype, which fixes the flux of experience—we see
in Mapplethorpe's gaze a reinscription of the fundamental *ambivalence*
of colonial fantasy, oscillating between sexual idealization of the racialized other and anxiety in defense of the identity of the white male
ego. Stuart Hall has underlined this splitting in the "imperial eye" by
suggesting that for every image of the black subject as a marauding,
menacing savage, native or slave, there is the comforting image of the
black as docile servant and amusing clown and entertainer. Commenting
on this bifurcation in racial representations, Hall describes it as the
expression of "both a nostalgia for an innocence lost forever to the
civilized, and the threat of civilization being over-run or undermined by
the recurrence of savagery, which is always lurking just below the sur-

face; or by an untutored sexuality threatening to 'break out.'"[7] In Mapplethorpe, we may discern three discreet camera codes through which this fundamental ambivalence is reenacted.

The first of these, which is most self-consciously acknowledged, could be called the *sculptural* code inasmuch as it is itself a subgenre of the nude. As Phillip pretends to put the shot, the idealized physique of a classical Greek male statue is superimposed on that most commonplace of stereotypes, the black man as sports hero, mythologically endowed with a "naturally" muscular physique and embodying essential capacities of strength, grace, and perfection: well hard. A major public arena, sport is a key site of white male ambivalence. The spectacle of black bodies triumphant in rituals of masculine competition reinforces the fixed idea that they are "all brawn and no brains," and yet because the white man is beaten at his own game—football, boxing, cricket, athletics—the Other is idolized to the point of envy. This schism is played out daily in the popular tabloid press. In the front-page headlines black males become visible as a threat, as muggers, rapists, terrorists, and guerrillas; their bodies become the imago of a savage and unstoppable capacity for destruction and violence. But turn to the back pages, the sports pages, and Mike Tyson and Frank Bruno, "Magic" Johnson and Daley Thompson are domesticated as national mascots and adopted pets, and any hint of antagonism is contained by paternalistic incorporation: they're not Other, they're okay because they're our boys, one of us. The national "shame" of England's demise and defeat in Test cricket at the hands of the West Indies is accompanied by the slavish admiration of Viv Richards's awesome physique: the high-speed West Indian bowler is both a threat and a winner. The ambivalence cuts deep into the recess of white male fears and fantasy. Recall those newsreel images of Hitler's reaction to Jesse Owens at the 1936 Olympics or, conversely, the phallic clenched-fist Black Power salute at the 1968 Olympics.

If Mapplethorpe's gaze is momentarily lost in admiration, it reasserts control by "feminizing" the Other into a decorative objet d'art. When Phillip is placed on a pedestal, he literally becomes putty in the hands of the white male artist, like others in this code; his body becomes raw material, mere plastic matter, to be molded, sculpted, and shaped into the aesthetic idealism of pure abstraction. In the picture of Derrick Cross, with the tilt of the pelvis, the black man's bum becomes a Brancusi. Commenting on the difference between moving and motionless pictures,

7. Stuart Hall, "The Whites of Their Eyes: Racist Ideologies and the Media," in *Silver Linings: Some Strategies for the Eighties*, ed. George Bridges and Rosalind Brunt (London: Lawrence Wishart, 1981), 41.

Christian Metz suggests an association among photography, silence, and death, for photographs invoke a residual "death effect" such that "the person who has been photographed is dead . . . dead for having been seen."[8] Under the intense scrutiny of Mapplethorpe's cool, detached gaze, it is as if each black model is made to die, if only to reincarnate their alienated essence as idealized aesthetic objects. We are not invited to imagine what their lives, histories, or experiences are like; they are silenced as subjects and in a sense "sacrificed" on the pedestal of the aesthetic ideal in order to affirm the omnipotence of the master subject, the I/eye who has the power of light and death.

In counterpoint there is a supplementary code of *portraiture* that "humanizes" the hard phallic lines and focuses on the face—the "window of the soul"—to introduce an element of realism into the scene. But any expressive connotation is denied by the direct look, which does not so much assert the presence of an autonomous subjectivity but rather, like the remote, aloof expressions of fashion models in glossy magazines, emphasizes maximum distance between the spectator and the unattainable object of desire. Look, but don't touch. The direct look to camera does not challenge the gaze of the white male artist, although it plays on the active/passive tension between seeing/being seen, because any potential disruption is contained by the subtextual work of the stereotype. Thus, in one portrait the "primitive" nature of the Negro is invoked by the profile; the face becomes an afterimage of a stereotypically "African" tribal mask; high cheekbones and matted dreadlocks connote wildness, danger, exotica. In another, the chiseled contours of a shaved head, honed by rivulets of sweat, summons up the criminal mug shot from the forensic files of police photography. It also recalls the anthropometric uses of photography in the colonial scene, measuring the cranium of the colonized so as to "show," by the documentary evidence of photography, the inherent inferiority of the Other. This aspect is overlaid with deeper ambivalence in the portrait of Terrel, whose grotesque grimace calls up the happy/sad mask of the nigger minstrel: humanized by racial pathos, the Sambo stereotype haunts the scene, evoking the black man's supposedly childlike dependency on ole Massa, which in turn fixes his social, legal, and existential "emasculation" at the hands of the white master.

Finally, two codes together—of *cropping* and *lighting*—interpenetrate the flesh and mortify it into a racial sex fetish, a juju doll from the dark side of the white man's imaginary. The body-whole is fragmented into details—chest, arms, torso, buttocks, penis—inviting a scopophilic dis-

8. Christian Metz, "Photography and Fetish," *October* 34 (Fall 1985): 85.

section of the parts that make up the whole. Indeed, like a talisman, each part is invested with the power to invoke the mystique of black male sexuality with more perfection than any empirically unified whole. The camera cuts away like a knife, allowing the spectator to inspect and scrutinize the "goods." In such fetishistic attention to detail, tiny scars and blemishes on the surface of black skin only heighten the sense of the technical perfectionism of the photographic print. The cropping and fragmentation of bodies—often "decapitated," so to speak—is a salient feature of pornography and has been seen from certain feminist positions as a form of male violence, a literal inscription of a sadistic impulse in the "male gaze," cutting up women's bodies into visual bits and pieces.[9] Whether or not this view is tenable, its effect here is to suggest aggression in the act of looking, but not as "racial violence" or racism-as-hate—on the contrary, aggression as the expression of frustration on the part of the ego who finds the object of his desires out of reach, unattainable. The cropping is analogous to striptease in this sense, as the exposure of successive body parts distances the erotogenic object and makes it untouchable so as to tantalize the drive to look, which reaches its aim in the denouement that unveils the woman's sex. Except here the unveiling that reduces the woman from angel to whore is substituted by the unconcealing of the black man's private parts, the fetishized penis as the forbidden totem of colonial fantasy.

As each fragment seduces the eye into intense fascination, we glimpse the dilation of a libidinal way of looking that spreads itself across the surface of black skin. Harsh contrasts of shadow and light draw the eye to focus on the dark and lovely texture of the black man's skin. According to Bhabha, unlike the sexual fetish per se, whose meanings are usually hidden as a hermeneutic secret, skin color functions in the signifying chain of "negrophobia" or is hypervalorized as a desirable attribute in "negrophilia"; the fetish of skin color as "the most visible of fetishes." Whether it is devalorized in the codes of racial discourse constitutes the most visible element in the articulation of what Stuart Hall calls "the ethnic signifier."[10] The shining surface of black skin serves several functions in its representation: it suggests the physical exertion of powerful bodies—black boxers always glisten like bronze in the illuminated square of the boxing ring—or as in pornography, it suggests intense sexual activity "just before" the photograph was taken, a metonymic stimulus to arouse spectatorial participation in the mise-en-scene of

9. Rosalind Coward, "Sexual Violence and Sexuality," *Feminist Review* 11 (Summer 1982): 17–22.

10. Stuart Hall, "Pluralism, Race, and Class in Caribbean Society," in *Race and Class in Post-Colonial Societies* (Paris: UNESCO, 1977), 150–82.

desire. In Mapplethorpe's pictures the spectacular brilliance of black skin is bound in a double articulation as a fixing agent for the repetition of colonial fantasy in the text. There is a subtle slippage between representer and represented as the shiny surface of black skin becomes consubstantial with the luxurious allure of the high-quality photographic print. As Victor Burgin has remarked, sexual fetishism dovetails with commodity fetishism to inflate the valorization of print texture in art photography as much as in fashion photography—the "glossies."[11] Here black skin and print surface are bound together to enhance the pleasure of the white spectator as much as the profitability of the art-world commodities exchanged between the artist and his dealers, collectors, and curators.

In everyday discourse "fetishism" probably connotes deviant or "kinky" sexuality, calling up images of leather and rubber wear as signs of sexual perversity. This is not a fortuitous example, for leather fashion fetishism has a sensuous appeal as a kind of "second skin." When one considers that such clothes are invariably black, rather than any other color, leather wear suggests a desire to simulate or imitate black skin. Freud's theorization of fetishism as a clinical phenomenon of sexual pathology or "perversion" is problematic in many ways, but the central notion of the fetish as metaphorical substitute for the absent phallus enables understanding of the psychic structure of disavowal or the splitting of levels of conscious and unconscious belief relevant to the ambiguous axis on which negrophilia and negrophobia intertwine.[12] For Freud, the little boy who is shocked to "see" in the little girl the absence of the penis, which he believes has been lost or castrated, encounters the recognition of sexual or genital difference, which is nevertheless denied or disavowed by the metaphorical substitute on which the adult fetishist depends for his access to sexual pleasure. Hence, to put the phenomenon in a linguistic formula, "*I know* (the woman has no penis), *but* (she does through the fetish)."[13]

Such splitting is captured precisely in *Man in a Polyester Suit* as the central focus on the black penis emerging from the unzipped trouser fly simultaneously affirms and denies that most fixed of racial myths in the white male imaginary, namely, that every black man has a monstrously large penis. The scale of the photograph foregrounds the size of the black dick, which thus signifies a threat, not the threat of racial difference as such but the fear that the Other is more sexually potent than his white

11. Victor Burgin, "Photography, Fantasy, Fiction," *Screen* 21 (Spring 1980): 54, reprinted in *Thinking Photography*, ed. Burgin (London: Macmillan, 1982), 177–216.
12. Sigmund Freud, "Fetishism" (1927), *Standard Edition*, 21: 147–57, and *Pelican Freud Library*, no. 7, "On Sexuality" (1977), 351–57.
13. John Ellis, "On Pornography," *Screen* 21 (Spring 1980): 100.

master. As a phobic object, the big black prick is a "bad object," a fixed point in the paranoid fantasies of the negrophobe, which Frantz Fanon found in the pathologies of his white psychiatric patients as much as in the normalized cultural artifacts and representations of his time. Then as now, in front of this picture "one is no longer aware of the Negro, but only of a penis; the Negro is eclipsed. He is turned into a penis. He is a penis."[14] The primal fantasy of the big black dick projects the fear of a threat not only to white womanhood but to civilization itself, as the anxiety of miscegenation, eugenic pollution, and racial degeneration is acted out through white male rituals of racial aggression—the historical lynching of black men in the United States routinely involved the literal castration of the Other's strange fruit. The myth of the black penis in supremacist ideology has been the target of enlightened liberal demystification as modern science has repeatedly embarked on the project of measuring empirical pricks to demonstrate its untruth. In post–Civil Rights, post–Black Power America, where liberal orthodoxy in public opinion provides no available legitimation for such folk myths, Mapplethorpe enacts a disavowal of this ideological "truth": I know (it's not true that all black men have huge penises) but (in my photo they do).

This presumably is the little joke acted out in the picture. But the racism it presupposes or complies with is effaced and whitewashed by the jokey irony of the contrast between the black man's private parts and his public attire in the cheap and tacky polyester business suit. The opposition of hidden and exposed, denuded and clothed, works around the nature/culture, savage/civilized binarisms of racial discourse. Sex is confirmed as the "nature" of black masculinity, as the polyester suit confirms the black man's failure to gain access to "culture." Even when the Other aims for respectability (the signified of the suit), his camouflage fails to conceal the fact that he essentially originates, like his dick, from somewhere anterior to civilization.

Finally, the tip of the penis shines. Like the "shine on the nose" that was the sexual fetish for Freud's patient, the shine on this emblematic object of Mapplethorpe's sex-race fantasy makes it all the more visible. But in this respect it merely recuperates what is commonplace: wherever naked black bodies appear in representations, they are saturated with sweat, always already wet with sex. Leni Riefenstahl's ethnographic images in The Last of the Nuba demonstrate the colonial roots of the negrophile's scopic fetishism: what is shown has precious little to do with the culture of African body adornment; rather, like a blank page, the very blackness of black skin acts as a tabula rasa for the inscription of

14. Frantz Fanon, Black Skin, White Masks (1952; London: Paladin, 1970), 120.

a look that speaks primarily of a white European sexuality. Riefenstahl admits that her fascination with this East African people originated not from an interest in their "culture" but from a photograph of two Nuba wrestlers by the English documentarist George Rodgers (which is reproduced, in homage, on the inside back cover of the book). In this sense her anthropological alibi for an ethnographic voyeurism is nothing more than the secondary elaboration and rationalization of the primal wish to see this lost image again and again.[15] Riefenstahl made her name as the author of cinematic spectacle in Nazi Germany, and surface similarities might suggest not only that racial fetishism involves a certain way of looking that is available to white women as well as white men but also a continuity in sensibility with Mapplethorpe which results in the similar aestheticization of politics. But to call Mapplethorpe a "fascist" would be pointless; it would merely enhance his celebrated reputation and persona as a "transgressive" artist in the late modern avant-garde. It is more useful, perhaps, to note that in his "thing" for black male bodies, Mapplethorpe silently reinscribes the ambivalent disavowal found in the most commonplace of utterances, "I'm not a racist, but . . . "

The fetishistic figuration of the black male body in Mapplethorpe's photography draws attention to the cultural politics of the fundamental ambivalence that inhabits the strange, uncharted, and theoretically "unknown" landscape of the white male imaginary, the "political unconscious" of white masculinity. The challenge of his work—and his highly ambiguous position in the structure of fear, fantasy, and fetishism that unfolds through the filigree of power wielded by his white male gaze— is at least to draw our attention to the ambivalent ways in which white people "look" at black people and to examine our own implication in them.

The Mirror Looks Back: Racial Fetishism Reconsidered (1989)

Returning to the scene some three years later I'm much more aware of how the ambivalence cuts both ways. In fact, I've actually changed my mind about Mapplethorpe and my earlier reading of his racial fetishism. I want therefore to suggest a revision of the preceding analysis not because I think it was wrong but because important changes in context

15. Leni Riefenstahl, *The Last of the Nuba* (London: Collins, 1976); discussed in Susan Sontag, "Fascinating Fascism," in *A Susan Sontag Reader* (New York: Vintage Books, 1983), 305–28.

demand a perspective that approaches ambivalence not as something that occurs "inside" the text, but as a complex "structure of feeling" experienced across the contingent relations among authors, texts, and readers, which are always historically specific to the context in which they arise.

Mapplethorpe died in early 1989 as a result of AIDS, and the "death of the author" has irrevocably changed the context in which we read, evaluate, and appraise his work. More specifically, subsequent to his major retrospective at the Whitney Museum, the censorship initiative led by Jesse Helms and the New Right against art deemed indecent or obscene has radically altered the cultural and political context of Mapplethorpe's significance as a gay artist. Under these changed conditions and circumstances it becomes possible, and indeed necessary, to reconsider the critique of racial fetishism in relation to the avowed homoeroticism of his black male nudes.

Another set of contemporary developments has also contributed to the change of context, that is, the new aesthetic practices that have emerged among black lesbian and gay artists in Britain and the United States. Black British photographers such as Rotimi Fani-Kayode and Sunil Gupta, and film and video artists such as Isaac Julien and Pratibha Parmar; black American artists such as Lyle Harris and Todd Grey in photography and Michelle Parkerson and Marlon Riggs in film and video have radically altered the context in which the politics of representation are being debated in a dialogue across black, gay, lesbian, and feminist discourses.[16] Taking these combined and uneven developments into account, I want to recontextualize what I previously described as the erotic objectification and aestheticization of racial "difference" in Mapplethorpe's black male nudes by proposing an alternative reading that revises the assumption that fetishism is necessarily a bad thing.

To call something fetishistic does not imply an affirmative judgment of aesthetic taste or cultural criticism; so I want to begin with the residual moralism of the term as it informs the angry tone of my earlier reading. I've only recently become aware of the logical slippage in my argument, which started with Foucault's distinction between author-name and author-function in order to distinguish Mapplethorpe's persona analytically from the ideological subject position inscribed in the

16. See Rotimi Fani-Kayode, *Black Male/White Male* (London: Gay Men's Press, 1987); the work of Sunil Gupta is featured in *Ten.8* magazine and in Pratibha Parmar's video *Memory Pictures* (1989); the films of Isaac Julien include *Territories* (1984, Sankofa Film and Video Collective), *This Is Not an AIDS Advertisement* (1987, Sankofa), and *Looking for Langston* (1988, Sankofa); Michelle Parkerson's film is *Storme: The Jewel Box Revue* (1987), and the films of Marlon Riggs include *Tongues Untied* (1989).

text, but which, by the end of the argument, had been conflated and reduced back to the commonsense abstractions "the white man"/"the black man," which are really methodological fictions or theoretical stereotypes—in any case somewhat reductive categories with which to conduct a critical reading of a complex cultural text. As a result, an equivalence was implied between Mapplethorpe as artist or author and the empty, impersonal, and anonymous place of the spectatorial position described as that of the white male subject.

In retrospect, I think the surreptitious return of ideological categories arose primarily out of my own ambivalent position in relation to the text. In other words, the logical slippage between author and enunciating subject discloses an ambivalence not so much on the part of Mapplethorpe or his photographs as on my part as a black gay male spectator situated somewhere always already *inside* its intertextual field.

Thus, on the one hand, the anger at the objectification of black male bodies was based on my identification with their subjectivity, an identification with the racialized Other which can best be described in Fanon's terms as a feeling that "I am laid bare. I am overdetermined from without. I am the slave not of the 'idea' that others have of me but of my own appearance. Already I am being dissected under white eyes. I am *fixed*. . . . Look, it's a Negro."[17] But on the other hand, I was also implicated as a desiring subject, as a gay reader in the text. Insofar as the objectified black male Other was also an image of the object choices that represent my own fantasies and desires, I was positioned in an identification with the white gay male subject position of the author. In this sense, sharing the same desire to look, I would actually inhabit the fantasy of power and mastery which I said was the projection of the white male subject. I now wonder as I wander back into the text whether the anger was not also the expression of a certain envy on my part, the effect of an imagined rivalry over the same idealized and unattainable object of homosexual desire? The element of aggression in textual analysis, or rather the anger that entered into my rhetoric of argumentation, might merely have concealed my own narcissistic participation in the ambivalent pleasures (and anxieties) the text makes available not only for white spectators but for black spectators as well.

Posing the issue of ambivalence and undecidability in this way not only underlines the role of the reader and the specific experiences, positions, and expectations that different readers bring to bear on the way they handle Mapplethorpe's text; it also demands a revision of the poststructuralist thesis concerning the death of the author. Since the

17. Fanon, *Black Skin/White Masks*, 82.

decentering of the subject announced by structuralism, commonsense notions of the author as origin of genius and creativity cannot be returned to the central place they once occupied in criticism and interpretation, but against the grain of theoretical antihumanism, the question of creative agency has made a dramatic return in the cultural practices of marginalized subjects whose work contests the cultural and ideological dominance of the "canon."

A common theme in black cultural practices as well as in lesbian, gay, and feminist countercultures is the retrieval and recovery of authors whose identities were previously invisible and "hidden from history." In regard to authorship in marginalized or subordinate cultural formations, it really *does* matter who is speaking. The universalizing authority by which the hegemonic white male bourgeois subject appropriated the right to speak on behalf of everyone, while denying the discourse of Others in the name of liberal-humanist "Man," is challenged and contested in each of the countercultures of modernity. The historical contestation of marginality in black, feminist, or gay cultural politics thus inevitably brings the issue of authorship and agency back into play in terms of the struggle to "come to voice" and gain access to the means of representation in the public sphere. The "death of the author" in Mapplethorpe's case thus entails acknowledgment of the implicit cultural politics of his homoeroticism, an aspect of his black male nudes that was underplayed in my earlier reading.

In the wake of the wholly contingent and arbitrary events brought about by the AIDS health crisis, the metropolitan spaces of gay male subculture have been changed irrevocably. In this context, Mapplethorpe's homoeroticism can be read alternatively as the photographic inscription of a highly stylized form of documentary reportage, a record of a style of life and a sexual ethics that has now largely disappeared. The importance of an urban gay male community was suggested by Mapplethorpe's comments in a television interview: "I was part of it. And that's where most of the photographers who move in that direction are at a disadvantage in that they're not part of it: they're voyeurs moving in. With me it was quite different. Often I had experienced some of those experiences which I later recorded, myself, firsthand, without a camera."[18] Mapplethorpe's perfectionist aesthetic may share formal similarities with the visual fetishism found in the avowedly heterosexual work of Helmut Newton or Edward Weston, but once he is situated in the biographical context and lived experience of a specifically urban gay male culture, Mapplethorpe can be seen to place himself in the visual

18. "Robert Mapplethorpe," *Arena*, BBC2 Television, transmitted 18 March 1988.

field by virtue of an ironic participant observation. As documentary reportage on gay male sexual identity in the 1970s, his images invoke a cool and distantiated ethnography whose descriptive clarity is measured by the author's own participation in the subcultural world that his photographs described. This historical and contextual dimension is emphasized by Mapplethorpe's statement that "it was a certain moment and I was in a perfect situation in that most of the people in the photographs were friends of mine and they trusted me. I felt almost an obligation to record those things. It was an obligation for me to do it, to make images that nobody's seen before and to do it in a way that's *aesthetic*."[19]

In other words, the critical difference entailed by the homoerotic specificity of Mapplethorpe's artistic practice reveals the salient *absence* of voyeurism in his work. Rather than reproduce the conventional subject-object hierarchy of the "male gaze," whose omnipotent eye sees but is never seen, Mapplethorpe's look not only turns back on itself in his many self-portraits (including the one with a bullwhip up his bum) but also, like a point-of-view shot in gay male pornography, implies a shared horizon of experiences with his models and subjects. Indeed, comments by Ken Moody, one of the models in *The Black Book*, overturn my previous inference that Mapplethorpe's visual fetishization of blackness was necessarily exploitative. Asked to evaluate the issue of objectification, Moody replied: "I don't honestly think of it as exploitation. . . . It's almost as if—and this is the conclusion I've come to, because I really haven't thought about it up to now—it's almost as if he wants to give a gift to this particular group. He wants to create something very beautiful and give it to them . . . and he is actually very giving."[20] Without overinterpreting such testimony, I think this biographical dimension of Mapplethorpe's relations with the black models enables a revision of racial fetishism that challenges the view that fetishization necessarily indicates a conservative cultural politics.

Once recontextualized as an avant-garde art practice located in the specific historical milieu of an urban gay male subculture, the shocking modernism enacted in Mapplethorpe's ambiguous and ironic appropriation of elements drawn from high and low culture—the superimposition of two ways of seeing, which appropriates everyday racial stereotypes as much as the canonical figuration of the fine-art nude—can be reread as a subversive deconstruction of the ethnocentrism that binds the two systems of representation together at opposite ends of the hierarchy of cultural value. What I mean to suggest is that instead of falling back on

19. Ibid., 24 March 1988.
20. Ibid.

the stabilizing and fixative function of the stereotype, what is experienced in the reception of Mapplethorpe's text as its characteristic "shock" effect betrays a radical *unfixing* that upsets and disrupts the spectator's horizon of expectations. The important but difficult question raised by Mapplethorpe's black male nudes—do they reinforce or undermine racist stereotypes?—is strictly undecidable or unresolvable as such, because it is thrown back from the author into the field of the spectator, where it is experienced precisely as that ambiguity which lures the eye and sets a trap for the gaze. "You want to see? Well take a look at this!"—to paraphrase Lacan;[21] rather than confirm the psychic structure of a universalized hegemonic white male subjectivity, the desire-to-look that Mapplethorpe arouses with such perverse precision can be seen to subvert the stability of such an ideological subject position by virtue of the ambivalent textual intermixing of elements drawn from opposite ends of dominant systems of representation.

Contextualized again in art-historical terms, in relation to similar aesthetic strategies in Pop Art in the 1960s, Mapplethorpe's ironic intermixing of the canonical, high-cultural nude with the filthy and degraded form of the commonplace stereotype does not reproduce either term of the binary relation between high and low culture *as it is*: rather, it upsets and disrupts the codification of culture and aesthetic "value" by demonstrating the interdependency between the two systems of representation. In this sense, the deconstructive aspects of Mapplethorpe's ambivalent way of looking enables me to turn my earlier reading around on a 180-degree axis to argue that the logic of fetishization as he uses it actually *makes visible* the supplementary and interdependent relation between elite and everyday culture, between "pure" and "polluted" types, between official and vernacular tastes, at issue in the representability of black male subjectivity.

In social, economic and political terms, black males constitute a significant population of "invisible men" in the late modern underclass: disempowered, disadvantaged, and disenfranchised by dominant relations of race, class, and gender.[22] What does it mean, therefore, for a modernist art practice (and a white gay male artist) to place some of the invisible men, who in all probability came from this underclass, onto the pedestal of a transcendent aesthetic ideal of bodily perfection, de-

21. Jacques Lacan, "Of the Gaze as *Objet Petit a*," in *The Four Fundamental Concepts of Psychoanalysis*, trans. Alan Sheridan (London: Penguin, 1979), 101.

22. See Robert Staples, *Black Masculinity: The Black Man's Role in American Society* (San Francisco: Black Scholar Press, 1982); see also Kobena Mercer and Isaac Julien, "Race, Sexual Politics, and Black Masculinity: A Dossier," in *Male Order: Unwrapping Masculinity*, ed. Jonathan Rutherford and Rowena Chapman (London: Lawrence and Wishart, 1988).

fined for the West by the originary value of the male nude in classical Greek sculpture? Doesn't such a strategy begin to unconceal the ethnocentric character of the liberal humanist values embodied in that normative aesthetic ideal? In this sense, the substitution of the black male as the embodiment of the aesthetic ideal can be seen to subvert the foundational myths of the canon itself. Precisely in the perversity of its modernist "shock" effect, Mapplethorpe's aesthetic strategy disturbs the spectator's ideological positioning by making invisible black men "visible" on the cultural pedestal of a universalized aesthetic ideal that historically always excluded black subjects from access to its system of aesthetic valorization. The irony of his eroticized intermixing of elements lies in the way in which members of one of the "lowest" social classes enter representation through one of the "highest" and most valued genres in Western art history.

In changing my mind in this way I do not want to minimize the unresolved political ambivalence of Mapplethorpe's individual positioning in the unequal interracial economy of the "look," but I do want to emphasize a *relational* approach that resists the attempt to impose closure on the difficulties his artwork presents. My earlier reading of racial fetishism was highly dependent on an analogy drawn from feminist cultural criticism. As the medium through which psychoanalytic concepts have enriched the interrogation of ideology and politics in cultural texts, feminist cultural theories have been radically enabling. The analogues that inform Homi Bhabha's rethinking of the stereotype in colonial discourse, for instance, show the important theoretical connections that such analogies facilitate in the study of race and ethnicity in representation. But there is also the risk that analogies flatten out the complex and indeterminate relations by which subjectivity is constituted in the overdetermined spaces *between* relations of race, gender, ethnicity, and sexuality. One way of acknowledging such complexity is to repeat the all-too-familiar "race, class, gender" mantra, but in my view such rhetoric, however necessary, inadvertently conceals the conceptual and political difficulties of theorizing "difference" in a way that speaks to the messy, ambivalent, and incomplete character of the "identities" we actually inhabit in our lived experiences. Coming back to the text, I want to suggest a dialogic reading of the context-bound relations among authors, texts, and readers in a way that opens an alternative departure into the cultural politics of difference, identity, and indeterminacy.

Consider, as a verbal analogue to the visual "statement" predicated in Mapplethorpe's images, the utterance |the black man is beautiful|. As a performative statement, the utterance takes on different meanings and connotations depending on the identity of the speaking subject who enunciates it. The same utterance cannot possibly mean the same thing when spoken by a white woman, a black woman, a white man, or a black man, because each of these "differences" alters its denotative value. Similarly, the same utterance engenders different meanings if the speaker is gay or straight. The intersecting variables of race, gender, sexuality, and class do indeed make a difference to one's positioning as a reader in the text. In the case of Mapplethorpe's work such indeterminacy dramatizes the fact that diverse and contradictory readings can be derived from the same textual system. I want to emphasize the political consequences of this indeterminacy in audience reception of Mapplethorpe's text. His photographs can confirm a racist reading as easily as they can produce an antiracist one; the images can elicit a homophobic reading as much as a homoerotic one. It all depends on the identity that different audiences and spectators bring to bear on the readings they produce.

It is crucial to note that over and above the moral objection to art deemed "indecent or obscene," Jesse Helms's proposed amendment to federal arts-funding policy also sought a much broader mandate for cultural censorship on the grounds of an ethical objection to art that "denigrates, debases or reviles a person, group or class of citizens on the basis of race, creed, sex, handicap or national origin."[23] What we see here is a rhetorical trope in the political discourse of the New Right which appropriates and rearticulates liberal/social democratic anti-discrimination legislation to promote and legitimate an antidemocratic politics of coercion. As V. N. Volosinov argued, the polyvalent or multi-accentual character of the key signs and signifiers in hegemonic political discourse means that they are subject to antagonistic efforts of articulation; they have no intrinsic or necessary place in the discourse of the Left or the Right, for ideological struggle consists precisely in the discursive struggle to articulate multiaccentual signs within one system of values rather than another.[24] It is quite conceivable that right-wing intellectuals could also produce a critique of racial fetishism in Mapplethorpe's work, but I suspect that this would be motivated by a very different cultural and political agenda from the one I had in mind in 1986. In the contemporary context, therefore, I've changed my mind about Mapplethorpe not for the fun of it but because I do *not* want a black gay critique to be appropriated into the antidemocratic closure sought by the New Right. The best way to forestall such neoconservative appropriations of Mapplethorpe's textual ambivalence, it seems to me, is to deepen and extend the work of critical reading.

23. *New York Times*, 28 September 1989.
24. V. N. Volosinov, *Marxism and the Philosophy of Language* (1929; Cambridge: Harvard University Press, 1973), 24.

In the work of Nigerian British photographer Rotimi Fani-Kayode, for instance, the reimaging of black male nudes enters into an explicitly dialogic or intertextual relationship with Mapplethorpe. The title of Fani-Kayode's first collection, *Black Male/White Male*,[25] reinscribes the tension of interracial binarism (and connotes ethnic antagonism as much as erotic attraction), which is a creative tension used to reopen the questions of identification, desire, and object choice etched across Mapplethorpe's homoeroticism. Despite formal similarities in the lighting and framing of beautiful black bodies in pictorial space, however, Fani-Kayode introduces salient differences. In contrast to Mapplethorpe's isolation effect, bodies are coupled and contextualized: in pictures such as *Technique of Ecstasy* the erotic conjunction of black men's bodies seems to sidestep the implied power relations of the interracial subject/object dichotomy.

If the textual strategies pursued by Fani-Kayode do indeed "make a difference" does this mean that the work is different *because* its author is black? No, not necessarily. What is at issue is not an essentialist argument that the racial or ethnic identity of the author guarantees the aesthetic, cultural, or political value of a text but, on the contrary, how elements of race and ethnicity enter into the overdetermination of the social relations in which authors and audiences participate in the construction of differing textual meanings.

One might point to the complexity of such dialogic relations of "difference" by way of two speculative questions. From the point of view of the reader, what would my response to the black nudes have been had I been told their author, Robert Mapplethorpe, was black? Had I constructed an image of Mapplethorpe's authorship along such hypothetical lines, I suspect I would have produced a rather different reading of racial fetishism from the one I did in 1986. And yet from the point of view of the author, when reading James Baldwin's first and most openly homosexual novel, *Giovanni's Room* (1957), how would one know from the narrator's voice that its author was not only a gay man but a black American?[26] Such questions are explored and interrogated in challenging and innovative ways in the film work of black British director Isaac Julien.

In *Looking for Langston* (1989), the question of authorial identity is invested with memory, fantasy, and desire. The film tracks the enigma of

25. See also Rotimi Fani-Kayode, "Traces of Ecstasy," *Ten.8*, no. 28 (1988): 36–42; and his contributions to *Ecstatic Antibodies*, ed. Sunil Gupta and Tessa Boffin (London: Arts Council of Great Britain, 1990).
26. Note that it was not until the 1980s, some thirty years after *Giovanni's Room*, that Baldwin figured black gay male characters in his novels, in *Just above My Head* (1982).

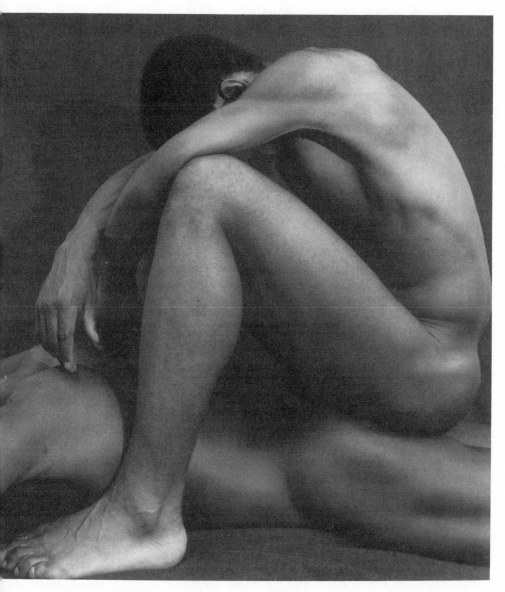

Rotimi Fani-Kayode. *Technique of Ecstasy.* 1987. (Estate of Rotimi Fani-Kayode.)

Langston Hughes's sexual identity as a point of entry into the highly ambiguous sexual and gender relations hidden in the subtexts of the "Harlem Renaissance" of the 1920s. Pursuing a dialogic aesthetic of critical reverie, rather than realist documentary, the film does not claim to discover an authentic, originary, or essential black gay male identity (for Langston Hughes or anyone else). Rather, it historicizes differences within black diaspora societies and emphasizes the diversity of black experiences and identities, both of which were signaled as key themes in Julien's earlier film *Territories* (1984), and across the work of the Sankofa Collective, especially *The Passion of Remembrance* (codirected with Maureen Blackwood, 1986).[27]

Julien's work makes a difference not because some mysterious black gay essence has been magically transferred onto acetate and celluloid but because as an artist he has made cultural and political choices that situate him in a dialogic position at the interface between different traditions. Hence, in one key scene in *Looking for Langston*, in which issues of voyeurism, objectification, and racial fetishism are foregrounded, we see the white protagonist leisurely leafing through *The Black Book*. Mapplethorpe's authorial presence ghosts the scene, and alongside intertextual allusions to Jean Cocteau and Jean Genet, the voices of James Baldwin, Toni Morrison, and Amiri Baraka all combine to emphasize the radical dialogism of Julien's artistic practice. It is through this relational approach that the film reopens the question of racial fetishism.

An exchange of looks between Langston and his mythic object of desire, called Beauty, provokes a hostile glare from Beauty's white partner. In the daydream that follows, Langston imagines himself coupled with Beauty, their bodies entwined on a bed in an image appropriated, or reaccentuated rather, from the photography of George Lynn Platt. As the *objet petit a* of both the white and the black man's gaze, Beauty becomes the signifier of desire and his desirability is enhanced precisely by the eroticized rivalry between the two looks. It is here that the trope of visual fetishization makes a subversive return in the closeup sequences that lovingly linger on the sensuous mouth of the actor portraying Beauty, with the rest of his face cast in shadow. As in Mapplethorpe's text, a strong emphasis on chiaroscuro lighting invests the fetishized fragment with a powerful erotogenic residue in which the "thick lips" of the Negro are hypervalorized as the iconic emblem of Beauty's desirability. In other words, Julien takes the risk of replicating the stereotype of the

27. See, Kobena Mercer, "Diaspora Culture and the Dialogic Imagination: The Aesthetics of Black Independent Film in Britain," in *BlackFrames: Critical Perspectives on Black Independent Cinema*, ed. Claire A. Watkins and Mbye Cham (Cambridge: MIT Press, 1988), 50–61.

"thick-lipped Negro" in order to revalorize that which has been historically devalorized, namely, the black subject as subject and not object of
desire. In my view, this is an artistic risk worth taking, for it is only by
intervening "in and against" the logic of fetishism in dominant regimes
of racial representation that Julien opens the liminal ambivalence of the
psychic and the social at stake in the subject positions inscribed in the
relay of "looks" among the three men.

The subversive return of "racial fetishism" in the work of black gay
artists raises important cultural and political issues for which we have
not yet invented an analytic or theoretical framework.[28] In the context of
debates on the "politics of representation" at issue in black British cultural production in the 1980s, Stuart Hall suggested that an open-
minded attitude will be an ethical prerequisite in responding to the new
"politics of criticism" that such complexity calls for. "Recently I've read
several articles about the photographic text of Robert Mapplethorpe, all
written by black critics or cultural practitioners," he said:

> These essays properly begin by identifying the tropes of fetishization,
> the fragmentation of the black image and its objectification, as the forms
> of their appropriation within the white, gay gaze. But as I read I know
> that something else is going on as well in both the production and the
> reading of those texts. The continuous circling around Mapplethorpe's
> work is not exhausted by being able to place him as the white fetishistic
> gay photographer; and this is because it is also marked by the surrep-
> titious return of desire—that deep ambivalence of identification which
> makes the categories in which we have previously thought and argued
> about black cultural politics extremely problematic. . . . What the new
> politics of representation does is to cross the questions of racism irre-
> vocably with questions of sexuality.[29]

As a critical inquiry into the imaginary spaces where race and gender
intersect in the visual representation of sexuality, my decidedly un-
decided reading of Mapplethorpe's beautiful black men may at least
contribute to the mapping of the political unconscious we all inhabit as
embodied subjects of identity, desire, and history.

28. I have sought to develop the new point of departure in my re-reading of Mapplethorpe in "Skin Head Sex Thing: Racial Difference and the Homoerotic Imaginary,"
in *How Do I Look? Queer Film and Video*, ed. Bad-Object Choices (Seattle: Bay Press,
1991), 169–210.
29. Stuart Hall, "New Ethnicities" in *Black Film/British Cinema*, ICA Document 7,
ed. Kobena Mercer (London: Institute of Contemporary Art/British Film Institute,
1988), 28.

Amor nel Cor

Jane Weinstock/Barbara Bloom

Barbara Bloom. *Lost and Found.* 1985. Engraved on crystal objects.

If I were in Paris . . . how I would love you! I would sicken, die, stupefy myself, from loving you; I would become nothing but a kind of sensitive plant which only your kisses would bring to life. No middle course! Life! And life is precisely that: love, love, sexual ecstasy. Or, something which resembles that but is its negation: namely, the Idea, the contemplation of the Immutable—in a word, Religion, in the broadest sense. I feel that you are too lacking in that, my love. I mean, it seems to me that you do not greatly adore Genius, that you do not tremble to your very entrails at the contemplation of the beautiful.

(Fragment of a letter from Gustave Flaubert to Louise Colet, 1846)

"If I could only be with you . . ." I can bear these words no longer. Upon reading them, I have, countless times, been moved to discern from them your desire to be with me—I have committed the crime of literally reading your words. Your desire lies elsewhere—you desire only this state of longing, itself. You construct it, prune it, guard over it—caring that it will never transpose itself into an active state. I must remind you, my dearest, that your precious suffering (of self-inflicted isolation) is not a pleasure shared by your object of desire—that you commit the sin of magnification— you transpose this state, call it by other names: Immutability, Religion, Idea—you bring out your soldiers and bodyguards— "Genius" . . .

(Fragment of a letter from Barbara Bloom to Gustave Flaubert, 1987)

There is something I love even more than your lovely body, and that is your self. Do you know what you lack, or rather what you sin against? Discernment. You find hidden meanings where they don't exist, in places where no one dreamed of concealing them. You exaggerate everything, you magnify, you carry things much too far. What shall I tell you? What shall I do? I'm at a loss. It takes courage to write to you, knowing that whatever I say wounds you. The caresses that cats give their females draw blood, and an exchange of jabs is part of their pleasure. Why do they keep doing it? Nature impels them: I must be the same as they.
(Fragment of a letter from Gustave Flaubert to Louise Colet, 1846)

It is just these attentions to detail, these hidden meanings and the careful deciphering of them, that have been our pleasure, our shared sport, and so often, our bond. And for someone who claims to walk the edge between the "divine and the banal"—how is it possible to speak against the microscopic gaze at life. Magnification (not exaggeration) reveals the hidden and underlying structures.

Acts of courage and adventure can be found in the precise formulations of the heart—and in dialogue with the other—a form of speech different from the formulation of abstractions, or the refinement of imitation—and offer an excitement perhaps more pleasurable than the physical thrill of drawing blood.
(Fragment of a letter from Barbara Bloom to Gustave Flaubert, 1987)

You tell me, my angel, that I have not initiated you into my inner life, into my most secret thoughts. Do you know what is most intimate, most hidden, in my heart, and what is most authentically myself? Two or three modest ideas about art, lovingly brooded over; that is all. The greatest events of my life have been a few thoughts, a few books. . . . I had formed quite a different idea of love. I thought it was something independent of everything, even of the person who inspired it. Absence, insult, infamy—all that does not affect it. When two persons love, they can go ten years without seeing each other and without suffering from it.
(Fragment of a letter from Gustave Flaubert to Louise Colet, 1846)

The Greeks have two words: *pothos*—desire for the absent being and *himeros*—the more burning desire for the present being. Isolate yourself, but then truly—leave me out of your dilemma—the drama in which you have me play the necessary other who is cast in the role of constantly drawing you out of your precious isolation—I did not solicit this part. You abuse me, not in the flesh—in this arena we meet as equals—but as someone who will *never* speak those words you long to hear: "So, dearest—come to me when you like—and in your absence I will love you all the more . . ." The words *I* long for are the ". . . ", the unmentionable pauses, the unspeakables—implicit silences which refer to moments spent together. Speak of our bodies, shock me, tease me, enrage me, for I am jealous of your pen, my rival—who accompanies you in your most rapturous states.
(Fragment of a letter from Barbara Bloom to Gustave Flaubert, 1987)

Dear Jane,

Thanks for your card. I couldn't decipher the stamp or postmark. The strange picture didn't reveal much more about your whereabouts. I assume that was your hotel dining room, and I started scrutinizing the silverware and dishes for signs of locality. But you know me, always looking for clues.

Did I read your condensed note correctly?:

. . . Sometimes I think fetishism when I see your work. You know, objects standing in for other objects, cups standing still, waiting to be filled. Something's missing. I don't really understand female fetishism. How can a woman miss something she never had. No loss. But something is gained. "Tea for Two" is as much about the cups as it is about the tea. And who are the two? . . .

When I got the card it reminded me of this text by K. Schippers:

In a painting from 1900, a woman is sleeping on a rumpled bed. She's lying on her back. Her left leg is painted somewhat awkwardly, and you can't tell if her foot is resting on the back of the knee of the other leg, or if it is floating somewhere in the air above it. The bed stands in a corner. Is this a hotel room or a bedroom in a house? The two different kinds of wallpaper (red flowers and green and red vertical stripes) seem like the walls of a cheap hotel room, but the table next to the bed seems something to the contrary.

So much silverware and so many objects aren't usually found on hotel room tables. And certainly not a teapot and teacups, these point to household conditions and not to travel.

The woman has the company of a small dog with a big bow, who lies asleep on the floor next to the bed. His fur and the drooping bed sheets and blankets have the same light-salmon color. It's as though the dog has taken on the color of the bed sheets in order not to be too conspicuous in this room. An eyewitness who knows that he'd better act as though he's seen nothing.

The painting is especially engaging because there is someone absent here who shortly before must have been present. You discern that not only by noticing the bed in disarray, the sleeping woman and the dog. On a table are two cups, more color than form. The table stands askew. It's a position which is somehow familiar to me, though I can't recall ever having seen a table in such a position. . . .

What is Bonnard attempting? . . . I want to take a better look at the silverware, perhaps I'll discover Bonnard's secrets if I don't neglect the details. As I walk forward, in the false hope that if I'm closer, the painting will gossip about itself, I recognize a teapot, but are the two blue forms two teacups, or a cup and a sugar bowl?

Schippers seems to be deciphering this image like a detective searching for clues to an implied narrative. He emphasizes that quality in Bonnard's paintings which makes them seem as though something (possibly quite intimate) has transpired before we are given a frozen glimpse of the place.

He glances at the woman's positions, her bed sheets, their disarray, the wallpaper, the placement of the furniture, the similarity between the dog and its boudoir surroundings. And last but not least, he finds in the dishes (their placement and quantity) evidence of the (not visible) presence of some Other.

I like best the last line: "I recognize a teapot, but are the two blue forms two teacups, or a cup and a sugar bowl?"—of course implying that if it were *two* cups, the presence (now absence) of this Other, the lover, could be surmised. And if it were only *one* cup and a sugar bowl, that would drastically alter the reading of the scene. This one cup would indicate something more solitary, a lingering Sunday brunch, something more autoerotic.

Or at least that doesn't supply us with visual evidence of the vanished lover.

I like how the crucial evidence is referred to as "two blue forms." This startles me out of my dreamy narrative state of mind, and reminds me that there is a subjective voice at work here. An interpretive gaze and voice, one that reads lascivious deeds into blue forms. And in doing so brings up the ever-present problems of abstraction and representation.

The precarious balancing point between abstraction and narrative representation seems to be my favorite fulcrum. Not only in this painting where "two blue forms" become the gates to various versions of a narrative; but I have an attraction to these images, moments, gestures, details into which we *read* meaning.

> Sometimes the metonymic object is a presence (engendering joy), sometimes it is an absence (engendering distress). What does my reading depend on? If I believe myself about to be gratified, the object will be favorable, if I see myself as abandoned, it will be sinister. . . . Aside from these fetishes, there is no other object in the amorous world.
>
> (from Roland Barthes, *A Lover's Discourse*)

Love,
Barbara

PS: I once received a letter from a friend whom I hadn't heard from in years. It was a chatty letter, written in an atypical flowery and padded style, which went on and on for pages with no terribly important news. And it was only after rereading the letter several times that I came to understand why she had written at all. Somewhere in the middle of her meanderings were two sentences which she had crossed out, but which were still quite legible. In these sentences she asked a direct favor of me. Directness was obviously not her forte. Obtuseness was more her style, and this peculiar typographic speaking/not speaking was a perfect subliminal solution to the awkwardness of bridging a long silence.

Dear Barbara:

I guess this is a correspondence about a fake correspondence based on a real correspondence. I don't know where that leaves our letters. They're real since they're received by the so-called Dear they supposedly address (unlike your letters to Flaubert). But their real destination isn't really you—I'm writing for other yous too.

I know what you're thinking, that Louise Colet's letters were also sent to more than one destination. What about the fact that Flaubert instructed his mistress to write to him *chez* his dear friend, Maxime du Camp? They say he feared his mother's disapproval. Or was it triangulation, with a flourish? And how do we know that Flaubert never indulged in exhibitionistic publication fantasies as his outpourings on Art and Love collected in Louise Colet's drawer.

We'll never know whether Flaubert's letters were written for Louise's eyes only, but we do know that it was Charles Bovary, not Flaubert, who suffered from and eventually died of literal-mindedness. Charles saw things as they appeared; the destination was the address on the envelope. As for Flaubert, "You say that I seriously loved that woman. It is not so. Only when I was writing to her."

Flaubert could thus dismiss the object of Colet's jealousy by pleading artistic license. He didn't love the recipient of these love letters, Madame X, the literal addressee. His letters traveled through her. And if these letters were fakes, maybe his correspondence with Madame Colet wasn't exactly the real thing either.

So even if he were alive, Flaubert could hardly object to your writing to him without ever sending a letter, or even a small token of your affection. For the object of his letters was beside the point. Although, if you had sent him your engraved crystal objects, he might have smashed them. You failed to appreciate his Genius, and you made a mockery of him: his words, his passion . . . on glass.

Shattering his Truths, your crystals would probably have seemed to

Flaubert a rather double-edged gift of love, another *Amor nel Cor*. Colet's last gift to him, her poison-pen poem, "Amor nel Cor" also hit below the belt—an appropriate point on the man who had written to her: "I want you to be a man down to the navel; below that, you get in my way, you disturb me—your female element ruins everything."

But it was this same man who also said, "Madame Bovary, c'est moi." And it was Madame Bovary who presented her unscrupulous lover, Rodolphe, with a signet ring bearing the words, "Amor nel cor." And it was Madame Colet who gave Flaubert a cigar holder engraved with "Amor nel Cor" before Emma Bovary even existed.

So I guess what we've got here is you (Barbara) identifying with a woman (Louise Colet) who's identified with a woman (Emma Bovary) by a man (Flaubert) who thinks he's a woman (Emma Bovary) when he's not busy being "the horses, the leaves, the wind, the sun," or a man.

Can you believe he said that, the part about the horses and the leaves? He didn't want to have it all; he was contemptuous of the bourgeoisie and its possessions. He just wanted to *be* it all, like God.

Now I'm going to watch "Sonny and Cher." Supposedly they haven't seen each other for years. They're on Letterman. Do you think David's a man of letters, too. Please let me know what you really think of Flaubert. And why *bonbonnières*?

Love,
Jane

Dear Jane,

Let's start at the end, the Ultima.

In Madame Bovary, Rodolphe writes a letter of rupture to Emma:

> Looking around for something to seal the letter with, his eyes fell on a signet ring (given him by Emma) with the motto "Amor nel Cor." "Scarcely appropriate under the circumstances but what the . . . " Whereupon he smoked three pipes and went to bed.

As you mentioned, it was a cigar holder with this inscription "Amor nel Cor"—"Love in the Heart"—Louise Colet had given Flaubert.

And it was Flaubert who wrote once to Louise that if other men feel nothing but contempt after sexual possession, he was not like them—that for him possession breeds affection. "Je suis comme les cigares on ne m'allume qu'en tirant." This, a pun: To light (*allumer*) a cigar, one "draws" (*tirer*), but *tirer* here refers to the expression *tirer un coup*—perform the sexual act. The more he makes love to a woman, the more he is attracted.

Perhaps not so for Rodolphe, who had an appetite for "drawing" on three pipes after writing his Ultima to Emma (not the usual clichéd act of "smoking after sex"). Perhaps his was a preferred form of climax.

Now let me get things straight. According to another author's voice, which speaks for Louise Colet (a man—Julian Barnes—from a chapter titled "Louise Colet's Version," from his novel *Flaubert's Parrot*). He has Colet say of Flaubert's sexual relations with prostitutes, grisettes, and perhaps with his male friends:

> I do not know precisely who, precisely when, precisely what, though I do know that Gustave was never tired of *double ententes* about *la pipe*. I also know he never tired of gazing at me as I lay on my front.[1]

I've tried, in vain, to find out the meaning of this French colloquialism. (In Dutch, "piping" someone is giving them a blow job.) That doesn't fit with the rest does it? Can you help with this?

Another anecdote written by the same voice of Louise Colet (Barnes) is particularly appropriate:

> Let me tell you how Gustave would humiliate me. When our love was young, we would exchange presents—small tokens, often meaningless in themselves, but which seemed to enclose the very essence of their donor. He feasted for months, for years, on a small pair of my slippers that I gave him; I expect he has burnt them by now. Once he sent me a paperweight, the very paperweight which had sat on his desk. I was greatly touched; it seemed the perfect gift from one writer to another; what had formerly held down his prose would now hold down my verses. Perhaps I commented on this once too often; perhaps I expressed my gratitude too sincerely. This is what Gustave told me; that it was no sadness for him to get rid of the paperweight, because he had another which did the work just as efficiently. Did I want to know what it was? If you wish, I replied. His new paperweight, he informed me, was a section of mizzenmast—he made a gesture of extravagant size—which his father had extracted with delivery forceps from the posterior of an old seaman. The seaman—Gustave continued as if this were the best story he had heard for many years—apparently claimed that he had no notion of how the section of mast had reached the position in which it was found. Gustave threw back his head and laughed. What intrigued him most was how, in that case, they knew from which mast the piece of wood had come.[2]

1. Julian Barnes, *Flaubert's Parrot* (New York: Alfred A. Knopf, 1985), 140–41.
2. Ibid., 146.

Forgive me for getting carried away with these sordid little details, this detective-work smut (the gems of research), but I thought that you would appreciate this fictional evidence coming from someone whom Flaubert preferred to address only "from the waist up."

It occurs to me that it is neither the pipe nor the cigar that should concern us, but Flaubert's pen. Perhaps this implement was Louise Colet's real rival. Flaubert boasted of his ability to "arouse himself with his pen." So if Flaubert wasn't really loving the women to whom he was writing rapturous letters, ink staining sheets of paper, I wonder then if he gnawed on the end of his trusted, beloved pen.

And I wonder whether the paperweight (no matter what kind of meaning Flaubert teased at) was meant to literally weigh down Louise Colet's poetry. Let's not forget that she was a poet, someone dedicated to the condensation of language. I can imagine that Louise, the recipient of a voluminous correspondence from Flaubert (often several letters in one day), never had her secret desire satisfied. Isn't this the ultimate love letter (from Goethe):

Why so I turn once again to writing?
Beloved, you must not ask such a question,
For the truth is, I have nothing to tell you,
All the same, your hands will hold this note.

Isn't the act of giving a gift always about contact, sensuality. You will be touching what I have touched—a third skin (that of the object) unites us.

Louise, had she known, would have been supported in her beliefs by what the Greeks thought about absence and presence—that desire is always the same, whether the object is present or absent, that ultimately the object is *always* absent. This isn't the same as languor. There are two words in the Greek language: *pothos*, desire for the absent being, and *himeros*, the more burning desire for the present being.

Flaubert wrote to her:

I had formed quite a different idea of love. I thought it was something independent of everything, even of the person who inspired it. Absence, insult, infamy—all that does not affect it. When two persons love, they can go ten years without seeing each other and without suffering from it.

"What a sentence!" Louise commented in the margin of his letter.

Louise was clearly suffering from absence. She admitted to her ambitiousness in Love—and compared their love to others'. "We could have been like George Sand and Chopin, even greater!"

But the French have a barometer for distance built into the language, and Gustave, in his letters to Louise sometimes addressed her as "tu" sometimes as "vous."

The even more famous French couple Sartre and de Beauvoir went so far as to address each other always as "vous." The French even have the possibility of declaring, "je vous aime"—a peculiar form of intimacy and distance, presence and absence.

In speaking for Louise Colet, I don't feel like a stand-in. Do you know the feeling, after leaving somewhere, realizing to yourself exactly what you *should* have said? A witty remark which is thought too late, a good retort conceived after the event. The French have a term for this, named after that inevitable staircase one is descending when the perfect words (too late) occur to you. They call it *esprit de l'escalier*.

In this case, descending the stairs seems to have taken a century and a half.

Love,
Barbara

PS: How was Sonny and Cher's reunion? How many years had it been since they were together? Just think about Peaches and Herb, the slick black duo who made the seventies hit single "Dedicated."

There is something you should know. Even though the duo is called Peaches and Herb, at last count Herb had switched partners twice. He keeps replacing his singing partner but continues to refer to his female other half as "Peaches." Is it just show-biz fickleness, artist's license, or Herb's own little monument to Ideal Love?

PPS: And while we're on the subject of The Ideal, I thought you might appreciate this text from *Paris Spleen* by Baudelaire:

> I once knew a certain Bénédicta who filled earth and air with the ideal, and whose eyes scattered the seeds of longing for greatness, beauty, and glory, for everything that makes a man believe in immortality.
>
> But this miraculous girl was too beautiful to live long; and so it was that only a few days after I had come to know her, she died, and I buried her with my own hands one day when Spring was swaying its censer over the graveyards. I buried her with my own hands and shut her into a coffin of scented and incorruptible wood like the coffers of India.
>
> And while my eyes still gazed on the spot where my treasure lay buried, all at once I saw a little creature who looked singularly like the deceased, stamping up and down on the fresh earth in a strange hysterical frenzy, and who said as she shrieked with laughter: "Look at me! I am the real Bénédicta! A perfect hussy! And to punish you for blindness and your folly, you shall love me as I am."

But I was furious and cried: "No! no! no!" And to emphasize my refusal I stamped so violently on the earth that my leg sank into the new-dug grave up to my knee; and now, like a wolf caught in a trap, I am held fast, perhaps forever, to the grave of the ideal.

Dear Barbara:

I can't find anything in my French dictionary about penises under "pipe." And I don't know what to do with Barnes's insinuations (via Colet) about Flaubert's homosexual desires. What does Barnes want? This attempt at parroting, is it a bid for parity? Is it parody?

Back to penises. Not that I care about Flaubert's and what he did with it. I'm more interested in what penises represent, to Flaubert, to Colet, to you. I'm not interested in when they stand but in what they stand for.

The relationship was already deteriorating when Flaubert wrote to Colet: "Women keep everything hidden. Their confidences are never the whole story. . . . when they tell you things, everything is so covered with sauce that the meat of the matter disappears." "The meat of the matter," substance, that's what penises stand for. As for women, they have nothing to stand for them; they simply stand for Lack. They lack, and their very existence says to men, "If you don't watch out, you could lack too."

Since the sight of the woman reminds the man of his penis's precarious position ("your female element ruins everything"), he tends to approach her with trepidation. To ward off his anxiety, he transforms an object—a shoe, a piece of velvet—into the penis she doesn't have. He says, "I know—but let's pretend."

But what about female fetishism? Does it exist? How can you lose what you never had? If your crystal becomes your fetish, some thing you're missing, is that because you identify with men? Or is there a fetishism specific to femininity? And what about Madame Bovary and her precious objects? If Flaubert's really Emma, does that make him a female fetishist?

I haven't figured this one out, but I do think of fetishism when I see your perfectly formed glass objects. How do they fit into your story, your "drama in which you (Flaubert) have me (Barbara) play the necessary Other who is cast in the role of constantly drawing you out of your precious isolation?" Are your crystals "the unspeakables" you speak of in your letter to Flaubert?

And what about other women, like the housewives who fill their homes with beloved objects and precious children? Are they fetishists trying to fill their lackluster lives?

Or maybe fetishism isn't really the issue? Maybe it's control, an anal economy? Freud certainly saw the obsessional housewife as a control maniac, but not one worth considering.

I'm beginning to feel like the obnoxious kid who won't stop asking questions.

Love,
Jane

Dear Jane,

Here's the courtroom Drama:

So, I too must "lack discernment. Finding hidden meanings where they don't exist, in places where no one dreamed of concealing them." I too must be "exaggerating everything, magnifying, carry things too far."

To all this I plead "Guilty," Your Honor. But I would like a moment of your time to defend myself against Flaubert's accusations and in doing so perhaps plead a case for all those who suffer from "housewife psychosis," those who spend hours cleaning and contemplating in great detail the objects that fill their cupboards.

This magnifying gaze made me think about Chantal Akerman's films, so I dug out this version of her script for *Jeanne Dielman, 23 Quai du Commerce, 1080 Bruxelles*. Even the title announces Akerman's interest in specificity, in detail, in "carrying things too far." The script begins:

The kitchen

A large, narrow kitchen, with tiles on the floor . . .

The repeated vibrations of a refrigerator . . . walls yellowy-white, covered to a certain height with tiles of a brighter white . . . modern functional furniture . . .

Next to the refrigerator at the rear of the room is a stove, to the left on the front burners is a kettle . . . a glass coffee pot.

In the foreground an aluminum sideboard with a drying rack.

A metal object falls into a container.

To the right, pushed against the wall, a table, in the length, set for breakfast, for four people.

Some spots of light on a cup, and on the kitchen towels that are drying on the radiator . . .

An orderly kitchen.

One could say that the repeated
vibrations of the refrigerator stress
the impression of order,
give it something inextricable . . .
The slow emphatic gaze
bestowed on this kitchen

is like a kind of violation,
which is greater than if
actual traces of life
were to be found.

So, She's at home, while He's out in the world. It's no wonder that she's learned to see the world in (through) these objects that surround her/make up her world. I'm not suggesting a kind of "Bluebird of Happiness" (in her own interior). And I don't think that these objects are symbols of either the Big Wide World Out There (perhaps gifts brought back to her) or clichéd symbols of her imprisonment. I think that her relationship to these objects is more complex.

The clue is in her magnifying gaze, the gaze that finds meaning where no one dreamed of concealing it. She's like a detective reading meaning into all the details. Her gaze is, by necessity, directed at the small. But what about me? I get out of the house. I travel. I'm not confined by those "four walls" and all they stand for. Why am I fascinated by the detail, the gesture, the clue, and their implicit narratives? What about my magnifying gaze? When you come right down to it, I probably believe that there are no places where hidden meanings aren't concealed.

But wait a minute, let's shift our focus for a moment from her to him. Flaubert had it figured out for himself. He saw two options, with no middle course. One was what he referred to as, "Life! and life is precisely that: love, love, sexual ecstasy." Or, his other opinion: "something which resembles that but is its negation: namely, the Idea, the contemplation of the Immutable—in a word, Religion, in the broadest sense." To this category of Big Terms he also added Genius and Art. It's clear what choices Flaubert made. The Life option would have necessarily included real women, and might inevitably lead to the dreads of all bachelors: Attachment, Responsibility, Sharing, etc.

It all reminds me of the age-old Adventure Story dilemma, ever present in literature from the *Iliad* to fairy tales, westerns, or James Bond. This is from Paul Zweig's *Adventurer*:

The adventure performed for the woman is also performed against her. In many written or filmed Westerns, for example, the main character is a drifter who arrives in a town where he gets mixed up in a local dispute involving the safety or the well-being of a woman. Inevitably things take their course and the woman falls in love with him. From this point the story works in two directions. The drifter is inspired by the woman; she reveals in him a strength which he had been reluctant to recognize in himself, even more reluctant to use. Because of the woman, he manages to win out, proving himself and guaranteeing her safety.

But his newly won strength of character is needed for another purpose now: to protect him from the woman, whose seduction he is able to
resist by riding off into the hills, still lonely but still unmarried.[3]

Flaubert's flights weren't off into the hills, on expeditions into the
Amazon jungle, or to the other end of the kingdom to behead a dreaded
dragon. But they were flights, and took him to realms far, far away. And
his "Idea of Love" fit perfectly into his suitcase. It suited him well to feel
that "when two persons love, they can go ten years without seeing each
other without suffering from it." Suffering is what Flaubert did when
Colet pressed him to follow through on some of his promises to come see
her, when she called him on his inability to do anything other than *write*
the words, "If I could only be with you." He even responded once with:

How rapturous your letter is, how ardent, how heartfelt! Because I tell
you I'll soon be coming, you approve everything in me, you shower me
with caresses and praise. You no longer reproach me for my whims, my
love of rhetoric, the refinements of my selfishness, etc. But should anything arise to prevent my coming, the whole thing would begin again,
would it not?

Well something inevitably arose and prevented his coming, and the
whole thing began again and again.

And I assume that when Louise faced the impossibility of confronting
Flaubert "face to face," she resorted to arguing "page to page" about his
inability (again) to show up for their afternoon rendezvous. And when
Louise tired of all this, she was left with her souvenirs (fetishes?).

Was Louise criminal to take Flaubert's words so literally, desiring a
one-to-one relationship between what was *said* and what was *done*?
And even after Flaubert assured her that the love letters he wrote to
Madame X were of no concern, since he "took this woman seriously only
while he was writing to her." Even after such a convincing explanation,
was Louise wrong to remain jealous?

We've gone over all this before: Flaubert's ability to arouse himself
with his pen, his literary license. (If I were on the review board I'd have
his literary license revoked.) His crime is far worse than any of Louise
Colet's misdemeanors: he imposed a State of Absence; he abstracted all
women, knowing them only as objects of desire and/or castrating vamps
trying to domesticate him.

3. Paul Zweig, *The Adventurer* (New York: Basic Books, 1974), 62–63.

I'm sure that Flaubert conveniently worked all this into his general disdain for the bourgeoisie = middle-class home = women.

So what was Louise Colet left with but dusting those treasures on the shelf?

Love,

Barbara

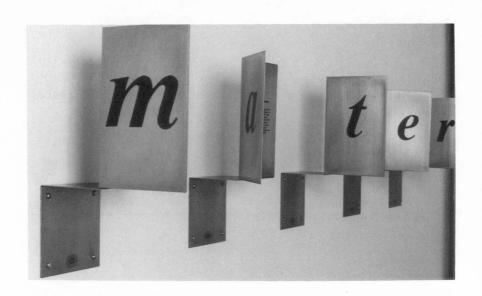

Mary Kelly. *Pecunia.* 1989.
16 × 6 × 11 inches.
Silkscreen on galvanized
steel. Details, *Mater* section.

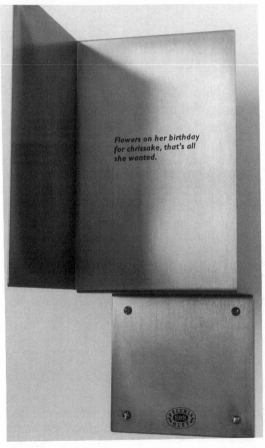

Flowers on her birthday for chrissake, that's all she wanted.

Mary Kelly. *Pecunia.* 1989.
16 × 6 × 11 inches.
Silkscreen on galvanized
steel. Details, *Conju* section.

She wanted her *and* she
wanted all of her clothes.

Mary Kelly. *Pecunia.* 1989.
16 × 6 × 11 inches.
Silkscreen on galvanized
steel. Details, *Soror* section.

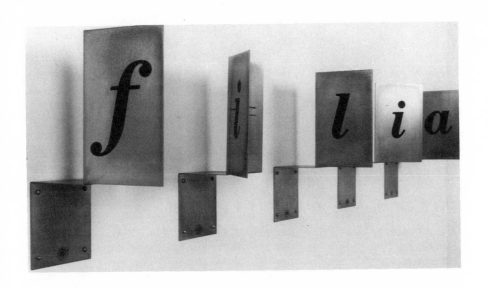

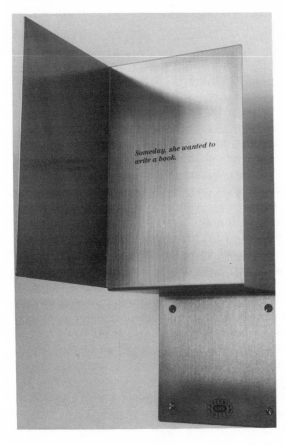

Mary Kelly. *Pecunia.* 1989. 16 × 6 × 11 inches. Silkscreen on galvanized steel. Details, *Filia* section.

The Smell of Money: Mary Kelly
in Conversation with Emily Apter

The following conversation with the artist Mary Kelly took place in April 1990 in New York City. Kelly's work includes *Post-Partum Document*, published in 1983, and *Interim*, shown in its entirety at the New Museum of Contemporary Art in New York in 1990.

Emily Apter: In a preface written for the book of your earlier work, *Post-Partum Document*, you explicitly stated that one of your principal concerns was to see whether some notion of female fetishism could be worked out according to the theoretical parameters of the installation. Emphasizing in the classic Freudian schema of male fetishism the strategic compensation of projected phallic loss through prosthetic substitutions, you then went on to discern a comparable (though different) female fetishism in the maternal reliquary, designed to ward off the fear of an impending "empty nest." *Post-Partum Document* "documents" the museological mania of the maternal collector/fetishist with a gently ironic sympathy. "First words set out in type, stained liners, hand imprints, comforter fragments, drawings, writings or even the plants and insects that were his gifts"—these are displayed through an affectionate but rigorously formal taxonomy.[1] A similar archival or ethnographic impulse is discernible in the "Pecunia" section of *Interim*. Could you describe the shifts and continuities in your treatment of female fetishism between the earlier and later work?

1. Mary Kelly, *Post-Partum Document* (London: Routledge and Kegan Paul, 1983), xvi.

Mary Kelly: First, there is a continuity in general between the two projects, which is established by the visual similarities of serial imagery and also by the way that I approach the subject matter. I would describe this, similarly, as ethnographic, that is, the artist as participant observer, recording the "rituals" of maternity or aging. One of the most important shifts, however, would concern the notion of female fetishism (although I would hesitate to use the term now). It was a central theme in *Post-Partum Document*, but only one of many in *Interim*, which layers several discourses within and across the different sections.

The woman's relation to the child is the classic example (but not acknowledged as such by Freud) of the trajectory of fetishism for the woman. The mother's memorabilia—the way she saves the lock of hair, the tooth, or school reports—signals a disavowal of the lack inscribed by separation from the child. In order to convey this sense of loss, and the subsequent "prosthetic substitution," I used found objects and arranged them in a parody of conventional museum display. But *Interim* does not use the "real thing," because it is an invocation of the fetish already once removed, a "representation." In "Corpus" the photo laminate and not the actual clothing enfolds an absent body; the simulated bar graph of "Potestas" also masquerades as minimal sculpture; a mediated version of the greeting card shapes the visual framework for "Pecunia."[2] All my material comes from popular sources, more exactly, what has been called "the everyday." Sentimentality is foregrounded in a way that seems either to justify or to reiterate your comparison of my work with Jeanne's (the maternal protagonist) preoccupations in Guy de Maupassant's [novel] *Une vie*. It is a self-indulgent replay of lost moments (the vanishing real, according to Jacques Lacan). Perhaps *Interim* illustrates the collector/fetishist you speak of, but I would like to distinguish this from the inverse, the fetishist/collector of *Post-Partum Document*. The maternal reliquary is in some sense esoteric. As is the case with "male" fetishism, it reveals an ambivalent but nevertheless passionate relation to her *object a*. This is closer to the clinical definition of the term *fetish*. There is a difference in the kind of object cathexis involved here; insofar as the mother (or woman as spectator in the position of the mother) cathects the trace, she places herself in the real. That is, she refuses the recognition of lack, perhaps only momentarily, in view of the artwork. But it is also important to remember that in psychoanalytic practice this "perversion" would pertain to specific forms of this refusal, something which this visualization can only mimic.

2. For the texts of "Pecunia" (published separately) see Mary Kelly, *Pecunia non olet* (New York: Top Stories, 1990).

In "Pecunia," the spectator (in the position of the older, postreproductive woman), senses a loss that is more overtly "presentified" in the "collection" of cards or the story's references to domestic objects. She is constituted in a relation of lack. But I think that here the castrating instance, so to speak, is also invoking something more fundamental or archaic. The woman's relation to her "things" is one of inaccessibility. The object is already lost, her desire repressed, because it is her own mother as signifier of The Real Other and not the child-as-phallus that figures as the lost object.

Actually, the two works, taken in their entirety, are not so schematically divided. For instance, as *Post-Partum Document* progresses from appropriated words and gestures to fabricated markings in section six, the fetishist does, in a sense, become collector. And in "Pecunia," when the narrative describes, say, the woman's addiction to the "smell of palest blue," the collector clearly slips into the place of fetishist. So there is always an imbrication of the two terms, but defined in different relations to the representation of feminine sexuality.

EA: You have invoked Michèle Montrelay's notions of "concentricity" and "precocious femininity" to describe the woman's autoconstruction as the phallus (fetish) of the Other's other, her regression to primal fantasies about where the child comes from, her "fix" on the child (or refusal to displace her/him). Could you clarify these terms and arguments as they relate to "Pecunia?" How do they allow us to revise the notion of female fetishism such that it may be defined as:

(1) (not) not feminine narcissism,

(2) (not) not masqueraded castration anxiety,

(3) (not) not obsessional neurosis.

MK: The reason I said that the term "female fetishism" no longer seems appropriate to me is that I would prefer to think about the way the category "woman" is constructed, to look at the various psychic identities that correspond to different moments (subjective, not chronological) in our lives. If fantasy is the instrument of desire, that is, the means by which the sexual drive is represented in terms of aims and objects, then we could speak of the fantasy of the "young" woman as profoundly narcissistic. She is the phallus; the whole body is phallicized, presented as the imaginary object of the Other's gaze. Fetishism in this case would concern the internalization of the split between being and having. Insofar as she is both subject and object of desire, she takes her own body, a part of it, and fetishizes it; that is to say, it constitutes a libidinal attachment that is the exclusive condition for sexual satisfaction. The "masculine" position is acknowledged or acted out, hence "perverse." On the other hand, the consequence of repressing this position is generally associated with the symptoms that define hysteria.

For the reproductive woman, or "mother," the child is the imaginary object, once a part of her, that comes to her as someone other than herself that she can love, as Freud says, with a "healthy" object love. Ironically, from the beginning, she is occupying the masculine position, that is, the position of the actively desiring subject. The child *is* the phallus for her. Fetishism here pertains to the separation and the inevitable loss of the child-as-phallus. Her imaginary object is maintained either anaclitically (feeding) or narcissistically (dressing), that is, by forming the child's functions (feces) or effects (clothes) into substitutes that can be controlled. Just as the fetishist described by Joan Copjec "knows what the other wants," the mother wants the child to be what-she-wants-it-to-be and believes the child wants to be it. Perhaps, when the mother's memorabilia is eroticized, not as emblems of desire but as her "piece of reality," we can speak of maternal perversity.

However, what the woman fears losing, beyond the pleasure of the child's body, is the closeness to her mother's body which she experiences in "being like her." According to Michèle Montrelay, it is the fantasy of "having the first object" that produces neurotic anxiety (not necessarily fetishism). This perverse relation to the mother's body is the result of what Montrelay has theorized as "censorship" rather than repression. It allows the woman to retain a "concentric" or archaic oral, anal organization of the drives, but at the same time, it disallows her access to sublimated pleasure.[3]

For the "older" woman there are various substitutes for the child, including philanthropy and pets—I know someone who is sending a birthday card to a friend's dog and who calls her cat "Baby"—as well as the contents and arrangement of the home, and especially her "collection" of precious (but not always valuable) things. She seems to slip along the equation phallus = child in the opposite direction, phallus = feces, suggesting a certain archaizing of the drives. Possibly, in this instance, fetishism represents a fixation of libidinal cathexis with regard to particular objects which she loves as she loved her child or her lover once loved her. Often the preoccupation with taste, texture, smell, and the eroticization of bodily processes indicates a specific form of perversity, i.e., coprophilia.

The repression of this perverse relation to the body produces, on the one hand, the real and imaginary illnesses identified with hypochondria and, on the other, the excessive order, cleanliness, attention to detail

3. Michèle Montrelay, *L'ombre et le nom: Sur la féminité* (Paris: Minuit, 1977), in particular, the section titled "Recherches sur la féminité," 57–81. For an English translation, see "Inquiry into Femininity," trans. Parveen Adams, *m/f* 1 (1978): 83–101.

that signals coprophobia. In "Character and Anal Eroticism," Freud defines it as a "reaction-formation against what is unclean and disturbing and should not be part of the body."[4]

EA: In the same essay Freud also linked coprophilia to the love of (filthy) lucre:

> Wherever the archaic way of thinking has prevailed or still prevails, in the old civilizations, in myths, fairy tales, superstition, in unconscious thinking, in dreams and in neuroses, money has been brought into the closest connection with filth.[5]

Just as this passage from Freud functioned as a significant intertext for Sandor Ferenczi's essay "The Ontogenesis of the Interest in Money," so Ferenczi's essay became a particularly important catalyst for you in the production of "Pecunia." Following Freud, Ferenczi speaks of childish anal retention in terms of the desire to hoard "dejecta" as so many "savings" for the future.[6] "Civilization," of course, prohibits the accumulation of excrement itself but sanctions its sanitized substitutes—sand, putty, rubber, and later, money. Ferenczi calls these material samples of deodorized and dehydrated filth "copro-symbols." (FC 323) Your work has always seemed to evince a fascination with copro-symbols.

MK: Well, not exactly. According to Ferenczi, money, specifically, is the supreme copro-symbol, but in "Pecunia" the woman's relation to money is shown to be problematic. She is configured with money only insofar as she herself is an object of exchange (i.e., the phallus for the other). As the narrative suggests, she signs the check "without conviction." Her signature fades, something fails at the point of entering into that system of exchange as subject of desire. Perhaps it is the difference between what Ferenczi called "intrinsic value" and "measurable value." In general (but by no means exclusively) the former characterizes the woman's relationship to things. Men for instance, have collections— stamps, cars, art, etc.—that add up in financial terms, while women collect items of sentimental worth. In "Mater," you may recall the "red Porsche" that features in the classified ad. It has no meaning for the mother except as signifier of someone else's desire. The last panel says, "She only wanted them to be happy." So I would say that the proximity

4. Sigmund Freud, "Character and Anal Eroticism" (1909), in *Standard Edition*, 9:172.

5. Ibid., 174.

6. Sandor Ferenczi, "The Ontogenesis of the Interest in Money," in *First Contributions to Psycho-analysis*, trans. Ernest Jones (London: Hogarth Press, 1952), 321, hereafter abbreviated *FC*.

Three gables and a country porch just visible beyond a cast-iron gate. It could be perfect. She imagined tidy evergreens and red azaleas against the brick facade. Instead, she found a thicket of dense bramble, a few wild poppies and an insipid cupid pissing in a seashell. That would have to go. She sealed its fate and carried on. A double-door, stained glass, she turned the key. It could be perfect with a little work—replaster, paint, remove the carpet and the hideous drapes. She planned, envisioning a floor of polished oak, a tasteful rug, an open fire. Perhaps it's Christmas, yes, a tree, clear lights, of course, with berry clusters, cabbage roses, ribbons, raffia and lace. He'd chop the wood and she'd prepare the goose. Where was the kitchen, anyway? She found it, much too small, a north extension possibly; a walk-in pantry, but too dark. She'd add a skylight, then a granite counter, porcelain sink, refrigerator, freezer, Aga range. Above her would-be-herbery, a window. She looked out—a partial view obstructed by the freeway, but the lot was large enough to have a pool, gazebo even, perfect! Scalloped tiles, it could be perfect, well, it could be, could be perfect, if

Mary Kelly. *Pecunia.* 1989. 16 × 6 × 11 inches. Silkscreen on galvanized steel.
Detail, *Conju* section.

for the woman of her mother's body, its affective force, constitutes a certain block or failure in the process of repression, and coprophilia is the symptomatic consequence. At another level though, you could say that the artwork is the desanitized version of this symptomology, and in that sense, like money, could be called a copro-symbol.

EA: The ensuing observation is part of my own response to the last two questions posed. In the "Conju" section of "Pecunia," the housewife cleans, throwing away tickets, receipts and lists, "removing the sallow wreath encrusted on the toilet bowl," and dreaming in the flashy cipher (readily traceable to Freud's famous *Glanz auf der Nase*) of polished oak floors, scalloped tiles, a porcelain sink. All these controlled and sparkling surfaces recall the passion for Meissen porcelain afflicting Bruce Chatwin's fictional character Utz.[7] Utz suffers from *Porzellankrankheit* ("porcelain sickness"), much as "Pecunia"'s allegorical spouse suffers from housewife's psychosis. Utz reminds us that the word *porcelain* derives etymologically from *porcella* ("little pig"), referring to the resemblance of a pig's back to the upper surface of the Venus shell. Of course, now thoughts turn to Botticelli's Venus rising out of her shell. Perhaps "Pecunia" similarly enshrines the goddess of love in a temple bedecked with hygienic appliances. The housewife's garden is, after all, blessed with an "insipid cupid pissing in a seashell."

MK: "Conju" is the most striking example of what I would call the coprophobic Imaginary. The wife's sublime (inaccessible) thing is invoked by the repeated phrase "it could be perfect." In another case she is "surrounded by an arc of abstinent light," her clean house provoking the consummate ecstasy of a Saint Teresa. This, however, is not perverse. It is the reaction against the repression of anal eroticism and the subsequent formation of what Freud called the anal character, notably the obsessional tendency that he ungraciously dubbed "housewife's psychosis."

EA: How does this coprophilic or coprophobic "archaizing of the drives" erupt into your figuration of the bourgeois woman inscribed within the claustrophobic socius of the family?

MK: The "bourgeois" woman, as you say, is not really represented in "Pecunia." None of the characters have financial security in that sense. Their problems with money are real, but their symptomatic relation to them is a consequence, perhaps, of this archaizing of the drives. "Filia" is a key series in this regard. The daughter was not brought up to think of herself as a breadwinner but nevertheless finds herself supporting both spouse and child. It should also be noted how frequent this is now. The

7. Bruce Chatwin, *Utz* (London: Penguin, 1988).

claustrophobic (one-income) wife-at-home family does not exist and perhaps, as Marx maintained so long ago, never did, except for a minority.

In "Filia" the reaction of one character upon spending the last of her savings is "he doesn't love me." This "irrationality" points to a psychic structure which underpins the social/sexual division which has produced this startling statistic: women own less than 1 percent of the world's wealth.

For both the boy and the girl, Freud maintains that anal eroticism provides a narcissistic pleasure in something that was once a part of the body, namely, feces. And for both, there is the contiguous belief that babies are produced in the same way. Then, during the phallic phase, the boy's organ is also seen to be detachable in fantasy, and Freud suggests that for the girl the clitoris assumes a similar function. He points out that castration constitutes a threat to this narcissistic integrity of the body, but whereas it ends the Oedipus complex for the boy, it only initiates it for the girl along the lines of the now-infamous equation penis = baby. Since pregnancy is infrequent and late, the wish is deferred but intensely cathected and, I would suggest, intimately linked to the tendency to coprophilia in women. The association of fecal production with reproduction persists and underlines the significance of menses in adolescence. For the boy, involvement in reproduction is conceptualized as loss and sublimated as the "father's gift" at a much earlier stage. Because the penis is his stake in the representation of lack, you could say he has already entered into an abstract system of exchange—phallus = gift = money, status, etc.—an infinite and interminable sliding of the signifier, as Lacan insists. But the woman identifies with the child as someone who was once a part of her. She has waited for the phallus to be given to her, never completely decathecting the eroticism of the anal stage and never effectively repressing the maternal body. Her achievements are tentative or temporary, that is to say, in addition to the project of mothering. So, when the children grow up, and especially with the onset of menopause, a certain representation of the feminine body (Montrelay's concentric, oral, anal schema) is posed as the woman's stake in representation. Phallocentricity here becomes the route to sublimated pleasure. This is true even if the woman has chosen not to have a child, because at this moment she realizes, this is really it!

So what makes this delayed oedipal passage finally possible? Clearly it happens for most women. I think it has something to do with the girl's preoedipal relation to the father. The familiar emphasis is on the symbolic dimension of the paternal metaphor. For instance, the child is given the father's name, the mother invokes it, the ego internalizes it, and the Law prevails. But what is the man's relationship to paternity beyond (or before) giving the name. [Julia] Kristeva suggests that there are two forms of primary identification—one projective (maternal) and the other introjective (paternal). The latter concerns a libidinal object, which is taken into the self already constituted as a phallic ideal. So, the father is both body and name, desire and meaning. Perhaps the equation money = filth should be prefaced with another, feces = body of the father. The main point here is that for the girl it is the remaking of this imaginary father, that is, taking his place or creating it within language, which defines "sublimational possibility." The phallocentric organization of the drives constitutes a kind of precondition for this. On the other hand, a denial of the imaginary father seems to be psychically linked to anal sadism. For women, this is usually expressed as a reaction which takes the form of overprotectiveness and sentimentality. Remaking the imaginary father is, I think, also instrumental in undoing a certain anxiety for women which is attached to the unconscious fear of being "like a man." And this I believe is the crisis for the older woman who, in "Filia," is described in the position of the father's precocious child in the final place which says, "Someday she wanted to write a book."

EA: In taking up in your logo Ferenczi's suppression of the "non" in "Pecunia non olet," you seem to be emphasizing the repression of anal eroticism within capitalism, its preference for *argent sec*, the "dry" (paper) currency that has come to replace primitive barter and, for that matter, the stickiness of real coins, within the sphere of global financial transactions (FC, 327). In alluding to the lurking threat of dirt's eternal return, you seem to be implying that capitalism, once demystified and desublimated, "stinks," even though it no longer "smells."

Do Freud and Marx converge in "Pecunia" through fantasms of commodified desire, or do you see the psychoanalytic and materialist fetish as anchored in definitions of value (libidinal surinvestment versus exchange value) so fundamentally separate that they ultimately fail to reward any effort at discursive cross-contamination?

MK: In The History of Sexuality, Michel Foucault defines the process of "desublimation" as one that channels rather than represses sexuality. He does not mean that sexuality is repressed for economic reasons but that it is controlled through circuits of the economy. The family, for instance, does not restrain sexuality but provides a support for it. In "Pecunia," the four sections—"Mater," "Conju," "Soror," "Filia"—survey "forms of alliance" as Foucault described concerns of kinship, names, possession, etc. Each section represents a set of social relations that the woman is designated to fulfill (or not): the agencies of mother, daughter, sister, wife. More important, because these relationships are "saturated with desire," I am trying to trace the way a psychic economy is ciphered through them. In other words, as Foucault insists, the alliance is linked to the economy not only as a contract for the transmission of wealth but also through a body that produces and consumes. So, the logo "Pecunia non olet" refers both to the materialist fetish-trademark, seal of authority, insignia of desire—and to the psychoanalytic fetish; that is, to the specific history of that discourse, to definitions of the perverse subject. Ferenczi is the obvious reference here.

Although Foucault was neither a Freudian nor a Marxist, his works perhaps provide the conditions of existence for a cross-contamination of the two discourses.

EA: Could you elaborate on how parts of "Pecunia" define a "perverse" subject?

MK: In its representation of the woman as perverse, "Soror" is important not only because the character transgresses the heterosexual imperative ("She wanted her *and* she wanted all of her clothes") but mostly because it questions the psychoanalytic injunction to define the feminine on the side of repression by mocking the conventions of so-called perversity. This mockery may be heard in the phrase, "She decided to put on her chain bracelet, lace anklets and the like and live complexly a little longer."

EA: Soror's bric-a-bracomania (her fondness for kitsch objets d'art) poses another question concerning the aesthetic and class tensions surrounding the "high" representation of "low" art. How would you compare your work to that, say, of Jeff Koons (I am thinking specifically here of his large-scale porcelain model of Michael Jackson and pet). Does it contain a politics of bad taste?

MK: Yes, but the difference between my work and the tendency Koons represents concerns the degree of formal mediation, the conditions of exhibition, and the question of audience. Koons appropriates the low-art genre of one class for the amusement and consumption of another. This audience, more privileged in the economic sense, is consequently able to appreciate the criticality of his displacement. Perhaps the differences between the two types of audiences would take us/ back to Ferenczi's distinction between two types of collections, one based on intrinsic and the other on measurable value. *Interim* recuperates a stigmatized popular culture of sentimentality, but the approach is ethnographic and inclusive, that is, the audience for the work is included as the subject of it and the subjectivity the work parodies does not exclude my own.

Formally, the dimensions and typography ironically restate the style and humor of generic greeting cards but do not literally reproduce them. The galvanized steel invokes, but does not simulate, the look of sentiment. And in terms of presentation, there is an emphasis on intratextuality or cross-referencing among the sections rather than the perception of discrete objects.

EA: Ferenczi implies that the sensual deprivation induced by odorless capital is compensated for by a surcharge of visual or aural pleasure. Art, as visual pleasure, in this sense trades on money's lack. Ferenczi argues: "The eye takes pleasure at the sight of their [the coins'] luster and color, the ear at the metallic clink, the sense of touch at play with the round smooth disks, only the sense of smell comes away empty" (*FC*, 327). Do you see "Pecunia" as embodying this inverse ratio between visual pleasure and odorless capital?

MK: The surcharge of visual and aural pleasure . . . you could say the luster of the galvanized surface and the metallic clink of the steel . . . has another function. For the woman as spectator, the invocatory and olfactory residue is shaped, metaphorically, into a material presence. So possibly the archaic, coprophilic (or phobic) imaginary is thrown into relief so to speak, as a sort of trompe l'oeil. In this sense, the work trades on woman's lack, that is, femininity masquerading as lack. "Sending it up" is at the same time setting it at a distance. By taking herself out of circulation she, the spectator, is no longer the object of exchange but the subject or author of the transaction.

EA: Hal Foster's discussion in this volume of Dutch pronk still lifes—historic loci of mediation between the gilded dazzle of the commodity and the transparently shining value of the artistic "masterpiece"—seems relevant here. In your reading of "Pecunia," is the spectator's "glance" the vehicle for (critically) eliding the gleam of the domestic icon with the embossed finish of the work's galvanized steel surfaces?

MK: Well, I would like to say . . . eliding the gleam of your polished statement with my desire for the perfect viewer . . . Yes.

Bibliography

This bibliography lists most of the works cited in the essays composing this volume. It has been divided for convenience into six sections: Psychoanalysis, Sexology, Medicolegal Texts; Marxism, Economics; Sociology, Anthropology, Religion; Visual Culture, Performance Arts, Fashion; Literature, Textual Criticism, Theory; and History, Biography. With the exception of well-known literary works, the English translation of texts written in a foreign language is given whenever one exists. Since interest in many of these works is historical, the original publication date is usually indicated. Works by Freud are cited from the *Standard Edition of the Complete Psychological Works of Sigmund Freud*, 24 vols. (London: Hogarth Press, 1966–74).

Psychoanalysis, Sexology, Medicolegal Texts

Binet, Alfred. "Le fétichisme dans l'amour: Etude de psychologie morbide." *Revue philosophique* 24 (1887): 143–67, 252–74.

Bourget, Paul. *Essais de psychologie contemporaine*. Vol. 1. Paris: Plon, 1912.

Charcot, Jean-Martin, and Valentin Magnan. "Inversion du sens génital." *Archives du neurologie* 3 (1882): 53–60; 4 (1882) 296–322. Reprinted in *Inversion du sens génital et autres perversions sexuelles*, ed. Gérard Bonnet. Paris: Frénésie, 1987.

Chasseguet-Smirgel, Janine. *Creativity and Perversion*. New York: Norton, 1984.

Chevalier, Julien. *L'inversion sexuelle: Une maladie de la personnalité*. Lyon: Storck, 1893.

Cleisz, Dr. A. *Recherches des lois qui président à la création des sexes*. Paris: Rongier, 1889.

Clérambault, Gatian de Gaeton de. "Passion érotique des étoffes chez la femme."
   1908. In *Oeuvre psychiatrique*. Paris: Presses Universitaires de France, 1942.
Du Camp, Maxime. *Les convulsions de Paris*. Paris: Hachette, 1880.
Dupouy, Edmond. *Médecine et moeurs de l'ancienne Rome d'après les poètes
   latins*. Paris: Baillière, 1885.
Ellis, Havelock. "Eonism." 1906. In *Studies in the Psychology of Sex*, 2: pt. 2, 1–
   110. New York: Random House, 1936.
Esquirol, Etienne. *Mental Maladies: A Treatise on Insanity*. 1838. Facsimile of
   the 1845 English trans. of E. K. Hunt. Introduction by Raymond de Saussure.
   New York: Hafner, 1965.
Falret, Jules. "De la folie raisonnante." *Annales médico-pathologiques* (1866):
   406–7.
Fenichel, Otto. "The Symbolic Equation: Girl = Phallus." 1936. Trans. Henry
   Alden Bunker. *Psychoanalytic Quarterly* 18 (1949): 303–24.
Féré, Charles Samson. *The Evolution and Dissolution of the Sexual Instinct*. 2d
   rev. ed. Paris: Carrington, 1904.
Ferenczi, Sandor. "The Ontogenesis of the Interest in Money." 1914. In *First
   Contributions to Psycho-analysis*, trans. Ernest Jones, 319–31. London:
   Hogarth Press, 1952.
Flugel, J. C. *The Psychology of Clothes*. London: Hogarth Press, 1930.
Forel, Auguste. *La question sexuelle*. 5th rev. ed. Paris: Masson, 1922.
Freud, Sigmund. "Analysis of a Phobia in a Five-Year-Old Boy." 1910. In *Stan-
   dard Edition*, 10:5–149.
——. "Character and Anal Eroticism." 1909. In *Standard Edition*, 9:169–75.
——. "A Child Is Being Beaten: A Contribution to the Study of the Origin of
   Perversions." 1919. In *Standard Edition*, 17:179–204.
——. "Contributions to the Psychology of Love." 1911. In *Standard Edition*,
   11:165–75.
——. "Fetishism." 1927. In *Standard Edition*, 21:152–57.
——. "Freud and Fetishism: Previously Unpublished Minutes of the Vienna Psy-
   choanalytic Society." Ed. and trans. Louis Rose. *Psychoanalytic Quarterly* 57
   (1988): 147–66.
——. *The Interpretation of Dreams*. 1900. In *Standard Edition*, vols. 4 and 5.
——. "Medusa's Head." 1922. In *Standard Edition*, 18:273–74.
——. "My Views on the Part Played by Sexuality in the Aetiology of the Neu-
   roses." 1905. In *Standard Edition*, 7:271–79.
——. "Negation." 1925. In *Standard Edition*, 19:35–39.
——. "On Narcissism: An Introduction." 1914. In *Standard Edition*, 14:73–81.
——. "Psychogenesis of a Case of Homosexuality in a Woman." 1920. *Standard
   Edition*, 18:147–72.
——. "Repression." 1915. *Standard Edition*, 14:146–58.
——. "Sexuality in the Aetiology of the Neuroses." 1898. In *Standard Edition*,
   3:263–85.
——. "Some Psychical Consequences of the Anatomical Distinction between the
   Sexes." 1925. In *Standard Edition*, 19:248–58.
——. "Splitting of the Ego in the Process of Defence." 1938. In *Standard Edition*,
   23:275–78.
——. *Three Essays on the Theory of Sexuality*. 1905. In *Standard Edition*, 7:130–
   243.
Garnier, Paul-Emile. *Les fétichistes, pervertis, et invertis sexuels: Observations
   médico-légales*. Paris: Baillière, 1896.

Gock, H. "Beitrag zur Kenntnis der conträren Sexualempfindung." *Archiv für Psychiatrie und Nervenkrankheiten* 5 (1875): 564–75.

Greenacre, Phyllis. "Fetishism." In *Sexual Deviations*, ed. Ismond Rosen, 79–108. London: Oxford University Press, 1979.

Hammond, William A. *Sexual Impotence in the Male and Female*. New York: Birmingham, 1883.

Hirschfeld, Magnus. *Anomalies et perversions sexuelles*. Trans. Ann-Catherine Stier. Paris: Corréa, 1957.

———. *Die Transvestiten*. Berlin: Alfred Pulvermacher, 1910.

Hopkins, Juliet. "The Probable Role of Trauma in a Case of Foot and Shoe Fetishism: Aspects of the Psychotherapy of a Six Year Old Girl." *International Review of Psychoanalysis* 11 (1984): 79–91.

Huchard, Henri. "Caractère, moeurs, état mental hystériques." *Archives de neurologie* 3 (February 1882): 187–211.

Kohon, Gregorio. "Fetishism Revisited." *International Journal of Psychoanalysis* 68 (1987): 213–28.

Krafft-Ebing, Richard von. *Psychopathia Sexualis*. 1886. 12th ed. Trans. Harry Wedeck. New York: Putnam, 1965.

Lacan, Jacques. "Of the Gaze as *Objet Petit a*." 1964. In *Four Fundamental Concepts of Psychoanalysis*, trans. Alan Sheridan, 67–122. London: Penguin, 1979.

———. "On a Question Preliminary to any Possible Treatment of Psychosis." 1955–56. In *Ecrits: A Selection*, trans. Alan Sheridan, 179–225. London: Tavistock, 1977.

———. "The Signification of the Phallus." 1958. In *Ecrits: A Selection*, trans. Alan Sheridan, 281–91. London: Tavistock, 1977.

Lacan, Jacques, and Wladimir Granoff. "Fetishism: The Symbolic, the Imaginary and the Real." In *Perversions, Psychodynamics, and Therapy*, ed. Sandor Lorand, 265–75. London: Tavistock, 1956.

Laurent, Emile. *L'amour morbide: Etude de psychologie pathologique*. Paris: Société d'éducation scientifique, 1891.

———. *Les bisexués: Gynécomastes et hermaphrodites*. Paris: Carré, 1894.

———. *Fétichistes et érotomanes*. Paris: Vigot, 1905.

Legludic, Henri. *Notes et observations de médecine légale: Attentats aux moeurs*. Paris: Masson, 1896.

Legrand du Saulle, Henri. *Les hystériques*. Paris: Ballière, 1883.

Lorand, Sandor. "Fetishism in *Statu Nascendi*." *International Journal of Psychoanalysis* 11 (October 1930): 419–27.

Magnan, Valentin. *Des anomalies, des aberrations, et des perversions sexuelles*. Paris: Delahaye, 1885.

Mallet, Joséphine. *La femme en prison*. Paris: Moulins, 1840.

Masson, Agnès. *Le travestissement: Essai de psycho-pathologie sexuelle*. Paris: Hippocrate, 1935.

Moll, Albert. *Perversions of the Sex Instinct*. 1891. Trans. Maurice Popkin. New York: AMS Press, 1976.

Moreau de Tours, Jacques-Joseph. *Des aberrations du sens génésique*. Paris, 1883.

Parent-Duchâtelet, Alexandre. *De la prostitution dans la ville de Paris*. Paris: Baillière, 1836.

Pontalis, Jean-Baptiste. Introduction to *Nouvelle revue de psychanalyse* 2 (Autumn 1970): 5–15.

Pouillon, Jean. "Fétiches sans fétichisme." *Nouvelle revue de psychanalyse* 2 (Autumn 1970): 135–47.

Reuss, Dr. Louis. "Des aberrations du sens génésique chez l'homme." *Annales d'hygiène publique et de médecine légale*, 3d ser., 16 (1886).

Roubaud, Dr. Félix. *Traité de l'impuissance et de la stérilité chez l'homme et chez la femme*. Paris: Baillière, 1855.

Roux, Joanny. *Psychologie de l'instinct sexuel*. Paris: Baillière, 1899.

Saint-Paul, Georges. *Perversion et perversités sexuelles: Une enquête médicale sur l'inversion*. Paris, 1896.

Stekel, Wilhelm. "The Psychology of Kleptomania." In *Twelve Essays on Sex and Psychoanalysis*, ed. and trans. S. A. Tannenbaum. New York: Eugenics, 1932.

——. *Sexual Aberrations: The Phenomena of Fetishism in Relation to Sex*. 1923. 2 vols. Trans. S. Parker. New York: Liveright, 1930. (Orig. title *Der Fetischismus dargestellt für Arzte und Kriminalogen*.)

——. Trélat, Ulysse. *La folie lucide*. Paris: Delahaye, 1861.

Virey, Julien Joseph. *De la femme*. Paris, 1823.

Westphal, C. "Die conträre Sexualempfindung." *Archiv für Psychiatrie und Nervenkrankheiten* 2 (1869): 73–108.

Marxism, Economics

Althusser, Louis. *For Marx*. 1967. Trans. Ben Brewster. London: Verso, 1979.

——. *Lenin and Philosophy and Other Essays*. Trans. Ben Brewster. New York: Monthly Review Press, 1971.

Althusser, Louis, et al. *Reading Capital*. 1968. Trans. Ben Brewster. London: Verso, 1979.

Amariglio, Jack. "Marxism against Economic Science: Althusser's Legacy." *Research in Political Economy* 10 (1987): 159–94.

Amariglio, Jack, Antonio Callari, and Stephen Cullenberg. "Analytical Marxism: A Critical Overview." *Review of Social Economy* 47 (Winter 1989): 415–32.

Balibar, Etienne. "The Vacillation of Ideology." Trans. Andrew Ross and Constance Penley. In *Marxism and the Interpretation of Culture*, ed. Cary Nelson and Lawrence Grossberg, 159–209. Urbana: University of Illinois Press, 1988.

Baudrillard, Jean. *For a Critique of the Political Economy of the Sign*. 1972. Trans. Charles Levin. St. Louis: Telos Press, 1981.

——. *The Mirror of Production*. 1973. Trans. Mark Poster. St. Louis: Telos Press, 1975.

Brewster, Ben. "Fetishism in *Capital* and *Reading Capital*." *Economy and Society* 5 (1976): 344–51.

Bukharin, Nicolai. *Economic Theory of the Leisure Class*. 1919. New York: Monthly Review Press, 1972.

——. *Historical Materialism*. 1921. Ann Arbor: University of Michigan Press, 1969.

Callari, Antonio. "The Classicals' Analysis of Capitalism." Ph.D. diss., University of Massachusetts, Amherst, 1981.

——. "History, Epistemology, and the Labor Theory of Value." *Research in Political Economy* 9 (1986): 69–93.

Carver, Terrell. "Marx's Commodity Fetishism." *Inquiry* 18 (1975): 39–63.

Cornforth, Maurice. *Historical Materialism*. New York: International, 1954.

Cottrell, Allin. "Value Theory and the Critique of Essentialism." *Economy and Society* 10, no. 2 (1981): 235–42.

Cutler, Anthony, Barry Hindess, Paul Q. Hirst, and Athar Hussain. *Marx's "Capital" and Capitalism Today.* Vol. 1. London: Routledge and Kegan Paul, 1977.

De Vroey, Michel. "Value, Production, and Exchange." In Ian Steedman et al., *The Value Controversy,* 173–201. London: Verso, 1981.

Elster, Jon. *Making Sense of Marx.* Cambridge: Cambridge University Press, 1985.

Finelli, Roberto. "Some Thoughts on the Modern in the Works of Smith, Hegel, and Marx." *Rethinking Marxism* 2 (Summer 1989): 111–31.

Fischer, Norman. "The Ontology of Abstract Labor." *Review of Radical Political Economics* 14 (Summer 1982): 27–35.

Geras, Norman. "Essence and Appearance: Aspects of Fetishism in Marx's *Capital.*" *New Left Review* 65 (1971): 69–85.

Godelier, Maurice. "Fetishism, Religion, and Marx's General Theories concerning Ideology." In *Perspectives in Marxist Anthropology,* trans. Robert Brain, 169–85. Cambridge: Cambridge University Press, 1977.

Greider, William. *Secrets of the Temple: How the Federal Reserve Runs the Country.* New York: Simon and Schuster, 1987.

Harvey, David. *The Limits to Capital.* Oxford: Basil Blackwell, 1984.

Henry, Michel. *Marx: A Philosophy of Human Reality.* 1976. Trans. Kathleen McLaughlin. Bloomington: Indiana University Press, 1983.

Hindess, Barry, and Paul Q. Hirst. *Mode of Production and Social Formation.* London: Macmillan, 1977.

Howard, M. C., and J. E. King. *The Political Economy of Marx.* London: Longman, 1975.

Hunt, E. K. "Marx's Concept of Human Nature and the Labor Theory of Value." *Review of Radical Political Economics* 14 (Summer 1982): 7–25.

Kennedy, Duncan. "The Role of Law in Economic Thought: Essays on the Fetishism of Commodities." *American University Law Review* 34 (Summer 1985): 939–1001.

Laclau, Ernesto. *New Reflections on the Revolution of Our Time.* London: Verso, 1990.

Laclau, Ernesto, and Chantal Mouffe. *Hegemony and Socialist Strategy.* London: Verso, 1985.

Lebowitz, Michael. "Is 'Analytical Marxism' Marxism?" *Science and Society* 52 (Summer 1988): 191–214.

Lecourt, Dominique. *Marxism and Epistemology.* London: New Left Books, 1975.

Levine, Andrew, Elliott Sober, and Erik Olin Wright. "Marxism and Methodological Individualism." *New Left Review* 162 (March-April 1987): 67–84.

Lipietz, Alain. *The Enchanted World: Inflation, Credit, and the World Crisis.* Trans. Ian Patterson. London: Verso, 1985.

Lippi, Marco. *Value and Naturalism in Marx.* Trans. Hilary Steedman. London: New Left Books, 1979.

Lukács, Georg. *History and Class Consciousness.* 1923. Trans. Rodney Livingstone. Cambridge: MIT Press, 1971.

Mandel, Ernest. *The Formation of the Economic Thought of Karl Marx.* Trans. Brian Pearce. New York: Monthly Review Press, 1971.

——. *Marxist Economic Theory.* Vol. 1. Trans. Brian Pearce. New York: Monthly Review Press, 1970.

Marx, Karl. *Capital: A Critique of Political Economy.* Vol. 1. 1867. Trans. Ben Fowkes. New York: Vintage, 1977.

——. *Capital: A Critigue of Political Economy.* Vol. 3. 1894. Trans. David Fernbach. New York: Random House, 1981.

——. *The Class Struggles in France, 1848–50.* 1850. Trans. Paul Jackson. In *Surveys from Exile,* ed. David Fernbach, 7–142. New York: Random House, 1974.

——. "Concerning Feuerbach." Written 1845. In *Early Writings,* trans. Rodney Livingstone and Gregor Benton, 421–23. New York: Vintage, 1975.

——. "A Contribution to the Critique of Hegel's 'Philosophy of Right': Introduction." 1844. In *Critique of Hegel's Philosophy of Right,* trans. Annette Jolin and Joseph O'Malley, 129–42. Cambridge: Cambridge University Press, 1977.

——. *Contribution to the Critique of Political Economy.* 1859. Ed. Maurice Dobb. Trans. S. W. Ryazanskaya. New York: International, 1970.

——. "Critique of Hegel's Doctrine of the State." Written 1843. In *Early Writings,* trans. Rodney Livingstone and Gregor Benton, 57–198. New York: Vintage, 1975.

——. *Critique of Hegel's "Philosophy of Right."* Written 1843–44. Trans. Annette Jolin and Joseph O'Malley. Cambridge: Cambridge University Press, 1977.

——. "Critique of the Gotha Programme." 1875. Trans. Joris de Bres. In *The First International and After,* ed. David Fernbach, 339–59. New York: Random House, 1974.

——. "Debates on the Law on Theft of Wood." 1842. In Karl Marx and Frederick Engels, *Collected Works,* 1:224–63. Moscow: Progress, 1976.

——. "Difference between the Democritean and Epicurean Philosophy of Nature." 1841. In Karl Marx and Frederick Engels, *Collected Works,* 1:25–105. Moscow: Progress, 1976.

——. "Economic and Philosophic Manuscripts." Written 1844. In *Early Writings,* trans. Rodney Livingstone and Gregor Benton, 279–400. New York: Vintage, 1975.

——. "Exzerpte zur Geschichte der Kunst und der Religion." Written 1842. In *Marx-Engels Gesamtausgabe,* 2: pt. 1, 320–34, 342–67. Berlin: Dietz, 1976.

——. *Grundrisse: Foundations of the Critique of Political Economy.* Written 1857–58. Trans. Martin Nicolaus. New York: Random House, 1973.

——. "The Leading Article in No. 179 of the *Kölnische Zeitung.*" In Karl Marx and Friedrich Engels, *Collected Works,* 1:189. New York: International, 1975.

——. *The Poverty of Philosophy.* 1846–47. Introduction by F. Engels. New York: International, 1963.

——. *Theories of Surplus Value.* Vol. 4 of Capital. Part 3. Written 1861–63. Trans. Jack Cohen and S. W. Ryazanskaya. Moscow: Progress, 1971.

Marx, Karl, and Frederick Engels. *The German Ideology.* Written 1845–46. 3d rev. ed. Moscow: Progress, 1976.

Meister, Robert. *Political Identity: Thinking through Marx.* London: Basil Blackwell, 1990.

Ollman, Bertell. *Alienation.* Cambridge: Cambridge University Press, 1975.

Plekhanov, Georgi. *The Development of the Monist View of History.* 1894. New York: International, 1972.

Polanyi, Karl. *The Great Transformation.* Boston: Beacon Press, 1957.

——. *Primitive, Archaic, and Modern Economies.* Ed. George Dalton. Boston: Beacon Press, 1971.

Rancière, Jacques. "The Concept of 'Critique' and the 'Critique of Political Economy' (from the 1844 Manuscript to Capital)." 1967. Trans. Ben Brewster. Economy and Society 5 (1976): 352–376.

——. "How to Use Lire 'Le Capital.'" Trans. Tanya Asad. Economy and Society 5 (1976): 377–84.

——. "On the Theory of Ideology (the Politics of Althusser)." Radical Philosophy 7 (1974): 2–15.

Resnick, Stephen, and Richard Wolff. Knowledge and Class. Chicago: University of Chicago Press, 1987.

Robinson, Joan. Economic Philosophy. Garden City, N. Y.: Doubleday, 1964.

Roemer, John. Free to Lose. Cambridge: Harvard University Press, 1988.

Roemer, John, ed. Analytical Marxism. Cambridge: Cambridge University Press, 1986.

Rose, Nikolas. "Fetishism and Ideology." Ideology and Consciousness 2 (Autumn 1977): 27–54.

Rubin, Isaac Illich. A History of Economic Thought. 1929. Afterword by C. Colliot-Thélène. London: Ink Links, 1979.

Ruccio, David. "The Merchant of Venice, or Marxism in the Mathematical Mode." Rethinking Marxism 1 (Winter 1988): 36–68.

Sayer, Derek. Marx's Method. Hassocks, Sussex: Harvester Press, 1983.

Sève, Lucien. 1969. Man in Marxist Theory and the Psychology of Personality. Trans. John McGreal. Hassocks, Sussex: Harvester Press, 1978.

Shaikh, Anwar. "Neo-Ricardian Economics: A Wealth of Algebra, a Poverty of Theory." Review of Radical Political Economics 14 (Summer 1982): 67–83.

Smith, Adam. Lectures in Jurisprudence. 1763. Ed. R. L. Meek, D. D. Raphael, and P. G. Stein. Indianapolis: Liberty Press, 1978.

Sweezy, Paul. 1942. The Theory of Capitalist Development. New York: Monthly Review Press, 1970.

Tucker, D. F. B. Marxism and Individualism. New York: St. Martin's Press, 1980.

Volosinov, V. N. Marxism and the Philosophy of Language. 1929. Trans. Ladislav Matejka and I. R. Titunik. New York: Seminar Press, 1973.

Weeks, John. Capital and Exploitation. London: Edward Arnold, 1981.

Wolff, Richard, Bruce Roberts, and Antonio Callari. "Marx's (not Ricardo's) Transformation Problem: A Radical Reconceptualization." History of Political Economy 14, no. 4 (1982): 564–82.

Žižek, Slavoj. The Sublime Object of Ideology. London: Verso, 1989.

Sociology, Anthropology, Religion

Abrams, Philip. "Notes on the Difficulty of Studying the State." Journal of Historical Sociology 1, no. 1 (1988): 58–89.

Alviella, Goblet d'. "Origines de l'idolâtrie." In Revue de l'histoire des religions, ed. Jean Réville, 12:1–25. Paris: Leroux, 1885.

Anderson, Benedict. Imagined Communities. London: Verso, 1983.

Aristotle. Nicomachean Ethics. Trans. H. Rackham. Loeb Classical Library, vol. 19. Cambridge: Harvard University Press, 1975.

Avineri, Shlomo. Hegel's Theory of the Modern State. Cambridge: Cambridge University Press, 1972.

Bakunin, Michael. God and the State. Written 1870–72. New York: Dover, 1970.

Bastian, Adolf. "Die Fetische." In Der Mensch in der Geschichte, 2:11–23. Leipzig: Wigand, 1860.

Bazard, Saint-Emand. Développement religieux de l'homme: Fétichisme, polythéisme, monothéisme Juif et Chrétien. 1829. In Oeuvres de Saint-Simon et d'Enfantin, 41:121–48. Aalen: Otto Zeller, 1964.

Bosman, Willem. A New and Accurate Description of the Coast of Guinea. 1704. London: Cass, 1967.

Böttiger, Karl August. Ideen zur Kunst-Mythologie. Dresden: 1826.

Bridges, E. Lucas. Uttermost Part of the Earth. London: Hodder and Stoughton, 1951.

Brosses, Charles de. Du culte des dieux fétiches, ou Parallèle de l'ancienne religion de l'Egypte avec la religion actuelle de Nigritie. Geneva, 1760.

——. "Mémoire sur l'oracle de Dodone." Mémoires de littérature de l'Académie royale des inscriptions et belles-lettres 35 (1770): 89–132.

Comte, Auguste. "First Theological Phase: Fetichism." 1840. In The Positive Philosophy of Auguste Comte, trans. Harriet Martineau, 545–61. New York: Eckler, n.d. Original title: Cours de philosophie positive.

——. "Positive Theory of the Age of Fetichism, or General Account of the Spontaneous Regime of Humanity." In System of Positive Polity, or Treatise on Sociology, Instituting the Religion of Humanity, trans. J. H. Bridges et al., 3:65–130. Paris: Carilian-Goeury and Dalmont, 1853.

Constant, Benjamin. De la religion considérée dans sa source, ses formes, et ses développements. Paris: Bossange, 1824.

Corrigan, Philip, and Derek Sayer, eds. The Great Arch: English State Formation as Cultural Revolution. Oxford: Basil Blackwell, 1985.

Cushing, Frank H. Zuni Fetishes. 1883. Las Vegas: KC Publications, 1974.

Dulaure, Jacques Antoine. The Gods of Generation: A History of Phallic Cults among Ancients and Moderns. 1805. New York: Panurge Press, 1933.

Dupuis, Charles François. The Origin of All Religious Worship. 1794. New Orleans, 1872.

Durkheim, Emile. The Elementary Forms of Religious Life. 1912. Trans. Joseph Ward Swain. New York: Free Press, 1965.

——. Professional Ethics and Civic Morals. 1904. London: Routledge, 1957.

——. The Rules of Sociological Method. 1895. Trans. Sarah A. Solovay and John H. Mueller. New York: Free Press, 1964.

Durkheim, Emile, and Marcel Mauss. Primitive Classification. 1903. Trans. Rodney Needham. Chicago: University of Chicago Press, 1963.

Ellis, A. B. The Land of Fetish. London: Chapman and Hall, 1883.

Fanon, Frantz. Black Skin, White Masks. 1952. London: Paladin, 1970.

Giddens, Anthony. The Constitution of Society. Berkeley: University of California Press, 1984.

Glave, E. J. "Fetishism in Congo Land." Century Magazine 41 (April 1891): 825–36.

Gutierrez, Gustavo. The Power of the Poor in History. Trans. Robert R. Barr. Maryknoll, N.Y.: Orbis Books, 1984.

Haddon, A. C. Magic and Fetishism. London: Constable, 1906.

Hegel, G. W. F. Lectures on the Philosophy of Religion. 1832. 3 vols. Trans. Rev. E. B. Speirs and J. Burdon Sanderson. New York: Humanities Press, 1974.

——. The Philosophy of History. 1837. Trans. J. Sibree. New York: Dover, 1956.

——. Philosophy of Mind. 1817. Trans. A. V. Miller. Oxford: Clarendon Press, 1971.

Helvétius, Claude Adrien. *De l'esprit*. 1758. In *Oeuvres d'Helvétius*, vol. 1. Paris: Briand, 1794.

Hobbes, Thomas. *Leviathan; or, The Matter, Forme and Power of a Commonwealth Ecclesiasticall and Civil*. 1651. New York: Macmillan, 1962.

Holbach, Paul Henri Thiery, Baron d'. "Serpent-Fetish." 1765. In *Essays on the "Encyclopédie" of Diderot and D'Alembert*, ed. John Lough, 170–72. London: Oxford University Press, 1968.

Hollier, Denis, ed. *The College of Sociology, 1937–39*. Minneapolis: University of Minnesota Press, 1988.

Hume, David. *The Natural History of Religion*. 1757. Ed. H. E. Root. Stanford: Stanford University Press, 1957.

Jevons, Frank Byron. *An Introduction to the History of Religion*. 3d ed. London: Methuen, 1896.

Kant, Immanuel. *Religion within the Limits of Reason Alone*. 1793. Trans. Theodore M. Greene and Hoyt H. Hudson. New York: Harper and Row, 1960.

Keesing, Roger. "Rethinking Mana." *Journal of Anthropological Research* 40 (1984): 137–56.

Kingsley, Mary H. "The Fetish View of the Human Soul." *Folk-Lore* 8 (June 1897): 138–51.

Knight, Robert Payne. *A Discourse on the Worship of Priapus*. London: Dilettanti Society, 1786.

Lang, Andrew. "Fetishism and the Infinite." In *Custom and Myth*, 212–242. London: Longmans, Green, 1893.

———. "Mr. Max Müller and Fetishism." *Mind* 16 (October 1879): 453–469.

Lévi-Strauss, Claude. *The Savage Mind*. 1962. Chicago: University of Chicago Press, 1966.

———. "The Structural Study of Myth." 1955. In *Structural Anthropology*, trans. Claire Jacobson and Brooke Grundfest Schoepf, 202–38. Garden City, N.Y.: Doubleday, 1967.

———. *Totemism*. 1962. Trans. Rodney Needham. Boston: Beacon Press, 1963.

———. "A Writing Lesson." 1955. In *Tristes Tropiques: An Anthropological Study of Primitive Societies in Brazil*, trans. John Russell, 286–297. New York: Atheneum, 1968.

Lewes, G. H. "Ages of Fetishism and Polytheism." 1853. In *Comte's Philosophy of Science*, 273–287. London: Bell, 1897.

McLennan, J. F. "The Worship of Plants and Animals: Part I, Totems and Totemism." *Fortnightly Review*, n.s., 34 (1869): 407–27.

Mauss, Marcel. "L'art et le myth d'après M. Wundt." 1906. In *Oeuvres*, vol. 2: *Représentations collectives et diversité des civilisations*, ed. Victor Karady, 195–227. Paris: Minuit, 1968.

———. *The Gift: Forms and Functions of Exchange in Ancient Societies*. 1925. Trans. Ian Cunnison. New York: Norton, 1967.

Meiners, Christoph. *Allgemeine kritische Geschichte der Religionen*. 2 vols. Hannover, 1806, 1807.

Mill, John Stuart. "Sir William Hamilton's Theory of Causation." 1865. In *Collected Works of John Stuart Mill*, vol. 9, 286–300. Toronto: University of Toronto Press, 1963.

———. "Theism." Written 1868–70. In *Collected Works of John Stuart Mill*, 10:429–89. Toronto: University of Toronto Press, 1963.

———. "Utility of Religion." Written 1850s. In *Collected Works of John Stuart Mill*, 10:402–28. Toronto: University of Toronto Press, 1963.

Milligan, Robert H., Rev. "The Dark Side of the Dark Continent: The Mental and Moral Degradation of Fetishism." *Missionary Review of the World* 40 (December 1917): 890–903.

Müller, F. Max. "Is Fetishism a Primitive Form of Religion?" In *Lectures on the Origin and Growth of Religion*, 54–131. London: Longmans, Green, 1882.

Nassau, Robert. *Fetishism in West Africa*. London: Duckworth, 1905.

———. "The Philosophy of Fetishism." *Journal of the Royal African Society* 17 (1903–4): 257–70.

Needham, Rodney. "Skulls and Causality." *Man*, n.s., 11 (1977): 71–78.

Nietzsche, Friedrich. *Beyond Good and Evil*. 1886. Trans. Walter Kaufmann. New York: Vintage, 1966.

Nina-Rodrigues, Dr. *L'animisme fétichiste des nègres de Bahia*. Bahia, Brazil: Resi, 1900.

Parsons, Talcott. *The Structure of Social Action: A Study in Social Theory with Special Reference to a Group of Recent European Writers*. New York: Free Press, 1937.

Radcliffe-Brown, A. R. Preface to *African Political Systems*, ed. Meyer Fortes and E. E. Evans-Pritchard, xi–xxiii. 1940. New York: Oxford University Press, 1970.

Reinhard, Philipp Christian. *Abriss einer Geschichte der Entstehung und Aubbildung der religiösen Ideen*. Jena, 1794.

Saussaye, P. D. Chantepie de la. *Manual of the Science of Religion*. Trans. Beatrice S. Colyer-Fergusson. London: Longmans, Green, 1891.

Schultz, Fritz. *Fetishism: A Contribution to the Anthropology of Religion*. 1871. Trans. J. Fitzgerald. New York: Humboldt, 1885.

Spencer, Baldwin, and F. J. Gillen. *The Native Tribes of Central Australia*. 1899. New York: Dover, 1968.

Spencer, Herbert. "Idol-Worship and Fetich-Worship." *Popular Science Monthly* 8 (1875): 158–164.

———. "The Origin of Animal Worship." 1870. In *Essays Scientific, Political, and Speculative*, 308–30. New York: Appleton, 1904.

Stanner, W. E. H. "Reflections on Durkheim and Aboriginal Religion." In *Social Organization: Essays Presented to Raymond Firth*, ed. Maurice Freedman, 217–40. Chicago: Aldine, 1967.

———. "Religion, Totemism, and Symbolism." In *White Men Got No Dreaming*, 106–43. Canberra: Australian National University Press, 1979.

Sumner, William Graham, and Albert Galloway Keller. "Fetishism." In *The Science of Society*, 2:979–1016. New Haven: Yale University Press, 1927.

Taylor, W. "Review of D. Heynig, *Theorie der Sämmthchen Religions arten*." *Monthly Magazine, or British Register* 11 (1801): 646.

Tiele, C. P. *Elements of the Science of Religion*. Vol. 1. New York: Scribner's, 1897.

Tylor, E. B. "The Religion of Savages." *Fortnightly Review* 6 (1866): 71–86.

Weber, Max. "Politics as a Vocation." 1919. In *From Max Weber: Essays in Sociology*, trans. Hans Gerth and C. Wright Mills, 77–128. London: Routledge and Kegan Paul, 1948.

Wundt, Wilhelm. *Elements of Folk Psychology*. 1912. Trans. Edward Leroy Schaub. New York: Macmillan, 1916.

Visual Culture, Performance Arts, Fashion

Alpers, Svetlana. *The Art of Describing: Dutch Art in the Seventeenth Century*. Chicago: University of Chicago Press, 1983.

——. "Describe or Narrate? A Problem in Realistic Representation." *New Literary History* 8 (1976–77): 15–41.

——. *Rembrandt's Enterprise: The Studio and the Market.* Chicago: University of Chicago Press, 1988.

Barthes, Roland. "The World as Object." In *Calligram: Essays in New Art History from France,* ed. Norman Bryson, 106–15. Cambridge: Cambridge University Press, 1988.

Baudelaire, Charles. *Art in Paris, 1845–1862.* Ed. and trans. Jonathan Mayne. New York: Phaidon, 1965.

——. *The Painter of Modern Life and Other Essays.* Ed. and trans. Jonathan Mayne. London: Phaidon, 1964.

Baudrillard, Jean. "The Trompe-l'Oeil." In *Calligram: Essays in New Art History from France,* ed. Norman Bryson, 53–62. Cambridge: Cambridge University Press, 1988.

Benjamin, Walter. "Surrealism: The Last Snapshot of the European Intelligentsia." 1929. In *Reflections,* trans. Edmund Jephcott, 177–92. New York: Harcourt Brace Jovanovich, 1978.

Bergstrom, Ingvar. *Dutch Still-Life Painting.* Trans. Christina Hedstrom and Gerald Taylor. London: Faber and Faber, 1956.

Boime, Albert. "The Case of Rosa Bonheur: Why Should a Woman Want to Be More Like a Man?" *Art History* 4, no. 4 (1981): 384–95.

Bryson, Norman. "Chardin and the Text of Still Life." *Critical Inquiry* 15 (Winter 1989): 227–52.

——. "The Gaze in the Expanded Field." In *Vision and Visuality,* ed. Hal Foster, 86–108. Seattle: Dia Art Foundation/Bay Press, 1988.

——. *Tradition and Desire: From David to Delacroix.* Cambridge: Cambridge University Press, 1984.

Burgin, Victor. "Photography, Phantasy, Function." In *Thinking Photography,* ed. Victor Burgin, 177–216. London: Macmillan, 1982.

Clair, Jean. *Méduse.* Paris: Gallimard, 1989.

Clark, T. J. *The Painting of Modern Life.* New York: Knopf, 1984.

Copjec, Joan. "The Sartorial Superego." *October* 50 (Fall 1989): 57–96.

Dijkstra, Bram. *Idols of Perversity.* New York: Oxford University Press, 1986.

Doane, Mary Ann. "Film and the Masquerade: Theorising the Female Spectator." *Screen* 23 (September–October 1982): 74–87.

——. "Masquerade Reconsidered: Further Thoughts on the Female Spectator." *Discourse* 11 (Fall–Winter 1988–89): 42–54.

——. "Technophilia: Technology, Representation, and the Feminine." In *Body/Politics: Women and the Discourses of Science,* ed. Mary Jacobus, Evelyn Fox Keller, and Sally Shuttleworth, 163–76. London: Routledge, 1990.

——. "Veiling over Desire: Close-ups of the Woman." In *Feminism and Psychoanalysis,* ed. Richard Feldstein and Judith Roof, 105–141. Ithaca: Cornell University Press, 1989.

Dufay, Pierre. *Le pantalon féminin.* Paris: Carrington, 1916.

Dyer, Richard. "Don't Look Now—the Male Pin-up." *Screen* 16 (Autumn 1982): 61–73.

Ellis, John. "On Pornography." *Screen* 21 (Spring 1980): 81–108.

Fani-Kayode, Rotimi. *Black Male/White Male.* London: Gay Men's Press, 1987.

——. "Traces of Ecstacy." *Ten.8,* no. 28 (1988): 36–42.

Farwell, Beatrice. *The Cult of Images: Baudelaire and the 19th-Century Media Explosion.* Santa Barbara, Calif.: University of Santa Barbara Art Museum, 1977.

Finney, Gail. *Women in Modern Drama.* Ithaca: Cornell University Press, 1989.

Flobert, Laure-Paul. "La femme et le costume masculin." *Le vieux papier, Bulletin de la Société archéologique, historique, et artistique* 10, no. 67 (1911): 359–60.

Foster, Hal. *(Dis)agreeable Objects.* New York: New Museum of Contemporary Art, 1986.

——. *The Future of an Illusion, or The Contemporary Artist as Cargo Cultist.* Boston: Institute of Contemporary Art, 1986.

Freund, Giselle. *Photography and Society.* Boston: David Godine, 1983.

Fried, Michael. *Absorption and Theatricality: Painting and Beholder in the Age of Diderot.* Berkeley: University of California Press, 1980.

Garafola, Lynn. "The Travesty Dancer in Nineteenth-Century Ballet," *Dance Research Journal* 17–18 (Fall–Spring 1985–1986): 35–40.

Gilbert, Elliot. "'Tumult of Images': Wilde, Beardsley, and *Salomé.*" *Victorian Studies* 26 (Winter 1983): 133–60.

Grand-Carteret, John. *La femme en culotte.* Paris: Flammarion, n.d. [1899].

Gribble, Francis. "The Origin of the Cancan." *Dancing Times* (April 1933): 19–21.

Guest, Ivor. *The Ballet of the Second Empire.* Middletown, Conn., Wesleyan University Press, 1974.

——. "Dandies and Dancers." *Dance Perspectives* 37 (Spring 1969).

——. "Queens of the Cancan." *Dance and Dancers* (December 1952): 14–16.

——. *The Romantic Ballet in Paris.* London: Pitman, 1966.

Hall, Stuart. "New Ethnicities." In *Black Film/British Cinema*, ICA document 7, ed. Kobena Mercer, 27–31. London: Institute of Contemporary Art/British Film Insitute, 1988.

——. "The Whites of Their Eyes: Racist Ideologies and the Media." In *Silver Linings: Some Strategies for the Eighties*, ed. George Bridges and Rosalind Brunt, 28–52. London: Lawrence Wishart, 1981.

Hansen, Miriam. "Benjamin, Cinema, and Experience: 'The Blue Flower in the Land of Technology.'" *New German Critique* 40 (Winter 1987): 179–224.

Kelly, Mary. *Pecunia non olet.* New York: Top Stories, 1990.

——. *Post-Partum Document.* London: Routledge and Kegan Paul, 1983.

Kunzle, David. *Fashion and Fetishism.* Totowa, N.J.: Rowman and Littlefield, 1982.

Loliée, Frédéric. *Les femmes du second empire.* Paris: Talladier, 1954.

McCauley, Elizabeth Ann. *A. A. E. Disdéri and the Carte-de-Visite.* New Haven: Yale University Press, 1985.

Mapplethorpe, Robert. *The Black Book.* Introduction by Ntozake Shange. Munich: Schirmer/Mosel, 1986.

——. *Black Males.* Introduction by Edmund White. Amsterdam: Gallerie Jurka, 1982.

——. *Robert Mapplethorpe, 1970–1983.* Introduction by Allan Hollinghurst. London: Institute of Contemporary Arts, 1983.

Marin, Louis. "Toward a Theory of Reading in the Visual Arts: Poussin's *The Arcadian Shepherds.*" In *The Reader in the Text*, ed. Susan R. Suleiman, 293–324. Princeton: Princeton University Press, 1980.

Mercer, Kobena. "Diaspora Culture and the Dialogic Imagination: The Aesthetics of Black Independent Film in Britain." In *BlackFrames: Critical Perspectives on Black Independent Cinema*, ed. Claire A. Watkins and Mbye Cham, 50–61. Cambridge: MIT Press, 1988.

Mercer, Kobena, and Isaac Julien. "Race, Sexual Politics, and Black Masculinity: A Dossier." In *Male Order: Unwrapping Masculinity*, ed. Jonathan Rutherford and Rowena Chapman, 97–164. London: Lawrence and Wishart, 1988

Merleau-Ponty, Maurice. *The Visible and the Invisible.* 1964. Trans. Alphonso Lingis. Evanston, Ill.: Northwestern University Press, 1968.

Metz, Christian. "Photography and Fetish." *October* 34 (Fall 1985): 81–90.

Mulvey, Laura. "Visual Pleasure and Narrative Cinema." *Screen* 16 (Autumn 1975): 6–18.

Needham, Gerald. "Manet, *Olympia*, and Pornographic Photography." In *Woman as Sex Object: Studies in Erotic Art, 1730–1970*, ed. Thomas B. Hess and Linda Nochlin, 80–89. New York: Newsweek Books, 1972.

Nochlin, Linda. "The Origin without an Original." *October* 37 (Summer 1986): 76–86.

Olson, Nancy. *Gavarni: The Carnival Lithographs.* New Haven: Yale University Press, 1979.

Perrot, Philippe. *Le travail des apparences, ou Les transformations du corps féminin, XVIII–XIXe siècle.* Paris: Seuil, 1984.

Pick, Daniel. *Faces of Degeneration: A European Disorder, c. 1848–c. 1918.* Cambridge: Cambridge University Press, 1989.

"Pierson's portretten van 'La Castiglione.'" *Foto* (December 1974): 36–39.

Reifenstahl, Leni. *The Last of the Nuba.* London: Collins, 1976.

Ross, Novelene Sue. *Manet's Bar at the Folies-Bergères and the Myths of Popular Illustration.* Ann Arbor: University of Michigan Press, 1982.

Sagne, Jean. *L'atelier du photographe, 1840–1940.* Paris: Presses de la Renaissance, 1984.

Schama, Simon. *The Embarrassment of Riches: An Interpretation of Dutch Culture in the Golden Age.* Berkeley: University of California Press, 1988.

Scheid, Uwe. *Das erotische Image.* Dortmund: Die bibliophilen Taschenbücher, 1984.

Segal, Sam. *A Prosperous Past: The Sumptuous Still Life in the Netherlands, 1600–1700.* The Hague: SDU, 1988.

Silverman, Debora. *Art Nouveau in Fin-de-Siècle France.* Berkeley: University of California Press, 1989.

Silverman, Kaja. *The Acoustic Mirror: The Female Voice in Psychoanalysis and Cinema.* Bloomington: Indiana University Press, 1988.

———. "Fragments of a Fashionable Discourse." In *Studies in Entertainment*, ed. Tania Modleski, 138–52. Bloomington: Indiana University Press, 1986.

Sobchack, Vivian. "The Active Eye: A Phenomenology of Cinematic Vision." *Quarterly Review of Film and Video* 12, no. 3 (1990): 21–36.

———. *The Address of the Eye: A Phenomenology of Film Experience.* Princeton: Princeton University Press, 1992.

Steele, Valerie. *Fashion and Eroticism.* Oxford: Oxford University Press, 1985.

———. *Paris Fashion.* New York: Oxford University Press, 1988.

Sterling, Charles. *Still Life Painting: From Antiquity to the Twentieth Century.* 2d rev. ed. New York: Harper and Row, 1981.

Strumingher, Laura. "The Vésuviennes: Images of Women Warriors in 1848 and Their Significance for French History." *History of European Ideas* 8, no. 4–5 (1987): 451–88.

Tyl, Pierre. "Mayer et Pierson (2)." In *Prestige de la photographie*, no. 7, 36–63. Paris: e. p. a., 1979.

Valverde, Marina. "The Love of Finery: Fashion and the Fallen Woman in

Nineteenth-Century Social Discourse." *Victorian Studies* (Winter 1989): 168–88.

Williamson, Judith. *Decoding Advertisement*. London: Marian Boyars, 1985.

Xavier, Boniface, and Félix-Auguste Duvert. *Les cabinets particuliers: Folie-vaudeville en un acte*. Paris: Barba, 1832.

Literature, Textual Criticism, Theory

Apter, Emily. *Feminizing the Fetish: Psychoanalysis and Narrative Obsession in Turn-of-the-Century France*. Ithaca: Cornell University Press, 1991.

Arnold, Matthew. *Culture and Anarchy*. 1869. Cambridge: Cambridge University Press, 1971.

Barbey d'Aurevilly, Jules. "Les bas-bleus." 1875. In *La femme au 19e siècle*, ed. Nicole Priollaud, 93–96. Paris: Liana Levi, 1983.

Barthes, Roland. "Myth Today." 1957. In *Mythologies*, trans. Annette Lavers, 109–59. New York: Hill and Wang, 1972.

——. *S/Z*. 1970. Trans. Richard Miller. New York: Hill and Wang, 1974.

Beckson, Karl, ed. *Oscar Wilde: The Critical Heritage*. London: Routledge and Kegan Paul, 1970.

Benjamin, Walter. "The Paris of the Second Empire in Baudelaire: The *Flâneur*." 1935. In *Charles Baudelaire*, trans. Harry Zohn, 35–66. London: Verso, 1983.

——. "On Some Motifs in Baudelaire." 1939. In *Illuminations*, ed. Hannah Arendt, trans. Harry Zohn, 186–92. New York: Schocken, 1969.

Bernhardt, Sarah. *My Double Life*. London: Heinemann, c. 1907.

Bernheimer, Charles. "'Castration' as Fetish." *Paragraph* 14 (1991): 1–9.

Bersani, Leo. *The Death of Stéphane Mallarmé*. Cambridge: Cambridge University Press, 1982.

Bhabha, Homi K. "Introduction: Narrating the Nation." In *Nation and Narration*, ed. Homi K. Bhabha, 1–7. London: Routledge, 1990.

——. "Of Mimicry and Man: The Ambivalence of Colonial Discourse." In *October: The First Decade, 1976–1986*, ed. Annette Michelson, Rosalind Krauss, Douglas Crimp, and Joan Copjec, 317–25. Cambridge: MIT Press, 1987.

——. "The Other Question: The Stereotype and Colonial Discourse." *Screen* 24 (Winter 1983): 18–36.

Birkett, Jennifer. *The Sins of the Fathers: Decadence in France, 1870–1914*. London: Quartet, 1986.

Booth, Wayne C. *A Rhetoric of Irony*. Chicago: University of Chicago Press, 1974.

Boswell, John. "Revolutions, Universals, and Sexual Categories." *Salmagundi* 58–59 (Fall 1983): 89–113.

Bowlby, Rachel. *Just Looking: Consumer Culture in Dreiser, Gissing, and Zola*. New York: Methuen, 1985.

Bruno, G. [pseud.]. *Le tour de France par deux enfants*. Paris: Belin, 1981.

Burke, Edmund. *A Philosophical Inquiry into the Origin of Our Idea of the Sublime and Beautiful*. 1756. Ed. Adam Phillips. New York: Oxford University Press, 1990.

Burne, Glenn S. *Remy de Gourmont: His Ideas and Influence in England and America*. Carbondale: Southern Illinois University Press, 1963.

Chatwin, Bruce. *Utz*. London: Penguin, 1988.

Cheyfitz, Eric. *The Trans-Parent*. Baltimore: Johns Hopkins University Press, 1981.

Coleridge, Samuel Taylor. *The Friend, I.* 1809–10. In *The Collected Works of Samuel Taylor Coleridge*, 4:1. Princeton: Princeton University Press, 1969.
——. *The Statesman's Manual.* 1839. Ed. W. G. T. Shedd. New York: Harper and Brothers, 1875.
Courtivron, Isabelle de. "Weak Men and Fatal Women: The Sand Image." In *Homosexualities and French Literature: Cultural Contexts, Critical Texts*, ed. George Stambolian and Elaine Marks, 210–27. Ithaca: Cornell University Press, 1979.
Coward, Rosalind. "Sexual Violence and Sexuality." *Feminist Review* 11 (Summer 1982): 17–22.
Coward, Rosalind, and John Ellis. *Language and Materialism.* London: Routledge and Kegan Paul, 1977.
Culler, Jonathan. *Ferdinand de Saussure.* Harmondsworth, Eng.: Penguin Books, 1977.
——. "The Uses of *Madame Bovary*." In *Flaubert and Postmodernism*, ed. Naomi Schor and Henry Majewski, 1–12. Lincoln: University of Nebraksa Press, 1984
Davidson, Arnold. "How to Do the History of Psychoanalysis: A Reading of Freud's *Three Essays on the Theory of Sexuality*." *Critical Inquiry* 13 (Winter 1987): 252–77.
——. "Sex and the Emergence of Sexuality," *Critical Inquiry* 14 (Autumn 1987): 16–48.
Dellamora, Richard. "Traversing the Feminine in Oscar Wilde's *Salomé*." In *Men Writing the Feminine*, ed. Thaïs Morgan. Forthcoming from Illinois University Press.
De Man, Paul. "Aesthetic Formalization: Kleist's *Uber das Marionettentheater*." In *The Rhetoric of Romanticism*, 263–90. New York: Columbia University Press, 1984.
——. *Allegories of Reading.* New Haven: Yale University Press, 1979.
——. "The Epistemology of Metaphor." *Critical Inquiry* 5 (Autumn 1978): 13–30.
——. "Phenomenality and Materiality in Kant." In *Hermeneutics: Questions and Prospects*, ed. Gary Shapiro and Alan Sica, 121–44. Amherst: University of Massachusetts Press, 1984.
Derrida, Jacques. *The Archaeology of the Frivolous.* 1973. Trans. John P. Leavey. Pittsburgh: Dusquene University Press, 1980.
——. *Glas.* 1974. Trans. John P. Leavey, Jr., and Richard Rand. Lincoln: University of Nebraska Press, 1986.
——. "La main de Heidegger (*Geschlecht* II)." In *Psyché*, 415–51. Paris: Galilée, 1987.
——. *Positions.* Trans. Alan Bass. Chicago: University of Chicago Press, 1981.
——. "Signature Event Context." In *Margins of Philosophy*, trans. Alan Bass, 307–30. Chicago: University of Chicago Press, 1982.
——. "White Mythology: Metaphor in the Text of Philosophy." In *Margins of Philosophy*, trans. Alan Bass, 207–71. Chicago: University of Chicago Press, 1982.
Eberhardt, Isabelle. *Lettres et journaliers.* Ed. Eglal Errera. Paris: Actes du Sud, 1987.
Esch, Deborah. "'Think of a Kitchen Table': Hume, Woolf, and the Translation of Example." In *Literature as Philosophy, Philosophy as Literature*, ed. Donald G. Marshall, 262–76. Iowa City: University of Iowa Press, 1987.
Felman, Shoshana. *Writing and Madness: (Literature/Philosophy/Psychoanalysis).* Trans. Martha Noel Evans. Ithaca: Cornell University Press, 1985.

Finkelkraut, Alain. *La défaite de la pensée*. Paris: Gallimard, 1987.

Flaubert, Gustave. *Mémoires d'un fou*. Written 1836–38. In *Oeuvres complètes*, vol. 1. Paris: Seuil, 1964.

——. *Sentimental Education*. 1869. Trans. Robert Baldick. Harmondsworth, Eng.: Penguin Books, 1964.

——. *Trois contes*. 1877. Paris: Gallimard, 1973.

Fontanier, Pierre. *Les figures du discours*. 1821–1830. Ed. Gérard Genette. Paris: Flammarion, 1977.

Foucault, Michel. *The History of Sexuality*. 1976. Vol. 1: *An Introduction*. Trans. Richard Howard. New York: Vintage, 1980.

——. "What Is an Author?" 1969. In *Language, Counter-Memory, Practice*, trans. Donald F. Bouchard and Sherry Simon, 113–38. Oxford: Basil Blackwell, 1977.

France, Anatole. *Le jardin d'Epicure*. Paris: Calmann-Lévy, 1894.

Garber, Marjorie. "Spare Parts: The Surgical Construction of Gender," *Differences* 1, no. 3 (1989): 137–59.

Genet, Jean. *The Thief's Journal*. 1949. Trans. Bernard Frechtman. Harmondsworth, Eng.: Penguin, 1967.

Gilman, Sander L. *Difference and Pathology: Stereotypes of Sexuality, Race, and Madness*. Ithaca: Cornell University Press, 1985.

Ginsburg, Michal Peled. *Flaubert Writing: A Study in Narrative Strategies*. Stanford: Stanford University Press, 1986.

Girard, René. "Scandal and the Dance: Salome in the Gospel of Mark." *New Literary History* 15 (Winter 1984): 311–24.

Girardet, Raoul. *Le nationalisme français, 1871–1914*. Paris: Armand Colin, 1966.

Goncourt, Edmond and Jules. *Pages from the Goncourt Journal*. Ed. and trans. Robert Baldick. London: Oxford University Press, 1963.

Gourmont, Remy de. *La culture des idées*. 1900. Paris: Mercure de France, 1983.

——. *Le joujou patriotisme*. 1891. Annotated edition by Jean-Pierre Rioux. Paris: Pauvert, 1967.

Goux, Jean-Joseph. *Symbolic Economies*. 1973. Trans. Jennifer Curtiss Gage. Ithaca: Cornell University Press, 1990.

Greenberg, David. *The Construction of Homosexuality*. Chicago: University of Chicago Press, 1988.

Grojnowski, Daniel. *Jules Laforgue et "l'originalité."* Neuchâtel: A la Baconnière, 1988.

Hall, Stuart. "Pluralism, Race, and Class in Caribbean Society." In *Race and Class in Post-Colonial Societies*, 150–82. Paris: UNESCO, 1977.

Haraway, Donna. "A Manifesto for Cyborgs: Science, Technology, and Socialist Feminism in the 1980s." *Socialist Review* 80 (March–April 1985): 65–108.

Heath, Stephen. *The Sexual Fix*. New York, Schocken, 1984.

Hegel, G. F. W. *Aesthetics: Lectures on Fine Art*. 1835–38. 2 vols. Trans. T. M. Knox. Oxford: Clarendon Press, 1975.

Heidegger, Martin. "Martin Heidegger: An Interview." 1970. Trans. Vincent Guagliardo and Robert Pambrun. *Listening* 6 (Winter 1971).

Hertz, Neil. "Medusa's Head: Male Hysteria under Political Pressure." *Representations* 4 (Fall 1983): 27–54.

Hollier, Denis. "How to Not Take Pleasure in Talking about Sex." *Enclitic* 8 (Spring–Fall 1984): 84–93.

Huysmans, Joris-Karl. *A rebours*. 1884. Paris: Gallimard, 1977.

Irigaray, Luce. "Women on the Market." 1977. In *This Sex Which Is Not One*, trans. Catherine Porter with Carolyn Burke, 170–91. Ithaca: Cornell University Press, 1985.

Jameson, Fredric. *Postmodernism, or The Cultural Logic of Late Capitalism*. Durham, N.C.: Duke University Press, 1991.

JanMohamed, Abdul R. "The Economy of Manichean Allegory: The Function of Racial Difference in Colonialist Literature." In *"Race," Writing, and Difference*, ed. Henry Louis Gates, Jr., 78–106. Chicago: University of Chicago Press, 1986

Jardine, Alice. "Bodies and Technologies." In *Discussions in Contemporary Culture*, ed. Hal Foster, 151–58. Seattle: Bay Press, 1989.

Jauss, Hans Robert. *Toward an Aesthetic of Reception*. Trans. Timothy Bahti. Minneapolis: University of Minnesota Press, 1982.

Kofman, Sarah. *The Enigma of Woman: Woman in Freud's Writings*. 1980. Trans. Catherine Porter. Ithaca: Cornell University Press, 1985.

——. *Les fins de l'homme: Lectures de Derrida*. Paris: Galilée, 1984.

Kristeva, Julia. *Desire in Language: A Semiotic Approach to Literature and Art*. Trans. Thomas Gora, Alice Jardine, and Leon S. S. Roudiez. New York: Columbia University Press, 1980.

Lang, Candace. *Irony/Humor: Critical Paradigms*. Baltimore: Johns Hopkins University Press, 1988.

Laqueur, Thomas W. "Amor Veneris, vel Dulcedo Appeletur." In *Fragments for a History of the Human Body, Part III, Zone 5*, ed. Michel Feher, 90–131. New York: Zone, 1989.

Mallarmé, Stéphane. *Oeuvres complètes*. Paris: Gallimard, 1945.

Mannoni, Octave. "Je sais bien, mais quand même..." In *Clefs pour l'imaginaire*, 9–33. Paris: Seuil, 1969.

Mauge, Annelise. *L'identité masculine en crise au tournant du siècle*. Paris: Rivages, 1987.

Mehlman, Jeffrey. "Future of an Allusion: Lacan with Léon Bloy." In *Legacies of Anti-Semitism in France*, 23–33. Minneapolis: University of Minnesota Press, 1983.

——. "The Paranoid Style in French Prose: Bloy, Céline, Lacan." *Oxford Literary Review* 12, nos. 1–2 (1990): 139–54.

——. "Perspectives: On de Man and *Le Soir*." In *Responses*, ed. Werner Hamacher, Neil Hertz, and Thomas Keenan, 324–33. Lincoln: University of Nebraska Press, 1989.

——. "Prosopopeia Revisited." *Romanic Review* 81, no. 1 (1990): 137–43.

——. *Revolution and Repetition*. Berkeley: University of California Press, 1977.

Meltzer, Françoise. *Salome and the Dance of Writing*. Chicago: University of Chicago Press, 1986.

Miller, Christopher L. *Blank Darkness: Africanist Discourse in French*. Chicago: University of Chicago Press, 1985.

Miller, Nancy. "Changing the Subject: Authorship, Writing, and the Reader." In *Feminist Studies/Critical Studies*, ed. Teresa De Lauretis, 102–20. Bloomington: Indiana University Press, 1986.

Mitchell, W. J. T. *Iconology: Image, Text, Ideology*. Chicago: University of Chicago Press, 1986.

Montrelay, Michèle. "Inquiry into Femininity." Trans. Parveen Adams. *m/f* 1 (1978): 83–101.

Mudimbe, V. Y. *The Invention of Africa: Gnosis, Philosophy, and the Order of Knowledge.* Bloomington: Indiana University Press, 1988.

Muecke, D. C. *Irony and the Ironic.* London: Methuen, 1970.

Pietz, William. "The Problem of the Fetish." Parts 1, 2, and 3a. *Res* 9 (Spring 1985): 5–17; 13 (Spring 1987): 23–45; 16 (Autumn 1988): 105–123.

Puttenham, George. *The Arte of English Poesie.* 1589. Kent, Ohio: Kent State University Press, 1970.

Robinson, Sally. "Misappropriations of the Feminine," *Sub-stance* 59 (1989): 48–70.

Sand, Georges. *Histoire de ma vie.* Paris: Gallimard, 1970.

Saussure, Ferdinand de. *Course in General Linguistics.* 1915. Trans. Wade Baskin. New York: McGraw-Hill, 1966.

Schor, Naomi. "Female Fetishism: The Case of George Sand." *Poetics Today* 6, no. 1–2 (1985): 301–10. Reprinted in *The Female Body in Western Culture: Contemporary Perspectives,* ed. Susan Rubin Suleiman, 363–72. Cambridge: Harvard University Press, 1986.

——. *Reading in Detail: Aesthetics and the Feminine.* New York: Methuen, 1987.

Seidler, Victor J. "Reason, Desire, and Male Sexuality." In *The Cultural Construction of Sexuality,* ed. Pat Caplan, 82–112. London: Tavistock, 1987.

Shapiro, Ann-Louise. "Disordered Bodies/Disorderly Acts: Medical Discourse and the Female Criminal in Nineteenth-Century Paris." *Genders* 4 (Spring 1989): 68–86.

Showalter, Elaine. *Sexual Anarchy: Gender and Culture at the Fin de Siècle.* New York: Viking, 1990.

Sieburth, Richard. *Instigations: Ezra Pound and Remy de Gourmont.* Cambridge: Harvard University Press, 1978.

Smith, Paul. *Discerning the Subject.* Minneapolis: University of Minnesota Press, 1988.

Sontag, Susan. "Fascinating Fascism." In *A Susan Sontag Reader,* 305–328. New York: Vintage Books, 1983.

Spackman, Barbara. *Decadent Genealogies: The Rhetoric of Sickness from Baudelaire to D'Annunzio.* Ithaca: Cornell University Press, 1989.

Spivak, Gayatri Chakravorty. "Scattered Speculations on the Question of Value." In *In Other Worlds,* 154–75. London: Routledge, 1988.

——. "Some Concept Metaphors of Political Economy in Derrida's Texts." *Left-wright/Intervention* 20 (1986): 88–97.

——. "Speculations on Reading Marx: After Reading Derrida." In *Post-structuralism and the Question of History,* ed. Derek Attridge et al., 30–62. Cambridge: Cambridge University Press, 1987.

Staples, Robert. *Black Masculinity: The Black Man's Role in American Society.* San Francisco: Black Scholar Press, 1982.

Suleiman, Susan Rubin. "Interpreting Ironies." *Diacritics* 6 (Summer 1976): 15–21.

——. "Pornography, Transgression, and the Avant-Garde: Bataille's Story of the Eye." In *The Poetics of Gender,* ed. Nancy K. Miller, 117–36. New York: Columbia University Press, 1986.

Warning, Rainer. "Irony and the 'Order of Discourse' in Flaubert." *New Literary History* 13 (Winter 1982): 253–86.

Weeks, Jeffrey. *Sexuality and Its Discontents.* London: Routledge, 1985.

White, Hayden. *Metahistory: The Historical Imagination in Nineteenth-Century Europe.* Baltimore: Johns Hopkins University Press, 1973.

Wilde, Oscar. "The Decay of Lying." In *Aesthetes and Decadents of the 1890s*, ed. Karl Beckson. Chicago: Academy, 1981.

——. *Letters of Oscar Wilde*. Ed. Rupert Hart-Davis. London: Rupert Hart-Davis, 1962.

——. *The Picture of Dorian Gray and Other Writings*. New York: Bantam, 1982.

Williams, Raymond. *Keywords: A Vocabulary of Culture and Society*. New York: Oxford University Press, 1976.

Williams, Rosalind. *Dream Worlds*. Berkeley: University of California Press, 1982.

Zagona, Helen Grace. *The Legend of Salome and the Principle of Art for Art's Sake*. Geneva: Droz, 1960.

History, Biography

Ackerman, Robert. *J. G. Frazier: His Life and Work*. Cambridge: Cambridge University Press, 1987.

Bidelman, Patrick Kay. *Pariahs Stand Up! The Founding of the Liberal Feminist Movement in France, 1858–1889*. Westport: Greenwood Press, 1982.

Birken, Lawrence. *Consuming Desire: Sexual Science and the Emergence of the Culture of Abundance, 1871–1914*. Ithaca: Cornell University Press, 1988.

Bonnet, Marie-Jo. *Un choix sans équivoque: Recherches historiques sur les relations amoureuses entre les femmes, XVIe–XXe siècle*. Paris: Denoël, 1981.

Canguilhem, Georges. *On the Normal and the Pathological*. Trans. Carolyn R. Fawcett. Boston: Reidel, 1978.

Chauncey, George, Jr. "From Sexual Inversion to Homosexuality: Medicine and the Changing Conceptualization of Female Deviance." *Salmagundi* 58–59 (1982–83): 114–46.

Clayson, Susan Hollis. "Representations of Prostitution in Early Third-Republic France." Ph.D. diss., UCLA, 1984.

Corbin, Alain. "Commercial Sexuality in Nineteenth-Century France." *Representations* 14 (Spring 1986): 209–19.

——. "La grande peur de la syphilis." In *Peurs et terreurs face à la contagion*, ed. Jean-Pierre Bardet et al., 328–48. Paris: Fayard, 1988.

——. *Women for Hire: Prostitution and Sexuality in France after 1850*. 1978. Trans. Alan Sheridan. Cambridge: Harvard University Press, 1990.

Darmon, Pierre. *Trial by Impotence: Virility and Marriage in Pre-revolutionary France*. 1979. Trans. Paul Keegan. London: Chatto and Windus, 1985.

David, Georges. "La stérilité masculine: Le déni du mâle." *Le genre humain* 10 (1984): 23–38.

Decaux, Alain. *La Castiglione: Dame de coeur de l'Europe*. Paris: Le Livre Contemporaine, 1959.

Ellenberger, Henri. *The Discovery of the Unconscious: The History and Evolution of Dynamic Psychiatry*. New York: Basic Books, 1970.

Ellmann, Richard. *Oscar Wilde*. New York: Vintage, 1987.

Gould, Stephen Jay. *The Mismeasure of Man*. New York: Norton, 1981.

Harris, Ruth. *Murders and Madness: Medicine, Law, and Society in the Fin de Siècle*. Oxford: Clarendon, 1989.

Hause, Steven C., with Anne R. Kenney. *Women's Suffrage and Social Politics in the French Third Republic*. Princeton: Princeton University Press, 1984.

Labrachérie, Pierre. *Napoléon III et son temps*. Paris: Julliard, 1976.

Lanteri-Laura, Georges. *Lecture des perversions: Histoire de leur appropriation médicale.* Paris: Masson, 1978.

Lukes, Steven. *Emile Durkheim: His Life and Work.* Harmondsworth, Eng.: Penguin Books, 1973.

McLaren, Angus. *Reproductive Rituals: The Perception of Fertility in England from the Sixteenth Century to the Nineteenth Century.* London: Methuen, 1984.

———. *Sexuality and the Social Order: The Debate over the Fertility of Women and Workers in France, 1770–1920.* New York: Holmes and Meier, 1983.

Miller, Michael B. *The Bon Marché.* Princeton: Princeton University Press, 1981.

Montesquiou, Robert de. *La divine comtesse: Etude d'après Mme de Castiglione.* Paris: Goupil, 1913.

Moses, Claire. *French Feminism in the Nineteenth Century.* Albany: SUNY Press 1984.

Mosse, George. *Nationalism and Sexuality.* Madison: University of Wisconsin Press, 1988.

Nye, Robert A. *Crime, Madness, and Politics in Modern France: The Medical Concept of National Decline.* Princeton: Princeton University Press, 1984.

———. "The History of Sexuality in Context: National Sexological Traditions." *Science in Context* 4 (Autumn 1991): 387–406.

———. "Honor, Impotence, and Male Sexuality in Nineteenth-Century French Medicine." *French Historical Studies* 16 (Spring 1988): 48–71.

———. "Sex Difference and Male Homosexuality in French Medical Discourse." *Bulletin of the History of Medicine* 63 (1989): 32–51.

O'Brien, Patricia. "The Kleptomania Diagnosis: Bourgeois Women and Theft in Late Nineteenth-Century France." *Journal of Social History* (Fall 1983): 65–77.

Offen, Karen. "Depopulation, Nationalism, and Feminism in *Fin-de-Siècle* France." *American Historical Review* 89 (June 1984): 648–76.

———. "Liberty, Equality, and Justice for Women: The Theory and Practice of Feminism in Nineteenth-Century Europe." In *Becoming Visible*, ed. Renate Bridenthal, Claudia Koonz, and Susan Stuard, 335–74. 2d edition. New York: Houghton Mifflin, 1987.

Ripa, Yannick. "Contribution à une histoire des femmes, des médecins, et de la folie, 1838–1860." Diss., Université de Paris VII, 1983.

Ronsin, Francis. *La grève des ventres.* Paris: Denoël, 1980.

Siegel, Jerrold. *Bohemian Paris.* New York: Viking, 1986.

Smith, Bonnie. *Changing Lives.* Lexington, Mass.: D.C. Heath, 1989.

Spengler, Joseph. *France Faces Depopulation.* Durham, N.C.: Duke University Press, 1938.

Stengers, Jean, and Anne Van Neck. *Histoire d'une grande peur: La masturbation.* Brussels: Editions de l'Université de Bruxelles, 1984.

Thomas, Edith. *The Women Incendiaries.* Trans. James and Starr Atkinson. New York: Braziller, 1966.

Walkowitz, Judith. *Prostitution and Victorian Society: Women, Class, and the State.* Cambridge: Cambridge University Press, 1980.

Contributors

Jack Amariglio teaches economics at Merrimack College and is the editor of the journal *Rethinking Marxism*. He has published on Marxian economics and on theories of ideology.

Emily Apter is Professor of French and Italian at the University of California at Davis. Her books include *André Gide and the Codes of Homotextuality* and *Feminizing the Fetish: Psychoanalysis and Narrative Obsession in Turn-of-the-Century France*.

Charles Bernheimer is Professor of Romance Languages and Comparative Literature at the University of Pennsylvania. His books include *Figures of Ill Repute: Representing Prostitution in Nineteenth-Century France* and *Flaubert and Kafka: Studies in Psychopoetic Structure*.

Barbara Bloom is an artist practicing in New York City and Cologne, Germany. Her major works include *L'esprit de l'escalier*.

Antonio Callari is Associate Professor of Economics at Franklin and Marshall College. He has published on Marxian theory and is currently working on a history of economics.

Hal Foster is Associate Professor of Art History at Cornell University and an editor of the journal *October*. His books include *Recodings: Art, Spectacle, Cultural Politics* and *The Anti-aesthetic: Essays on Postmodern Culture*.

383

Elizabeth Grosz is Associate Professor in the Institute for Critical and Cultural Studies at Monash University. She is the author of *Jacques Lacan: A Feminist Introduction* and *Sexual Subversions: Three French Feminists*.

Thomas Keenan is Assistant Professor of English at Princeton University. He is coeditor of *The Wartime Journalism of Paul de Man, 1939–1943*.

Mary Kelly is an artist practicing in New York City. She also teaches in the Independent Study Program at the Whitney Museum. Her major works include *Post-Partum Document* and *Interim*.

Jann Matlock is Assistant Professor of Romance Languages at Harvard University. Her forthcoming book is titled *Scenes of Seduction: Prostitution, Hysteria, and Reading Difference in Nineteenth-Century France*.

Jeffrey Mehlman is Professor of French at Boston University. His books include *Revolution and Repetition* and *Legacies of Anti-Semitism in France*.

Kobena Mercer is Assistant Professor of Art History at University of California at Santa Cruz. Books he has edited include *BlackFrames: Critical Perspectives on Black Independent Cimema* and *Male Order: Unwrapping Masculinity*.

Robert A. Nye is Professor of History at the University of Oklahoma. He is the author of *Crime, Madness, and Politics in Modern France: The Medical Concept of National Decline* and *The Origins of Crowd Psychology: Gustave le Bon and the Crisis of Mass Democracy in the Third Republic*.

William Pietz lives in Santa Cruz, California. He has published on the history of the idea of fetishism and the impact of colonialism on social theory.

Naomi Schor is Professor of Romance Studies at Duke University. Her books include *Breaking the Chain: Women, Theory, and French Realist Fiction* and *Reading in Detail: Aesthetics and the Feminine*.

Abigail Solomon-Godeau is Assistant Professor of Art History at the University of California, Santa Barbara. Her books include *Photography* *at the Dock: Essays on Photographic History, Institutions, and Practices* and *Sexual Difference: Both Sides of the Camera.*

Michael Taussig is Professor of Performance Studies at New York University. His books include *The Devil and Commodity Fetishism in South America* and *Shamanism, Colonialism, and the Wild Man: A Study in Terror and Healing.*

Jane Weinstock is a film maker and critic practicing in New York City. Her films include *Sigmund Freud's Dora: A Case of Mistaken Identity* and, for German television, *Voices of Silence.*

Index

Library of Congress Cataloging-in-Publication Data

Fetishism as cultural discourse / edited by Emily Apter and William
  Pietz.
     p. cm.
  Includes bibliographical references and index.
  ISBN 0-8014-2522-0 (cloth : alk. paper). — ISBN 0-8014-9757-4 (paper : alk.
  paper)
  1. Fetishism. 2. Marx, Karl, 1818–1883. Kapital. I. Apter,
Emily S. II. Pietz, William.
HQ79.F47   1993
306.77—dc20   92-31984